Matthew Henry's Concise Commen

(Psalm 73 to Acts)

Psalm Chapter 73

Chapter Outline

The psalmist's temptation.	(1–14)
How he gained a victory over it.	(15–20)
How he profited by it.	(21–28)

Verses 1-14

The psalmist was strongly tempted to envy the prosperity of the wicked; a common temptation, which has tried the graces of many saints. But he lays down the great principle by which he resolved to abide. It is the goodness of God. This is a truth which cannot be shaken. Good thoughts of God will fortify against Satan's temptations. The faith even of strong believers may be sorely shaken, and ready to fail. There are storms that will try the firmest anchors. Foolish and wicked people have sometimes a great share of outward prosperity. They seem to have the least share of the troubles of this life; and they seem to have the greatest share of its comforts. They live without the fear of God, yet they prosper, and get on in the world. Wicked men often spend their lives without much sickness, and end them without great pain; while many godly persons scarcely know what health is, and die with great sufferings. Often the wicked are not frightened, either by the remembrance of their sins, or the prospect of their misery, but they die without terror. We cannot judge men's state beyond death, by what passes at their death. He looked abroad, and saw many of God's people greatly at a loss. Because the wicked are so very daring, therefore his people return hither; they know not what to say to it, and the rather, because they drink deep of the bitter cup of affliction. He spoke feelingly when he spoke of his own troubles; there is no disputing against sense, except by faith. From all this arose a strong temptation to cast off religion. But let us learn that the true course of sanctification consists in cleansing a man from all pollution both of soul and body. The heart is cleansed by the blood of Christ laid hold upon by faith; and by the begun works of the

Lord's Spirit, manifested in the hearty resolution, purpose, and study of holiness, and a blameless course of life and actions, the hands are cleansed. It is not in vain to serve God and keep his ordinances.

Verses 15-20

The psalmist having shown the progress of his temptation, shows how faith and grace prevailed. He kept up respect for God's people, and with that he restrained himself from speaking what he had thought amiss. It is a sign that we repent of the evil thoughts of the heart, if we suppress them. Nothing gives more offence to God's children, than to say it is vain to serve God; for there is nothing more contrary to their universal experience. He prayed to God to make this matter plain to him; and he understood the wretched end of wicked people; even in the height of their prosperity they were but ripening for ruin. The sanctuary must be the resort of a tempted soul. The righteous man's afflictions end in peace, therefore he is happy; the wicked man's enjoyments end in destruction, therefore he is miserable. The prosperity of the wicked is short and uncertain, slippery places. See what their prosperity is; it is but a vain show, it is only a corrupt imagination, not substance, but a mere shadow; it is as a dream, which may please us a little while we are slumbering, yet even then it disturbs our repose.

Verses 21-28

God would not suffer his people to be tempted, if his grace were not sufficient, not only to save them from harm, but to make them gainers by it. This temptation, the working of envy and discontent, is very painful. In reflecting upon it, the psalmist owns it was his folly and ignorance thus to vex himself. If good men, at any time, through the surprise and strength of temptation, think, or speak, or act amiss, they will reflect upon it with sorrow and shame. We must ascribe our safety in temptation, and our victory, not to our own wisdom, but to the gracious presence of God with us, and Christ's intercession for us. All who commit themselves to God, shall be guided with the counsel both of his word and of his Spirit, the best counsellors here, and shall be received to his glory in another world; the believing hopes and prospects of which will reconcile us to all dark providences. And the psalmist was hereby quickened to cleave the closer to God. Heaven itself could not make us happy without the presence and love of our God. The world and all its glory vanishes. The body will fail by sickness, age, and death; when the flesh fails, the conduct, courage, and comfort fail. But Christ Jesus, our Lord, offers to be all in all to every poor sinner, who renounces all other portions and confidences. By sin we are all far from God. And a profession Christ, if we go on in sin, will increase our condemnation. May we draw near, and keep near, to our God, by faith and prayer, and find it good to do so. Those that with an upright heart put their trust in God, shall never want matter for thanksgiving to him. Blessed Lord, who hast so graciously promised to become our portion in the next world, prevent us from choosing any other in this.

Chapter 74

Chapter Outline

Verses 1-11

This psalm appears to describe the destruction of Jerusalem and the temple by the Chaldeans. The deplorable case of the people of God, at the time, is spread before the Lord, and left with him. They plead the great things God had done for them. If the deliverance of Israel out of Egypt was encouragement to hope that he would not cast them off, much more reason have we to believe, that God will not cast off any whom Christ has redeemed with his own blood. Infidels and persecutors may silence faithful ministers, and shut up places of worship, and say they will destroy the people of God and their religion together. For a long time they may prosper in these attempts, and God's oppressed servants may see no prospect of deliverance; but there is a remnant of believers, the seed of a future harvest, and the despised church has survived those who once triumphed over her. When the power of enemies is most threatening, it is comfortable to flee to the power of God by earnest prayer.

Verses 12-17

The church silences her own complaints. What God had done for his people, as their King of old, encouraged them to depend on him. It was the Lord's doing, none besides could do it. This providence was food to faith and hope, to support and encourage in difficulties. The God of Israel is the God of nature. He that is faithful to his covenant about the day and the night, will never cast off those whom he has chosen. We have as much reason to expect affliction, as to expect night and winter. But we have no more reason to despair of the return of comfort, than to despair of day and summer. And in the world above we shall have no more changes.

Verses 18-23

The psalmist begs that God would appear for the church against their enemies. The folly of such as revile his gospel and his servants will be plain to all. Let us call upon our God to enlighten the dark nations of the earth; and to rescue his people, that the poor and needy may praise his name. Blessed Saviour, thou art the same yesterday, to-day, and for ever. Make thy people more than conquerors. Be thou, Lord, all in all to them in every situation and circumstances; for then thy poor and needy people will praise thy name.

Chapter 75

Chapter Outline

The psalmist declares his resolution of executing judgment.   (1–5)

He rebukes the wicked, and concludes with resolutions to praise God.   (6–10)

Verses 1-5

We often pray for mercy, when in pursuit of it; and shall we only once or twice give thanks, when we obtain it? God shows that he is nigh to us in what we call upon him for. Public trusts are to be managed uprightly. This may well be applied to Christ and his government. Man's sin threatened to destroy the whole creation; but Christ saved the world from utter ruin. He who is made of God to us wisdom, bids us be wise. To the proud, daring sinners he says, Boast not of your power, persist not in contempt. All the present hopes and future happiness of the human race spring from the Son of God.

Verses 6-10

No second causes will raise men to preferment without the First Cause. It comes neither from the east, nor from the west, nor from the south. He mentions not the north; the same word that signifies the north, signifies the secret place; and from the secret of God's counsel it does come. From God alone all must receive their doom. There are mixtures of mercy and grace in the cup of affliction, when it is put into the hands of God's people; mixtures of the curse, when it is put into the hands of the wicked. God's people have their share in common calamities, but the dregs of the cup are for the wicked. The exaltation of the Son of David will be the subject of the saints' everlasting praises. Then let sinners submit to the King of righteousness, and let believers rejoice in and obey him.

Chapter 76

Chapter Outline

The psalmist speaks of God's power.   (1–6)

All have to fear and to trust in him.   (7–12)

Verses 1-6

Happy people are those who have their land filled with the knowledge of God! happy persons that have their hearts filled with that knowledge! It is the glory and happiness of a people to have God among them by his ordinances. Wherein the enemies of the church deal proudly, it will appear that God is above them. See the power of God's rebukes. With pleasure may Christians apply this to the advantages bestowed by the Redeemer.

Verses 7-12

God's people are the meek of the earth, the quiet in the land, that suffer wrong, but do none. The righteous God seems to keep silence long, yet, sooner or later, he will make judgment to be heard. We live in an angry, provoking world; we often feel much, and are apt to fear more, from the wrath of man. What will not turn to his praise, shall not be suffered to break out. He can set bounds to the wrath of man, as he does to the raging sea; hitherto it shall come, and no further. Let all submit to God. Our prayers and praises, and especially our hearts, are the presents we should bring to the Lord. His name is glorious, and he is the proper object of our fear. He shall cut off the spirit of princes; he shall slip it off easily, as we slip off a flower from the stalk, or a bunch of grapes from the vine; so the word signifies. He can dispirit the most daring: since there is no contending with God, it is our wisdom, as it is our duty, to submit to him. Let us seek his favour as our portion, and commit all our concerns to him.

Chapter 77

Chapter Outline

The psalmist's troubles and temptation. (1–10)

He encourages himself by the remembrance (11–20)
of God's help of his people.

Verses 1-10

Days of trouble must be days of prayer; when God seems to have withdrawn from us, we must seek him till we find him. In the day of his trouble the psalmist did not seek for the diversion of business or amusement, but he sought God, and his favor and grace. Those that are under trouble of mind, must pray it away. He pored upon the trouble; the methods that should have relieved him did but increase his grief. When he remembered God, it was only the Divine justice and wrath. His spirit was overwhelmed, and sank under the load. But let not the remembrance of the comforts we have lost, make us unthankful for those that are left. Particularly he called to remembrance the comforts with which he supported himself in former sorrows. Here is the language of a sorrowful, deserted soul, walking in darkness; a common case even among those that fear the Lord, Isa 50:10. Nothing wounds and pierces like the thought of God's being angry. God's own people, in a cloudy and dark day, may be tempted to make wrong conclusions about their spiritual state, and that of God's kingdom in the world. But we must not give way to such fears. Let faith answer them from the Scripture. The troubled fountain will work itself clear again; and the recollection of former times of joyful experience often raises a hope, tending to relief. Doubts and fears proceed from the want and weakness of faith. Despondency and distrust under affliction, are too often the infirmities of believers, and, as such, are to be thought upon by us with sorrow and shame. When, unbelief is working in us, we must thus suppress its risings.

Verses 11-20

The remembrance of the works of God, will be a powerful remedy against distrust of his promise and goodness; for he is God, and changes not. God's way is in the sanctuary. We are sure that God is holy in all his works. God's ways are like the deep waters, which cannot be fathomed; like the way of a ship, which cannot be tracked. God brought Israel out of Egypt. This was typical of the great redemption to be wrought out in the fulness of time, both by price and power. If we have harboured doubtful thoughts, we should, without delay, turn our minds to meditate on that God, who spared not his own Son, but delivered him up for us all, that with him, he might freely give us all things.

Chapter 78

Chapter Outline

Attention called for.	(1–8)
The history of Israel.	(9–39)
Their settlement in Canaan.	(40–55)
The mercies of God to Israel contrasted with their ingratitude.	(56–72)

Verses 1-8

These are called dark and deep sayings, because they are carefully to be looked into. The law of God was given with a particular charge to teach it diligently to their children, that the church may abide for ever. Also, that the providences of God, both in mercy and in judgment, might encourage them to conform to the will of God. The works of God much strengthen our resolution to keep his commandments. Hypocrisy is the high road to apostacy; those that do not set their hearts right, will not be stedfast with God. Many parents, by negligence and wickedness, become murderers of their children. But young persons, though they are bound to submit in all things lawful, must not obey sinful orders, or copy sinful examples.

Verses 9-39

Sin dispirits men, and takes away the heart. Forgetfulness of God's works is the cause of disobedience to his laws. This narrative relates a struggle between God's goodness and man's badness. The Lord hears all our murmurings and distrusts, and is much displeased. Those that will not believe the power of God's mercy, shall feel the fire of his indignation. Those cannot be said to trust in God's salvation as their happiness at last, who can not trust his providence in the way to it. To all that by faith and prayer, ask, seek, and knock, these doors of heaven shall at any time be opened; and our distrust of God is a great aggravation of our sins. He expressed his resentment of their provocation; not in denying what they sinfully lusted after, but in granting it to them. Lust is contented with nothing. Those that indulge their lust, will never be estranged from it. Those hearts are hard indeed, that will neither be melted by the mercies of the Lord, nor broken by his judgments. Those that sin still, must expect to be in trouble still. And the reason why we live with so little comfort, and to so little purpose, is, because we do not live by faith. Under these rebukes they professed repentance, but they were not sincere, for they were not constant. In Israel's history we have a picture of our own hearts and lives. God's patience, and warnings, and mercies, imbolden them to harden their hearts against his word. And the history of kingdoms is much the same. Judgments and mercies have been little attended to, until the measure of their sins has been full. And higher advantages have not kept churches from declining from the commandments of God. Even true believers recollect, that for many a year they abused the kindness of Providence. When they come to heaven, how will they admire the Lord's patience and mercy in bringing them to his kingdom!

Verses 40-55

Let not those that receive mercy from God, be thereby made bold to sin, for the mercies they receive will hasten its punishment; yet let not those who are under Divine rebukes for sin, be discouraged from repentance. The Holy One of Israel will do what is most for his own glory, and what is most for their good. Their forgetting former favours, led them to limit God for the future. God made his own people to go forth like sheep; and guided them in the wilderness, as a shepherd his flock, with all care and tenderness. Thus the true Joshua, even Jesus, brings his church out of the wilderness; but no earthly Canaan, no worldly advantages, should make us forget that the church is in the wilderness while in this world, and that there remaineth a far more glorious rest for the people of God.

Verses 56-72

After the Israelites were settled in Canaan, the children were like their fathers. God gave them his testimonies, but they turned back. Presumptuous sins render even Israelites hateful to God's holiness, and exposed to his justice. Those whom the Lord forsakes become an easy prey to the destroyer. And sooner or later, God will disgrace his enemies. He set a good government over his people; a monarch after his own heart. With good reason does the psalmist make this finishing, crowning instance of God's favour to Israel; for David was a type of Christ, the great and good Shepherd, who was humbled first, and then exalted; and of whom it was foretold, that he should be filled with the Spirit of wisdom and understanding. On the uprightness of his heart, and the skilfulness of his hands, all his subjects may rely; and of the increase of his government and peace there shall be no end. Every trial of human nature hitherto, confirms the testimony of Scripture, that the heart is deceitful above all things, and desperately wicked, and nothing but being created anew by the Holy Ghost can cure the ungodliness of any.

Chapter 79

Chapter Outline

Verses 1-5

God is complained to: whither should children go but to a Father able and willing to help them? See what a change sin made in the holy city, when the heathen were suffered to pour in upon them. God's own people defiled it by their sins, therefore he suffered their enemies to defile it by their insolence. They desired that God would be reconciled. Those who desire God's favour as better than life, cannot but dread his wrath as worse than death. In every affliction we should first beseech the Lord to cleanse away the guilt of our sins; then he will visit us with his tender mercies.

Verses 6-13

Those who persist in ignorance of God, and neglect of prayer, are the ungodly. How unrighteous soever men were, the Lord was righteous in permitting them to do what they did. Deliverances from trouble are mercies indeed, when grounded upon the pardon of sin; we should therefore be more earnest in prayer for the removal of our sins than for the removal of afflictions. They had no hopes but from God's mercies, his tender mercies. They plead no merit, they pretend to none, but, Help us for the glory of thy name; pardon us for thy name's sake. The Christian forgets not that he is often bound in the chain of his sins. The world to him is a prison; sentence of death is passed upon him, and he knows not how soon it may be executed. How fervently should he at all times pray, O let the sighing of a prisoner come before thee, according to the greatness of thy power preserve thou those that are appointed to die! How glorious will the day be, when, triumphant over sin and sorrow, the church beholds the adversary disarmed for ever! while that church shall, from age to age, sing the praises of her great Shepherd and Bishop, her King and her God.

Chapter 80

Chapter Outline

Verses 1-7

He that dwelleth upon the mercy-seat, is the good Shepherd of his people. But we can neither expect the comfort of his love, nor the protection of his arm, unless we partake of his converting grace. If he is really angry at the prayers of his people, it is because, although they pray, their ends are not right, or there is some secret sin indulged in them, or he will try their patience and perseverance in prayer. When God is displeased with his people, we must expect to see them in tears, and their enemies in triumph. There is no salvation but from God's favour; there is no conversion to God but by his own grace.

Verses 8-16

The church is represented as a vine and a vineyard. The root of this vine is Christ, the branches are believers. The church is like a vine, needing support, but spreading and fruitful. If a vine do not bring forth fruit, no tree is so worthless. And are not we planted as in a well-cultivated garden, with every means of being fruitful in works of righteousness? But the useless leaves of profession, and the empty boughs of notions and forms, abound far more than real piety. It was wasted and ruined. There was a good reason for this change in God's way toward them. And it is well or ill with us, according as we are under God's smiles or frowns. When we consider the state of the purest part of the visible church, we cannot wonder that it is visited with sharp corrections. They request that God would help the vine. Lord, it is formed by thyself, and for thyself, therefore it may, with humble confidence, be committed to thyself.

Verses 17-19

The Messiah, the Protector and Saviour of the church, is the Man of God's right hand; he is the Arm of the Lord, for all power is given to him. In him is our strength, by which we are enabled to persevere to the end. The vine, therefore, cannot be ruined, nor can any fruitful branch perish; but the unfruitful will be cut off and cast into the fire. The end of our redemption is, that we should serve Him who hath redeemed us, and not go back to our old sins.

Chapter 81

Chapter Outline

God is praised for what he has done for his people. (1–7)

Their obligations to him. (8–16)

Verses 1-7

All the worship we can render to the Lord is beneath his excellences, and our obligations to him, especially in our redemption from sin and wrath. What God had done on Israel's behalf, was kept in remembrance by public solemnities. To make a deliverance appear more gracious, more glorious, it is good to observe all that makes the trouble we are delivered from appear more grievous. We ought never to forget the base and ruinous drudgery to which Satan, our oppressor, brought us. But when, in distress of conscience, we are led to cry for deliverance, the Lord answers our prayers, and sets us at liberty. Convictions of sin, and trials by affliction, prove his regard to his people. If the Jews, on their solemn feast-days, were thus to call to mind their redemption out of Egypt, much more ought we, on the Christian sabbath, to call to mind a more glorious redemption, wrought out for us by our Lord Jesus Christ, from worse bondage.

Verses 8-16

We cannot look for too little from the creature, nor too much from the Creator. We may have enough from God, if we pray for it in faith. All the wickedness of the world is owing to man's wilfulness. People are not religious, because they will not be so. God is not the Author of their sin, he leaves them to the lusts of their own hearts, and the counsels of their own heads; if they do not well, the blame must be upon themselves. The Lord is unwilling that any should perish. What enemies sinners are to themselves! It is sin that makes our troubles long, and our salvation slow. Upon the same conditions of faith and obedience, do Christians hold those spiritual and eternal good things, which the pleasant fields and fertile hills of Canaan showed forth. Christ is the Bread of life; he is the Rock of salvation, and his promises are as honey to pious minds. But those who reject him as their Lord and Master, must also lose him as their Saviour and their reward.

Chapter 82

Chapter Outline

An exhortation to judges.   (1–5)

The doom of evil rulers.   (6–8)

Verses 1-5

Magistrates are the mighty in authority for the public good. Magistrates are the ministers of God's providence, for keeping up order and peace, and particularly in punishing evil-doers, and protecting those that do well. Good princes and good judges, who mean well, are under Divine direction; and bad ones, who mean ill, are under Divine restraint. The authority of God is to be submitted to, in those governors whom his providence places over us. But when justice is turned from what is right, no good can be expected. The evil actions of public persons are public mischiefs.

Verses 6-8

It is hard for men to have honour put upon them, and not to be proud of it. But all the rulers of the earth shall die, and all their honour shall be laid in the dust. God governs the world. There is a righteous God to whom we may go, and on whom we may depend. This also has respect to the kingdom of the Messiah. Considering the state of affairs in the world, we have need to pray that the Lord Jesus would speedily rule over all nations, in truth, righteousness, and peace.

Chapter 83

Chapter Outline

The designs of the enemies of Israel. (1–8)

Earnest prayer for their defeat. (9–18)

Verses 1-8

Sometimes God seems not to be concerned at the unjust treatment of his people. But then we may call upon him, as the psalmist here. All wicked people are God's enemies, especially wicked persecutors. The Lord's people are his hidden one; the world knows them not. He takes them under his special protection. Do the enemies of the church act with one consent to destroy it, and shall not the friends of the church be united? Wicked men wish that there might be no religion among mankind. They would gladly see all its restraints shaken off, and all that preach, profess, or practise it, cut off. This they would bring to pass if it were in their power. The enemies of God's church have always been many: this magnifies the power of the Lord in preserving to himself a church in the world.

Verses 9-18

All who oppose the kingdom of Christ may here read their doom. God is the same still that ever he was; the same to his people, and the same against his and their enemies. God would make their enemies like a wheel; unsettled in all their counsels and resolves. Not only let them be driven away as stubble, but burnt as stubble. And this will be the end of wicked men. Let them be made to fear thy name, and perhaps that will bring them to seek thy name. We should desire no confusion to our enemies and persecutors but what may forward their conversion. The stormy tempest of Divine vengeance will overtake them, unless they repent and seek the pardoning mercy of their offended Lord. God's triumphs over his enemies, clearly prove that he is, according to his name JEHOVAH, an almighty Being, who has all power and perfection in himself. May we fear his wrath, and yield ourselves to be his willing servants. And let us seek deliverance by the destruction of our fleshly lusts, which war against the soul.

Chapter 84

Chapter Outline

The psalmist expresses his affection to the ordinances of God.   (1–7)

His desire towards the God of the ordinances.   (8–12)

Verses 1-7

The ordinances of God are the believer's solace in this evil world; in them he enjoys the presence of the living God: this causes him to regret his absence from them. They are to his soul as the nest to the bird. Yet they are only an earnest of the happiness of heaven; but how can men desire to enter that holy habitation, who complain of Divine ordinances as wearisome? Those are truly happy, who go forth, and go on in the exercise of religion, in the strength of the grace of Jesus Christ, from whom all our sufficiency is. The pilgrims to the heavenly city may have to pass through many a valley of weeping, and many a thirsty desert; but wells of salvation shall be opened for them, and consolations sent for their support. Those that press forward in their Christian course, shall find God add grace to their graces. And those who grow in grace, shall be perfect in glory.

Verses 8-12

In all our addresses to God, we must desire that he would look on Christ, his Anointed One, and accept us for his sake: we must look to Him with faith, and then God will with favour look upon the face of the Anointed: we, without him, dare not show our faces. The psalmist pleads love to God's ordinances. Let us account one day in God's courts better than a thousand spent elsewhere; and deem the meanest place in his service preferable to the highest earthly preferment. We are here in darkness, but if God be our God, he will be to us a Sun, to enlighten and enliven us, to guide and direct us. We are here in danger, but he will be to us a Shield, to secure us from the fiery darts that fly thick about us. Through he has not promised to give riches and dignities, he has promised to give grace and glory to all that seek them in his appointed way. And what is grace, but heaven begun below, in the knowledge, love, and service of God? What is glory, but the completion of this happiness, in being made like to him, and in fully enjoying him for ever? Let it be our care to walk uprightly, and then let us trust God to give us every thing that is good for us. If we cannot go to the house of the Lord, we may go by faith to the Lord of the house; in him we shall be happy, and may be easy. That man is really happy, whatever his outward circumstances may be, who trusts in the Lord of hosts, the God of Jacob.

Chapter 85

Chapter Outline

Prayers for the continuance of former mercies.　　　　　　　　　　　　　　(1–7)

Trust in God's goodness.　　　　　　　　　　　　　　　　　　　　　　　(8–13)

Verses 1-7

The sense of present afflictions should not do away the remembrance of former mercies. The favour of God is the fountain of happiness to nations, as well as to particular persons. When God forgives sin, he covers it; and when he covers the sin of his people, he covers it all. See what the pardon of sin is. In compassion to us, when Christ our Intercessor has stood before thee, thou hast turned away thine anger. When we are reconciled to God, then, and not till then, we may expect the comfort of his being reconciled to us. He shows mercy to those to whom he grants salvation; for salvation is of mere mercy. The Lord's people may expect sharp and tedious afflictions when they commit sin; but when they return to him with humble prayer, he will make them again to rejoice in him.

Verses 8-13

Sooner or later, God will speak peace to his people. If he do not command outward peace, yet he will suggest inward peace; speaking to their hearts by his Spirit. Peace is spoken only to those who turn from sin. All sin is folly, especially backsliding; it is the greatest folly to return to sin. Surely God's salvation is nigh, whatever our difficulties and distresses are. Also, his honour is secured, that glory may dwell in our land. And the truth of the promises is shown by the Divine mercy in sending the Redeemer. The Divine justice is now satisfied by the great atonement. Christ, the way, truth, and life, sprang out of the earth when he took our nature upon him, and Divine justice looked upon him well pleased and satisfied. For his sake all good things, especially his Holy Spirit, are given to those who ask him. Through Christ, the pardoned sinner becomes fruitful in good works, and by looking to and trusting in the Saviour's righteousness, finds his feet set in the way of his steps. Righteousness is a sure guide, both in meeting God, and in following him

Chapter 86

Chapter Outline

The psalmist pleads his earnestness, and the mercy of God, as reasons why his prayer should be heard.　　　　　　　　　　　　　　　　　　　　(1–7)

He renews his requests for help and comfort.　　　　　　　　　　　　　(8–17)

Verses 1-7

Our poverty and wretchedness, when felt, powerfully plead in our behalf at the throne of grace. The best self-preservation is to commit ourselves to God's keeping. I am one whom thou favourest, hast set apart for thyself, and made partaker of sanctifying grace. It is a great encouragement to prayer, to feel that we have received the converting grace of God, have learned to trust in him, and to be his servants. We may expect comfort from God, when we keep up our communion with God. God's goodness appears in two things, in giving and forgiving. Whatever others do, let us call upon God, and commit our case to him; we shall not seek in vain.

Verses 8-17

Our God alone possesses almighty power and infinite love. Christ is the way and the truth. And the believing soul will be more desirous to be taught the way and the truth. And the believing soul will be more desirous to be taught the way and the truth of God, in order to walk therein, than to be delivered out of earthly distress. Those who set not the Lord before them, seek after believers' souls; but the compassion, mercy, and truth of God, will be their refuge and consolation. And those whose parents were the servants of the Lord, may urge this as a plea why he should hear and help them. In considering David's experience, and that of the believer, we must not lose sight of Him, who though he was rich, for our sakes became poor, that we through his poverty might be rich.

Chapter 87

Chapter Outline

The glory of the church.   (1–3)

It is filled with the Divine blessing.   (4–7)

Verses 1-3

Christ himself is the Foundation of the church, which God has laid. Holiness is the strength and firmness of the church. Let us not be ashamed of the church of Christ in its meanest condition, nor of those that belong to it, since such glorious things are spoken of it. Other foundation can no man lay than that is laid, even Jesus Christ. The glorious things spoken of Zion by the Spirit, were all typical of Christ, and his work and offices; of the gospel church, its privileges and members; of heaven, its glory and perfect happiness.

Verses 4-7

The church of Christ is more glorious and excellent than the nations of the earth. In the records of heaven, the meanest of those who are born again stand registered. When God renders to every man according to his works, he shall observe who enjoyed the privileges of his sanctuary. To them much was given, and of them much will be required. Let those that dwell in Zion, mark this, and live up to their profession. Zion's songs shall be sung with joy and triumph. The springs of the joy of a carnal worldling are in wealth and pleasure; but of a gracious soul, in the word of God and prayer. All grace and consolation are derived from Christ, through his ordinances, to the souls of believers.

Chapter 88

Chapter Outline

The psalmist pours out his soul to God in lamentation.	(1–9)
He wrestles by faith, in his prayer to God for comfort.	(10–18)

Verses 1-9

The first words of the psalmist are the only words of comfort and support in this psalm. Thus greatly may good men be afflicted, and such dismal thoughts may they have about their afflictions, and such dark conclusion may they make about their end, through the power of melancholy and the weakness of faith. He complained most of God's displeasure. Even the children of God's love may sometimes think themselves children of wrath and no outward trouble can be so hard upon them as that. Probably the psalmist described his own case, yet he leads to Christ. Thus are we called to look unto Jesus, wounded and bruised for our iniquities. But the wrath of God poured the greatest bitterness into his cup. This weighed him down into darkness and the deep.

Verses 10-18

Departed souls may declare God's faithfulness, justice, and lovingkindness; but deceased bodies can neither receive God's favours in comfort, nor return them in praise. The psalmist resolved to continue in prayer, and the more so, because deliverance did not come speedily. Though our prayers are not soon answered, yet we must not give over praying. The greater our troubles, the more earnest and serious we should be in prayer. Nothing grieves a child of God so much as losing sight of him; nor is there any thing he so much dreads as God's casting off his soul. If the sun be clouded, that darkens the earth; but if the sun should leave the earth, what a dungeon would it be! Even those designed for God's favours, may for a time suffer his terrors. See how deep those terrors wounded the psalmist. If friends are put far from us by providences, or death, we have reason to look upon it as affliction. Such was the calamitous state of a good man. But the pleas here used were peculiarly suited to Christ. And we are not to think that the holy Jesus suffered for us only at Gethsemane and on Calvary. His whole life was labour and sorrow; he was afflicted as never man was, from his youth up. He was prepared for that death of which he tasted through life. No man could share in the sufferings by which other men were to be redeemed. All forsook him, and fled. Oftentimes, blessed Jesus, do we forsake thee; but do not forsake us, O take not thy Holy Spirit from us.

Chapter 89

Chapter Outline

God's mercy and truth, and his covenant.	(1–4)
The glory and perfection of God.	(5–14)
The happiness of those in communion with him.	(15–18)
God's covenant with David, as a type of Christ.	(19–37)
A calamitous state lamented, Prayer for redress.	(38–52)

Verses 1-4

Though our expectations may be disappointed, yet God's promises are established in the heavens, in his eternal counsels; they are out of the reach of opposers in hell and earth. And faith in the boundless mercy and everlasting truth of God, may bring comfort even in the deepest trials.

Verses 5-14

The more God's works are known, the more they are admired. And to praise the Lord, is to acknowledge him to be such a one that there is none like him. Surely then we should feel and express reverence when we worship God. But how little of this appears in our congregations, and how much cause have we to humble ourselves on this account! That almighty power which smote Egypt, will scatter the enemies of the church, while all who trust in God's mercy will rejoice in his name; for mercy and truth direct all he does. His counsels from eternity, and their consequences to eternity, are all justice and judgment.

Verses 15-18

Happy are those who so know the joyful sound of the gospel as to obey it; who experience its power upon their hearts, and bring forth the fruit of it in their lives. Though believers are nothing in themselves, yet having all in Christ Jesus, they may rejoice in his name. May the Lord enable us to do so. The joy of the Lord is the strength of his people; whereas unbelief dispirits ourselves and discourages others. Though it steals upon us under a semblance of humility, yet it is the very essence of pride. Christ is the Holy One of Israel; and in him was that peculiar people more blessed than in any other blessing.

Verses 19-37

The Lord anointed David with the holy oil, not only as an emblem of the graces and gifts he received, but as a type of Christ, the King Priest, and Prophet, anointed with the Holy Ghost without measure. David after his anointing, was persecuted, but none could gain advantage against him. Yet all this was a faint shadow of the Redeemer's sufferings, deliverance, glory, and authority, in whom alone these predictions and promises are fully brought to pass. He is the mighty God. This is the Redeemer appointed for us, who alone is able to complete the work of our salvation. Let us seek an interest in these blessings, by the witness of the Holy Spirit in our hearts. As the Lord corrected the posterity of David for their transgressions, so his people shall be corrected for their sins. Yet it is but a rod, not a sword; it is to correct, not to destroy. It is a rod in the hand of God, who is wise, and knows what he does; gracious, and will do what is best. It is a rod which they shall never feel, but when there is need. As the sun and moon remain in heaven, whatever changes there seem to be in them, and again appear in due season; so the covenant of grace made in Christ, whatever alteration seems to come to it, should not be questioned.

Verses 38-52

Sometimes it is not easy to reconcile God's providences with his promises, yet we are sure that God's works fulfil his word. When the great Anointed One, Christ himself, was upon the cross, God seemed to have cast him off, yet did not make void his covenant, for that was established for ever. The honour of the house of David was lost. Thrones and crowns are often laid in the dust; but there is a crown of glory reserved for Christ's spiritual seed, which fadeth not away. From all this complaint learn what work sin makes with families, noble families, with families in which religion has appeared. They plead with God for mercy. God's unchangeableness and faithfulness assure us that He will not cast off those whom he has chosen and covenanted with. They were reproached for serving him. The scoffers of the latter days, in like manner, reproach the footsteps of the Messiah when they ask, Where is the promise of his coming? 2Pe 3:3, 4. The records of the Lord's dealings with the family of David, show us his dealings with his church, and with believers. Their afflictions and distresses may be grievous, but he will not finally cast them off. Self-deceivers abuse this doctrine, and others by a careless walk bring themselves into darkness and distress; yet let the true believer rely on it for encouragement in the path of duty, and in bearing the cross. The psalm ends with praise, even after this sad complaint. Those who give God thanks for what he has done, may give him thanks for what he will do. God will follow those with his mercies, who follow him with praises.

Chapter 90

Chapter Outline

The eternity of God, the frailty of man.   (1–6)

Submission to Divine chastisements.   (7–11)

Prayer for mercy and grace.   (12–17)

Verses 1-6

It is supposed that this psalm refers to the sentence passed on Israel in the wilderness, Nu 14. The favour and protection of God are the only sure rest and comfort of the soul in this evil world. Christ Jesus is the refuge and dwelling-place to which we may repair. We are dying creatures, all our comforts in the world are dying comforts, but God is an ever-living God, and believers find him so. When God, by sickness, or other afflictions, turns men to destruction, he thereby calls men to return unto him to repent of their sins, and live a new life. A thousand years are nothing to God's eternity: between a minute and a million of years there is some proportion; between time and eternity there is none. All the events of a thousand years, whether past or to come, are more present to the Eternal Mind, than what was done in the last hour is to us. And in the resurrection, the body and soul shall both return and be united again. Time passes unobserved by us, as with men asleep; and when it is past, it is as nothing. It is a short and quickly-passing life, as the waters of a flood. Man does but flourish as the grass, which, when the winter of old age comes, will wither; but he may be mown down by disease or disaster.

Verses 7-11

The afflictions of the saints often come from God's love; but the rebukes of sinners, and of believers for their sins, must be seen coming from the displeasure of God. Secret sins are known to God, and shall be reckoned for. See the folly of those who go about to cover their sins, for they cannot do so. Our years, when gone, can no more be recalled than the words that we have spoken. Our whole life is toilsome and troublesome; and perhaps, in the midst of the years we count upon, it is cut off. We are taught by all this to stand in awe. The angels that sinned know the power of God's anger; sinners in hell know it; but which of us can fully describe it? Few seriously consider it as they ought. Those who make a mock at sin, and make light of Christ, surely do not know the power of God's anger. Who among us can dwell with that devouring fire?

Verses 12-17

Those who would learn true wisdom, must pray for Divine instruction, must beg to be taught by the Holy Spirit; and for comfort and joy in the returns of God's favour. They pray for the mercy of God, for they pretend not to plead any merit of their own. His favour would be a full fountain of future joys. It would be a sufficient balance to former griefs. Let the grace of God in us produce the light of good works. And let Divine consolations put gladness into our hearts, and a lustre upon our countenances. The work of our hands, establish thou it; and, in order to that, establish us in it. Instead of wasting our precious, fleeting days in pursuing fancies, which leave the possessors for ever poor, let us seek the forgiveness of sins, and an inheritance in heaven. Let us pray that the work of the Holy Spirit may appear in converting our hearts, and that the beauty of holiness may be seen in our conduct.

Chapter 91

Chapter Outline

The safety of those who have God for their refuge.	(1–8)
Their favour with Him.	(9–16)

Verses 1-8

He that by faith chooses God for his protector, shall find all in him that he needs or can desire. And those who have found the comfort of making the Lord their refuge, cannot but desire that others may do so. The spiritual life is protected by Divine grace from the temptations of Satan, which are as the snares of the fowler, and from the contagion of sin, which is a noisome pestilence. Great security is promised to believers in the midst of danger. Wisdom shall keep them from being afraid without cause, and faith shall keep them from being unduly afraid. Whatever is done, our heavenly Father's will is done; and we have no reason to fear. God's people shall see, not only God's promises fulfilled, but his threatenings. Then let sinners come unto the Lord upon his mercy-seat, through the Redeemer's name; and encourage others to trust in him also.

Verses 9-16

Whatever happens, nothing shall hurt the believer; though trouble and affliction befal, it shall come, not for his hurt, but for good, though for the present it be not joyous but grievous. Those who rightly know God, will set their love upon him. They by prayer constantly call upon him. His promise is, that he will in due time deliver the believer out of trouble, and in the mean time be with him in trouble. The Lord will manage all his worldly concerns, and preserve his life on earth, so long as it shall be good for him. For encouragement in this he looks unto Jesus. He shall live long enough; till he has done the work he was sent into this world for, and is ready for heaven. Who would wish to live a day longer than God has some work to do, either by him or upon him? A man may die young, yet be satisfied with living. But a wicked man is not satisfied even with long life. At length the believer's conflict ends; he has done for ever with trouble, sin, and temptation.

Chapter 92

Chapter Outline

Praise is the business of the sabbath.	(1–6)
The wicked shall perish, but God's people shall be exalted.	(7–15)

Verses 1-6

It is a privilege that we are admitted to praise the Lord, and hope to be accepted in the morning, and every night; not only on sabbath days, but every day; not only in public, but in private, and in our families. Let us give thanks every morning for the mercies of the night, and every night for the mercies of the day; going out, and coming in, let us bless God. As He makes us glad, through the works of his providence for us, and of his grace in us, and both through the great work of redemption, let us hence be encouraged. As there are many who know not the designs of Providence, nor care to know them, those who through grace do so, have the more reason to be thankful. And if distant views of the great Deliverer so animated believers of old, how should we abound in love and praise!

Verses 7-15

God sometimes grants prosperity to wicked men in displeasure; yet they flourish but for a moment. Let us seek for ourselves the salvation and grace of the gospel, that being daily anointed by the Holy Spirit, we may behold and share the Redeemer's glory. It is from his grace, by his word and Spirit, that believers receive all the virtue that keeps them alive, and makes them fruitful. Other trees, when old, leave off bearing, but in God's trees the strength of grace does not fail with the strength of nature. The last days of the saints are sometimes their best days, and their last work their best work: perseverance is sure evidence of sincerity. And may every sabbath, while it shows forth the Divine faithfulness, find our souls resting more and more upon the Lord our righteousness.

Chapter 93

The majesty, power, and holiness of Christ's kingdom.
—The Lord might have displayed only his justice, holiness, and awful power, in his dealings with fallen men; but he has been pleased to display the riches of his mercy, and the power of his renewing grace. In this great work, the Father has given all power to his Son, the Lord from heaven, who has made atonement for our sins. He not only can pardon, but deliver and protect all who trust in him. His word is past, and all the saints may rely upon it. Whatever was foretold concerning the kingdom of the Messiah, must be fulfilled in due time. All his people ought to be very strictly pure. God's church is his house; it is a holy house, cleansed from sin, and employed in his service. Where there is purity, there shall be peace. Let all carefully look if this kingdom is set up in their hearts.

Chapter 94

Chapter Outline

The danger and folly of persecutors.   (1–11)

Comfort and peace to the persecuted.   (12–23)

Verses 1-11

We may with boldness appeal to God; for he is the almighty Judge by whom every man is judged. Let this encourage those who suffer wrong, to bear it with silence, committing themselves to Him who judges righteously. These prayers are prophecies, which speak terror to the sons of violence. There will come a day of reckoning for all the hard speeches which ungodly sinners have spoken against God, his truths, and ways, and people. It would hardly be believed, if we did not witness it, that millions of rational creatures should live, move, speak, hear, understand, and do what they purpose, yet act as if they believed that God would not punish the abuse of his gifts. As all knowledge is from God, no doubt he knows all the thoughts of the children of men, and knows that the imaginations of the thoughts of men's hearts are only evil, and that continually. Even in good thoughts there is a want of being fixed, which may be called vanity. It concerns us to keep a strict watch over our thoughts, because God takes particular notice of them. Thoughts are words to God.

Verses 12-23

That man is blessed, who, under the chastening of the Lord, is taught his will and his truths, from his holy word, and by the Holy Spirit. He should see mercy through his sufferings. There is a rest remaining for the people of God after the days of their adversity, which shall not last always. He that sends the trouble, will send the rest. The psalmist found succour and relief only in the Lord, when all earthly friends failed. We are beholden, not only to God's power, but to his pity, for spiritual supports; and if we have been kept from falling into sin, or shrinking from our duty, we should give him the glory, and encourage our brethren. The psalmist had many troubled thoughts concerning the case he was in, concerning the course he should take, and what was likely to be the end of it. The indulgence of such contrivances and fears, adds to care and distrust, and renders our views more gloomy and confused. Good men sometimes have perplexed and distressed thoughts concerning God. But let them look to the great and precious promises of the gospel. The world's comforts give little delight to the soul, when hurried with melancholy thoughts; but God's comforts bring that peace and pleasure which the smiles of the world cannot give, and which the frowns of the world cannot take away. God is his people's Refuge, to whom they may flee, in whom they are safe, and may be secure. And he will reckon with the wicked. A man cannot be more miserable than his own wickedness will make him, if the Lord visit it upon him.

Chapter 95

Chapter Outline

part. An exhortation to praise God.   (1–7)

A warning not to tempt Him.   (7–11)

Verses 1-7

Whenever we come into God's presence, we must come with thanksgiving. The Lord is to be praised; we do not want matter, it were well if we did not want a heart. How great is that God, whose the whole earth is, and the fulness thereof; who directs and disposes of all!, The Lord Jesus, whom we are here taught to praise, is a great God; the mighty God is one of his titles, and God over all, blessed for evermore. To him all power is given, both in heaven and earth. He is our God, and we should praise him. He is our Saviour, and the Author of our blessedness. The gospel church is his flock, Christ is the great and good Shepherd of believers; he sought them when lost, and brought them to his fold.

Verses 7-11

Christ calls upon his people to hear his voice. You call him Master, or Lord; then be his willing, obedient people. Hear the voice of his doctrine, of his law, and in both, of his Spirit: hear and heed; hear and yield. Christ's voice must be heard to-day. This day of opportunity will not last always; improve it while it is called to-day. Hearing the voice of Christ is the same with believing. Hardness of heart is at the bottom of all distrust of the Lord. The sins of others ought to be warnings to us not to tread in their steps. The murmurings of Israel were written for our admonition. God is not subject to such passions as we are; but he is very angry at sin and sinners. That certainly is evil, which deserves such a recompence; and his threatenings are as sure as his promises. Let us be aware of the evils of our hearts, which lead us to wander from the Lord. There is a rest ordained for believers, the rest of everlasting refreshment, begun in this life, and perfected in the life to come. This is the rest which God calls his rest.

Chapter 96

Chapter Outline

Verses 1-9

When Christ finished his work on earth, and was received into his glory in heaven, the church began to sing a new song unto him, and to bless his name. His apostles and evangelists showed forth his salvation among the heathen, his wonders among all people. All the earth is here summoned to worship the Lord. We must worship him in the beauty of holiness, as God in Christ, reconciling the world unto himself. Glorious things are said of him, both as motives to praise and matter of praise.

Verses 10-13

We are to hope and pray for that time, when Christ shall reign in righteousness over all nations. He shall rule in the hearts of men, by the power of truth, and the Spirit of righteousness. His coming draws nigh; this King, this Judge standeth before the door, but he is not yet come. The Lord will accept the praises of all who seek to promote the kingdom of Christ. The sea can but roar, and how the trees of the wood can show that they rejoice we know not; but He that searches the heart knows what is the mind of the Spirit, and understands the words, the broken language of the weakest. Christ will come to judge the earth, to execute just vengeance on his enemies, and to fulfil his largest promises to his people. What then are we? Would that day be welcome to us? If this be not our case, let us now begin to prepare to meet our God, by seeking the pardon of our sins, and the renewal of our souls to holiness.

Chapter 97

Chapter Outline

The Lord Jesus reigns in power that cannot be resisted.	(1–7)
His care of his people, and his provision for them.	(8–12)

Verses 1-7

Though many have been made happy in Christ, still there is room. And all have reason to rejoice in Christ's government. There is a depth in his counsels, which we must not pretend to fathom; but still righteousness and judgment are the habitation of his throne. Christ's government, though it might be matter of joy to all, will yet be matter of terror to some; but it is their own fault that it is so. The most resolute and daring opposition will be baffled at the presence of the Lord. And the Lord Jesus will ere long come, and put an end to idol worship of every kind.

Verses 8-12

The faithful servants of God may well rejoice and be glad, because he is glorified; and whatever tends to his honour, is his people's pleasure. Care is taken for their safety. But something more is meant than their lives. The Lord will preserve the souls of his saints from sin, from apostasy, and despair, under their greatest trials. He will deliver them out of the hands of the wicked one, and preserve them safe to his heavenly kingdom. And those that rejoice in Christ Jesus, and in his exaltation, have fountains of joy prepared for them. Those that sow in tears, shall reap in joy. Gladness is sure to the upright in heart; the joy of the hypocrite is but for a moment. Sinners tremble, but saints rejoice at God's holiness. As he hates sin, yet freely loves the person of the repentant sinner who believes in Christ, he will make a final separation between the person he loves and the sin he hates, and sanctify his people wholly, body, soul, and spirit.

Chapter 98

Chapter Outline

Verses 1-3

A song of praise for redeeming love is a new song, a mystery hidden from ages and generations. Converts sing a new song, very different from what they had sung. If the grace of God put a new heart into our breasts, it will put a new song into our mouths. Let this new song be sung to the praise of God, in consideration of the wonders he has wrought. The Redeemer has overcome all difficulties in the way of our redemption, and was not discouraged by the services or sufferings appointed him. Let us praise him for the discoveries made to the world of the work of redemption; his salvation and his righteousness fulfilling the prophecies and promises of the Old Testament. In pursuance of this design, God raised up his Son Jesus to be not only a Light to lighten the Gentiles, but the glory of his people Israel. Surely it behoves us to inquire whether his holy arm hath gotten the victory in our hearts, over the power of Satan, unbelief, and sin? If this be our happy case, we shall exchange all light songs of vanity for songs of joy and thanksgiving; our lives will celebrate the Redeemer's praise.

Verses 4-9

Let all the children of men rejoice in the setting up the kingdom of Christ, for all may benefit by it. The different orders of rational creatures in the universe, seem to be described in figurative language in the reign of the great Messiah. The kingdom of Christ will be a blessing to the whole creation. We expect his second coming to begin his glorious reign. Then shall heaven and earth rejoice, and the joy of the redeemed shall be full. But sin and its dreadful effects will not be utterly done away, till the Lord come to judge the world in righteousness. Seeing then that we look for such things, let us give diligence that we may be found of him in peace, without spot, and blameless.

Chapter 99

Chapter Outline

The happy government God's people are under.   (1–5)

Its happy administration.   (6–9)

Verses 1-5

God governs the world by his providence, governs the church by his grace, and both by his Son. The inhabitants of the earth have cause to tremble, but the Redeemer still waits to be gracious. Let all who hear, take warning, and seek his mercy. The more we humble ourselves before God, the more we exalt him; and let us be thus reverent, for he is holy.

Verses 6-9

The happiness of Israel is made out by referring to the most useful governors of that people. They in every thing made God's word and law their rule, knowing that they could not else expect that their prayers should be answered. They all wonderfully prevailed with God in prayer; miracles were wrought at their request. They pleaded for the people, and obtained answers of peace. Our Prophet and High Priest, of infinitely greater dignity than Moses, Aaron, or Samuel, has received and declared to us the will of the Father. Let us not only exalt the Lord with our lips, but give him the throne in our heart; and while we worship him upon his mercy-seat, let us never forget that he is holy.

Chapter 100

An exhortation to praise God, and rejoice in him.
—This song of praise should be considered as a prophecy, and even used as a prayer, for the coming of that time when all people shall know that the Lord he is God, and shall become his worshippers, and the sheep of his pasture. Great encouragement is given us, in worshipping God, to do it cheerfully. If, when we strayed like wandering sheep, he has brought us again to his fold, we have indeed abundant cause to bless his name. The matter of praise, and the motives to it, are very important. Know ye what God is in himself, and what he is to you. Know it; consider and apply it, then you will be more close and constant, more inward and serious, in his worship. The covenant of grace set down in the Scriptures of the Old and New Testament, with so many rich promises, to strengthen the faith of every weak believer, makes the matter of God's praise and of his people's joys so sure, that how sad soever our spirits may be when we look to ourselves, yet we shall have reason to praise the Lord when we look to his goodness and mercy, and to what he has said in his word for our comfort.

Chapter 101

David's vow and profession of godliness.

—In this psalm we have David declaring how he intended to regulate his household, and to govern his kingdom, that he might stop wickedness, and encourage godliness. It is also applicable to private families, and is the householder's psalm. It teaches all that have any power, whether more or less, to use it so as to be a terror to evil-doers, and a praise to them that do well. The chosen subject of the psalm is God's mercy and judgment. The Lord's providences concerning his people are commonly mixed; mercy and judgment. God has set the one over against the other, both to do good, like showers and sunshine. When, in his providence, he exercises us with the mixture of mercy and judgment, we must make suitable acknowledgments to him for both. Family mercies and family afflictions are both calls to family religion. Those who are in public stations are not thereby excused from care in governing their families; they are the more concerned to set a good example of ruling their own houses well. Whenever a man has a house of his own, let him seek to have God to dwell with him; and those may expect his presence, who walk with a perfect heart, in a perfect way. David resolves to practise no evil himself. He further resolves not to keep bad servants, nor to employ those about him that are wicked. He will not admit them into his family, lest they spread the infection of sin. A froward heart, one that delights to be cross and perverse, is not fit for society, the bond of which is Christian love. Nor will he countenance slanderers, those who take pleasure in wounding their neighbour's reputation. Also, God resists the proud, and false, deceitful people, who scruple not to tell lies, or commit frauds. Let every one be zealous and diligent to reform his own heart and ways, and to do this early; ever mindful of that future, most awful morning, when the King of righteousness shall cut off all wicked doers from the heavenly Jerusalem.

Chapter 102

Chapter Outline

A sorrowful complaint of great afflictions.	(1–11)
Encouragement by expecting the performances of God's promises to his church.	(12–22)
The unchangeableness of God.	(23–28)

Verses 1-11

The whole word of God is of use to direct us in prayer; but here, is often elsewhere, the Holy Ghost has put words into our mouths. Here is a prayer put into the hands of the afflicted; let them present it to God. Even good men may be almost overwhelmed with afflictions. It is our duty and interest to pray; and it is comfort to an afflicted spirit to unburden itself, by a humble representation of its griefs. We must say, Blessed be the name of the Lord, who both gives and takes away. The psalmist looked upon himself as a dying man; My days are like a shadow.

Verses 12-22

We are dying creatures, but God is an everlasting God, the protector of his church; we may be confident that it will not be neglected. When we consider our own vileness, our darkness and deadness, and the manifold defects in our prayers, we have cause to fear that they will not be received in heaven; but we are here assured of the contrary, for we have an Advocate with the Father, and are under grace, not under the law. Redemption is the subject of praise in the Christian church; and that great work is described by the temporal deliverance and restoration of Israel. Look down upon us, Lord Jesus; and bring us into the glorious liberty of thy children, that we may bless and praise thy name.

Verses 23-28

Bodily distempers soon weaken our strength, then what can we expect but that our months should be cut off in the midst; and what should we do but provide accordingly? We must own God's hand in it; and must reconcile this to his love, for often those that have used their strength well, have it weakened; and those who, as we think, can very ill be spared, have their days shortened. It is very comfortable, in reference to all the changes and dangers of the church, to remember that Jesus Christ is the same yesterday, to-day, and for ever. And in reference to the death of our bodies, and the removal of friends, to remember that God is an everlasting God. Do not let us overlook the assurance this psalm contains of a happy end to all the believer's trials. Though all things are changing, dying, perishing, like a vesture folding up and hastening to decay, yet Jesus lives, and thus all is secure, for he hath said, Because I live ye shall live also.

Chapter 103

Chapter Outline

Verses 1-5

By the pardon of sin, that is taken away which kept good things from us, and we are restored to the favor of God, who bestows good things on us. Think of the provocation; it was sin, and yet pardoned: how many the provocations, yet all pardoned! God is still forgiving, as we are still sinning and repenting. The body finds the melancholy consequences of Adam's offence, it is subject to many infirmities, and the soul also. Christ alone forgives all our sins; it is he alone who heals all our infirmities. And the person who finds his sin cured, has a well-grounded assurance that it is forgiven. When God, by the graces and comforts of his Spirit, recovers his people from their decays, and fills them with new life and joy, which is to them an earnest of eternal life and joy, they may then be said to return to the days of their youth, Job 33:25.

Verses 6-14

Truly God is good to all: he is in a special manner good to Israel. He has revealed himself and his grace to them. By his ways we may understand his precepts, the ways he requires us to walk in; and his promises and purposes. He always has been full of compassion. How unlike are those to God, who take every occasion to chide, and never know when to cease! What would become of us, if God should deal so with us? The Scripture says a great deal of the mercy of God, and we all have experienced it. The father pities his children that are weak in knowledge, and teaches them; pities them when they are froward, and bears with them; pities them when they are sick, and comforts them; pities them when they are fallen, and helps them to rise; pities them when they have offended, and, upon their submission, forgives them; pities them when wronged, and rights them: thus the Lord pities those that fear him. See why he pities. He considers the frailty of our bodies, and the folly of our souls, how little we can do, how little we can bear; in all which his compassion appears.

Verses 15-18

How short is man's life, and uncertain! The flower of the garden is commonly more choice, and will last the longer, for being sheltered by the garden-wall, and the gardener's care; but the flower of the field, to which life is here compared, is not only withering in itself, but exposed to the cold blasts, and liable to be cropt and trod on by the beasts of the field. Such is man. God considers this, and pities him; let him consider it himself. God's mercy is better than life, for it will outlive it. His righteousness, the truth of his promise, shall be unto children's children, who tread in the footsteps of their forefathers' piety. Then shall mercy be preserved to them.

Verses 19-22

He who made all, rules all, and both by a word of power. He disposes all persons and things to his own glory. There is a world of holy angels who are ever praising him. Let all his works praise him. Such would have been our constant delight, if we had not been fallen creatures. Such it will in a measure become, if we are born of God. Such it will be for ever in heaven; nor can we be perfectly happy till we can take unwearied pleasure in perfect obedience to the will of our God. And let the feeling of each redeemed heart be, Bless the Lord, O my soul.

Chapter 104

Chapter Outline

Verses 1-9

Every object we behold calls on us to bless and praise the Lord, who is great. His eternal power and Godhead are clearly shown by the things which he hath made. God is light, and in him is no darkness at all. The Lord Jesus, the Son of his love, is the Light of the world.

Verses 10-18

When we reflect upon the provision made for all creatures, we should also notice the natural worship they render to God. Yet man, forgetful ungrateful man, enjoys the largest measure of his Creator's kindness. the earth, varying in different lands. Nor let us forget spiritual blessings; the fruitfulness of the church through grace, the bread of everlasting life, the cup of salvation, and the oil of gladness. Does God provide for the inferior creatures, and will he not be a refuge to his people?

Verses 19-30

We are to praise and magnify God for the constant succession of day and night. And see how those are like to the wild beasts, who wait for the twilight, and have fellowship with the unfruitful works of darkness. Does God listen to the language of mere nature, even in ravenous creatures, and shall he not much more interpret favourably the language of grace in his own people, though weak and broken groanings which cannot be uttered? There is the work of every day, which is to be done in its day, which man must apply to every morning, and which he must continue in till evening; it will be time enough to rest when the night comes, in which no man can work. The psalmist wonders at the works of God. The works of art, the more closely they are looked upon, the more rough they appear; the works of nature appear more fine and exact. They are all made in wisdom, for they all answer the end they were designed to serve. Every spring is an emblem of the resurrection, when a new world rises, as it were, out of the ruins of the old one. But man alone lives beyond death. When the Lord takes away his breath, his soul enters on another state, and his body will be raised, either to glory or to misery. May the Lord send forth his Spirit, and new-create our souls to holiness.

Verses 31-35

Man's glory is fading; God's glory is everlasting: creatures change, but with the Creator there is no variableness. And if mediation on the glories of creation be so sweet to the soul, what greater glory appears to the enlightened mind, when contemplating the great work of redemption! There alone can a sinner perceive ground of confidence and joy in God. While he with pleasure upholds all, governs all, and rejoices in all his works, let our souls, touched by his grace, meditate on and praise him.

Chapter 105

Chapter Outline

A solemn call to praise and serve the Lord.	(1–7)
His gracious dealings with Israel.	(8–23)
Their deliverance from Egypt, and their settlement in Canaan.	(24–45)

Verses 1-7

Our devotion is here stirred up, that we may stir up ourselves to praise God. Seek his strength; that is, his grace; the strength of his Spirit to work in us that which is good, which we cannot do but by strength derived from him, for which he will be sought. Seek to have his favour to eternity, therefore continue seeking it while living in this world; for he will not only be found, but he will reward those that diligently seek him.

Verses 8-23

Let us remember the Redeemer's marvellous works, his wonders, and the judgments of his mouth. Though true Christians are few number, strangers and pilgrims upon earth, yet a far better inheritance than Canaan is made sure to them by the covenant of God; and if we have the anointing of the Holy Spirit, none can do us any harm. Afflictions are among our mercies. They prove our faith and love, they humble our pride, they wean us from the world, and quicken our prayers. Bread is the staff which supports life; when that staff is broken, the body fails and sinks to the earth. The word of God is the staff of spiritual life, the food and support of the soul: the sorest judgment is a famine of hearing the word of the Lord. Such a famine was sore in all lands when Christ appeared in the flesh; whose coming, and the blessed effect of it, are shadowed forth in the history of Joseph. At the appointed time Christ was exalted as Mediator; all the treasures of grace and salvation are at his disposal, perishing sinners come to him, and are relieved by him.

Verses 24-45

As the believer commonly thrives best in his soul when under the cross; so the church also flourishes most in true holiness, and increases in number, while under persecution. Yet instruments shall be raised up for their deliverance, and plagues may be expected by persecutors. And see the special care God took of his people in the wilderness. All the benefits bestowed on Israel as a nation, were shadows of spiritual blessings with which we are blessed in Christ Jesus. Having redeemed us with his blood, restored our souls to holiness, and set us at liberty from Satan's bondage, he guides and guards us all the way. He satisfies our souls with the bread of heaven, and the water of life from the Rock of salvation, and will bring us safely to heaven. He redeems his servants from all iniquity, and purifies them unto himself, to be a peculiar people, zealous of good works.

Chapter 106

Chapter Outline

Verses 1-5

None of our sins or sufferings should prevent our ascribing glory and praise to the Lord. The more unworthy we are, the more is his kindness to be admired. And those who depend on the Redeemer's righteousness will endeavour to copy his example, and by word and deed to show forth his praise. God's people have reason to be cheerful people; and need not envy the children of men their pleasure or pride.

Verses 6-12

Here begins a confession of sin; for we must acknowledge that the Lord has done right, and we have done wickedly. We are encouraged to hope that though justly corrected, yet we shall not be utterly forsaken. God's afflicted people own themselves guilty before him. God is distrusted because his favours are not remembered. If he did not save us for his own name's sake, and to the praise of his power and grace, we should all perish.

Verses 13-33

Those that will not wait for God's counsel, shall justly be given up to their own hearts' lusts, to walk in their own counsels. An undue desire, even for lawful things, becomes sinful. God showed his displeasure for this. He filled them with uneasiness of mind, terror of conscience, and self-reproach. Many that fare deliciously every day, and whose bodies are healthful, have leanness in their souls: no love to God, no thankfulness, no appetite for the Bread of life, and then the soul must be lean. Those wretchedly forget themselves, that feast their bodies and starve their souls. Even the true believer will see abundant cause to say, It is of the Lord's mercies that I am not consumed. Often have we set up idols in our hearts, cleaved to some forbidden object; so that if a greater than Moses had not stood to turn away the anger of the Lord, we should have been destroyed. If God dealt severely with Moses for unadvised words, what do those deserve who speak many proud and wicked words? It is just in God to remove those relations that are blessings to us, when we are peevish and provoking to them, and grieve their spirits.

Verses 34-48

The conduct of the Israelites in Canaan, and God's dealings with them, show that the way of sin is down-hill; omissions make way for commissions: when they neglected to destroy the heathen, they learned their works. One sin led to many more, and brought the judgments of God on them. Their sin was, in part, their own punishment. Sinners often see themselves ruined by those who led them into evil. Satan, who is a tempter, will be a tormentor. At length, God showed pity to his people for his covenant's sake. The unchangeableness of God's merciful nature and love to his people, makes him change the course of justice into mercy; and no other change is meant by God's repentance. Our case is awful when the outward church is considered. When nations professing Christianity, are so guilty as we are, no wonder if the Lord brings them low for their sins. Unless there is general and deep repentance, there can be no prospect but of increasing calamities. The psalm concludes with prayer for completing the deliverance of God's people, and praise for the beginning and progress of it. May all the people of the earth, ere long, add their Amen.

Chapter 107

Chapter Outline

God's providential care of the children of men in distresses, in banishment, and dispersion.	(1–9)
In captivity.	(10–16)
In sickness.	(17–22)
Danger at sea.	(23–32)
God's hand is to be seen by his own people.	(33–43)

Verses 1-9

In these verses there is reference to the deliverance from Egypt, and perhaps that from Babylon: but the circumstances of travellers in those countries are also noted. It is scarcely possible to conceive the horrors suffered by the hapless traveller, when crossing the trackless sands, exposed to the burning rays of the sum. The words describe their case whom the Lord has redeemed from the bondage of Satan; who pass through the world as a dangerous and dreary wilderness, often ready to faint through troubles, fears, and temptations. Those who hunger and thirst after righteousness, after God, and communion with him, shall be filled with the goodness of his house, both in grace and glory.

Verses 10-16

This description of prisoners and captives intimates that they are desolate and sorrowful. In the eastern prisons the captives were and are treated with much severity. Afflicting providences must be improved as humbling providences; and we lose the benefit, if our hearts are unhumbled and unbroken under them. This is a shadow of the sinner's deliverance from a far worse confinement. The awakened sinner discovers his guilt and misery. Having struggled in vain for deliverance, he finds there is no help for him but in the mercy and grace of God. His sin is forgiven by a merciful God, and his pardon is accompanied by deliverance from the power of sin and Satan, and by the sanctifying and comforting influences of God the HolySpirit.

Verses 17-22

If we knew no sin, we should know no sickness. Sinners are fools. They hurt their bodily health by intemperance, and endanger their lives by indulging their appetites. This their way is their folly. The weakness of the body is the effect of sickness. It is by the power and mercy of God that we are recovered from sickness, and it is our duty to be thankful. All Christ's miraculous cures were emblems of his healing diseases of the soul. It is also to be applied to the spiritual cures which the Spirit of grace works. He sends his word, and heals souls; convinces, converts them, makes them holy, and all by the word. Even in common cases of recovery from sickness, God in his providence speaks, and it is done; by his word and Spirit the soul is restored to health and holiness.

Verses 23-32

Let those who go to sea, consider and adore the Lord. Mariners have their business upon the tempestuous ocean, and there witness deliverances of which others cannot form an idea. How seasonable it is at such a time to pray! This may remind us of the terrors and distress of conscience many experience, and of those deep scenes of trouble which many pass through, in their Christian course. Yet, in answer to their cries, the Lord turns their storm into a calm, and causes their trials to end in gladness.

Verses 33-43

What surprising changes are often made in the affairs of men! Let the present desolate state of Judea, and of other countries, explain this. If we look abroad in the world, we see many greatly increase, whose beginning was small. We see many who have thus suddenly risen, as suddenly brought to nothing. Worldly wealth is uncertain; often those who are filled with it, ere they are aware, lose it again. God has many ways of making men poor. The righteous shall rejoice. It shall fully convince all those who deny the Divine Providence. When sinners see how justly God takes away the gifts they have abused, they will not have a word to say. It is of great use to us to be fully assured of God's goodness, and duly affected with it. It is our wisdom to mind our duty, and to refer our comfort to him. A truly wise person will treasure in his heart this delightful psalm. From it, he will fully understand the weakness and wretchedness of man, and the power and loving-kindness of God, not for our merit, but for his mercy's sake.

Chapter 108

—We may usefully select passages from different psalms, as here, Ps 57; 60, to help our devotions, and enliven our gratitude. When the heart is firm in faith and love, the tongue, being employed in grateful praises, is our glory. Every gift of the Lord honours and profits the possessor, as it is employed in God's service and to his glory. Believers may pray with assured faith and hope, for all the blessings of salvation; which are secured to them by the faithful promise and covenant of God. Then let them expect from him help in every trouble, and victory in every conflict. Whatever we do, whatever we gain, God must have all the glory. Lord, visit all our souls with this salvation, with this favour which thou bearest to thy chosen people.

Chapter 109

Chapter Outline

David complains of his enemies.	(1–5)
He prophesies their destruction.	(6–20)
Prayers and praises.	(21–31)

Verses 1-5

It is the unspeakable comfort of all believers, that whoever is against them, God is for them; and to him they may apply as to one pleased to concern himself for them. David's enemies laughed at him for his devotion, but they could not laugh him out of it.

Verses 6-20

The Lord Jesus may speak here as a Judge, denouncing sentence on some of his enemies, to warn others. When men reject the salvation of Christ, even their prayers are numbered among their sins. See what hurries some to shameful deaths, and brings the families and estates of others to ruin; makes them and theirs despicable and hateful, and brings poverty, shame, and misery upon their posterity: it is sin, that mischievous, destructive thing. And what will be the effect of the sentence, "Go, ye cursed," upon the bodies and souls of the wicked! How it will affect the senses of the body, and the powers of the soul, with pain, anguish, horror, and despair! Think on these things, sinners, tremble and repent.

Verses 21-31

The psalmist takes God's comforts to himself, but in a very humble manner. He was troubled in mind. His body was wasted, and almost worn away. But it is better to have leanness in the body, while the soul prospers and is in health, than to have leanness in the soul, while the body is feasted. He was ridiculed and reproached by his enemies. But if God bless us, we need not care who curses us; for how can they curse whom God has not cursed; nay, whom he has blessed? He pleads God's glory, and the honour of his name. Save me, not according to my merit, for I pretend to none, but according to thy-mercy. He concludes with the joy of faith, in assurance that his present conflicts would end in triumphs. Let all that suffer according to the will of God, commit the keeping of their souls to him. Jesus, unjustly put to death, and now risen again, is an Advocate and Intercessor for his people, ever ready to appear on their behalf against a corrupt world, and the great accuser.

Chapter 110

Christ's kingdom.
—Glorious things are here spoken of Christ. Not only he should be superior to all the kings of the earth, but he then existed in glory as the eternal Son of God. Sitting is a resting posture: after services and sufferings, to give law, to give judgment. It is a remaining posture: he sits like a king for ever. All his enemies are now in a chain, but not yet made his footstool. And his kingdom, being set up, shall be kept up in the world, in despite of all the powers of darkness. Christ's people are a willing people. The power of the Spirit, going with the power of the world, to the people of Christs, is effectual to make them willing. They shall attend him in the beautiful attire of holiness; which becomes his house for ever. And he shall have many devoted to him. The dew of our youth, even in the morning of our days, ought to be consecrated to our Lord Jesus. Christ shall not only be a King, but a Priest. He is God's Minister to us, and our Advocate with the Father, and so is the Mediator between God and man. He is a Priest of the order of Melchizedek, which was before that of Aaron, and on many accounts superior to it, and a more lively representation of Christ's priesthood. Christ's sitting at the right hand of God, speaks as much terror to his enemies as happiness to his people. The effect of this victory shall be the utter ruin of his enemies. We have here the Redeemer saving his friends, and comforting them. He shall be humbled; he shall drink of the brook in the way. The wrath of God, running in the curse of the law, may be considered as the brook in the way of his undertaking. Christ drank of the waters of affliction in his way to the throne of glory. But he shall be exalted. What then are we? Has the gospel of Christ been to us the power of God unto salvation? Has his kingdom been set up in our hearts? Are we his willing subjects? Once we knew not our need of his salvation, and we were not willing that he should reign over us. Are we willing to give up every sin, to turn from a wicked, insnaring world, and rely only on his merits and mercy, to have him for our Prophet, Priest, and King? and do we desire to be holy? To those who are thus changed, the Saviour's sacrifice, intercession, and blessing belong.

Chapter 111

The Lord is to be praised for his works.

—The psalmist resolves to praise God himself. Our exhortations and our examples should agree together. He recommends the works of the Lord, as the proper subject, when we are praising him; and the dealings of his providence toward the world, the church, and particular persons. All the works of the Lord are spoken of as one, it is his work; so admirably do all the dispensations of his providence centre in one design. The works of God, humbly and diligently sought into, shall all be found just and holy. God's pardoning sin is the most wonderful of all his works, and ought to be remembered to his glory. He will ever be mindful of his covenant; he has ever been so, and he ever will be so. His works of providence were done according to the truth of the Divine promises and prophecies, and so were verity, or truth; and by him who has a right to dispose of the earth as he pleases, and so are judgment, or righteous: and this holds good of the work of grace upon the heart of man, ver. #(7, 8). All God's commandments are sure; all have been fulfilled by Christ, and remain with him for a rule of walk and conversation to us. He sent redemption unto his people, out of Egypt at first, and often afterwards; and these were typical of the great redemption, which in the fulness of time was to be wrought out by the Lord Jesus. Here his everlasting righteousness shines forth in union with his boundless mercy. No man is wise who does not fear the Lord; no man acts wisely except as influenced by that fear. This fear will lead to repentance, to faith in Christ, to watchfulness and obedience. Such persons are of a good understanding, however poor, unlearned, or despised.

Chapter 112

The blessedness of the righteous.

—We have to praise the Lord that there are a people in the world, who fear him and serve him, and that they are a happy people; which is owing entirely to his grace. Their fear is not that which love casts out, but that which love brings in. It follows and flows from love. It is a fear to offend. This is both fear and trust. The heart touched by the Spirit of God, as the needle touched with the loadstone, turns direct and speedily to God, yet still with trembling, being filled with this holy fear. Blessings are laid up for the faithful and their children's children; and true riches are bestowed on them, with as much of this world's possessions as is profitable for them. In the darkest hours of affliction and trial, the light of hope and peace will spring up within them, and seasonable relief shall turn mourning into joy. From their Lord's example they learn to be kind and full of compassion, as well as just in all their dealings; they use discretion, that they may be liberal in that manner which appears most likely to do good. Envy and slander may for a time hide their true characters here, but they shall be had in everlasting remembrance. They need not fear evil tidings. A good man shall have a settled spirit. And it is the endeavour of true believers to keep their minds stayed upon God, and so to keep them calm and undisturbed; and God has promised them both cause to do so, and grace to do so. Trusting in the Lord is the best and surest way of establishing the heart. The heart of man cannot fix any where with satisfaction, but in the truth of God, and there it finds firm footing. And those whose hearts are established by faith, will patiently wait till they gain their point.

Compare all this with the vexation of sinners. The happiness of the saints is the envy of the wicked. The desire of the wicked shall perish; their desire was wholly to the world and the flesh, therefore when these perish, their joy is gone. But the blessings of the gospel are spiritual and eternal, and are conferred upon the members of the Christian church, through Christ their Head, who is the Pattern of all righteousness, and the Giver of all grace.

Chapter 113

An exhortation to praise God.
—God has praise from his own people. They have most reason to praise him; for those who attend him as his servants, know him best, and receive most of his favours, and it is easy, pleasant work to speak well of their Master. God's name ought to be praised in every place, from east to west. Within this wide space the Lord's name is to be praised; it ought to be so, though it is not. Ere long it will be, when all nations shall come and worship before him. God is exalted above all blessing and praise. We must therefore say, with holy admiration, Who is like unto the Lord our God? How condescending in him to behold the things in the earth! And what amazing condescension was it for the Son of God to come from heaven to earth, and take our nature upon him, that he might seek and save those that were lost! How vast his love in taking upon him the nature of man, to ransom guilty souls! God sometimes makes glorious his own wisdom and power, when, having some great work to do, he employs those least likely, and least thought of for it by themselves or others. The apostles were sent from fishing to be fishers of men. And this is God's constant method in his kingdom of grace. He takes men, by nature beggars, and even traitors, to be his favourites, his children, kings and priests unto him; and numbers them with the princes of his chosen people. He gives us all our comforts, which are generally the more welcome when long delayed, and no longer expected. Let us pray that those lands which are yet barren, may speedily become fruitful, and produce many converts to join in praising the Lord.

Chapter 114

An exhortation to fear God.
—Let us acknowledge God's power and goodness in what he did for Israel, applying it to that much greater work of wonder, our redemption by Christ; and encourage ourselves and others to trust in God in the greatest straits. When Christ comes for the salvation of his people , he redeems them from the power of sin and Satan, separates them from an ungodly world, forms them to be his people, and becomes their King. There is no sea, no Jordan, so deep, so broad, but, when God's time is come, it shall be divided and driven back. Apply this to the planting the Christian church in the world. What ailed Satan and his idolatries, that they trembled as they did? But especially apply it to the work of grace in the heart. What turns the stream in a regenerate soul? What affects the lusts and corruptions, that they fly back; that prejudices are removed, and the whole man becomes

new? It is at the presence of God's Spirit. At the presence of the Lord, not only mountains, but the earth itself may well tremble, since it has lain under a curse for man's sin. As the Israelites were protected, so they were provided for by miracles; such was that fountain of waters into which the flinty rock was turned, and that rock was Christ. The Son of God, the Rock of ages, gave himself to death, to open a fountain to wash away sins, and to supply believers with waters of life and consolation; and they need not fear that any blessing is too great to expect from his love. But let sinners fear before their just and holy Judge. Let us now prepare to meet our God, that we may have boldness before him at his coming.

Chapter 115

Chapter Outline

Glory to be ascribed to God. (1–8)

by trusting in him and praising him. (9–18)

Verses 1-8

Let no opinion of our own merits have any place in our prayers or in our praises. All the good we do, is done by the power of his grace; and all the good we have, is the gift of his mere mercy, and he must have all the praise. Are we in pursuit of any mercy, and wrestling with God for it, we must take encouragement in prayer from God only. Lord, do so for us; not that we may have the credit and comfort of it, but that they mercy and truth may have the glory of it. The heathen gods are senseless things. They are the works of men's hands: the painter, the carver, the statuary, can put no life into them, therefore no sense. The psalmist hence shows the folly of the worshippers of idols.

Verses 9-18

It is folly to trust in dead images, but it is wisdom to trust in the living God, for he is a help and a shield to those that trust in him. Wherever there is right fear of God, there may be cheerful faith in him; those who reverence his word, may rely upon it. He is ever found faithful. The greatest need his blessing, and it shall not be denied to the meanest that fear him. God's blessing gives an increase, especially in spiritual blessings. And the Lord is to be praised: his goodness is large, for he has given the earth to the children of men for their use. The souls of the faithful, after they are delivered from the burdens of the flesh, are still praising him; but the dead body cannot praise God: death puts an end to our glorifying him in this world of trial and conflict. Others are dead, and an end is thereby put to their service, therefore we will seek to do the more for God. We will not only do it ourselves, but will engage others to do it; to praise him when we are gone. Lord, thou art the only object for faith and love. Help us to praise thee while living and when dying, that thy name may be the first and last upon our lips: and let the sweet savour of thy name refresh our souls for ever.

Chapter 116

Chapter Outline

Verses 1-9

We have many reasons for loving the Lord, but are most affected by his loving-kindness when relieved out of deep distress. When a poor sinner is awakened to a sense of his state, and fears that he must soon sink under the just wrath of God, then he finds trouble and sorrow. But let all such call upon the Lord to deliver their souls, and they will find him gracious and true to his promise. Neither ignorance nor guilt will hinder their salvation, when they put their trust in the Lord. Let us all speak of God as we have found him; and have we ever found him otherwise than just and good? It is of his mercies that we are not consumed. Let those who labour and are heavy laden come to him, that they may find rest to their souls; and if at all drawn from their rest, let them haste to return, remembering how bountifully the Lord has dealt with them. We should deem ourselves bound to walk as in his presence. It is a great mercy to be kept from being swallowed up with over-much sorrow. It is a great mercy for God to hold us by the right hand, so that we are not overcome and overthrown by a temptation. But when we enter the heavenly rest, deliverance from sin and sorrow will be complete; we shall behold the glory of the Lord, and walk in his presence with delight we cannot now conceive.

Verses 10-19

When troubled, we do best to hold our peace, for we are apt to speak unadvisedly. Yet there may be true faith where there are workings of unbelief; but then faith will prevail; and being humbled for our distrust of God's word, we shall experience his faithfulness to it. What can the pardoned sinner, or what can those who have been delivered from trouble or distress, render to the Lord for his benefits? We cannot in any way profit him. Our best is unworthy of his acceptance; yet we ought to devote ourselves and all we have to his service. I will take the cup of salvation; I will offer the drink-offerings appointed by the law, in token of thankfulness to God, and rejoice in God's goodness to me. I will receive the cup of affliction; that cup, that bitter cup, which is sanctified to the saints, so that to them it is a cup of salvation; it is a means of spiritual health. The cup of consolation; I will receive the benefits God bestows upon me, as from his hand, and taste his love in them, as the portion not only of mine inheritance in the other world, but of my cup in this. Let others serve what masters they will, truly I am thy servant. Two ways men came to be servants. By birth. Lord, I was born in thy house; I am the son of thine handmaid, and therefore thine. It is a great mercy to be children of godly parents. By redemption. Lord, thou hast loosed my bonds, thou hast discharged me from them, therefore I am thy servant. The bonds thou hast loosed shall tie me faster unto thee. Doing good is sacrifice, with which God is well pleased; and this must accompany giving thanks to his name. Why should we offer that to the Lord which cost us nothing? The psalmist will pay his vows now; he will not delay the payment: publicly, not to make a boast, but to show he is not ashamed of God's service, and to invite others to join him. Such are true saints of God, in whose lives and deaths he will be glorified.

Chapter 117

All people called upon to praise God.
—Here is a solemn call to all nations to praise the Lord, and proper matter for that praise is suggested. We are soon weary of well-doing, if we keep not up the pious and devout affections with which the spiritual sacrifice of praise ought to be kindled and kept burning. This is a gospel psalm. The apostle, Ro 15:11, quotes it as a proof that the gospel was to be preached to the Gentile nations, and that it would be entertained by them. For many ages, in Judah only was God known, and his name praised; this call was not then given to any Gentiles. But the gospel of Christ is ordered to be preached to all nations, and by him those that were afar off are made nigh. We are among the persons to whom the Holy Spirit here speaks, whom he calls upon to join his ancient people in praising the Lord. Grace has thus abounded to millions of perishing sinners. Let us then listen to the offers of the grace of God, and pray for that time when all nations of the earth shall show forth his praises. And let us bless God for the unsearchable riches of gospel grace.

Chapter 118

Chapter Outline

It is good to trust in the Lord.   (1–18)
The coming of Christ in his kingdom.   (19–29)

Verses 1-18

The account the psalmist here gives of his troubles is very applicable to Christ: many hated him without a cause; nay, the Lord himself chastened him sorely, bruised him, and put him to grief, that by his stripes we might be healed. God is sometimes the strength of his people, when he is not their song; they have spiritual supports, though they want spiritual delights. Whether the believer traces back his comfort to the everlasting goodness and mercy of God, or whether he looks forward to the blessing secured to him, he will find abundant cause for joy and praise. Every answer to our prayers is an evidence that the Lord is on our side; and then we need not fear what man can do unto us; we should conscientiously do our duty to all, and trust in him alone to accept and bless us. Let us seek to live to declare the works of God, and to encourage others to serve him and trust in him. Such were the triumphs of the Son of David, in the assurance that the good pleasure of the Lord should prosper in his hand.

Verses 19-29

Those who saw Christ's day at so great a distance, saw cause to praise God for the prospect. The prophecy, ver. #(22, 23), may refer to David's preferment; but principally to Christ. 1. His humiliation; he is the Stone which the builders refused: they would go on in their building without him. This proved the ruin of those who thus made light of him. Rejecters of Christ are rejected of God. 2. His exaltation; he is the chief Cornerstone in the foundation. He is the chief Top-stone, in whom the building is completed, who must, in all things, have the pre-eminence. Christ's name is Wonderful; and the redemption he wrought out is the most amazing of all God's wondrous works. We will rejoice and be glad in the Lord's day; not only that such a day is appointed, but in the occasion of it, Christ's becoming the Head. Sabbath days ought to be rejoicing days, then they are to us as the days of heaven. Let this Saviour be my Saviour, my Ruler. Let my soul prosper and be in health, in that peace and righteousness which his government brings. Let me have victory over the lusts that war against my soul; and let Divine grace subdue my heart. The duty which the Lord has made, brings light with it, true light. The duty this privilege calls for, is here set forth; the sacrifices we are to offer to God in gratitude for redeeming love, are ourselves; not to be slain upon the altar, but living sacrifices, to be bound to the altar; spiritual sacrifices of prayer and praise, in which our hearts must be engaged. The psalmist praises God, and calls upon all about him to give thanks to God for the glad tidings of great joy to all people, that there is a Redeemer, even Christ the Lord. In him the covenant of grace is made sure and everlasting.

Chapter 119

The general scope and design of this psalm is to magnify the Divine law, and make it honourable. There are ten words by which Divine revelation is called in this psalm, and each expresses what God expects from us, and what we may expect from him. 1. God's law; this is enacted by him as our Sovereign. 2. His way; this is the rule of his providence. 3. His testimonies; they are solemnly declared to the world. 4. His commandments; given with authority. 5. His precepts; not left as indifferent matters to us. 6. His word, or saying; it is the declaration of his mind. 7. His judgments; framed in infinite wisdom. 8. His righteousness; it is the rule and standard of what is right. 9. His statutes; they are always binding. 10. His truth or faithfulness; it is eternal truth, it shall endure forever.

Verses 1-8

This psalm may be considered as the statement of a believer's experience. As far as our views, desires, and affections agree with what is here expressed, they come from the influences of the Holy Spirit, and no further. The pardoning mercy of God in Christ, is the only source of a sinner's happiness. And those are most happy, who are preserved most free from the defilement of sin, who simply believe God's testimonies, and depend on his promises. If the heart be divided between him and the world, it is evil. But the saints carefully avoid all sin; they are conscious of much evil that clogs them in the ways of God, but not of that wickedness which draws them out of those ways. The tempter would make men think they are at them out of those ways. The tempter would make men think they are at liberty to follow the word of God or not, as they please. But the desire and prayer of a good man agree with the will and command of God. If a man expects by obedience in one thing to purchase indulgence for disobedience in others, his hypocrisy will be detected; if he is not ashamed in this world, everlasting shame will be his portion. The psalmist coveted to learn the laws of God, to give God the glory. And believers see that if God forsakes them, the temper will be too hard for them.

Verses 9-16

To original corruption all have added actual sin. The ruin of the young is either living by no rule at all, or choosing false rules: let them walk by Scripture rules. To doubt of our own wisdom and strength, and to depend upon God, proves the purpose of holiness is sincere. God's word is treasure worth laying up, and there is no laying it up safe but in our hearts, that we may oppose God's precepts to the dominion of sin, his promises to its allurements, and his threatenings to its violence. Let this be our plea with Him to teach us his statutes, that, being partakers of his holiness, we may also partake of his blessedness. And those whose hearts are fed with the bread of life, should with their lips feed many. In the way of God's commandments there is the unsearchable riches of Christ. But we do not meditate on God's precepts to good purpose, unless our good thoughts produce good works. I will not only think of thy statutes, but do them with delight. And it will be well to try the sincerity of our obedience by tracing the spring of it; the reality of our love by cheerfulness in appointed duties.

Verses 17-24

If God deals in strict justice with us, we all perish. We ought to spend our lives in his service; we shall find true life in keeping his word. Those that would see the wondrous things of God's law and gospel, must beg him to give them understanding, by the light of his Spirit. Believers feel themselves strangers on earth; they fear missing their way, and losing comfort by erring from God's commandments. Every sanctified soul hungers after the word of God, as food which there is no living without. There is something of pride at the bottom of every wilful sin. God can silence lying lips; reproach and contempt may humble and do us good, and then they shall be removed. Do we find the weight of the cross is above that we are able to bear? He that bore it for us will enable us to bear it; upheld by him we cannot sink. It is sad when those who should protect the innocent, are their betrayers. The psalmist went on in duty, and he found comfort in the word of God. The comforts of the word of God are most pleasant to a gracious soul, when other comforts are made bitter; and those that would have God's testimonies to be their delight, must be advised by them. May the Lord direct us in exercising repentance of sin, and faith in Christ.

Verses 25-32

While the souls of the children of this world cleave to the earth as their portion, the children of light are greatly burdened, because of the remains of carnal affections in their hearts. It is unspeakable comfort to a gracious soul, to think with what tenderness all its complaints are received by a gracious God. We can talk of the wonders of redeeming love, when we understand the way of God's precepts, and walk in that way. The penitent melts in sorrow for sin: even the patient spirit may melt in the sense of affliction, it is then its interest to pour out its soul before God. The way of lying means all false ways by which men deceive themselves and others, or are deceived by Satan and his instruments. Those who know and love the law of the Lord, desire to know it more, and love it better. The way of serious godliness is the way of truth; the only true way to happiness: we must always have actual regard to it. Those who stick to the word of God, may in faith expect and pray for acceptance with God. Lord, never leave me to do that by which I shall shame myself, and do not thou reject my services. Those that are going to heaven, should still press forward. God, by his Spirit, enlarges the hearts of his people when he gives them wisdom. The believer prays to be set free from sin.

Verses 33-40

Teach me thy statutes, not the mere words, but the way of applying them to myself. God, by his Spirit, gives a right understanding. But the Spirit of revelation in the word will not suffice, unless we have the Spirit of wisdom in the heart. God puts his Spirit within us, causing us to walk in his statutes. The sin here prayed against is covetousness. Those that would have the love of God rooted in them, must get the love of the world rooted out; for the friendship of the world is enmity with God. Quicken me in thy way; to redeem time, and to do every duty with liveliness of spirit. Beholding vanity deadens us, and slackens our pace; a traveller must not stand gazing upon every object that presents itself to his view. The promises of God's word greatly relate to the preservation of the true believer. When Satan has drawn a child of God into worldly compliances, he will reproach him with the falls into which he led him. Victory must come from the cross of Christ. When we enjoy the sweetness of God's precepts, it will make us long for more acquaintance with them. And where God has wrought to will, he will work to do.

Verses 41-48

Lord, I have by faith thy mercies in view; let me by prayer prevail to obtain them. And when the salvation of the saints is completed, it will plainly appear that it was not in vain to trust in God's word. We need to pray that we may never be afraid or ashamed to own God's truths and ways before men. And the psalmist resolves to keep God's law, in a constant course of obedience, without backsliding. The service of sin is slavery; the service of God is liberty. There is no full happiness, or perfect liberty, but in keeping God's law. We must never be ashamed or afraid to own our religion. The more delight we take in the service of God, the nearer we come to perfection. Not only consent to his law as good, but take pleasure in it as good for us. Let me put forth all the strength I have, to do it. Something of this mind of Christ is in every true disciple.

Verses 49-56

Those that make God's promises their portion, may with humble boldness make them their plea. He that by his Spirit works faith in us, will work for us. The word of God speaks comfort in affliction.

If, through grace, it makes us holy, there is enough in it to make us easy, in all conditions. Let us be certain we have the Divine law for what we believe, and then let not scoffers prevail upon us to decline from it. God's judgments of old comfort and encourage us, for he is still the same. Sin is horrible in the eyes of all that are sanctified. Ere long the believer will be absent from the body, and present with the Lord. In the mean time, the statutes of the Lord supply subjects for grateful praise. In the season of affliction, and in the silent hours of the night, he remembers the name of the Lord, and is stirred up to keep the law. All who have made religion the first thing, will own that they have been unspeakable gainers by it.

Verses 57-64

True believers take the Lord for the portion of their inheritance, and nothing less will satisfy them. The psalmist prayed with his whole heart, knowing how to value the blessing he prayed for: he desired the mercy promised, and depended on the promise for it. He turned from by-paths, and returned to God's testimonies. He delayed not. It behoves sinners to hasten to escape; and the believer will be equally in haste to glorify God. No care or grief should take away God's word out of our minds, or hinder the comfort it bestows. There is no situation on earth in which a believer has not cause to be thankful. Let us feel ashamed that others are more willing to keep from sleep to spend the time in sinful pleasures, than we are to praise God. And we should be more earnest in prayer, that our hearts may be filled with his mercy, grace, and peace.

Verses 65-72

However God has dealt with us, he has dealt with us better than we deserve; and all in love, and for our good. Many have knowledge, but little judgment; those who have both, are fortified against the snares of Satan, and furnished for the service of God. We are most apt to wander from God, when we are easy in the world. We should leave our concerns to the disposal of God, seeing we know not what is good for us. Lord, thou art our bountiful Benefactor; incline our hearts to faith and obedience. The psalmist will go on in his duty with constancy and resolution. The proud are full of the world, and its wealth and pleasures; these make them senseless, secure, and stupid. God visits his people with affliction, that they may learn his statutes. Not only God's promises, but even his law, his percepts, though hard to ungodly men, are desirable, and profitable, because they lead us with safety and delight unto eternal life.

Verses 73-80

God made us to serve him, and enjoy him; but by sin we have made ourselves unfit to serve him, and to enjoy him. We ought, therefore, continually to beseech him, by his Holy Spirit, to give us understanding. The comforts some have in God, should be matter of joy to others. But it is easy to own, that God's judgments are right, until it comes to be our own case. All supports under affliction must come from mercy and compassion. The mercies of God are tender mercies; the mercies of a father, the compassion of a mother to her son. They come to us when we are not able to go to them. Causeless reproach does not hurt, and should not move us. The psalmist could go on in the way of his duty, and find comfort in it. He valued the good will of saints, and was desirous to keep up his communion with them. Soundness of heart signifies sincerity in dependence on God, and devotedness to him.

Verses 81-88

The psalmist sought deliverance from his sins, his foes, and his fears. Hope deferred made him faint; his eyes failed by looking out for this expected salvation. But when the eyes fail, yet faith must not. His affliction was great. He was become like a leathern bottle, which, if hung up in the smoke, is dried and shrivelled up. We must ever be mindful of God's statutes. The days of the believer's mourning shall be ended; they are but for a moment, compared with eternal happiness. His enemies used craft as well as power for his ruin, in contempt of the law of God. The commandments of God are true and faithful guides in the path of peace and safety. We may best expect help from God when, like our Master, we do well and suffer for it. Wicked men may almost consume the believer upon earth, but he would sooner forsake all than forsake the word of the Lord. We should depend upon the grace of God for strength to do every good work. The surest token of God's good-will toward us, is his good work in us.

Verses 89-96

The settling of God's word in heaven, is opposed to the changes and revolutions of the earth. And the engagements of God's covenant are established more firmly than the earth itself. All the creatures answer the ends of their creation: shall man, who alone is endued with reason, be the only unprofitable burden of the earth? We may make the Bible a pleasant companion at any time. But the word, without the grace of God, would not quicken us. See the best help for bad memories, namely, good affections; and though the exact words be lost, if the meaning remain, that is well. I am thine, not my own, not the world's; save me from sin, save me from ruin. The Lord will keep the man in peace, whose mind is stayed on him. It is poor perfection which one sees and end of. Such are all things in this world, which pass for perfections. The glory of man is but as the flower of the grass. The psalmist had seen the fulness of the word of God, and its sufficiency. The word of the Lord reaches to all cases, to all times. It will take us from all confidence in man, or in our own wisdom, strength, and righteousness. Thus shall we seek comfort and happiness from Christ alone.

Verses 97-104

What we love, we love to think of. All true wisdom is from God. A good man carries his Bible with him, if not in his hands, yet in his head and in his heart. By meditation on God's testimonies we understand more than our teachers, when we understand our own hearts. The written word is a more sure guide to heaven, than all the fathers, the teachers, and ancients of the church. We cannot, with any comfort or boldness, attend God in holy duties, while under guilt, or in any by-way. It was Divine grace in his heart, that enabled the psalmist to receive these instructions. The soul has its tastes as well as the body. Our relish for the word of God will be greatest, when that for the world and the flesh is least. The way of sin is a wrong way; and the more understanding we get by the precepts of God, the more rooted will be our hatred of sin; and the more ready we are in the Scriptures, the better furnished we are with answers to temptation.

Verses 105-112

The word of God directs us in our work and way, and a dark place indeed the world would be without it. The commandment is a lamp kept burning with the oil of the Spirit, as a light to direct us in the choice of our way, and the steps we take in that way. The keeping of God's commands here meant, was that of a sinner under a dispensation of mercy, of a believer having part in the covenant of grace. The psalmist is often afflicted; but with longing desires to become more holy, offers up daily prayers for quickening grace. We cannot offer any thing to God, that he will accept but what he is pleased to teach us to do. To have our soul or life continually in our hands, implies constant danger of life; yet he did not forget God's promises nor his precepts. Numberless are the snares laid by the wicked; and happy is that servant of God, whom they have not caused to err from his Master's precepts. Heavenly treasures are a heritage for ever; all the saints accept them as such, therefore they can be content with little of this world. We must look for comfort only in the way of duty, and that duty must be done. A good man, by the grace of God, brings his heart to his work, then it is done well.

Verses 113-120

Here is a dread of the risings of sin, and the first beginnings of it. The more we love the law of God, the more watchful we shall be, lest vain thoughts draw us from what we love. Would we make progress in keeping God's commands, we must be separate from evil-doers. The believer could not live without the grace of God; but, supported by his hand, his spiritual life shall be maintained. Our holy security is grounded on Divine supports. All departure from God's statutes is error, and will prove fatal. Their cunning is falsehood. There is a day coming which will put the wicked into everlasting fire, the fit place for the dross. See what comes of sin Surely we who fall so low in devout affections, should fear, lest a promise being left us of entering into heavenly rest, any of us should be found to come short of it, Heb 4:1.

Verses 121-128

Happy is the man, who, acting upon gospel principles, does justice to all around. Christ our Surety, having paid our debt and ransom, secures all the blessings of salvation to every true believer. The psalmist expects the word of God's righteousness, and no other salvation than what is secured by that word, which cannot fall to the ground. We deserve no favour form God; we are most easy when we cast ourselves upon God's mercy, and refer ourselves to it. If any man resolve to do God's will as his servant, he shall be made to know his testimonies. We must do what we can for the support of religion, and, after all, must beg of God to take the work into his own hands. It is hypocrisy to say we love God's commandments more than our worldly interests. The way of sin is a false way, being directly contrary to God's precepts, which are right: those that love and esteem God's law, hate sin, and will not be reconciled to it.

Verses 129-136

The wonders of redeeming love will fix the heart in adoration of them. The Scriptures show us what we were, what we are, and what we shall be. They show us the mercy and the justice of the Lord, the joys of heaven, and the pains of hell. Thus they give to the simple, in a few days, understanding of those matters, which philosophers for ages sought in vain. The believer, wearied with the cares of life and his conflicts with sin, pants for the consolations conveyed to him by means of the sacred word. And every one may pray, Look thou upon me, and be merciful unto me as thou usest to do unto those that love thy name. We must beg that the Holy Spirit would order our steps. The dominion of sin is to be dreaded and prayed against by every one. The oppression of men is often more than flesh and blood can bear; and He who knoweth our frame, will not refuse to remove it in answer to the prayers of his people. Whatever obscurity may appear as to the faith of the Old Testament believers, their confidence at the throne of grace can only be explained by their having obtained more distinct views of gospel privileges, through the sacrifices and services of their law, than is generally imagined. Go to the same place, plead the name and merits of Jesus, and you will not, you cannot plead in vain. Commonly, where there is a gracious heart, there is a weeping eye. Accept, O Lord, the tears our blessed Redeemer shed in the days of his flesh, for us who should weep for our brethren or ourselves.

Verses 137-144

God never did, and never can do wrong to any. The promises are faithfully performed by Him that made them. Zeal against sin should constrain us to do what we can against it, at least to do more in religion ourselves. Our love to the word of God is evidence of our love to God, because it is designed to make us partake his holiness. Men's real excellency always makes them low in their own eyes. When we are small and despised, we have the more need to remember God's precepts, that we may have them to support us. The law of God is the truth, the standard of holiness, the rule of happiness; but the obedience of Christ alone justifies the believer. Sorrows are often the lot of saints in this vale of tears; they are in heaviness through manifold temptations. There are delights in the word of God, which the saints often most sweetly enjoy when in trouble and anguish. This is life eternal, to know God and Jesus Christ whom he has sent, Joh 17:3. May we live the life of faith and grace here, and be removed to the life of glory hereafter.

Verses 145-152

Supplications with the whole heart are presented only by those who desire God's salvation, and who love his commandments. Whither should the child go but to his father? Save me from my sins, my corruptions, my temptations, all the hinderances in my way, that I may keep thy testimonies. Christians who enjoy health, should not suffer the early hours of the morning to glide away unimproved. Hope in God's word encourages us to continue in prayer. It is better to take time from sleep, than not to find time for prayer. We have access to God at all hours; and if our first thoughts in the morning are of God, they will help to keep us in his fear all the day long. Make me lively and cheerful. God knows what we need and what is good for us, and will quicken us. If we are employed in God's service, we need not fear those who try to set themselves as far as they can out of the reach of the convictions and commands of his law. When trouble is near, God is near. He is never far to seek. All his commandments are truth. And God's promises will be performed. All that ever trusted in God have found him faithful.

Verses 153-160

The closer we cleave to the word of God, both as our rule and as our stay, the more assurance we have of deliverance. Christ is the Advocate of his people, their Redeemer. Those who were quickened by his Spirit and grace, when they were dead in trespasses and sins, often need to have the work of grace revived in them, according to the word of promise. The wicked not only do not God's statutes, but they do not even seek them. They flatter themselves that they are going to heaven; but the longer they persist in sin, the further it is from them. God's mercies are tender; they are a fountain that can never be exhausted. The psalmist begs for God's reviving, quickening grace. A man, steady in the way of his duty, though he may have many enemies, needs to fear none. Those that hate sin truly, hate it as sin, as a transgression of the law of God, and a breaking of his word. Our obedience is only pleasing to God, and pleasant to ourselves, when it comes from a principle of love. All, in every age, who receive God's word in faith and love, find every saying in it faithful.

Verses 161-168

Those whose hearts stand in awe of God's word, will rather endure the wrath of man, than break the law of God. By the word of God we are unspeakable gainers. Every man hates to have a lie told him, but we should more hate telling a lie; by the latter we give an affront to God. The more we see the beauty of truth, the more we shall see the hateful deformity of a lie. We are to praise God even for afflictions; through grace we get good from them. Those that love the world have great vexation, for it does not answer what they expect; those that love God's word have great peace, for it outdoes what they expect. Those in whom this holy love reigns, will not perplex themselves with needless scruples, or take offence at their brethren. A good hope of salvation will engage the heart in doing the commandments. And our love to the word of God must subdue our lusts, and root out carnal affections: we must make heart work of it, or we make nothing of it. We must keep the commandments of God by obedience to them, and his promises by reliance on them. God's eye is on us at all times; this should make us very careful to keep his commandments.

Verses 169-176

The psalmist desired grace and strength to lift up his prayers, and that the Lord would receive and notice them. He desired to know more of God in Christ; to know more of the doctrines of the word, and the duties of religion. He had a deep sense of unworthiness, and holy fear that his prayer should not come before God; Lord, what I pray for is, what thou hast promised. We have learned nothing to purpose, if we have not learned to praise God. We should always make the word of God the rule of our discourse, so as never to transgress it by sinful speaking, or sinful silence. His own hands are not sufficient, nor can any creature lend him help; therefore he looks up to God, that the hand that had made him may help him. He had made religion his deliberate choice. There is an eternal salvation all the saints long for, and therefore they pray that God would help their way to it. Let thy judgments help me; let all ordinances and all providences, (both are God's judgments,) further me in glorifying God; let them help me for that work. He often looks back with shame and gratitude to his lost estate. He still prays for the tender care of Him who purchased his flock with his own blood, that he may receive from him the gift of eternal life. Seek me, that is, Find me; for God never seeks in vain. Turn me, and I shall be turned. Let this psalm be a touchstone by which to try our hearts, and our lives. Do our hearts, cleansed in Christ's blood, make these prayers, resolutions and confessions our own? Is God's word the standard of our faith, and the law of our practice? Do we use it as pleas with Christ for what we need? Happy those who live in such delightful exercises.

Chapter 120

Chapter Outline

The psalmist prays to God to deliver him from false and malicious tongues.   (1–4)

He complains of wicked neighbours.   (5–7)

Verses 1-4

The psalmist was brought into great distress by a deceitful tongue. May every good man be delivered from lying lips. They forged false charges against him. In this distress, he sought God by fervent prayer. God can bridle their tongues. He obtained a gracious answer to this prayer. Surely sinners durst not act as they do, if they knew, and would be persuaded to think, what will be in the end thereof. The terrors of the Lord are his arrows; and his wrath is compared to burning coals of juniper, which have a fierce heat, and keep fire very long. This is the portion of the false tongue; for all that love and make a lie, shall have their portion in the lake that burns eternally.

Verses 5-7

It is very grievous to a good man, to be cast into, and kept in the company of the wicked, from whom he hopes to be for ever separated. See here the character of a good man; he is for living peaceably with all men. And let us follow David as he prefigured Christ; in our distress let us cry unto the Lord, and he will hear us. Let us follow after peace and holiness, striving to overcome evil with good.

Chapter 121

The safety of the godly.

—We must not rely upon men and means, instruments and second causes. Shall I depend upon the strength of the hills? upon princes and great men? No; my confidence is in God only. Or, we must lift up our eyes above the hills; we must look to God who makes all earthly things to us what they are. We must see all our help in God; from him we must expect it, in his own way and time. This psalm teaches us to comfort ourselves in the Lord, when difficulties and dangers are greatest. It is almighty wisdom that contrives, and almighty power that works the safety of those that put themselves under God's protection. He is a wakeful, watchful Keeper; he is never weary; he not only does not sleep, but he does not so much as slumber. Under this shade they may sit with delight and assurance. He is always near his people for their protection and refreshment. The right hand is the working hand; let them but turn to their duty, and they shall find God ready to give them success. He will take care that his people shall not fall. Thou shalt not be hurt, neither by the open assaults, nor by the secret attempts of thine enemies. The Lord shall prevent the evil thou fearest, and sanctify, remove, or lighten the evil thou feelest. He will preserve the soul, that it be not defiled by sin, and disturbed by affliction; he will preserve it from perishing eternally. He will keep thee in life and death; going out to thy labour in the morning of thy days, and coming home to thy rest when the evening of old age calls thee in. It is a protection for life. The Spirit, who is their Preserver and Comforter, shall abide with them for ever. Let us be found in our work, assured that the blessings promised in this psalm are ours.

Chapter 122

Chapter Outline

Esteem for Jerusalem. (1–5)

Concern for its welfare. (6–9)

Verses 1-5

The pleasure and profit from means of grace, should make us disregard trouble and fatigue in going to them; and we should quicken one another to what is good. We should desire our Christian friends, when they have any good work in hand, to call for us, and take us with them. With what readiness should we think of the heavenly Jerusalem! How cheerfully should we bear the cross and welcome death, in hopes of a crown of glory! Jerusalem is called the beautiful city. It was a type of the gospel church, which is compact together in holy love and Christian communion, so that it is all as one city. If all the disciples of Christ were of one mind, and kept the unity of the Spirit in the bond of peace, their enemies would be deprived of their chief advantages against them. But Satan's maxim always has been, to divide that he may conquer; and few Christians are sufficiently aware of his designs.

Verses 6-9

Those who can do nothing else for the peace of Jerusalem, may pray for it. Let us consider all who seek the glory of the Redeemer, as our brethren and fellow-travellers, without regarding differences which do not affect our eternal welfare. Blessed Spirit of peace and love, who didst dwell in the soul of the holy Jesus, descend into his church, and fill those who compose it with his heavenly tempers; cause bitter contentions to cease, and make us to be of one mind. Love of the brethren and love to God, ought to stir us up to seek to be like the Lord Jesus in fervent prayer and unwearied labour, for the salvation of men, and the Divine glory.

Chapter 123

Confidence in God under contempt.
—Our Lord Jesus has taught us to look unto God in prayer as our Father in heaven. In every prayer a good man lifts up his soul to God; especially when in trouble. We desire mercy from him; we hope he will show us mercy, and we will continue waiting on him till it come. The eyes of a servant are to his master's directing hand, expecting that he will appoint him his work. And also to his supplying hand. Servants look to their master or their mistress for their portion of meat in due season. And to God we must look for daily bread, for grace sufficient; from him we must receive it thankfully. Where can we look for help but to our Master? And, further, to his protecting hand. If the servant is wronged and injured in his work, who should right him, but his master? And to his correcting hand. Whither should sinners turn but to him that smote them? They humble themselves under God's mighty hand. And lastly, to his rewarding hand. Hypocrites look to the world's hand, thence they have their reward; but true Christians look to God as their Master and their Rewarder. God's people find little mercy with men; but this is their comfort, that with the Lord there is mercy. Scorning and contempt have been, are, and are likely to be, the lot of God's people in this world. It is hard to bear; but the servants of God should not complain if they are treated as his beloved Son was. Let us then, when ready to faint under trials, look unto Jesus, and by faith and prayer cast ourselves upon the mercy of God.

Chapter 124

Chapter Outline

The deliverance of the church.   (1–5)
Thankfulness for the deliverance.   (6–8)

Verses 1-5

God suffers the enemies of his people sometimes to prevail very far against them, that his power may be seen the more in their deliverance. Happy the people whose God is Jehovah, a God all-sufficient. Besides applying this to any particular deliverance wrought in our days and the ancient times, we should have in our thoughts the great work of redemption by Jesus Christ, by which believers were rescued from Satan.

Verses 6-8

God is the Author of all our deliverances, and he must have the glory. The enemies lay snares for God's people, to bring them into sin and trouble, and to hold them there. Sometimes they seem to prevail; but in the Lord let us put our trust, and we shall not be put to confusion. The believer will ascribe all the honour of his salvation, to the power, mercy, and truth of God, and look back with wonder and thanksgiving on the way in which the Lord has led him. Let us rejoice that our help for the time to come is in him who made heaven and earth.

Chapter 125

Chapter Outline

The security of the righteous.   (1–3)

Prayer for them, The ruin of the wicked.   (4, 5)

Verses 1-3

All those minds shall be truly stayed, that are stayed on God. They shall be as Mount Zion, firm as it is; a mountain supported by providence, much more as a holy mountain supported by promise. They cannot be removed from confidence in God. They abide for ever in that grace which is the earnest of their everlasting continuance in glory. Committing themselves to God, they shall be safe from their enemies. Even mountains may moulder and come to nothing, and rocks be removed, but God's covenant with his people cannot be broken, nor his care of them cease. Their troubles shall last no longer than their strength will bear them up under them. The rod of the wicked may come, may fall upon the righteous, upon their persons, their estates, their liberties, their families names, on any thing that falls to their lot; only it cannot reach their souls. And though it may come upon their lot, it shall not rest thereon. The Lord will make all work together for their good. The wicked shall only prove a correcting rod, not a destroying sword; even this rod shall not remain upon them, lest they distrust the promise, thinking God has cast them off.

Verses 4, 5

God's promises should quicken our prayers. The way of holiness is straight; there are no windings or shiftings in it. But the ways of sinners are crooked. They shift from one purpose to another, and turn hither and thither to deceive; but disappointment and misery shall befal them. Those who cleave to the ways of God, though they may have trouble in their way, their end shall be peace.

The pleading of their Saviour for them, secures to them the upholding power and preserving grace of their God. Lord, number us with them, in time, and to eternity.

Chapter 126

Chapter Outline

Those returned out of captivity are to be thankful.   (1–3)

Those yet in captivity are encouraged.   (4–6)

Verses 1-3

It is good to observe how God's deliverances of the church are for us, that we may rejoice in them. And how ought redemption from the wrath to come, from the power of sin and of Satan, to be valued! The sinner convinced of his guilt and danger, when by looking to a crucified Saviour he receives peace to his conscience, and power to break off his sins, often can scarcely believe that the prospect which opens to him is a reality.

Verses 4-6

The beginnings of mercies encourage us to pray for the completion of them. And while we are in this world there will be matter for prayer, even when we are most furnished with matter for praise. Suffering saints are often in tears; they share the calamities of human life, and commonly have a greater share than others. But they sow in tears; they do the duty of an afflicted state. Weeping must not hinder sowing; we must get good from times of affliction. And they that sow, in the tears of godly sorrow, to the Spirit, shall of the Spirit reap life everlasting; and that will be a joyful harvest indeed. Blessed are those that mourn, for they shall be for ever comforted. When we mourn for our sins, or suffer for Christ's sake, we are sowing in tears, to reap in joy. And remember that God is not mocked; for whatever a man soweth that shall he reap, Ga 6:7–9. Here, O disciple of Jesus, behold an emblem of thy present labour and future reward; the day is coming when thou shalt reap in joy, plentiful shall be thy harvest, and great shall be thy joy in the Lord.

Chapter 127

The value of the Divine blessing.

—Let us always look to God's providence. In all the affairs and business of a family we must depend upon his blessing. 1. For raising a family. If God be not acknowledged, we have no reason to expect his blessing; and the best-laid plans fail, unless he crowns them with success. 2. For the safety of a family or a city. Except the Lord keep the city, the watchmen, though they neither slumber nor sleep, wake but in vain; mischief may break out, which even early discoveries may not be able to prevent. 3. For enriching a family. Some are so eager upon the world, that they are continually full of care, which makes their comforts bitter, and their lives a burden. All this is to get money; but all in vain, except God prosper them: while those who love the Lord, using due diligence in their lawful callings, and casting all their care upon him, have needful success, without uneasiness or vexation. Our care must be to keep ourselves in the love of God; then we may be easy, whether we have little or much of this world. But we must use the proper means very diligently. Children are God's gifts, a heritage, and a reward; and are to be accounted blessings, and not burdens: he who sends mouths, will send meat, if we trust in him. They are a great support and defence to a family. Children who are young, may be directed aright to the mark, God's glory, and the service of their generation; but when they are gone into the world, they are arrows out of the hand, it is too late to direct them then. But these arrows in the hand too often prove arrows in the heart, a grief to godly parents. Yet, if trained according to God's word, they generally prove the best defence in declining years, remembering their obligations to their parents, and taking care of them in old age. All earthly comforts are uncertain, but the Lord will assuredly comfort and bless those who serve him; and those who seek the conversion of sinners, will find that their spiritual children are their joy and crown in the day of Jesus Christ.

Chapter 128

The blessings of those who fear God.

—Only those who are truly holy, are truly happy. In vain do we pretend to be of those that fear God, if we do not make conscience of keeping stedfastly to his ways. Blessed is every one that fears the Lord; whether he be high or low, rich or poor in the world. If thou fear him and walk in his ways, all shall be well with thee while thou livest, better when thou diest, best of all in eternity. By the blessing of God, the godly shall get an honest livelihood. Here is a double promise; they shall have something to do, for an idle life is a miserable, uncomfortable life, and shall have health and strength, and power of mind to do it. They shall not be forced to live upon the labours of other people. It is as much a mercy as a duty, with quietness to work and eat our own bread. They and theirs shall enjoy what they get. Such as fear the Lord and walk in his ways, are the only happy persons, whatever their station in life may be. They shall have abundant comfort in their family relations. And they shall have all the good things God has promised, and which they pray for. A good man can have little comfort in seeing his children's children, unless he sees peace upon Israel. Every true believer rejoices in the prosperity of the church. Hereafter we shall see greater things, with the everlasting peace and rest that remain for the Israel of God.

Chapter 129

Chapter Outline

Thankfulness for former deliverances.   (1–4)

A believing prospect of the destruction of   (5–8)
the enemies of Zion.

Verses 1-4

The enemies of God's people have very barbarously endeavoured to wear out the saints of the Most High. But the church has been always graciously delivered. Christ has built his church upon a rock. And the Lord has many ways of disabling wicked men from doing the mischief they design against his church. The Lord is righteous in not suffering Israel to be ruined; he has promised to preserve a people to himself.

Verses 5-8

While God's people shall flourish as the loaded palm-tree, or the green and fruitful olive, their enemies shall wither as the grass upon the house-tops, which in eastern countries are flat, and what grows there never ripens; so it is with the designs of God's enemies. No wise man will pray the Lord to bless these mowers or reapers. And when we remember how Jesus arose and reigns; how his people have been supported, like the burning but unconsumed bush, we shall not fear.

Chapter 130

Chapter Outline

The psalmist's hope in prayer.   (1–4)

His patience in hope.   (5–8)

Verses 1-4

The only way of relief for a sin-entangled soul, is by applying to God alone. Many things present themselves as diversions, many things offer themselves as remedies, but the soul finds that the Lord alone can heal. And until men are sensible of the guilt of sin, and quit all to come at once to God, it is in vain for them to expect any relief. The Holy Ghost gives to such poor souls a fresh sense of their deep necessity, to stir them up in earnest applications, by the prayer of faith, by crying to God. And as they love their souls, as they are concerned for the glory of the Lord, they are not to be wanting in this duty. Why is it that these matters are so long uncertain with them? Is it not from sloth and despondency that they content themselves with common and customary applications to God? Then let us up and be doing; it must be done, and it is attended with safety. We are to humble ourselves before God, as guilty in his sight. Let us acknowledge our sinfulness; we cannot justify ourselves, or plead not guilty. It is our unspeakable comfort that there is forgiveness with him, for that is what we need. Jesus Christ is the great Ransom; he is ever an Advocate for us, and through him we hope to obtain forgiveness. There is forgiveness with thee, not that thou mayest be presumed upon, but that thou mayest be feared. The fear of God often is put for the whole worship of God. The only motive and encouragement for sinners is this, that there is forgiveness with the Lord.

Verses 5-8

It is for the Lord that my soul waits, for the gifts of his grace, and the working of his power. We must hope for that only which he has promised in his word. Like those who wish to see the dawn, being very desirous that light would come long before day; but still more earnestly does a good man long for the tokens of God's favour, and the visits of his grace. Let all that devote themselves to the Lord, cheerfully stay themselves on him. This redemption is redemption from all sin. Jesus Christ saves his people from their sins, both from the condemning and from the commanding power of sin. It is plenteous redemption; there is an all-sufficient fulness in the Redeemer, enough for all, enough for each; therefore enough for me, says the believer. Redemption from sin includes redemption from all other evils, therefore it is a plenteous redemption, through the atoning blood of Jesus, who shall redeem his people from all their sins. All that wait on God for mercy and grace, are sure to have peace.

Chapter 131

The psalmist's humility. Believers encouraged to trust in God.

—The psalmist aimed at nothing high or great, but to be content in every condition God allotted. Humble saints cannot think so well of themselves as others think of them. The love of God reigning in the heart, will subdue self-love. Where there is a proud heart, there is commonly a proud look. To know God and our duty, is learning sufficiently high for us. It is our wisdom not to meddle with that which does not belong to us. He was well reconciled to every condition the Lord placed him in. He had been as humble as a little child about the age of weaning, and as far from aiming at high things; as entirely at God's disposal, as the child at the disposal of the mother or nurse. We must become as little children, Mt 18:3. Our hearts are desirous of worldly things, cry for them, and are fond of them; but, by the grace of God, a soul that is made holy, is weaned from these things. The child is cross and fretful while in the weaning; but in a day or two it cares no longer for milk, and it can bear stronger food. Thus does a converted soul quiet itself under the loss of what it loved, and disappointments in what it hoped for, and is easy whatever happens. When our condition is not to our mind, we must bring our mind to our condition; then we are easy to ourselves and all about us; then our souls are as a weaned child. And thus the psalmist recommends confidence in God, to all the Israel of God, from his own experience. It is good to hope, and quietly to wait for the salvation of the Lord under every trial.

Chapter 132

Chapter Outline

David's care for the ark.   (1–10)

The promises of God.   (11–18)

Verses 1-10

David bound himself to find a place for the Lord, for the ark, the token of God's presence. When work is to be done for the Lord, it is good to tie ourselves to a time. It is good in the morning to fix upon work for the day, with submission to Providence, for we know not what a day may bring forth. And we should first, and without delay, seek to have our own hearts made a habitation of God through the Spirit. He prays that God would take up his dwelling in the habitation he had built; that he would give grace to the ministers of the sanctuary to do their duty. David pleads that he was the anointed of the Lord, and this he pleads as a type of Christ, the great Anointed. We have no merit of our own to plead; but, for His sake, in whom there is a fulness of merit, let us find favour. And every true believer in Christ, is an anointed one, and has received from the Holy One the oil of true grace. The request is, that God would not turn away, but hear and answer their petitions for his Son's sake.

Verses 11-18

The Lord never turns from us when we plead the covenant with his anointed Prophet, Priest, and King. How vast is the love of God to man, that he should speak thus concerning his church! It is his desire to dwell with us; yet how little do we desire to dwell with him! He abode in Zion till the sins of Israel caused him to give them up to the spoilers. Forsake us not, O God, and deliver us not in like manner, sinful though we are. God's people have a special blessing on common enjoyments, and that blessing puts peculiar sweetness into them. Zion's poor have reason to be content with a little of this world, because they have better things prepared for them. God will abundantly bless the nourishment of the new man, and satisfy the poor in spirit with the bread of life. He gives more than we ask, and when he gives salvation, he will give abundant joy. God would bring to nothing every design formed to destroy the house of David, until King Messiah should arise out of it, to sit upon the throne of his Father. In him all the promises centre. His enemies, who will not have him to reign over them, shall at the last day be clothed with shame and confusion for ever.

Chapter 133

The excellency of brotherly love.

—We cannot say too much, it were well if enough could be said, to persuade people to live together in peace. It is good for us, for our honour and comfort; and brings constant delight to those who live in unity. The pleasantness of this is likened to the holy anointing oil. This is the fruit of the Spirit, the proof of our union with Christ, and adorns his gospel. It is profitable as well as pleasing; it brings blessings numerous as the drops of dew. It cools the scorching heat of men's passions, as the dews cool the air and refresh the earth. It moistens the heart, and makes it fit to receive the good seed of the word, and to make it fruitful. See the proof of the excellency of brotherly love: where brethren dwell together in unity, the Lord commands the blessing. God commands the blessing; man can but beg a blessing. Believers that live in love and peace, shall have the God of love and peace with them now, and they shall shortly be with him for ever, in the world of endless love and peace. May all who love the Lord forbear and forgive one another, as God, for Christ's sake, hath forgiven them.

Chapter 134

An exhortation to bless the Lord.
—We must stir up ourselves to give glory to God, and encourage ourselves to hope for mercy and grace from him. It is an excellent plan to fill up all our spare minutes with pious meditations, and prayers and praises. No time would then be a burden, nor should we murder our hours by trifling conversation and vain amusements, or by carnal indulgences. We need desire no more to make us happy, than to be blessed of the Lord. We ought to beg spiritual blessings, not only for ourselves, but for others; not only, The Lord bless me, but, The Lord bless thee; thus testifying our belief that there is enough for others as well as for us, and showing our good will to others.

Chapter 135

Chapter Outline

God to be praised for his mercy.   (1–4)

For his power and judgments.   (5–14)

The vanity of idols.   (15–21)

Verses 1-4

The subject-matter of praise, is the blessings of grace flowing from the everlasting love of God. The name of God as a covenant God and Father in Christ, blessing us with all spiritual blessings in him, is to be loved and praised. The Lord chose a people to himself, that they might be unto him for a name and a praise. If they do not praise him for this distinguishing favour, they are the most unworthy and ungrateful of all people.

Verses 5-14

God is, and will be always, the same to his church, a gracious, faithful, wonder-working God. And his church is, and will be, the same to him, a thankful, praising people: thus his name endures for ever. He will return in ways of mercy to them, and will delight to do them good.

Verses 15-21

These verses arm believers against idolatry and all false worship, by showing what sort of gods the heathen worshipped. And the more deplorable the condition of the Gentile nations that worship idols, the more are we to be thankful that we know better. Let us pity, and pray for, and seek to benefit benighted heathens and deluded sinners. Let us endeavour to glorify his name, and recommend his truth, not only with our lips, but by holy lives, copying the example of Christ's goodness and truth.

Chapter 136

Chapter Outline

God to be praised as the Creator of the world.	(1–9)
As Israel's God and Saviour.	(10–22)
For his blessings to all.	(23–26)

Verses 1-9

Forgetful as we are, things must be often repeated to us. By "mercy" we understand the Lord's disposition to save those whom sin has rendered miserable and vile, and all the provision he has made for the redemption of sinners by Jesus Christ. The counsels of this mercy have been from everlasting, and the effects of it will endure for ever, to all who are interested in it. The Lord continues equally ready to show mercy to all who seek for it, and this is the source of all our hope and comfort.

Verses 10-22

The great things God did for Israel, when he brought them out of Egypt, were mercies which endured long to them; and our redemption by Christ, which was typified thereby, endures for ever. It is good to enter into the history of God's favours, and in each to observe, and own, that his mercy endureth for ever. He put them in possession of a good land; it was a figure of the mercy of our Lord Jesus Christ.

Verses 23-26

God's everlasting mercy is here praised for the redemption of his church; in all his glories, and all his gifts. Blessed be God, who has provided and made known to us salvation through his Son. May we know and feel his redeeming power, that we may serve him in righteousness all our days. May He who giveth food to all flesh, feed our souls unto eternal life, and enliven our affections by his grace, that we may give thanks and praise to his holy name, for his mercy endureth for ever. Let us trace up all the favours we receive to this true source, and offer praise continually.

Chapter 137

Chapter Outline

The Jews bewail their captivity.	(1–4)
Their affection for Jerusalem.	(5–9)

Verses 1-4

Their enemies had carried the Jews captive from their own land. To complete their woes, they insulted over them; they required of them mirth and a song. This was very barbarous; also profane, for no songs would serve but the songs of Zion. Scoffers are not to be compiled with. They do not say, How shall we sing, when we are so much in sorrow? but, It is the Lord's song, therefore we dare not sing it among idolaters.

Verses 5-9

What we love, we love to think of. Those that rejoice in God, for his sake make Jerusalem their joy. They stedfastly resolved to keep up this affection. When suffering, we should recollect with godly sorrow our forfeited mercies, and our sins by which we lost them. If temporal advantages ever render a profession, the worst calamity has befallen him. Far be it from us to avenge ourselves; we will leave it to Him who has said, Vengeance is mine. Those that are glad at calamities, especially at the calamities of Jerusalem, shall not go unpunished. We cannot pray for promised success to the church of God without looking to, though we do not utter a prayer for, the ruin of her enemies. But let us call to mind to whose grace and finished salvation alone it is, that we have any hopes of being brought home to the heavenly Jerusalem.

Chapter 138

Chapter Outline

Verses 1-5

When we can praise God with our whole heart, we need not be unwilling for the whole world to witness our gratitude and joy in him. Those who rely on his loving-kindness and truth through Jesus Christ, will ever find him faithful to his word. If he spared not his own Son, how shall he not with him freely give us all things? If God gives us strength in our souls, to bear the burdens, resist the temptations, and to do the duties of an afflicted state, if he strengthens us to keep hold of himself by faith, and to wait with patience for the event, we are bound to be thankful.

Verses 6-8

Though the Lord is high, yet he has respect to every lowly, humbled sinner; but the proud and unbelieving will be banished far from his blissful presence. Divine consolations have enough in them to revive us, even when we walk in the midst of troubles. And God will save his own people that they may be revived by the Holy Spirit, the Giver of life and holiness. If we give to God the glory of his mercy, we may take to ourselves the comfort. This confidence will not do away, but quicken prayer. Whatever good there is in us, it is God works in us both to will and to do. The Lord will perfect the salvation of every true believer, and he will never forsake those whom he has created anew in Christ Jesus unto good works.

Chapter 139

Chapter Outline

Verses 1-6

God has perfect knowledge of us, and all our thoughts and actions are open before him. It is more profitable to meditate on Divine truths, applying them to our own cases, and with hearts lifted to God in prayer, than with a curious or disputing frame of mind. That God knows all things, is omniscient; that he is every where, is omnipresent; are truths acknowledged by all, yet they are seldom rightly believed in by mankind. God takes strict notice of every step we take, every right step and every by step. He knows what rule we walk by, what end we walk toward, what company we walk with. When I am withdrawn from all company, thou knowest what I have in my heart. There is not a vain word, not a good word, but thou knowest from what thought it came, and with what design it was uttered. Wherever we are, we are under the eye and hand of God. We cannot by searching find how God searches us out; nor do we know how we are known. Such thoughts should restrain us from sin.

Verses 7-16

We cannot see God, but he can see us. The psalmist did not desire to go from the Lord. Whither can I go? In the most distant corners of the world, in heaven, or in hell, I cannot go out of thy reach. No veil can hide us from God; not the thickest darkness. No disguise can save any person or action from being seen in the true light by him. Secret haunts of sin are as open before God as the most open villanies. On the other hand, the believer cannot be removed from the supporting, comforting presence of his Almighty Friend. Should the persecutor take his life, his soul will the sooner ascend to heaven. The grave cannot separate his body from the love of his Saviour, who will raise it a glorious body. No outward circumstances can separate him from his Lord. While in the path of duty, he may be happy in any situation, by the exercise of faith, hope, and prayer.

Verses 17-24

God's counsels concerning us and our welfare are deep, such as cannot be known. We cannot think how many mercies we have received from him. It would help to keep us in the fear of the Lord all the day long, if, when we wake in the morning, our first thoughts were of him: and how shall we admire and bless our God for his precious salvation, when we awake in the world of glory! Surely we ought not to use our members and senses, which are so curiously fashioned, as instruments of unrighteousness unto sin. But our immortal and rational souls are a still more noble work and gift of God. Yet if it were not for his precious thoughts of love to us, our reason and our living for ever would, through our sins, prove the occasion of our eternal misery. How should we then delight to meditate on God's love to sinners in Jesus Christ, the sum of which exceeds all reckoning! Sin is hated, and sinners lamented, by all who fear the Lord. Yet while we shun them we should pray for them; with God their conversion and salvation are possible. As the Lord knows us thoroughly, and we are strangers to ourselves, we should earnestly desire and pray to be searched and proved by his word and Spirit. if there be any wicked way in me, let me see it; and do thou root it out of me. The way of godliness is pleasing to God, and profitable to us; and will end in everlasting life. It is the good old way. All the saints desire to be kept and led in this way, that they may not miss it, turn out of it, or tire in it.

Chapter 140

Chapter Outline

David encourages himself in God.   (1–7)

He prays for, and prophesies the destruction   (8–13)
of, his persecutors.

Verses 1-7

The more danger appears, the more earnest we should be in prayer to God. All are safe whom the Lord protects. If he be for us, who can be against us? We should especially watch and pray, that the Lord would hold up our goings in his ways, that our footsteps slip not. God is as able to keep his people from secret fraud as from open force; and the experience we have had of his power and care, in dangers of one kind, may encourage us to depend upon him in other dangers.

Verses 8-13

Believers may pray that God would not grant the desires of the wicked, nor further their evil devices. False accusers will bring mischief upon themselves, even the burning coals of Divine vengeance. And surely the righteous shall dwell in God's presence, and give him thanks for evermore. This is true thanksgiving, even thanks-living: this use we should make of all our deliverances, we should serve God the more closely and cheerfully. Those who, though evil spoken of and ill-used by men, are righteous in the sight of God, being justified by the righteousness of Christ, which is imputed to them, and received by faith, as the effect of which, they live soberly and righteously; these give thanks to the Lord, for the righteousness whereby they are made righteous, and for every blessing of grace, and mercy of life.

Chapter 141

Chapter Outline

David prays for God's acceptance and   (1–4)
assistance.

That God would appear for his rescue.   (5–10)

Verses 1-4

Make haste unto me. Those that know how to value God's gracious presence, will be the more fervent in their prayers. When presented through the sacrifice and intercession of the Saviour, they will be as acceptable to God as the daily sacrifices and burnings of incense were of old. Prayer is a spiritual sacrifice, it is the offering up the soul and its best affections. Good men know the evil of tongue sins. When enemies are provoking, we are in danger of speaking unadvisedly. While we live in an evil world, and have such evil hearts, we have need to pray that we may neither be drawn nor driven to do any thing sinful. Sinners pretend to find dainties in sin; but those that consider how soon sin will turn into bitterness, will dread such dainties, and pray to God to take them out of their sight, and by his grace to turn their hearts against them. Good men pray against the sweets of sin.

Verses 5-10

We should be ready to welcome the rebuke of our heavenly Father, and also the reproof of our brethren. It shall not break my head, if it may but help to break my heart: we must show that we take it kindly. Those who slighted the word of God before, will be glad of it when in affliction, for that opens the ear to instruction. When the world is bitter, the word is sweet. Let us lift our prayer unto God. Let us entreat him to rescue us from the snares of Satan, and of all the workers of iniquity. In language like this psalm, O Lord, would we entreat that our poor prayers should set forth our only hope, our only dependence on thee. Grant us thy grace, that we may be prepared for this employment, being clothed with thy righteousness, and having all the gifts of thy Spirit planted in our hearts.

Chapter 142

David's comfort in prayer.
—There can be no situation so distressing or dangerous, in which faith will not get comfort from God by prayer. We are apt to show our troubles too much to ourselves, poring upon them, which does us no service; whereas, by showing them to God, we might cast the cares upon him who careth for us, and thereby ease ourselves. Nor should we allow any complaint to ourselves or others, which we cannot make to God. When our spirits are overwhelmed by distress, and filled with discouragement; when we see snares laid for us on every side, while we walk in his way, we may reflect with comfort that the Lord knoweth our path. Those who in sincerity take the Lord for their God, find him all-sufficient, as a Refuge, and as a Portion: every thing else is a refuge of lies, and a portion of no value. In this situation David prayed earnestly to God. We may apply it spiritually; the souls of believers are often straitened by doubts and fears. And it is then their duty and interest to beg of God to set them at liberty, that they may run the way of his commandments. Thus the Lord delivered David from his powerful persecutors, and dealt bountifully with him. Thus he raised the crucified Redeemer to the throne of glory, and made him Head over all things for his church. Thus the convinced sinner cries for help, and is brought to praise the Lord in the company of his redeemed people; and thus all believers will at length be delivered from this evil world, from sin and death, and praise their Saviour for ever.

Chapter 143

Chapter Outline

David complains of his enemies and distresses.   (1–6)

He prays for comfort, guidance, and deliverance.   (7–12)

Verses 1-6

We have no righteousness of our own to plead, therefore must plead God's righteousness, and the word of promise which he has freely given us, and caused us to hope in. David, before he prays for the removal of his trouble, prays for the pardon of his sin, and depends upon mercy alone for it. He bemoans the weight upon his mind from outward troubles. But he looks back, and remembers God's former appearance for his afflicted people, and for him in particular. He looks round, and notices the works of God. The more we consider the power of God, the less we shall fear the face or force of man. He looks up with earnest desires towards God and his favour. This is the best course we can take, when our spirits are overwhelmed. The believer will not forget, that in his best actions he is a sinner. Meditation and prayer will recover us from distresses; and then the mourning soul strives to return to the Lord as the infant stretches out its hands to the indulgent mother, and thirsts for his consolations as the parched ground for refreshing rain.

Verses 7-12

David prays that God would be well pleased with him, and let him know that he was so. He pleads the wretchedness of his case, if God withdrew from him. But the night of distress and discouragement shall end in a morning of consolation and praise. He prays that he might be enlightened with the knowledge of God's will; and this is the first work of the Spirit. A good man does not ask the way in which is the most pleasant walking, but what is the right way. Not only show me what thy will is, but teach me how to do it. Those who have the Lord for their God, have his Spirit for their Guide; they are led by the Spirit. He prays that he might be enlivened to do God's will. But we should especially seek the destruction of our sins, our worst enemies, that we may be devotedly God's servants.

Chapter 144

Chapter Outline

David acknowledges the great goodness of God, and prays for help.   (1–8)

He prays for the prosperity of his kingdom.   (9–15)

Verses 1-8

When men become eminent for things as to which they have had few advantages, they should be more deeply sensible that God has been their Teacher. Happy those to whom the Lord gives that noblest victory, conquest and dominion over their own spirits. A prayer for further mercy is fitly begun with a thanksgiving for former mercy. There was a special power of God, inclining the people of Israel to be subject to David; it was typical of the bringing souls into subjection to the Lord Jesus. Man's days have little substance, considering how many thoughts and cares of a never-dying soul are employed about a poor dying body. Man's life is as a shadow that passes away. In their highest earthly exaltation, believers will recollect how mean, sinful, and vile they are in themselves; thus they will be preserved from self-importance and presumption. God's time to help his people is, when they are sinking, and all other helps fail.

Verses 9-15

Fresh favours call for fresh returns of thanks; we must praise God for the mercies we hope for by his promise, as well as those we have received by his providence. To be saved from the hurtful sword, or from wasting sickness, without deliverance from the dominion of sin and the wrath to come, is but a small advantage. The public prosperity David desired for his people, is stated. It adds much to the comfort and happiness of parents in this world, to see their children likely to do well. To see them as plants, not as weeds, not as thorns; to see them as plants growing, not withered and blasted; to see them likely to bring forth fruit unto God in their day; to see them in their youth growing strong in the Spirit. Plenty is to be desired, that we may be thankful to God, generous to our friends, and charitable to the poor; otherwise, what profit is it to have our garners full? Also, uninterrupted peace. War brings abundance of mischiefs, whether it be to attack others or to defend ourselves. And in proportion as we do not adhere to the worship and service of God, we cease to be a happy people. The subjects of the Saviour, the Son of David, share the blessings of his authority and victories, and are happy because they have the Lord for their God.

Chapter 145

Chapter Outline

David extols the power, goodness, and   (1–9)
mercy of the Lord.

The glory of God's kingdom, and his care   (10–21)
of those that love him.

Verses 1-9

Those who, under troubles and temptations, abound in fervent prayer, shall in due season abound in grateful praise, which is the true language of holy joy. Especially we should speak of God's wondrous work of redemption, while we declare his greatness. For no deliverance of the Israelites, nor the punishment of sinners, so clearly proclaims the justice of God, as the cross of Christ exhibits it to the enlightened mind. It may be truly said of our Lord Jesus Christ, that his words are words of goodness and grace; his works are works of goodness and grace. He is full of compassion; hence he came into the world to save sinners. When on earth, he showed his compassion both to the bodies and souls of men, by healing the one, and making wise the other. He is of great mercy, a merciful High Priest, through whom God is merciful to sinners.

Verses 10-21

All God's works show forth his praises. He satisfies the desire of every living thing, except the unreasonable children of men, who are satisfied with nothing. He does good to all the children of men; his own people in a special manner. Many children of God, who have been ready to fall into sin, to fall into despair, have tasted his goodness in preventing their falls, or recovering them speedily by his graces and comforts. And with respect to all that are heavy laden under the burden of sin, if they come to Christ by faith, he will ease them, he will raise them. He is very ready to hear and answer the prayers of his people. He is present every where; but in a special way he is nigh to them, as he is not to others. He is in their hearts, and dwells there by faith, and they dwell in him. He is nigh to those that call upon him, to help them in all times of need. He will be nigh to them, that they may have what they ask, and find what they seek, if they call upon him in truth and sincerity. And having taught men to love his name and holy ways, he will save them from the destruction of the wicked. May we then love his name, and walk in his ways, while we desire that all flesh should bless his holy name for ever and ever.

Chapter 146

Chapter Outline

Why we should not trust in men.   (1–4)

Why we should trust in God.   (5–10)

Verses 1-4

If it is our delight to praise the Lord while we live, we shall certainly praise him to all eternity. With this glorious prospect before us, how low do worldly pursuits seem! There is a Son of man in whom there is help, even him who is also the Son of God, who will not fail those that trust in him. But all other sons of men are like the man from whom they sprung, who, being in honour, did not abide. God has given the earth to the children of men, but there is great striving about it. Yet, after a while, no part of the earth will be their own, except that in which their dead bodies are laid.

And when man returns to his earth, in that very day all his plans and designs vanish and are gone: what then comes of expectations from him?

Verses 5-10

The psalmist encourages us to put confidence in God. We must hope in the providence of God for all we need as to this life, and in the grace of God for that which is to come. The God of heaven became a man that he might become our salvation. Though he died on the cross for our sins, and was laid in the grave, yet his thoughts of love to us did not perish; he rose again to fulfil them. When on earth, his miracles were examples of what he is still doing every day. He grants deliverance to captives bound in the chains of sin and Satan. He opens the eyes of the understanding. He feeds with the bread of life those who hunger for salvation; and he is the constant Friend of the poor in spirit, the helpless: with him poor sinners, that are as fatherless, find mercy; and his kingdom shall continue for ever. Then let sinners flee to him, and believers rejoice in him. And as the Lord shall reign for ever, let us stir up each other to praise his holy name.

Chapter 147

Chapter Outline

The people of God are exhorted to praise him for his mercies and care.	(1–11)
For the salvation and prosperity of the church.	(12–20)

Verses 1-11

Praising God is work that is its own wages. It is comely; it becomes us as reasonable creatures, much more as people in covenant with God. He gathers outcast sinners by his grace, and will bring them into his holy habitation. To those whom God heals with the consolations of his Spirit, he speaks peace, assures them their sins are pardoned. And for this, let others praise him also. Man's knowledge is soon ended; but God's knowledge is a dept that can never be fathomed. And while he telleth the number of the stars, he condescends to hear the broken-hearted sinner. While he feeds the young ravens, he will not leave his praying people destitute. Clouds look dull and melancholy, yet without them we could have no rain, therefore no fruit. Thus afflictions look black and unpleasant; but from clouds of affliction come showers that make the soul to yield the peaceable fruits of righteousness. The psalmist delights not in things wherein sinners trust and glory; but a serious and suitable regard to God is, in his sight, of very great price. We are not to be in doubt between hope and fear, but to act under the gracious influences of hope and fear united.

Verses 12-20

The church, like Jerusalem of old, built up and preserved by the wisdom, power, and goodness of God, is exhorted to praise him for all the benefits and blessings vouchsafed to her; and these are represented by his favours in the course of nature. The thawing word may represent the gospel of Christ, and the thawing wind the Spirit of Christ; for the Spirit is compared to the wind, Joh 3:8. Converting grace softens the heart that was hard frozen, and melts it into tears of repentance, and makes good reflections to flow, which before were chilled and stopped up. The change which the thaw makes is very evident, yet how it is done no one can say. Such is the change wrought in the conversion of a soul, when God's word and Spirit are sent to melt it and restore it to itself.

Chapter 148

Chapter Outline

The creatures placed in the upper world called on to praise the Lord. (1–6)

Also the creatures of this lower world, especially his own people. (7–14)

Verses 1-6

We, in this dark and sinful world, know little of the heavenly world of light. But we know that there is above us a world of blessed angels. They are always praising God, therefore the psalmist shows his desire that God may be praised in the best manner; also we show that we have communion with spirits above, who are still praising him. The heavens, with all contained in them, declare the glory of God. They call on us, that both by word and deed, we glorify with them the Creator and Redeemer of the universe.

Verses 7-14

Even in this world, dark and bad as it is, God is praised. The powers of nature, be they ever so strong, so stormy, do what God appoints them, and no more. Those that rebel against God's word, show themselves to be more violent than even the stormy winds, yet they fulfil it. View the surface of the earth, mountains and all hills; from the barren tops of some, and the fruitful tops of others, we may fetch matter for praise. And assuredly creatures which have the powers of reason, ought to employ themselves in praising God. Let all manner of persons praise God. Those of every rank, high and low. Let us show that we are his saints by praising his name continually. He is not only our Creator, but our Redeemer; who made us a people near unto him. We may by "the Horn of his people" understand Christ, whom God has exalted to be a Prince and a Saviour, who is indeed the defence and the praise of all his saints, and will be so for ever. In redemption, that unspeakable glory is displayed, which forms the source of all our hopes and joys. May the Lord pardon us, and teach our hearts to love him more and praise him better.

Chapter 149

Chapter Outline

Joy to all the people of God.   (1–5)

Terror to their enemies.   (6–9)

Verses 1-5

New mercies continually demand new songs of praise, upon earth and in heaven. And the children of Zion have not only to bless the God who made them, but to rejoice in him, as having created them in Christ Jesus unto good works, and formed them saints as well as men. The Lord takes pleasure in his people; they should rejoice in Him. When the Lord has made sinners feel their wants and unworthiness, he will adorn them with the graces of his Spirit, and cause them to bear his image, and rejoice in his happiness for ever. Let his saints employ their waking hours upon their beds in songs of praise. Let them rejoice, even upon the bed of death, assured that they are going to eternal rest and glory.

Verses 6-9

Some of God's servants of old were appointed to execute vengeance according to his word. They did not do it from personal revenge or earthly politics, but in obedience to God's command. And the honour intended for all the saints of God, consists in their triumphs over the enemies of their salvation. Christ never intended his gospel should be spread by fire and sword, or his righteousness by the wrath of man. But let the high praises of God be in our mouths, while we wield the sword of the word of God, with the shield of faith, in warfare with the world, the flesh, and the devil. The saints shall be more than conquerors over the enemies of their souls, through the blood of the Lamb and the word of his testimony. The completing of this will be in the judgement of the great day. Then shall the judgement be executed. Behold Jesus, and his gospel church, chiefly in her millennial state. He and his people rejoice in each other; by their prayers and efforts they work with him, while he goes forth in the chariots of salvation, conquering sinners by grace, or in chariots of vengeance, to destroy his enemies.

Chapter 150

A psalm of praise.

—We are here stirred up to praise God. Praise God for his sanctuary, and the privileges we enjoy by having it among us; praise him because of his power and glory in the firmament. Those who praise the Lord in heaven, behold displays of his power and glory which we cannot now conceive. But the greatest of all his mighty acts is known in his earthly sanctuary. The holiness and the love of our God are more displayed in man's redemption, than in all his other works. Let us praise our God and Saviour for it. We need not care to know what instruments of music are mentioned. Hereby is meant that in serving God we should spare no cost or pains. Praise God with strong faith; praise him with holy love and delight; praise him with entire confidence in Christ; praise him with believing triumph over the powers of darkness; praise him by universal respect to all his commands; praise him by cheerful submission to all his disposals; praise him by rejoicing in his love, and comforting ourselves in his goodness; praise him by promoting the interests of the kingdom of his grace; praise him by lively hope and expectation of the kingdom of his glory. Since we must shortly breathe our last, while we have breath let us praise the Lord; then we shall breathe our last with comfort. Let every thing that hath breath praise the Lord. Praise ye the Lord. Such is the very suitable end of a book inspired by the Spirit of God, written for the work of praise; a book which has supplied the songs of the church for more than three thousand years; a book which is quoted more frequently than any other by Christ and his apostles; a book which presents the loftiest ideas of God and his government, which is fitted to every state of human life, which sets forth every state of religious experience, and which bears simple and clear marks of its Divine origin.

Proverbs

The subject of this book may be thus stated by an enlargement on the opening verses. 1. The Proverbs of Solomon, the son of David, king of Israel. 2. Which treat of the knowledge of wisdom, of piety towards God, of instruction and moral discipline, of the understanding wise and prudent counsels. 3. Which treat of the attainment of instruction in wisdom, which wisdom is to be shown in the conduct of life, and consists in righteousness with regard to our fellow-creatures. 4. Which treat of the giving to the simple sagacity to discover what is right, by supplying them with just principles, and correct views of virtue and vice; and to the young man knowledge, so that he need not err through ignorance; and discretion, so that by pondering well these precepts, he may not err through obstinacy. Take the proverbs of other nations, and we shall find great numbers founded upon selfishness, cunning, pride, injustice, national contempt, and animosities. The principles of the Proverbs of Solomon are piety, charity, justice, benevolence, and true prudence. Their universal purity proves that they are the word of God.

Chapter 1

Chapter Outline

The use of the Proverbs.	(1–6)
Exhortations to fear God and obey parents.	(7–9)
To avoid the enticings of sinners.	(10–19)
The address of Wisdom to sinners.	(20–33)

Verses 1-6

The lessons here given are plain, and likely to benefit those who feel their own ignorance, and their need to be taught. If young people take heed to their ways, according to Solomon's Proverbs, they will gain knowledge and discretion. Solomon speaks of the most important points of truth, and a greater than Solomon is here. Christ speaks by his word and by his Spirit. Christ is the Word and the Wisdom of God, and he is made to us wisdom.

Verses 7-9

Fools are persons who have no true wisdom, who follow their own devices, without regard to reason, or reverence for God. Children are reasonable creatures, and when we tell them what they must do, we must tell them why. But they are corrupt and wilful, therefore with the instruction there is need of a law. Let Divine truths and commands be to us most honourable; let us value them, and then they shall be so to us.

Verses 10-19

Wicked people are zealous in seducing others into the paths of the destroyer: sinners love company in sin. But they have so much the more to answer for. How cautious young people should be! "Consent thou not." Do not say as they say, nor do as they do, or would have thee to do; have no fellowship with them. Who could think that it should be a pleasure to one man to destroy another! See their idea of worldly wealth; but it is neither substance, nor precious. It is the ruinous mistake of thousands, that they overvalue the wealth of this world. Men promise themselves in vain that sin will turn to their advantage. The way of sin is down-hill; men cannot stop themselves. Would young people shun temporal and eternal ruin, let them refuse to take one step in these destructive paths. Men's greediness of gain hurries them upon practices which will not suffer them or others to live out half their days. What is a man profited, though he gain the world, if he lose his life? much less if he lose his soul?

Verses 20-33

Solomon, having showed how dangerous it is to hearken to the temptations of Satan, here declares how dangerous it is not to hearken to the calls of God. Christ himself is Wisdom, is Wisdoms. Three sorts of persons are here called by Him: 1. Simple ones. Sinners are fond of their simple notions of good and evil, their simple prejudices against the ways of God, and flatter themselves in their wickedness. 2. Scorners. Proud, jovial people, that make a jest of every thing. Scoffers at religion, that run down every thing sacred and serious. 3. Fools. Those are the worst of fools that hate to be taught, and have a rooted dislike to serious godliness. The precept is plain; Turn you at my reproof. We do not make a right use of reproofs, if we do not turn from evil to that which is good. The promises are very encouraging. Men cannot turn by any power of their own; but God answers, Behold, I will pour out my Spirit unto you. Special grace is needful to sincere conversion. But that grace shall never be denied to any who seek it. The love of Christ, and the promises mingled with his reproofs, surely should have the attention of every one. It may well be asked, how long men mean to proceed in such a perilous path, when the uncertainty of life and the consequences of dying without Christ are considered? Now sinners live at ease, and set sorrow at defiance; but their calamity will come. Now God is ready to hear their prayers; but then they shall cry in vain. Are we yet despisers of wisdom? Let us hearken diligently, and obey the Lord Jesus, that we may enjoy peace of conscience and confidence in God; be free from evil, in life, in death, and for ever.

Chapter 2

Chapter Outline

Verses 1-9

Those who earnestly seek heavenly wisdom, will never complain that they have lost their labour; and the freeness of the gift does not do away the necessity of our diligence, Joh 6:27 Let them seek, and they shall find it; let them ask, and it shall be given them. Observe who are thus favoured. They are the righteous, on whom the image of God is renewed, which consists in righteousness. If we depend upon God, and seek to him for wisdom, he will enable us to keep the paths of judgment.

Verses 10-22

If we are truly wise, we shall be careful to avoid all evil company and evil practices. When wisdom has dominion over us, then it not only fills the head, but enters into the heart, and will preserve, both against corruptions within and temptations without. The ways of sin are ways of darkness, uncomfortable and unsafe: what fools are those who leave the plain, pleasant, lightsome paths of uprightness, to walk in such ways! They take pleasure in sin; both in committing it, and in seeing others commit it. Every wise man will shun such company. True wisdom will also preserve from those who lead to fleshly lusts, which defile the body, that living temple, and war against the soul. These are evils which excite the sorrow of every serious mind, and cause every reflecting parent to look upon his children with anxiety, lest they should be entangled in such fatal snares. Let the sufferings of others be our warnings. Our Lord Jesus deters from sinful pleasures, by the everlasting torments which follow them. It is very rare that any who are caught in this snare of the devil, recover themselves; so much is the heart hardened, and the mind blinded, by the deceitfulness of this sin. Many think that this caution, besides the literal sense, is to be understood as a caution against idolatry, and subjecting the soul to the body, by seeking any forbidden object. The righteous must leave the earth as well as the wicked; but the earth is a very different thing to them. To the wicked it is all the heaven they ever shall have; to the righteous it is the place of preparation for heaven. And is it all one to us, whether we share with the wicked in the miseries of their latter end, or share those everlasting joys that shall crown believers?

Chapter 3

Chapter Outline

Verses 1-6

In the way of believing obedience to God's commandments health and peace may commonly be enjoyed; and though our days may not be long upon earth, we shall live for ever in heaven. Let not mercy and truth forsake thee; God's mercy in promising, and his truth in performing: live up to them, keep up thine interest in them, and take the comfort of them. We must trust in the Lord with all our hearts, believing he is able and wise to do what is best. Those who know themselves, find their own understandings a broken reed, which, if they lean upon, will fail. Do not design any thing but what is lawful, and beg God to direct thee in every case, though it may seem quite plain. In all our ways that prove pleasant, in which we gain our point, we must acknowledge God with thankfulness. In all our ways that prove uncomfortable, and that are hedged up with thorns, we must acknowledge him with submission. It is promised, He shall direct thy paths; so that thy way shall be safe and good, and happy at last.

Verses 7-12

There is not a greater enemy to the fear of the Lord in the heart, than self-conceit of our own wisdom. The prudence and sobriety which religion teaches, tend not only to the health of the soul, but to the health of the body. Worldly wealth is but poor substance, yet, such as it is, we must honour God with it; and those that do good with what they have, shall have more to do more good with. Should the Lord visit us with trials and sickness, let us not forget that the exhortation speaks to us as to children, for our good. We must not faint under an affliction, be it ever so heavy and long, not be driven to despair, or use wrong means for relief. The father corrects the son whom he loves, because he loves him, and desires that he may be wise and good. Afflictions are so far from doing God's children any hurt, that, by the grace of God, they promote their holiness.

Verses 13-20

No precious jewels or earthly treasures are worthy to be compared with true wisdom, whether the concerns of time or eternity be considered. We must make wisdom our business; we must venture all in it, and be willing to part with all for it. This Wisdom is the Lord Jesus Christ and his salvation, sought and obtained by faith and prayer. Were it not for unbelief, remaining sinfulness, and carelessness, we should find all our ways pleasantness, and our paths peace, for his are so; but we too often step aside from them, to our own hurt and grief. Christ is that Wisdom, by whom the worlds were made, and still are in being; happy are those to whom he is made of God wisdom. He has wherewithal to make good all his promises.

Verses 21-26

Let us not suffer Christ's words to depart from us, but keep sound wisdom and discretion; then shall we walk safely in his ways. The natural life, and all that belongs to it, shall be under the protection of God's providence; the spiritual life, and all its interests, under the protection of his grace, so that we shall be kept from falling into sin or trouble.

Verses 27-35

Our business is to observe the precepts of Christ, and to copy his example; to do justice, to love mercy, and to beware of covetousness; to be ready for every good work, avoiding needless strife, and bearing evils, if possible, rather than seeking redress by law. It will be found there is little got by striving. Let us not envy prosperous oppressors; far be it from the disciples of Christ to choose any of their ways. These truths may be despised by the covetous and luxurious, but everlasting contempt will be the portion of such scorners, while Divine favour is shown to the humble believer.

Chapter 4

Chapter Outline

Exhortation to the study of wisdom.   (1–13)

Cautions against bad company, Exhortation   (14–27)
to faith and holiness.

Verses 1-13

We must look upon our teachers as our fathers: though instruction carry in it reproof and correction, bid it welcome. Solomon's parents loved him, therefore taught him. Wise and godly men, in every age of the world, and rank in society, agree that true wisdom consists in obedience, and is united to happiness. Get wisdom, take pains for it. Get the rule over thy corruptions; take more pains to get this than the wealth of this world. An interest in Christ's salvation is necessary. This wisdom is the one thing needful. A soul without true wisdom and grace is a dead soul. How poor, contemptible, and wretched are those, who, with all their wealth and power, die without getting understanding, without Christ, without hope, and without God! Let us give heed to the sayings of Him who has the words of eternal life. Thus our path will be plain before us: by taking, and keeping fast hold of instruction, we shall avoid being straitened or stumbling.

Verses 14-27

The way of evil men may seem pleasant, and the nearest way to compass some end; but it is an evil way, and will end ill; if thou love thy God and thy soul, avoid it. It is not said, Keep at a due distance, but at a great distance; never think you can get far enough from it. The way of the righteous is light; Christ is their Way, and he is the Light. The saints will not be perfect till they reach heaven, but there they shall shine as the sun in his strength. The way of sin is as darkness. The way of the wicked is dark, therefore dangerous; they fall into sin, but know not how to avoid it. They fall into trouble, but never seek to know wherefore God contends with them, nor what will be in the end of it. This is the way we are bid to shun. Attentive hearing the word of God, is a good sign of a work of grace begun in the heart, and a good means of carrying it on. There is in the word of God a proper remedy for all diseases of the soul. Keep thy heart with all diligence. We must set a strict guard upon our souls; keep our hearts from doing hurt, and getting hurt. A good reason is given; because out of it are the issues of life. Above all, we should seek from the Lord Jesus that living water, the sanctifying Spirit, issuing forth unto everlasting life. Thus we shall be enabled to put away a froward mouth and perverse lips; our eyes will be turned from beholding vanity, looking straight forward, and walking by the rule of God's word, treading in the steps of our Lord and Master. Lord, forgive the past, and enable us to follow thee more closely for the time to come.

Chapter 5

Chapter Outline

Exhortations to wisdom. The evils of licentiousness.   (1–14)

Remedies against licentiousness, The miserable end of the wicked.   (15–23)

Verses 1-14

Solomon cautions all young men, as his children, to abstain from fleshly lusts. Some, by the adulterous woman, here understand idolatry, false doctrine, which tends to lead astray men's minds and manners; but the direct view is to warn against seventh-commandment sins. Often these have been, and still are, Satan's method of drawing men from the worship of God into false religion. Consider how fatal the consequences; how bitter the fruit! Take it any way, it wounds. It leads to the torments of hell. The direct tendency of this sin is to the destruction of body and soul. We must carefully avoid every thing which may be a step towards it. Those who would be kept from harm, must keep out of harm's way. If we thrust ourselves into temptation we mock God when we pray, Lead us not into temptation. How many mischiefs attend this sin! It blasts the reputation; it wastes time; it ruins the estate; it is destructive to health; it will fill the mind with horror. Though thou art merry now, yet sooner or later it will bring sorrow. The convinced sinner reproaches himself, and makes no excuse for his folly. By the frequent acts of sin, the habits of it become rooted and confirmed. By a miracle of mercy true repentance may prevent the dreadful consequences of such sins; but this is not often; far more die as they have lived. What can express the case of the self-ruined sinner in the eternal world, enduring the remorse of his conscience!

Verses 15-23

Lawful marriage is a means God has appointed to keep from these destructive vices. But we are not properly united, except as we attend to God's word, seeking his direction and blessing, and acting with affection. Ever remember, that though secret sins may escape the eyes of our fellow-creatures, yet a man's ways are before the eyes of the Lord, who not only sees, but ponders all his goings. Those who are so foolish as to choose the way of sin, are justly left of God to themselves, to go on in the way to destruction.

Chapter 6

Chapter Outline

Verses 1-5

If we live as directed by the word of God, we shall find it profitable even in this present world. We are stewards of our worldly substance, and have to answer to the Lord for our disposal of it; to waste it in rash schemes, or such plans as may entangle us in difficulties and temptations, is wrong. A man ought never to be surety for more than he is able and willing to pay, and can afford to pay, without wronging his family; he ought to look upon every sum he is engaged for, as his own debt. If we must take all this care to get our debts to men forgiven, much more to obtain forgiveness with God. Humble thyself to him, make sure of Christ as thy Friend, to plead for thee; pray earnestly that thy sins may be pardoned, and that thou mayest be kept from going down to the pit.

Verses 6-11

Diligence in business is every man's wisdom and duty; not so much that he may attain worldly wealth, as that he may not be a burden to others, or a scandal to the church. The ants are more diligent than slothful men. We may learn wisdom from the meanest insects, and be shamed by them. Habits of indolence and indulgence grow upon people. Thus life runs to waste; and poverty, though at first at a distance, gradually draws near, like a traveller; and when it arrives, is like an armed man, too strong to be resisted. All this may be applied to the concerns of our souls. How many love their sleep of sin, and their dreams of worldly happiness! Shall we not seek to awaken such? Shall we not give diligence to secure our own salvation?

Verses 12-19

If the slothful are to be condemned, who do nothing, much more those that do all the ill they can. Observe how such a man is described. He says and does every thing artfully, and with design. His ruin shall come without warning, and without relief. Here is a list of things hateful to God. Those sins are in a special manner provoking to God, which are hurtful to the comfort of human life. These things which God hates, we must hate in ourselves; it is nothing to hate them in others. Let us shun all such practices, and watch and pray against them; and avoid, with marked disapproval, all who are guilty of them, whatever may be their rank.

Verses 20-35

The word of God has something to say to us upon all occasions. Let not faithful reproofs ever make us uneasy. When we consider how much this sin abounds, how heinous adultery is in its own nature, of what evil consequence it is, and how certainly it destroys the spiritual life in the soul, we shall not wonder that the cautions against it are so often repeated. Let us notice the subjects of this chapter. Let us remember Him who willingly became our Surety, when we were strangers and enemies. And shall Christians, who have such prospects, motives, and examples, be slothful and careless? Shall we neglect what is pleasing to God, and what he will graciously reward? May we closely watch every sense by which poison can enter our minds or affections.

Chapter 7

Chapter Outline

Verses 1-5

We must lay up God's commandments safely. Not only, Keep them, and you shall live; but, Keep them as those that cannot live without them. Those that blame strict and careful walking as needless and too precise, consider not that the law is to be kept as the apple of the eye; indeed the law in the heart is the eye of the soul. Let the word of God dwell in us, and so be written where it will be always at hand to be read. Thus we shall be kept from the fatal effects of our own passions, and the snares of Satan. Let God's word confirm our dread of sin, and resolutions against it.

Verses 6-27

Here is an affecting example of the danger of youthful lusts. It is a history or a parable of the most instructive kind. Will any one dare to venture on temptations that lead to impurity, after Solomon has set before his eyes in so lively and plain a manner, the danger of even going near them? Then is he as the man who would dance on the edge of a lofty rock, when he has just seen another fall headlong from the same place. The misery of self-ruined sinners began in disregard to God's blessed commands. We ought daily to pray that we may be kept from running into temptation, else we invite the enemies of our souls to spread snares for us. Ever avoid the neighbourhood of vice. Beware of sins which are said to be pleasant sins. They are the more dangerous, because they most easily gain the heart, and close it against repentance. Do nothing till thou hast well considered the end of it. Were a man to live as long as Methuselah, and to spend all his days in the highest delights sin can offer, one hour of the anguish and tribulation that must follow, would far outweigh them.

Chapter 8

Chapter Outline

Verses 1-11

The will of God is made known by the works of creation, and by the consciences of men, but more clearly by Moses and the prophets. The chief difficulty is to get men to attend to instruction. Yet attention to the words of Christ, will guide the most ignorant into saving knowledge of the truth. Where there is an understanding heart, and willingness to receive the truth in love, wisdom is valued above silver and gold.

Verses 12-21

Wisdom, here is Christ, in whom are all the treasures of wisdom and knowledge; it is Christ in the word, and Christ in the heart; not only Christ revealed to us, but Christ revealed in us. All prudence and skill are from the Lord. Through the redemption of Christ's precious blood, the riches of his grace abound in all wisdom and prudence. Man found out many inventions for ruin; God found one for our recovery. He hates pride and arrogance, evil ways and froward conversation; these render men unwilling to hear his humbling, awakening, holy instructions. True religion gives men the best counsel in all difficult cases, and helps to make their way plain. His wisdom makes all truly happy who receive it in the love of Christ Jesus. Seek him early, seek him earnestly, seek him before any thing else. Christ never said, Seek in vain. Those who love Christ, are such as have seen his loveliness, and have had his love shed abroad in their hearts; therefore they are happy. They shall be happy in this world, or in that which is beyond compare better. Wealth gotten by vanity will soon be diminished, but that which is well got, will wear well; and that which is well spent upon works of piety and charity, will be lasting. If they have not riches and honour in this world, they shall have that which is infinitely better. They shall be happy in the grace of God. Christ, by his Spirit, guides believers into all truth, and so leads them in the way of righteousness; and they walk after the Spirit. Also, they shall be happy in the glory of God hereafter. In Wisdom's promises, believers have goods laid up, not for days and years, but for eternity; her fruit therefore is better than gold.

Verses 22-31

The Son of God declares himself to have been engaged in the creation of the world. How able, how fit is the Son of God to be the Saviour of the world, who was the Creator of it! The Son of God was ordained, before the world, to that great work. Does he delight in saving wretched sinners, and shall not we delight in his salvation?

Verses 32-36

Surely we should hearken to Christ's voice with the readiness of children. Let us all be wise, and not refuse such mercy. Blessed are those who hear the Saviour's voice, and wait on him with daily reading, meditation, and prayer. The children of the world find time for vain amusements, without neglecting what they deem the one thing needful. Does it not show contempt of Wisdom's instructions, when people professing godliness, seek excuses for neglecting the means of grace? Christ is Wisdom, and he is Life to all believers; nor can we obtain God's favour, unless we find Christ, and are found in him. Those who offend Christ deceive themselves; sin is a wrong to the soul. Sinners die because they will die, which justifies God when he judges.

Chapter 9

Chapter Outline

Verses 1-12

Christ has prepared ordinances to which his people are admitted, and by which nourishment is given here to those that believe in him, as well as mansions in heaven hereafter. The ministers of the gospel go forth to invite the guests. The call is general, and shuts out none that do not shut out themselves. Our Saviour came, not to call the righteous, but sinners; not the wise in their own eyes, who say they see. We must keep from the company and foolish pleasures of the ungodly, or we never can enjoy the pleasures of a holy life. It is vain to seek the company of wicked men in the hope of doing them good; we are far more likely to be corrupted by them. It is not enough to forsake the foolish, we must join those that walk in wisdom. There is no true wisdom but in the way of religion, no true life but in the end of that way. Here is the happiness of those that embrace it. A man cannot be profitable to God; it is for our own good. Observe the shame and ruin of those who slight it. God is not the Author of sin: and Satan can only tempt, he cannot force. Thou shalt bear the loss of that which thou scornest: it will add to thy condemnation.

Verses 13-18

How diligent the tempter is, to seduce unwary souls into sin! Carnal, sensual pleasure, stupifies conscience, and puts out the sparks of conviction. This tempter has no solid reason to offer; and where she gets dominion in a soul, all knowledge of holy things is lost and forgotten. She is very violent and pressing. We need to seek and pray for true wisdom, for Satan has many ways to withdraw our souls from Christ. Not only worldly lusts and abandoned seducers prove fatal to the souls of men; but false teachers, with doctrines that flatter pride and give liberty to lusts, destroy thousands. They especially draw off such as have received only partial serious impressions. The depths of Satan are depths of hell; and sin, without remorse, is ruin, ruin without remedy. Solomon shows the hook; those that believe him, will not meddle with the bait. Behold the wretched, empty, unsatisfying, deceitful, and stolen pleasure sin proposes; and may our souls be so desirous of the everlasting enjoyment of Christ, that on earth we may live to him, daily, by faith, and ere long be with him in glory.

Chapter 10

Through the whole of the Proverbs, we are to look for somewhat beyond the first sense the passage may imply, and this we shall find to be Christ. He is the Wisdom so often spoken of in this book.

Verse 1

The comfort of parents much depends on their children; and this suggests to both, motives to their duties.

Verses 2, 3

Though the righteous may be poor, the Lord will not suffer him to want what is needful for spiritual life.

Verse 4

Those who are fervent in spirit, serving the Lord, are likely to be rich in faith, and rich in good works.

Verse 5

Here is just blame of those who trifle away opportunities, both for here and for hereafter.

Verse 6

Abundance of blessings shall abide on good men; real blessings.

Verse 7

Both the just and the wicked must die; but between their souls there is a vast difference.

Verse 8

The wise in heart puts his knowledge in practice.

Verse 9

Dissemblers, after all their shuffling, will be exposed.

Verse 10

Trick and artifice will be no excuse for iniquity.

Verse 11

The good man's mouth is always open to teach, comfort, and correct others.

Verse 12

Where there is hatred, every thing stirs up strife. By bearing with each other, peace and harmony are preserved.

Verse 13

Those that foolishly go on in wicked ways, prepare rods for themselves.

Verse 14

Whatever knowledge may be useful, we must lay it up, that it may not be to seek when we want it. The wise gain this wisdom by reading, by hearing the word, by meditation, by prayer, by faith in Christ, who is made of God unto us wisdom.

Verse 15

This refers to the common mistakes both of rich and poor, as to their outward condition. Rich people's wealth exposes them to many dangers; while a poor man may live comfortably, if he is content, keeps a good conscience, and lives by faith.

Verse 16

Perhaps a righteous man has no more than what he works hard for, but that labour tends to life.

Verse 17

The traveller that has missed his way, and cannot bear to be told of it, and to be shown the right way, must err still.

Verse 18

He is especially a fool who thinks to hide anything from God; and malice is no better.

Verse 19

Those that speak much, speak much amiss. He that checks himself is a wise man, and therein consults his own peace.

Verses 20, 21

The tongue of the just is sincere, freed from the dross of guile and evil design. Pious discourse is spiritual food to the needy. Fools die for want of a heart, so the word is; for want of thought.

Verse 22

That wealth which is truly desirable, has no vexation of spirit in the enjoyment; no grief for the loss; no guilt by the abuse of it. What comes from the love of God, has the grace of God for its companion.

Verse 23

Only foolish and wicked men divert themselves with doing harm to others, or tempting to sin.

Verse 24

The largest desire of eternal blessings the righteous can form, will be granted.

Verse 25

The course of prosperous sinners is like a whirlwind, which soon spends itself, and is gone.

Verse 26

As vinegar sets the teeth on edge, and as the smoke causes the eyes to smart, so the sluggard vexes his employer.

Verses 27, 28

What man is he that loves life? Let him fear God, and that will secure to him life enough in this world, and eternal life in the other.

Verse 29

The believer grows stronger in faith, and obeys with increased delight.

Verse 30

The wicked would be glad to have this earth their home for ever, but it cannot be so. They must die and leave all their idols behind.

Verses 31, 32

A good man discourses wisely for the benefit of others. But it is the sin, and will be the ruin of a wicked man, that he speaks what is displeasing to God, and provoking to those he converses with. The righteous is kept by the power of God; and nothing shall be able to separate him from the love of God which is in Christ Jesus.

Chapter 11

Verse 1

However men may make light of giving short weight or measure, and however common such crimes may be, they are an abomination to the Lord.

Verse 2

Considering how safe, and quiet, and easy the humble are, we see that with the lowly is wisdom.

Verse 3

An honest man's principles are fixed, therefore his way is plain.

Verse 4

Riches will stand men in no stead in the day of death.

Verses 5, 6

The ways of wickedness are dangerous. And sin will be its own punishment.

Verse 7

When a godly man dies, all his fears vanish; but when a wicked man dies, his hopes vanish.

Verse 8

The righteous are often wonderfully kept from going into dangerous situations, and the ungodly go in their stead.

Verse 9

Hypocrites delude men into error and sin by artful objections against the truths of God's word.

Verses 10, 11

Nations prosper when wicked men are cast down.

Verse 12

A man of understanding does not judge of others by their success.

Verse 13

A faithful man will not disclose what he is trusted with, unless the honour of God and the real good of society require it.

Verse 14

We shall often find it to our advantage to advise with others.

Verse 15

The welfare of our families, our own peace, and our ability to pay just debts, must not be brought into danger. But here especially let us consider the grace of our Lord Jesus Christ in becoming Surety even for enemies.

Verse 16

A pious and discreet woman will keep esteem and respect, as strong men keep possession of wealth.

Verse 17

A cruel, froward, ill-natured man, is vexatious to those that are, and should be to him as his own flesh, and punishes himself.

Verse 18

He that makes it his business to do good, shall have a reward, as sure to him as eternal truth can make it.

Verse 19

True holiness is true happiness. The more violent a man is in sinful pursuits, the more he hastens his own destruction.

Verse 20

Nothing is more hateful to God, than hypocrisy and double dealing, which are here signified. God delights in such as aim and act with uprightness.

Verse 21

Joining together in sin shall not protect the sinners.

Verse 22

Beauty is abused by those who have not discretion or modesty with it. This is true of all bodily endowments.

Verse 23

The wicked desire mischief to others, but it shall return upon themselves.

Verse 24

A man may grow poor by not paying just debts, not relieving the poor, not allowing needful expenses. Let men be ever so saving of what they have, if God appoints, it comes to nothing.

Verse 25

Both in temporal and spiritual things, God commonly deals with his people according to the measure by which they deal with their brethren.

Verse 26

We must not hoard up the gifts of God's bounty, merely for our own advantage.

Verse 27

Seeking mischief is here set against seeking good; for those that are not doing good are doing hurt, even to themselves.

Verse 28

The true believer is a branch of the living Vine. When those that take root in the world wither, those who are grafted into Christ shall be fruitful.

Verse 29

He that brings trouble upon himself and his family, by carelessness, or by wickedness, shall be unable to keep and enjoy what he gets, as a man is unable to hold the wind, or to satisfy himself with it.

Verse 30

The righteous are as trees of life; and their influence upon earth, like the fruits of that tree, support and nourish the spiritual life in many.

Verse 31

Even the righteous, when they offend on earth, shall meet with sharp corrections; much more will the wicked meet the due reward of their sins. Let us then seek those blessings which our Surety purchased by his sufferings and death; let us seek to copy his example, and to keep his commandments.

Chapter 12

Verse 1

Those who have grace, will delight in the instructions given them. Those that stifle their convictions, are like brutes.

Verse 2

The man who covers selfish and vicious designs under a profession of religion or friendship, will be condemned.

Verse 3

Though men may advance themselves by sinful arts, they cannot settle and secure themselves. But those who by faith are rooted in Christ, are firmly fixed.

Verse 4

A wife who is pious, prudent, and looks well to the ways of her household, who makes conscience of her duty, and can bear crosses; such a one is an honour and comfort to her husband. She that is the reverse of this, preys upon him, and consumes him.

Verse 5

Thoughts are not free; they are under the Divine knowledge, therefore under the Divine command. It is a man's shame to act with deceit, with trick and design.

Verse 6

Wicked people speak mischief to their neighbours. A man may sometimes do a good work with one good word.

Verse 7

God's blessing is often continued to the families of godly men, while the wicked are overthrown.

Verse 8

The apostles showed wisdom by glorying in shame for the name of Christ.

Verse 9

He that lives in a humble state, who has no one to wait upon him, but gets bread by his own labour, is happier than he that glories in high birth or gay attire, and wants necessaries.

Verse 10

A godly man would not put even an animal to needless pain. But the wicked often speak of others as well used, when they would not endure like treatment for a single day.

Verse 11

It is men's wisdom to mind their business, and follow an honest calling. But it is folly to neglect business; and the grace of God teaches men to disdain nothing but sin.

Verse 12

When the ungodly see others prosper by sin, they wish they could act in the same way. But the root of Divine grace, in the heart of the righteous, produces other desires and purposes.

Verse 13

Many a man has paid dear in this world for the transgression of his lips.

Verse 14

When men use their tongues aright, to teach and comfort others, they enjoy acceptance through Christ Jesus; and the testimony of their conscience, that they in some measure answer the end of their being.

Verse 15

A fool, in the sense of Scripture, means a wicked man, one who acts contrary to the wisdom that is from above. His rule is, to do what is right in his own eyes.

Verse 16

A foolish man is soon angry, and is hasty in expressing it; he is ever in trouble and running into mischief. It is kindness to ourselves to make light of injuries and affronts, instead of making the worst of them.

Verse 17

It is good for all to dread and detest the sin of lying, and to be governed by honesty.

Verse 18

Whisperings and evil surmises, like a sword, separate those that have been dear to each other. The tongue of the wise is health, making all whole.

Verse 19

If truth be spoken, it will hold good; whoever may be disobliged, still it will keep its ground.

Verse 20

Deceit and falsehood bring terrors and perplexities. But those who consult the peace and happiness of others have joy in their own minds.

Verse 21

If men are sincerely righteous, the righteous God has engaged that no evil shall happen to them. But they that delight in mischief shall have enough of it.

Verse 22

Make conscience of truth, not only in words, but in actions.

Verse 23

Foolish men proclaim to all the folly and emptiness of their minds.

Verse 24

Those who will not take pains in an honest calling, living by tricks and dishonesty, are paltry and beggarly.

Verse 25

Care, fear, and sorrow, upon the spirits, deprive men of vigour in what is to be done, or courage in what is to be borne. A good word from God, applied by faith, makes the heart glad.

Verse 26

The righteous is abundant; though not in this world's goods, yet in the graces and comforts of the Spirit, which are the true riches. Evil men vainly flatter themselves that their ways are not wrong.

Verse 27

The slothful man makes no good use of the advantages Providence puts in his way, and has no comfort in them. The substance of a diligent man, though not great, does good to him and his family. He sees that God gives it to him in answer to prayer.

Verse 28

The way of religion is a straight, plain way; it is the way of righteousness. There is not only life at the end, but life in the way; all true comfort.

Chapter 13

Verse 1

There is great hope of those that reverence their parents. There is little hope of any who will not hear those that deal faithfully with them.

Verse 2

By our words we must be justified or condemned, Mt 12:37.

Verse 3

He that thinks before he speaks, that suppresses evil if he have thought it, keeps his soul from a great deal both of guilt and grief. Many a one is ruined by an ungoverned tongue.

Verse 4

The slothful desire the gains the diligent get, but hate the pains the diligent take; therefore they have nothing. This is especially true as to the soul.

Verse 5

Where sin reigns, the man is loathsome. If his conscience were awake, he would abhor himself, and repent in dust and ashes.

Verse 6

An honest desire to do right, preserves a man from fatal mistakes, better than a thousand fine-drawn distinctions.

Verse 7

Some who are really poor, trade and spend as if they were rich: this is sin, and will be shame, and it will end accordingly. Some that are really rich, would be thought to be poor: in this there is want of gratitude to God, want of justice and charity to others. There are many hypocrites, empty of grace, who will not be convinced of their poverty. There are many fearing Christians, who are spiritually rich, yet think themselves poor; by their doubts, and complaints, and griefs, they make themselves poor.

Verse 8

Great riches often tempt to violence against those that possess them; but the poor are free from such perils.

Verse 9

The light of the righteous is as that of the sun, which may be eclipsed and clouded, but will continue: the Spirit is their Light, he gives a fulness of joy: that of the wicked is as a lamp of their own kindling, easily put out.

Verse 10

All contentions, whether between private persons, families, churches, or nations, are begun and carried forward by pride. Disputes would be easily prevented or ended, if it were not for pride.

Verse 11

Wealth gotten by dishonesty or vice, has a secret curse, which will speedily waste it.

Verse 12

The delay of what is anxiously hoped for, is very painful to the mind; obtaining it is very pleasant. But spiritual blessings are chiefly intended.

Verse 13

He that stands in awe of God, and reverences his word, shall escape destruction, and be rewarded for his godly fear.

Verse 14

The rule by which the wise regulate their conduct, is a fountain yielding life and happiness.

Verse 15

The way of sinners is hard upon others, and hard to the sinner himself. The service of sin is slavery; the road to hell is strewed with the thorns and thistles that followed the curse.

Verse 16

It is folly to talk of things of which we know nothing, and to undertake what we are no way fit for.

Verse 17

Those that are wicked, and false to Christ and to the souls of men, do mischief, and fall into mischief; but those that are faithful, find sound words healing to others and to themselves.

Verse 18

He that scorns to be taught, will certainly be brought down.

Verse 19

There are in man strong desires after happiness; but never let those expect any thing truly sweet to their souls, who will not be persuaded to leave their sins.

Verse 20

Multitudes are brought to ruin by bad company. And all that make themselves wicked will be destroyed.

Verse 21

When God pursues sinners he is sure to overtake them; and he will reward the righteous.

Verse 22

The servant of God who is not anxious about riches, takes the best method of providing for his children.

Verse 23

The poor, yet industrious, thrive, though in a homely manner, while those who have great riches are often brought to poverty for want of judgment.

Verse 24

He acts as if he hated his child, who, by false indulgence, permits sinful habits to gather strength, which will bring sorrow here, and misery hereafter.

Verse 25

It is the misery of the wicked, that even their sensual appetites are always craving. The righteous feeds on the word and ordinances, to the satisfying of his soul with the promises of the gospel, and the Lord Jesus Christ, who is the Bread of life.

Chapter 14

Verse 1

A woman who has no fear of God, who is wilful and wasteful, and indulges her ease, will as certainly ruin her family, as if she plucked her house down.

Verse 2

Here are grace and sin in their true colours. Those that despise God's precepts and promises, despise God and all his power and mercy.

Verse 3

Pride grows from that root of bitterness which is in the heart. The root must be plucked up, or we cannot conquer this branch. The prudent words of wise men get them out of difficulties.

Verse 4

There can be no advantage without something which, though of little moment, will affright the indolent.

Verse 5

A conscientious witness will not dare to represent anything otherwise than according to his knowledge.

Verse 6

A scorner treats Divine things with contempt. He that feels his ignorance and unworthiness will search the Scriptures in a humble spirit.

Verse 7

We discover a wicked man if there is no savour of piety in his discourse.

Verse 8

We are travellers, whose concern is, not to spy out wonders, but to get to their journey's end; to understand the rules we are to walk by, also the ends we are to walk toward. The bad man cheats himself, and goes on in his mistake.

Verse 9

Foolish and profane men consider sin a mere trifle, to be made light of rather than mourned over. Fools mock at the sin-offering; but those that make light of sin, make light of Christ.

Verse 10

We do not know what stings of conscience, or consuming passions, torment the prosperous sinner. Nor does the world know the peace of mind a serious Christian enjoys, even in poverty and sickness.

Verse 11

Sin ruins many great families; whilst righteousness often raises and strengthens even mean families.

Verse 12

The ways of carelessness, of worldliness, and of sensuality, seem right to those that walk in them; but self-deceivers prove self-destroyers. See the vanity of carnal mirth.

Verse 14

Of all sinners backsliders will have the most terror when they reflect on their own ways.

Verse 15

Eager readiness to believe what others say, has ever proved mischievous. The whole world was thus ruined at first. The man who is spiritually wise, depends on the Saviour alone for acceptance. He is watchful against the enemies of his salvation, by taking heed to God's word.

Verse 16

Holy fear guards against every thing unholy.

Verse 17

An angry man is to be pitied as well as blamed; but the revengeful is more hateful.

Verse 18

Sin is the shame of sinners; but wisdom is the honour of the wise.

Verse 19

Even bad men acknowledge the excellency of God's people.

Verse 20

Friendship in the world is governed by self-interest. It is good to have God our Friend; he will not desert us.

Verse 21

To despise a man for his employment or appearance is a sin.

Verse 22

How wisely those consult their own interest, who not only do good, but devise it!

Verse 23

Labour of the head, or of the hand, will turn to some good account. But if men's religion runs all out in talk and noise, they will come to nothing.

Verse 24

The riches of men of wisdom and piety enlarge their usefulness.

Verse 25

An upright man will venture the displeasure of the greatest, to bring truth to light.

Verses 26, 27

Those who fear the Lord so as to obey and serve him, have a strong ground of confidence, and will be preserved. Let us seek to this Fountain of life, that we may escape the snares of death.

Verse 28

Let all that wish well to the kingdom of Christ, do what they can, that many may be added to his church.

Verse 29

A mild, patient man is one that learns of Christ, who is Wisdom itself. Unbridled passion is folly made known.

Verse 30

An upright, contented, and benevolent mind, tends to health.

Verse 31

To oppress the poor is to reproach our Creator.

Verse 32

The wicked man has his soul forced from him; he dies in his sins, under the guilt and power of them. But godly men, though they have pain and some dread of death, have the blessed hope, which God, who cannot lie, has given them.

Verse 33

Wisdom possesses the heart, and thus regulates the affections and tempers.

Verse 34

Piety and holiness always promote industry, sobriety, and honesty.

Verse 35

The great King who reigns over heaven and earth, will reward faithful servants who honour his gospel by the proper discharge of the duties of their stations: he despises not the services of the lowest.

Chapter 15

Verse 1

A right cause will be better pleaded with meekness than with passion. Nothing stirs up anger like grievous words.

Verse 2

He that has knowledge, is to use it aright, for the good of others.

Verse 3

Secret sins, services, and sorrows, are under God's eye. This speaks comfort to saints, and terror to sinners.

Verse 4

A good tongue is healing to wounded consciences, by comforting them; to sin-sick souls, by convincing them; and it reconciles parties at variance.

Verse 5

If instruction is despised, reprove men rather than suffer them to go on undisturbed in the way to ruin.

Verse 6

The wealth of worldly men increases their fears and suspicions, adds strength to their passions, and renders the fear of death more distressing.

Verse 7

We use knowledge aright when we disperse it; but the heart of the foolish has nothing to disperse that is good.

Verses 8, 9

The wicked put other things in the stead of Christ's atonement, or in the place of holy obedience. Praying graces are his gift, and the work of his Spirit, with which he is well pleased.

Verse 10

He that hates reproof shall perish in his sins, since he would not be parted from them.

Verse 11

There is nothing that can be hid from the eyes of God, not even man's thoughts.

Verse 12

A scorner cannot bear to reflect seriously within his own heart.

Verse 13

A gloomy, impatient, unthankful spirit, springing from pride and undue attachment to worldly objects, renders a man uneasy to himself and others.

Verse 14

A wise man seeks to gain more wisdom, growing in grace and in the knowledge of Christ. But a carnal mind rests contented, flattering itself.

Verse 15

Some are much in affliction, and of a sorrowful spirit. Such are to be pitied, prayed for, and comforted. And others serve God with gladness of heart, and it prompts their obedience, yet they should rejoice with trembling.

Verses 16, 17

Believers often have enough when worldly eyes see little; the Lord is with them, without the cares, troubles, and temptations which are with the wealth of the wicked.

Verse 18

He that is slow to anger, not only prevents strife, but appeases it, if kindled.

Verse 19

Those who have no heart to their work, pretend that they cannot do their work without hardship and danger. And thus many live always in doubt about their state, because always in neglect of some duty.

Verse 20

Those who treat an aged mother or a father with contempt or neglect, show their own folly.

Verse 21

Such as are truly wise, study that their thoughts, words, and actions should be regular, sincere, and holy.

Verse 22

If men will not take time and pains to deliberate, they are not likely to bring any thing to pass.

Verse 23

Wisdom is needed to suit our discourse to the occasions.

Verse 24

A good man sets his affections on things above; his way leads directly thither.

Verse 25

Pride is the ruin of multitudes. But those who are in affliction God will support.

Verse 26

The thoughts of wicked men offend Him who knows the heart.

Verse 27

The covetous man lets none of his family have rest or enjoyment. And greediness of gain often tempts to projects that bring ruin.

Verse 28

A good man is proved to be a wise man by this; he governs his tongue well.

Verse 29

God sets himself at a distance from those who set him at defiance.

Verse 30

How delightful to the humbled soul to hear the good report of salvation by the Lord Jesus Christ!

Verse 31

Faithful, friendly reproofs help spiritual life, and lead to eternal life.

Verse 32

Sinners undervalue their own souls; therefore they prefer the body before the soul, and wrong the soul to please the body.

Verse 33

The fear of the Lord will dispose us to search the Scriptures with reverence; and it will cause us to follow the leadings of the Holy Spirit. While we humbly place all our dependence on the grace of God, we are exalted in the righteousness of Christ.

Chapter 16

Verse 1

The renewing grace of God alone prepares the heart for every good work. This teaches us that we are not sufficient of ourselves to think or speak any thing wise and good.

Verse 2

Ignorance, pride, and self-flattery render us partial judges respecting our own conduct.

Verse 3

Roll the burden of thy care upon God, and leave it with him, by faith and dependence on him.

Verse 4

God makes use of the wicked to execute righteous vengeance on each other; and he will be glorified by their destruction at last.

Verse 5

Though sinners strengthen themselves and one another, they shall not escape God's judgments.

Verse 6

By the mercy and truth of God in Christ Jesus, the sins of believers are taken away, and the power of sin is broken.

Verse 7

He that has all hearts in his hand, can make a man's enemies to be at peace with him.

Verse 8

A small estate, honestly come by, will turn to better account than a great estate ill-gotten.

Verse 9

If men make God's glory their end, and his will their rule, he will direct their steps by his Spirit and grace. 10. Let kings and judges of the earth be just, and rule in the fear of God.

Verse 11

To observe justice in dealings between man and man is God's appointment.

Verse 12

The ruler that uses his power aright, will find that to be his best security.

Verse 13

Put those in power who know how to speak to the purpose.

Verses 14, 15

Those are fools, who, to obtain the favour of an earthly prince, throw themselves out of God's favour.

Verse 16

There is joy and satisfaction of spirit, only in getting wisdom.

Verse 17

A sincerely religious man keeps at a distance from every appearance of evil. Happy is the man that walks in Christ, and is led by the Spirit of Christ.

Verse 18

When men defy God's judgments, and think themselves far from them, it is a sign they are at the door. Let us not fear the pride of others, but fear pride in ourselves.

Verse 19

Humility, though it exposes to contempt in the world, is much better than high-spiritedness, which makes God an enemy. He that understands God's word shall find good.

Verse 21

The man whose wisdom dwells in his heart, will be found more truly prudent than many who possess shining talents.

Verse 22

As waters to a thirsty land, so is a wise man to his friends and neighbours.

Verse 23

The wise man's self-knowledge, always suggests something proper to be spoken to others.

Verse 24

The word of God cures the diseases that weaken our souls.

Verse 25

This is caution to all, to take heed of deceiving themselves as to their souls.

Verse 26

We must labour for the meat which endureth to everlasting life, or we must perish.

Verses 27, 28

Ungodly men bestow more pains to do mischief than would be needful to do good. The whisperer separates friends: what a hateful, but how common a character!

Verses 29, 30

Some do all the mischief they can by force and violence, and are blind to the result.

Verse 31

Old people especially should be found in the way of religion and godliness.

Verse 32

To overcome our own passions, requires more steady management, than obtaining victory over an enemy.

Verse 33

All the disposal of Providence concerning our affairs, we must look upon to be the determining what we referred to God; and we must be reconciled to them accordingly. Blessed are those that give themselves up to the will of God; for he knows what is good for them.

Chapter 17

Verse 1

These words recommend family love and peace, as needful for the comfort of human life.

Verse 2

The wise servant is more deserving, and more likely to appear one of the family, than a profligate son.

Verse 3

God tries the heart by affliction. He thus has often shown the sin remaining in the heart of the believer.

Verse 4

Flatterers, especially false teachers, are welcome to those that live in sin.

Verse 5

Those that laugh at poverty, treat God's providence and precepts with contempt.

Verse 6

It is an honour to children to have wise and godly parents continued to them, even after they are grown up and settled in the world.

Verse 7

A fool, in Solomon's Proverbs, signifies a wicked man, whom excellent speech does not become, because his conversation contradicts it.

Verse 8

Those who set their hearts upon money, will do any thing for it. What influence should the gifts of God have on our hearts!

Verse 9

The way to preserve peace is to make the best of every thing; not to notice what has been said or done against ourselves.

Verse 10

A gentle reproof will enter, not only into the head, but into the heart of a wise man.

Verse 11

Satan, and the messengers of Satan, shall be let loose upon an evil man.

Verse 12

Let us watch over our own passions, and avoid the company of furious men.

Verse 13

To render evil for good is devilish. He that does so, brings a curse upon his family.

Verse 14

What danger there is in the beginning of strife! Resist its earliest display; and leave it off, if it were possible, before you begin.

Verse 15

It is an offence to God to acquit the guilty, or to condemn those who are not guilty.

Verse 16

Man's neglect of God's favour and his own interest is very absurd.

Verse 17

No change of outward circumstances should abate our affection for our friends or relatives. But no friend, except Christ, deserves unlimited confidence. In Him this text did receive, and still receives its most glorious fulfilment.

Verse 18

Let not any wrong their families. Yet Christ's becoming Surety for men, was a glorious display of Divine wisdom; for he was able to discharge the bond.

Verse 19

If we would keep a clear conscience and a quiet mind, we must shun all excitements to anger. And a man who affects a style of living above his means, goes the way to ruin.

Verse 20

There is nothing got by ill designs. And many have paid dear for an unbridled tongue.

Verse 21

This speaks very plainly what many wise and good men feel very strongly, how grievous it is to have a foolish, wicked child.

Verse 22

It is great mercy that God gives us leave to be cheerful, and cause to be cheerful, if by his grace he gives us hearts to be cheerful.

Verse 23

The wicked are ready to part with their money, though loved, that they may not suffer for their crimes.

Verse 24

The prudent man keeps the word of God continually in view. But the foolish man cannot fix his thoughts, nor pursue any purpose with steadiness.

Verse 25

Wicked children despise the authority of their father, and the tenderness of their mother.

Verse 26

It is very wrong to find fault for doing what is duty.

Verses 27, 28

A man may show himself to be a wise man, by the good temper of his mind, and by the good government of his tongue. He is careful when he does speak, to speak to the purpose. God knows his heart, and the folly that is bound there; therefore he cannot be deceived in his judgment as men may be.

Chapter 18

Verse 1

If we would get knowledge and grace, we must try all methods of improving ourselves.

Verse 2

Those make nothing to purpose, of learning or religion, whose only design is to have something to make a show with.

Verse 3

As soon as sin entered, shame followed.

Verse 4

The well-spring of wisdom in the heart of a believer, continually supplies words of wisdom.

Verse 5

The merits of a cause must be looked to, not the person.

Verses 6, 7

What mischief bad men do to themselves by their ungoverned tongues!

Verse 8

How base are those that sow contention! and what fatal effects may be expected from small beginnings of jealousy!

Verse 9

Omissions of duty, and in duty, are fatal to the soul, as well as commissions of sin.

Verses 10, 11

The Divine power, made known in and through our Lord Jesus Christ, forms a strong tower for the believer, who relies on the Lord. How deceitful the defence of the rich man, who has his portion and treasure in this world! It is a strong city and a high wall only in his own conceit; for it will fail when most in need. They will be exposed to the just wrath of that Judge whom they despised as a Saviour.

Verse 12

After the heart has been lifted up with pride, a fall comes. But honour shall be the reward of humility.

Verse 13

Eagerness, with self-conceit, will expose to shame.

Verse 14

Firmness of mind supports under many pains and trials. But when the conscience is tortured with remorse, no human fortitude can bear the misery; what then will hell be?

Verse 15

We must get knowledge, not only into our heads, but into our hearts.

Verse 16

Blessed be the Lord, who makes us welcome to come to his throne, without money and without price. May his gifts make room for him in our souls.

Verse 17

It is well to listen to our enemies, that we may form a better judgment of ourselves.

Verse 18

It was customary sometimes to refer matters to God, by casting lots, with solemn prayer. The profaning the lot, by using it in matters of diversion, or coveting what belongs to others, forms an objection to this now.

Verse 19

Great care must be taken to prevent quarrels among relations and those under obligations to each other. Wisdom and grace make it easy to forgive; but corruption makes it difficult.

Verse 20

The belly is here put for the heart, as elsewhere; and what that is filled with, our satisfaction will be accordingly, and our inward peace.

Verse 21

Many a one has caused his own death, or the death of others, by a false or injurious tongue.

Verse 22

A good wife is a great blessing to a man, and it is a token of Divine favour.

Verse 23

Poverty tells men they must not order or demand. And at the throne of God's grace we are all poor, and must use entreaties.

Verse 24

Christ Jesus never will forsake those who trust in and love him. May we be such friends to others, for our Master's sake. Having loved his own, which were in the world, he loved them unto the end; and we are his friends if we do whatever he commands us, Joh 15:14.

Chapter 19

Verse 1

A poor man who fears God, is more honourable and happy, than a man without wisdom and grace, however rich or advanced in rank.

Verse 2

What good can the soul do, if without knowledge? And he sins who will not take time to ponder the path of his feet.

Verse 3

Men run into troubles by their own folly, and then fret at the appointments of God.

Verse 4

Here we may see how strong is men's love of money.

Verse 5

Those that tell lies in discourse, are in a fair way to be guilty of bearing false-witness.

Verse 6

We are without excuse if we do not love God with all our hearts. His gifts to us are past number, and all the gifts of men to us are fruits of his bounty.

Verse 7

Christ was left by all his disciples; but the Father was with him. It encourages our faith that he had so large an experience of the sorrows of poverty.

Verse 8

Those only love their souls aright that get true wisdom.

Verse 9

Lying is a damning, destroying sin.

Verse 10

A man that has not wisdom and grace, has no right or title to true joy. It is very unseemly for one who is a servant to sin, to oppress God's free-men.

Verse 11

He attains the most true glory who endeavours most steadily to overcome evil with good.

Verse 12

Christ is a King, whose wrath against his enemies will be as the roaring of a lion, and his favour to his people as the refreshing dew.

Verse 13

It shows the vanity of the world, that we are liable to the greatest griefs where we promise ourselves the greatest comfort.

Verse 14

A discreet and virtuous wife is more valuable than house and riches.

Verse 15

A sluggish, slothful disposition makes men poor; it brings them to want. And this applies both to the present life and that which is to come.

Verse 16

If we keep God's word, God's word will keep us from every thing really hurtful. We abuse the doctrine of free grace, if we think that it does away the necessity and advantage of obedience. Those that live at random must die. This truth is clearly taught in words enough to alarm the stoutest sinner.

Verse 17

God has chosen the poor of this world, to be rich in faith, and heirs of his kingdom.

Verse 18

When parents keep under foolish tenderness, they do their best to render children a comfort to them, and happy in themselves.

Verse 19

The spared and spoiled child is likely to become a man of great wrath.

Verse 20

Those that would be wise in their latter end, must be taught and ruled when young.

Verse 21

What should we desire, but that all our purposes may agree with God's holy will?

Verse 22

It is far better to have a heart to do good, and want ability for it, than to have ability for it, and want a heart to it.

Verse 23

Those that live in the fear of God, shall get safety, satisfaction, and true and complete happiness.

Verse 24

Indolence, when indulged, so grows upon people, that they have no heart to do the most needful things for themselves.

Verse 25

A gentle rebuke goes farthest with a man of understanding.

Verse 26

The young man who wastes his father's substance, or makes his aged mother destitute, is hateful, and will come to disgrace.

Verse 27

It is the wisdom of young men to dread hearing such talk as puts loose and evil principles into the mind.

Verse 28

Those are the worst of sinners, who are glad of an opportunity to sin.

Verse 29

The unbelief of man shall not make God's threatenings of no effect. Christ himself, when bearing sins not his own, was not spared. Justice and judgment took hold of our blessed Surety; and will God spare obstinate sinners?

Chapter 20

Verse 1

It seems hard to believe that men of the greatest abilities, as well as the ignorant, should render themselves fools and madmen, merely for the taste or excitement produced by strong liquors.

Verse 2

How formidable kings are to those who provoke them! how much more foolish then is it to provoke the King of kings!

Verse 3

To engage in quarrels is the greatest folly that can be. Yield, and even give up just demands, for peace' sake.

Verse 4

He who labours and endures hardship in his seed-time for eternity, will be properly diligent as to his earthly business.

Verse 5

Though many capable of giving wise counsel are silent, yet something may be drawn from them, which will reward those who obtain it.

Verse 6

It is hard to find those that have done, and will do more good than they speak, or care to hear spoken of.

Verse 7

A good man is not liable to uneasiness in contriving what he shall do, or in reflecting on what he has done, as those who walk in deceit. And his family fare better for his sake.

Verse 8

If great men are good men, they may do much good, and prevent very much evil.

Verse 9

Some can say, Through grace, we are cleaner than we have been; but it was the work of the Holy Spirit.

Verse 10

See the various deceits men use, of which the love of money is the root. The Lord will not bless what is thus gotten.

Verse 11

Parents should observe their children, that they may manage them accordingly.

Verse 12

All our powers and faculties are from God, and are to be employed for him.

Verse 13

Those that indulge themselves, may expect to want necessaries, which should have been gotten by honest labour.

Verse 14

Men use arts to get a good bargain, and to buy cheap; whereas a man ought to be ashamed of a fraud and a lie.

Verse 15

He that prefers true knowledge to riches, follows the ways of religion and happiness. If we really believed this truth, the word of God would be valued as it deserves, and the world would lose its tempting influence.

Verse 16

Those ruin themselves who entangle themselves in rash suretiship. Also those who are in league with abandoned women. Place no confidence in either.

Verse 17

Wealth gotten by fraud may be sweet, for the carnal mind takes pleasure in the success of wicked devices; but it will be bitter in the reflection.

Verse 18

Especially we need advice in spiritual warfare. The word and Spirit of God are the best counsellors in every point.

Verse 19

Those dearly buy their own praise, who put confidence in a man because he speaks fairly.

Verse 20

An undutiful child will become very miserable. Never let him expect any peace or comfort.

Verse 21

An estate suddenly raised, is often as suddenly ruined.

Verse 22

Wait on the Lord, attend his pleasure, and he will protect thee.

Verse 23

A bargain made by fraud will prove a losing bargain in the end.

Verse 24

How can we form plans, and conduct business, independently of the Lord?

Verse 25

The evasions men often use with their own consciences show how false and deceitful man is.

Verse 26

Justice should crush the wicked, and separate them from the virtuous.

Verse 27

The rational soul and conscience are as a lamp within us, which should be used in examining our dispositions and motives with the revealed will of God.

Verse 28

Mercy and truth are the glories of God's throne.

Verse 29

Both young and old have their advantages; and let neither despise or envy the other.

Verse 30

Severe rebukes sometimes do a great deal of good. But such is the corruption of nature, that men are loth to be rebuked for their sins. If God uses severe afflictions, to purify our hearts and fit us for his service, we have cause to be very thankful.

Chapter 21

Verse 1

The believer, perceiving that the Lord rules every heart as he sees fit, like the husbandman who turns the water through his grounds as he pleases, seeks to have his own heart, and the hearts of others, directed in his faith, fear, and love.

Verse 2

We are partial in judging ourselves and our actions.

Verse 3

Many deceive themselves with a conceit that outward devotions will excuse unrighteousness.

Verse 4

Sin is the pride, the ambition, the glory, the joy, and the business of wicked men.

Verse 5

The really diligent employ foresight as well as labour.

Verse 6

While men seek wealth by unlawful practices, they seek death.

Verse 7

Injustice will return upon the sinner, and will destroy him here and for ever.

Verse 8

The way of mankind by nature is froward and strange.

Verse 9

It is best to shun bitter contention by pouring out the heart before God. For by prudence and patience, with constant prayer, the cross may be removed.

Verse 10

The evil desires of a wicked man's heart, lead to baseness in his conduct.

Verse 11

The simple may be made wise by punishments on the wicked, and by instructions to those who are willing to be taught.

Verse 12

Good men envy not the prosperity of evil-doers; they see there is a curse on them.

Verse 13

Such as oppress the poor by beating down wages, such as will not relieve according to their ability those in distress, and those in authority who neglect to do justice, stop their ears at the cry of the poor. But doubtless care is to be used in the exercise of charity.

Verse 14

If money can conquer the fury of the passions, shall reason, the fear of God, and the command of Christ, be too weak to bridle them?

Verse 15

There is true pleasure only in the practice of religion.

Verse 16

Of all wanderers in the ways of sin, those are in the most dangerous condition who turn aside into the ways of darkness. Yet there is hope even for them in the all-sufficient Saviour; but let them flee to him without delay.

Verse 17

A life of worldly pleasure brings ruin on men.

Verse 18

The righteous is often delivered out of trouble, and the wicked comes in his stead, and so seems as a ransom for him.

Verse 19

Unbridled passions spoil the comfort of all relations.

Verse 20

The plenty obtained by prudence, industry, and frugality, is desirable. But the foolish misspend what they have upon their lusts.

Verse 21

True repentance and faith will lead him that relies on the mercy of God in Christ, to follow after righteousness and mercy in his own conduct.

Verse 22

Those that have wisdom, often do great things, even against those confident of their strength.

Verse 23

It is our great concern to keep our souls from being entangled and disquieted.

Verse 24

Pride and haughtiness make men passionate; such continually deal in wrath, as if it were their trade to be angry.

Verses 25, 26

Here is the misery of the slothful; their hands refuse to labour in an honest calling, by which they might get an honest livelihood; yet their hearts cease not to covet riches, pleasures, and honours, which cannot be obtained without labour. But the righteous and industrious have their desires satisfied.

Verse 27

When holiness is pretended, but wickedness intended, that especially is an abomination.

Verse 28

The doom of a false witness is certain.

Verse 29

A wicked man bids defiance to the terrors of the law and the rebukes of Providence. But a good man asks, What does God require of me?

Verses 30, 31

Means are to be used, but, after all, our safety and salvation are only of the Lord. In our spiritual warfare we must arm ourselves with the whole armour of God; but our strength must be in the Lord, and in the power of his might.

Chapter 22

Verse 1

We should be more careful to do that by which we may get and keep a good name, than to raise or add unto a great estate.

Verse 2

Divine Providence has so ordered it, that some are rich, and others poor, but all are guilty before God; and at the throne of God's grace the poor are as welcome as the rich.

Verse 3

Faith foresees the evil coming upon sinners, and looks to Jesus Christ as the sure refuge from the storm.

Verse 4

Where the fear of God is, there will be humility. And much is to be enjoyed by it; spiritual riches, and eternal life at last.

Verse 5

The way of sin is vexatious and dangerous. But the way of duty is safe and easy.

Verse 6

Train children, not in the way they would go, that of their corrupt hearts, but in the way they should go; in which, if you love them, you would have them go. As soon as possible every child should be led to the knowledge of the Saviour.

Verse 7

This shows how important it is for every man to keep out of debt. As to the things of this life, there is a difference between the rich and the poor; but let the poor remember, it is the Lord that made the difference.

Verse 8

The power which many abuse, will soon fail them.

Verse 9

He that seeks to relieve the wants and miseries of others shall be blessed.

Verse 10

Profane scoffers and revilers disturb the peace.

Verse 11

God will be the Friend of a man in whose spirit there is no guile; this honour have all the saints.

Verse 12

God turns the counsels and designs of treacherous men to their own confusion.

Verse 13

The slothful man talks of a lion without, but considers not his real danger from the devil, that roaring lion within, and from his own slothfulness, which kills him.

Verse 14

The vile sin of licentiousness commonly besots the mind beyond recovery.

Verse 15

Sin is foolishness, it is in the heart, there is an inward inclination to sin: children bring it into the world with them; and it cleaves close to the soul. We all need to be corrected by our heavenly Father.

Verse 16

We are but stewards, and must distribute what God intrusts to our care, according to his will.

Verses 17-21

To these words, to this knowledge, the ear must be bowed down, and the heart applied by faith and love. To live a life of delight in God and dependence on him, is the foundation of all practical religion. The way to know the certainty of the word of truth, is to make conscience of our duty.

Verses 22, 23

He that robs and oppresses the poor, does so at his peril. And if men will not appear for them, God will.

Verses 24, 25

Our corrupt hearts have so much tinder in them, that it is dangerous to have to do with those that throw about the sparks of their passion.

Verses 26, 27

Every man ought to be just to himself, and his family; those are not so, who, by folly or other carelessness, waste what they have.

Verse 28

We are taught not to trespass on another man's right. And it is hard to find a truly industrious man. Such a man will rise. Seest thou a man diligent in the business of religion? He is likely to excel. Let us then be diligent in God's work.

Chapter 23

Verses 1-3

God's restraints of the appetite only say, Do thyself no harm.

Verses 4, 5

Be not of those that will be rich. The things of this world are not happiness and a portion for a soul; those that hold them ever so fast, cannot hold them always, cannot hold them long.

Verses 6-8

Do not make thyself burdensome to any, especially those not sincere. When we are called by God to his feast, and to let our souls delight themselves, Isa 25:6; 55:2, we may safely partake of the Bread of life.

Verse 9

It is our duty to take all fit occasions to speak of Divine things; but if what a wise man says will not be heard, let him hold his peace.

Verses 10, 11

The fatherless are taken under God's special protection. He is their Redeemer, who will take their part; and he is mighty, almighty.

Verses 12-16

Here is a parent instructing his child to give his mind to the Scriptures. Here is a parent correcting his child: accompanied with prayer, and blessed of God, it may prove a means of preventing his destruction. Here is a parent encouraging his child, telling him what would be for his good. And what a comfort it would be, if herein he answered his expectation!

Verses 17, 18

The believer's expectation shall not be disappointed; the end of his trials, and of the sinner's prosperity, is at hand.

Verses 19-28

The gracious Saviour who purchased pardon and peace for his people, with all the affection of a tender parent, counsels us to hear and be wise, and is ready to guide our hearts in his way. Here we have an earnest call to young people, to attend to the advice of their godly parents. If the heart be guided, the steps will be guided. Buy the truth, and sell it not; be willing to part with any thing for it. Do not part with it for pleasures, honours, riches, or any thing in this world. The heart is what the great God requires. We must not think to divide the heart between God and the world; he will have all or none. Look to the rule of God's word, the conduct of his providence, and the good examples of his people. Particular cautions are given against sins most destructive to wisdom and grace in the soul. It is really a shame to make a god of the belly. Drunkenness stupifies men, and then all goes to ruin. Licentiousness takes away the heart that should be given to God. Take heed of any approaches toward this sin, it is very hard to retreat from it. It bewitches men to their ruin.

Verses 29-35

Solomon warns against drunkenness. Those that would be kept from sin, must keep from all the beginnings of it, and fear coming within reach of its allurements. Foresee the punishment, what it will at last end in, if repentance prevent not. It makes men quarrel. Drunkards wilfully make woe and sorrow for themselves. It makes men impure and insolent. The tongue grows unruly; the heart utters things contrary to reason, religion, and common civility. It stupifies and besots men. They are in danger of death, of damnation; as much exposed as if they slept upon the top of a mast, yet feel secure. They fear no peril when the terrors of the Lord are before them; they feel no pain when the judgments of God are actually upon them. So lost is a drunkard to virtue and honour, so wretchedly is his conscience seared, that he is not ashamed to say, I will seek it again. With good reason we were bid to stop before the beginning. Who that has common sense would contract a habit, or sell himself to a sin, which tends to such guilt and misery, and exposes a man every day to the danger of dying insensible, and awaking in hell? Wisdom seems in these chapters to take up the discourse as at the beginning of the book. They must be considered as the words of Christ to the sinner.

Chapter 24

Verses 1, 2

Envy not sinners. And let not a desire ever come into thy mind, Oh that I could shake off restraints!

Verses 3-6

Piety and prudence in outward affairs, both go together to complete a wise man. By knowledge the soul is filled with the graces and comforts of the spirit, those precious and pleasant riches. The spirit is strengthened for the spiritual work and the spiritual warfare, by true wisdom.

Verses 7-9

A weak man thinks wisdom is too high for him, therefore he will take no pains for it. It is bad to do evil, but worse to devise it. Even the first risings of sin in the heart are sin, and must be repented of. Those that strive to make others hateful, make themselves so.

Verse 10

Under troubles we are apt to despair of relief. But be of good courage, and God shall strengthen thy heart.

Verses 11, 12

If a man know that his neighbour is in danger by any unjust proceeding, he is bound to do all in his power to deliver him. And what is it to suffer immortal souls to perish, when our persuasions and example may be the means of preventing it?

Verses 13, 14

We are quickened to the study of wisdom by considering both the pleasure and the profit of it. All men relish things that are sweet to the palate; but many have no relish for the things that are sweet to the purified soul, and that make us wise unto salvation.

Verses 15, 16

The sincere soul falls as a traveller may do, by stumbling at some stone in his path; but gets up, and goes on his way with more care and speed. This is rather to be understood of falls into affliction, than falls into actual sin.

Verses 17, 18

The pleasure we are apt to take in the troubles of an enemy is forbidden.

Verses 19, 20

Envy not the wicked their prosperity; be sure there is no true happiness in it.

Verses 21, 22

The godly in the land, will be quiet in the land. There may be cause to change for the better, but have nothing to do with them that are given change.

Verses 23-26

The wisdom God giveth, renders a man fit for his station. Every one who finds the benefit of the right answer, will be attached to him that gave it.

Verse 27

We must prefer necessaries before conveniences, and not go in debt.

Verses 28, 29

There are three defaults in a witness pointed out.

Verses 30-34

See what a blessing the husbandman's calling is, and what a wilderness this earth would be without it. See what great difference there is in the management even of worldly affairs. Sloth and self-indulgence are the bane of all good. When we see fields overgrown with thorns and thistles, and the fences broken down, we see an emblem of the far more deplorable state of many souls. Every vile affection grows in men's hearts; yet they compose themselves to sleep. Let us show wisdom by doubling our diligence in every good thing.

Chapter 25

Verses 1-3

God needs not search into any thing; nothing can be hid from him. But it is the honour of rulers to search out matters, to bring to light hidden works of darkness.

Verses 4, 5

For a prince to suppress vice, and reform his people, is the best way to support his government.

Verses 6, 7

Religion teaches us humility and self-denial. He who has seen the glory of the Lord in Christ Jesus, will feel his own unworthiness.

Verses 8-10

To be hasty in beginning strife, will bring into difficulties. War must at length end, and might better be prevented. It is so in private quarrels; do all thou canst to settle the matter.

Verses 11, 12

A word of counsel, or reproof, rightly spoken, is especially beautiful, as fine fruit becomes still more beautiful in silver baskets.

Verse 13

See what ought to be the aim of him that is trusted with any business; to be faithful. A faithful minister, Christ's messenger, should be thus acceptable to us.

Verse 14

He who pretends to have received or given that which he never had, is like the morning cloud, that disappoints those who look for rain.

Verse 15

Be patient to bear a present hurt. Be mild to speak without passion; for persuasive language is the most effectual to prevail over the hardened mind.

Verse 16

God has given us leave to use grateful things, but we are cautioned against excess.

Verse 17

We cannot be upon good terms with our neighbours, without discretion as well as sincerity. How much better a Friend is God than any other friend! The oftener we come to him, the more welcome.

Verse 18

A false testimony is dangerous in every thing.

Verse 19

Confidence in an unfaithful man is painful and vexatious; when we put any stress on him, he not only fails, but makes us feel for it.

Verse 20

We take a wrong course if we think to relieve those in sorrow by endeavouring to make them merry.

Verses 21, 22

The precept to love even our enemies is an Old Testament commandment. Our Saviour has shown his own great example in loving us when we were enemies.

Verse 23

Slanders would not be so readily spoken, if they were not readily heard. Sin, if it receives any check, becomes cowardly.

Verse 24

It is better to be alone, than to be joined to one who is a hinderance to the comfort of life.

Verse 25

Heaven is a country afar off; how refreshing is good news from thence, in the everlasting gospel, which signifies glad tidings, and in the witness of the Spirit with our spirits that we are God's children!

Verse 26

When the righteous are led into sin, it is as hurtful as if the public fountains were poisoned.

Verse 27

We must be, through grace, dead to the pleasures of sense, and also to the praises of men.

Verse 28

The man who has no command over his anger, is easily robbed of peace. Let us give up ourselves to the Lord, and pray him to put his Spirit within us, and cause us to walk in his statutes.

Chapter 26

Verse 1

Honour is out of season to those unworthy and unfit for it.

Verse 2

He that is cursed without cause, the curse shall do him no more harm than the bird that flies over his head.

Verse 3

Every creature must be dealt with according to its nature, but careless and profligate sinners never will be ruled by reason and persuasion. Man indeed is born like the wild ass's colt; but some, by the grace of God, are changed.

Verses 4, 5

We are to fit our remarks to the man, and address them to his conscience, so as may best end the debate.

Verses 6-9

Fools are not fit to be trusted, nor to have any honour. Wise sayings, as a foolish man delivers and applies them, lose their usefulness.

Verse 10

This verse may either declare how the Lord, the Creator of all men, will deal with sinners according to their guilt, or, how the powerful among men should disgrace and punish the wicked.

Verse 11

The dog is a loathsome emblem of those sinners who return to their vices, 2Pe 2:22.

Verse 12

We see many a one who has some little sense, but is proud of it. This describes those who think their spiritual state to be good, when really it is very bad.

Verse 13

The slothful man hates every thing that requires care and labour. But it is foolish to frighten ourselves from real duties by fancied difficulties. This may be applied to a man slothful in the duties of religion.

Verse 14

Having seen the slothful man in fear of his work, here we find him in love with his ease. Bodily ease is the sad occasion of many spiritual diseases. He does not care to get forward with his business. Slothful professors turn thus. The world and the flesh are hinges on which they are hung; and though they move in a course of outward services, yet they are not the nearer to heaven.

Verse 15

The sluggard is now out of his bed, but he might have lain there, for any thing he is likely to bring to pass in his work. It is common for men who will not do their duty, to pretend they cannot. Those that are slothful in religion, will not be at the pains to feed their souls with the bread of life, nor to fetch in promised blessings by prayer.

Verse 16

He that takes pains in religion, knows he is working for a good Master, and that his labour shall not be in vain.

Verse 17

To make ourselves busy in other men's matters, is to thrust ourselves into temptation.

Verses 18, 19

He that sins in jest, must repent in earnest, or his sin will be his ruin.

Verses 20-22

Contention heats the spirit, and puts families and societies into a flame. And that fire is commonly kindled and kept burning by whisperers and backbiters.

Verse 23

A wicked heart disguising itself, is like a potsherd covered with the dross of silver.

Verses 24-26

Always distrust when a man speaks fair unless you know him well. Satan, in his temptations, speaks fair, as he did to Eve; but it is madness to give credit to him.

Verse 27

What pains men take to do mischief to others! but it is digging a pit, it is rolling a stone, hard work; and they prepare mischief to themselves.

Verse 28

There are two sorts of lies equally detestable. A slandering lie, the mischief of this every body sees. A flattering lie, which secretly works ruin. A wise man will be more afraid of a flatterer than of a slanderer.

Chapter 27

Verse 1

We know not what a day may bring forth. This does not forbid preparing for to-morrow, but presuming upon to-morrow. We must not put off the great work of conversion, that one thing needful.

Verse 2

There may be occasion for us to justify ourselves, but not to praise ourselves.

Verses 3, 4

Those who have no command of their passions, sink under the load.

Verses 5, 6

Plain and faithful rebukes are better, not only than secret hatred, but than love which compliments in sin, to the hurt of the soul.

Verse 7

The poor have a better relish of their enjoyments, and are often more thankful for them, than the rich. In like manner the proud and self-sufficient disdain the gospel; but those who hunger and thirst after righteousness, find comfort from the meanest book or sermon that testifies of Christ Jesus.

Verse 8

Every man has his proper place in society, where he may be safe and comfortable.

Verses 9, 10

Depend not for relief upon a kinsman, merely for kindred's sake; apply to those who are at hand, and will help in need. But there is a Friend that sticketh closer than a brother, and let us place entire confidence in him.

Verse 11

An affectionate parent urges his son to prudent conduct that should gladden his heart. The good conduct of Christians is the best answer to all who find fault with the gospel.

Verse 12

Where there is temptation, if we thrust ourselves into it, there will be sin, and punishment will follow.

Verse 13

An honest man may be made a beggar, but he is not honest that makes himself one.

Verse 14

It is folly to be fond of being praised; it is a temptation to pride.

Verses 15, 16

The contentions of a neighbour may be like a sharp shower, troublesome for a time; the contentions of a wife are like constant rain.

Verse 17

We are cautioned to take heed whom we converse with. And directed to have in view, in conversation, to make one another wiser and better.

Verse 18

Though a calling be laborious and despised, yet those who keep to it, will find there is something to be got by it. God is a Master who has engaged to honour those who serve him faithfully.

Verse 19

One corrupt heart is like another; so are sanctified hearts: the former bear the same image of the earthly, the latter the same image of the heavenly. Let us carefully watch our own hearts, comparing them with the word of God.

Verse 20

Two things are here said to be never satisfied, death and sin. The appetites of the carnal mind for profit or pleasure are always desiring more. Those whose eyes are ever toward the Lord, are satisfied in him, and shall for ever be so.

Verse 21

Silver and gold are tried by putting them into the furnace and fining-pot; so is a man tried by praising him.

Verse 22

Some are so bad, that even severe methods do not answer the end; what remains but that they should be rejected? The new-creating power of God's grace alone is able to make a change.

Verses 23-27

We ought to have some business to do in this world, and not to live in idleness, and not to meddle with what we do not understand. We must be diligent and take pains. Let us do what we can, still the world cannot be secured to us, therefore we must choose a more lasting portion; but by the blessing of God upon our honest labours, we may expect to enjoy as much of earthly blessings as is good for us.

Chapter 28

Verse 1

Sin makes men cowards. Whatever difficulties the righteous meet in the way of duty, they are not daunted.

Verse 2

National sins disturb the public repose.

Verse 3

If needy persons get opportunities of oppressing, their extortion will be more severe than that of the more wealthy.

Verse 4

Wicked people strengthen one another in wicked ways.

Verse 5

If a man seeks the Lord, it is a good sign that he understands much, and it is a good means of understanding more.

Verse 6

An honest, godly, poor man, is better than a wicked, ungodly, rich man; has more comfort in himself, and is a greater blessing to the world.

Verse 7

Companions of riotous men not only grieve their parents, but shame them.

Verse 8

That which is ill got, though it may increase much, will not last long. Thus the poor are repaid, and God is glorified.

Verse 9

The sinner at whose prayers God is angry, is one who obstinately refuses to obey God's commands.

Verse 10

The success of ungodly men is their own misery.

Verse 11

Rich men are so flattered, that they think themselves superior to others.

Verse 12

There is glory in the land when the righteous have liberty.

Verse 13

It is folly to indulge sin, and excuse it. He who covers his sins, shall not have any true peace. He who humbly confesses his sins, with true repentance and faith, shall find mercy from God. The Son of God is our great atonement. Under a deep sense of our guilt and danger, we may claim salvation from that mercy which reigns through righteousness unto eternal life, by Jesus Christ our Lord.

Verse 14

There is a fear which causes happiness. Faith and love will deliver from the fear of eternal misery; but we should always fear offending God, and fear sinning against him.

Verse 15

A wicked ruler, whatever we may call him, this scripture calls a roaring lion, and a ranging bear.

Verse 16

Oppressors want understanding; they do not consult their own honour, ease, and safety.

Verse 17

The murderer shall be haunted with terrors. None shall desire to save him from deserved punishment, nor pity him.

Verse 18

Uprightness will give men holy security in the worst times; but the false and dishonest are never safe.

Verse 19

Those who are diligent, take the way to live comfortably.

Verse 20

The true way to be happy, is to be holy and honest; not to raise an estate suddenly, without regard to right or wrong.

Verse 21

Judgment is perverted, when any thing but pure right is considered.

Verse 22

He that hastens to be rich, never seriously thinks how quickly God may take his wealth from him, and leave him in poverty.

Verse 23

Upon reflection, most will have a better opinion of a faithful reprover than of a soothing flatterer.

Verse 24

Here is the wickedness of those who think it no sin to rob their parents, by wheedling them or threatening them, or by wasting what they have, and running into debt.

Verse 25

Those make themselves always easy, that live in continual dependence upon God and his grace, and live by faith.

Verse 26

A fool trusts to his own strength, merit, and righteousness. And trusts to his own heart, which is not only deceitful above all things, but which has often deceived him.

Verse 27

A selfish man not only will not look out for objects of compassion, but will look off from those that call for his attention.

Verse 28

When power is put into the hands of the wicked, wise men decline public business. If the reader will go diligently over this and the other chapters, in many places where at first he may suppose there is least of Christ, still he will find what will lead to him.

Chapter 29

Verse 1

If God wounds, who can heal? The word of God warns all to flee from the wrath to come, to the hope set before us in Jesus Christ.

Verse 2

The people have cause to rejoice or mourn, as their rulers are righteous or wicked.

Verse 3

Divine wisdom best keeps us from ruinous lusts.

Verse 4

The Lord Jesus is the King who will minister true judgment to the people.

Verse 5

Flatterers put men off their guard, which betrays them into foolish conduct.

Verse 6

Transgressions always end in vexations. Righteous men walk at liberty, and walk in safety.

Verse 7

This verse is applicable to compassion for the distress of the poor, and the unfeeling disregard shown by the wicked.

Verse 8

The scornful mock at things sacred and serious. Men who promote religion, which is true wisdom, turn away the wrath of God.

Verse 9

If a wise man dispute with a conceited wrangler, he will be treated with anger or ridicule; and no good is done.

Verse 10

Christ told his disciples that they should be hated of all men. The just, whom the blood-thirsty hate, gladly do any thing for their salvation.

Verse 11

He is a fool who tells every thing he knows, and can keep no counsel.

Verse 12

One who loves flatterers, and hearkens to slanderers, causes his servants to become liars and false accusers.

Verse 13

Some are poor, others have a great deal of deceitful riches. They meet in the business of this world; the Lord gives to both the comforts of this life. To some of both sorts he gives his grace.

Verse 14

The rich will look to themselves, but the poor and needy the prince must defend and plead for.

Verse 15

Parents must consider the benefit of due correction, and the mischief of undue indulgence.

Verse 16

Let not the righteous have their faith and hope shocked by the increase of sin and sinners, but let them wait with patience.

Verse 17

Children must not be suffered to go without rebuke when they do amiss.

Verse 18

How bare does a place look without Bibles and ministers! and what an easy prey is it to the enemy of souls! That gospel is an open vision, which holds forth Christ, which humbles the sinner and exalts the Saviour, which promotes holiness in the life and conversation: and these are precious truths to keep the soul alive, and prevent it from perishing.

Verse 19

Here is an unprofitable, slothful, wicked servant; one that serves not from conscience, or love, but from fear.

Verse 20

When a man is self-conceited, rash, and given to wrangling, there is more hope of the ignorant and profligate.

Verse 21

Good usage to a servant does not mean indulgence, which would ruin even a child. The body is a servant to the soul; those that humour it, and are over-tender of it, will find it forget its place.

Verse 22

An angry, passionate disposition makes men provoking to one another, and provoking to God.

Verse 23

Only those who humble themselves shall be exalted and established.

Verse 24

The receiver is as bad as the thief.

Verse 25

Many are ashamed to own Christ now; and he will not own them in the day of judgment. But he that trusts in the Lord will be saved from this snare.

Verse 26

The wisest course is, to look to God, and seek the favour of the Ruler of rulers; for every creature is that to us which God makes it to be.

Verse 27

The just man abhors the sins of the wicked, and shuns their company. Christ exposed the wickedness of men, yet prayed for the wicked when they were crucifying him. Hatred to sin in ourselves and others, is a needful branch of the Christian temper. But all that are unholy, have rooted hatred to godliness.

Chapter 30

Verses 1-6

Agur speaks of himself as wanting a righteousness, and having done very foolishly. And it becomes us all to have low thoughts of ourselves. He speaks of himself as wanting revelation to guide him in the ways of truth and wisdom. The more enlightened people are, the more they lament their ignorance; the more they pray for clearer, still clearer discoveries of God, and his rich grace in Christ Jesus. In ver.#(4), there is a prophetic notice of Him who came down from heaven to be our Instructor and Saviour, and then ascended into heaven to be our Advocate. The Messiah is here spoken of as a Person distinct from the Father, but his name as yet secret. The great Redeemer, in the glories of his providence and grace, cannot be found out to perfection. Had it not been for Christ, the foundations of the earth had sunk under the load of the curse upon the ground, for man's sin. Who, and what is the mighty One that doeth all this? There is not the least ground to suspect anything wanting in the word of God; adding to his words opens the way to errors and corruptions.

Verses 7-9

Agur wisely prayed for a middle state, that he might be kept at a distance from temptations; he asked daily bread suited to his station, his family, and his real good. There is a remarkable similarity between this prayer and several clauses of the Lord's prayer. If we are removed from vanity and lies; if we are interested in the pardoning love of Christ, and have him for our portion; if we walk with God, then we shall have all we can ask or think, as to spiritual things. When we consider how those who have abundance are prone to abuse the gift, and what it is to suffer want, Agur's prayer will ever be found a wise one, though seldom offered. Food convenient; what is so for one, may not be so for another; but we may be sure that our heavenly Father will supply all our need, and not suffer us to want anything good for us; and why should we wish for more?

Verse 10

Slander not a servant to his master, accuse him not in small matters, to make mischief.

Verses 11-14

In every age there are monsters of ingratitude who ill-treat their parents. Many persuade themselves they are holy persons, whose hearts are full of sin, and who practise secret wickedness. There are others whose lofty pride is manifest. There have also been cruel monsters in every age.

Verses 15-17

Cruelty and covetousness are two daughters of the horseleech, that still cry, "Give, give," and they are continually uneasy to themselves. Four things never are satisfied, to which these devourers are compared. Those are never rich that are always coveting. And many who have come to a bad end, have owned that their wicked courses began by despising their parents' authority.

Verses 18-20

Four things cannot be fully known. The kingdom of nature is full of marvels. The fourth is a mystery of iniquity; the cursed arts by which a vile seducer gains the affections of a female; and the arts which a vile woman uses to conceal her wickedness.

Verses 21-23

Four sorts of persons are very troublesome. Men of low origin and base spirit, who, getting authority, become tyrants. Foolish and violent men indulging in excesses. A woman of a contentious spirit and vicious habits. A servant who has obtained undue influence. Let those whom Providence has advanced from low beginnings, carefully watch against that sin which most easily besets them.

Verses 24-28

Four things that are little, are yet to be admired. There are those who are poor in the world, and of small account, yet wise for their souls and another world.

Verses 29-33

We may learn from animals to go well; also to keep our temper under all provocations. We must keep the evil thought in our minds from breaking out into evil speeches. We must not stir up the passions of others. Let nothing be said or done with violence, but every thing with softness and calmness. Alas, how often have we done foolishly in rising up against the Lord our King! Let us humble ourselves before him. And having found peace with Him, let us follow peace with all men.

Chapter 31

Chapter Outline

Verses 1-9

When children are under the mother's eye, she has an opportunity of fashioning their minds aright. Those who are grown up, should often call to mind the good teaching they received when children. The many awful instances of promising characters who have been ruined by vile women, and love of wine, should warn every one to avoid these evils. Wine is to be used for want or medicine. Every creature of God is good, and wine, though abused, has its use. By the same rule, due praise and consolation should be used as cordials to the dejected and tempted, not administered to the confident and self-sufficient. All in authority should be more carefully temperate even than other men; and should be protectors of those who are unable or afraid to plead their own cause. Our blessed Lord did not decline the bitterest dregs of the cup of sorrow put into his hands; but he puts the cup of consolation into the hands of his people, and causes those to rejoice who are in the deepest distress.

Verses 10-31

This is the description of a virtuous woman of those days, but the general outlines equally suit every age and nation. She is very careful to recommend herself to her husband's esteem and affection, to know his mind, and is willing that he rule over her. 1. She can be trusted, and he will leave such a wife to manage for him. He is happy in her. And she makes it her constant business to do him good. 2. She is one that takes pains in her duties, and takes pleasure in them. She is careful to fill up time, that none be lost. She rises early. She applies herself to the business proper for her, to women's business. She does what she does, with all her power, and trifles not. 3. She makes what she does turn to good account by prudent management. Many undo themselves by buying, without considering whether they can afford it. She provides well for her house. She lays up for hereafter. 4. She looks well to the ways of her household, that she may oblige all to do their duty to God and one another, as well as to her. 5. She is intent upon giving as upon getting, and does it freely and cheerfully. 6. She is discreet and obliging; every word she says, shows she governs herself by the rules of wisdom. She not only takes prudent measures herself, but gives prudent advice to others. The law of love and kindness is written in the heart, and shows itself in the tongue. Her heart is full of another world, even when her hands are most busy about this world. 7. Above all, she fears the Lord. Beauty recommends none to God, nor is it any proof of wisdom and goodness, but it has deceived many a man who made his choice of a wife by it. But the fear of God reigning in the heart, is the beauty of the soul; it lasts for ever. 8. She has firmness to bear up under crosses and disappointments. She shall reflect with comfort when she comes to be old, that she was not idle or useless when young. She shall rejoice in a world to come. She is a great blessing to her relations. If the fruit be good, the tree must have our good word. But she leaves it to her own works to praise her. Every one ought to desire this honour that cometh from God; and according to this standard we all ought to regulate our judgments. This description let all women daily study, who desire to be truly beloved and respected, useful and honourable. This passage is to be applied to individuals, but may it not also be applied to the church of God, which is described as a virtuous spouse? God by his grace has formed from among sinful men a church of true believers, to possess all the excellences here described.

Amos

Amos was a herdsman, and engaged in agriculture. But the same Divine Spirit influenced Isaiah and Daniel in the court, and Amos in the sheep-folds, giving to each the powers and eloquence needful for them. He assures the twelve tribes of the destruction of the neighbouring nations; and as they at that time gave themselves up to wickedness and idolatry, he reproves the Jewish nation with severity; but describes the restoration of the church by the Messiah, extending to the latter days.

Chapter 1

Judgments against the Syrians, Philistines, Tyrians, Edomites, and Ammonites.
—GOD employed a shepherd, a herdsman, to reprove and warn the people. Those to whom God gives abilities for his services, ought not to be despised for their origin, or their employment. Judgments are denounced against the neighbouring nations, the oppressors of God's people. The number of transgressions does not here mean that exact number, but many: they had filled the measure of their sins, and were ripe for vengeance. The method in dealing with these nations is, in part, the same, yet in each there is something peculiar. In all ages this bitterness has been shown against the Lord's people. When the Lord reckons with his enemies, how tremendous are his judgments!

Chapter 2

Chapter Outline

Judgments against Moab and Judah.	(1–8)
The ingratitude and ruin of Israel.	(9–16)

Verses 1-8

The evil passions of the heart break out in various forms; but the Lord looks to our motives, as well as our conduct. Those that deal cruelly, shall be cruelly dealt with. Other nations were reckoned with for injuries done to men; Judah is reckoned with for dishonour done to God. Judah despised the law of the Lord; and he justly gave them up to strong delusion; nor was it any excuse for their sin, that they were the lies, the idols, after which their fathers walked. The worst abominations and most grievous oppressions have been committed by some of the professed worshippers of the Lord. Such conduct leads many to unbelief and vile idolatry.

Verses 9-16

We need often to be reminded of the mercies we have received; which add much to the evil of the sins we have committed. They had helps for their souls, which taught them how to make good use of their earthly enjoyments, and were therefore more valuable. Faithful ministers are great blessings to any people; but it is God that raises them up to be so. Sinners' own consciences will witness that he has not been wanting to them in the means of grace. They did what they could to lead believers aside. Satan and his agents are busy to corrupt the minds of young people who look heavenward; they overcome many by drawing them to the love of mirth and pleasure, and into drinking company. Multitudes of young men who bade fair as professors of religion, have erred through strong drink, and have been undone for ever. The Lord complains of sin, especially the sins of his professing people, as a burden to him. And though his long-suffering be tired, his power is not, and so the sinner will find to his cost. When men reject God's word, adding obstinacy to sin, and this becomes the general character of a people, they will be given up to misery, notwithstanding all their boasted power and resources. May we then humble ourselves before the Lord, for all our ingratitude and unfaithfulness.

Chapter 3

Chapter Outline

Judgments against Israel.   (1–8)

The like to other nations.   (9–15)

Verses 1-8

The distinguishing favours of God to us, if they do not restrain from sin, shall not exempt from punishment. They could not expect communion with God, unless they first sought peace with him. Where there is not friendship, there can be no fellowship. God and man cannot walk together, except they are agreed. Unless we seek his glory, we cannot walk with him. Let us not presume on outward privileges, without special, sanctifying grace. The threatenings of the word and providence of God against the sin of man are certain, and certainly show that the judgments of God are at hand. Nor will God remove the affliction he has sent, till it has done its work. The evil of sin is from ourselves, it is our own doing; but the evil of trouble is from God, and is his doing, whoever are the instruments. This should engage us patiently to bear public troubles, and to study to answer God's meaning in them. The whole of the passage shows that natural evil, or troubles, and not moral evil, or sin, is here meant. The warning given to a careless world will increase its condemnation another day. Oh the amazing stupidity of an unbelieving world, that will not be wrought upon by the terrors of the Lord, and that despise his mercies!

Verses 9-15

That power which is an instrument of unrighteousness, will justly be brought down and broken. What is got and kept wrongfully, will not be kept long. Some are at ease, but there will come a day of visitation, and in that day, all they are proud of, and put confidence in, shall fail them. God will inquire into the sins of which they have been guilty in their houses, the robbery they have stored up, and the luxury in which they lived. The pomp and pleasantness of men's houses, do not fortify against God's judgments, but make sufferings the more grievous and vexatious. Yet a remnant, according to the election of grace, will be secured by our great and good Shepherd, as from the jaws of destruction, in the worst times.

Chapter 4

Chapter Outline

Israel is reproved.	(1–5)
Their impenitence shown.	(6–13)

Verses 1-5

What is got by extortion is commonly used to provide for the flesh, and to fulfil the lusts thereof. What is got by oppression cannot be enjoyed with satisfaction. How miserable are those whose confidence in unscriptural observances only prove that they believe a lie! Let us see to it that our faith, hope, and worship, are warranted by the Divine word.

Verses 6-13

See the folly of carnal hearts; they wander from one creature to another, seeking for something to satisfy, and labour for that which satisfies not; yet, after all, they will not incline their ear to Him in whom they might find all they can want. Preaching the gospel is as rain, and every thing withers where this rain is wanting. It were well if people were as wise for their souls as they are for their bodies; and, when they have not this rain near, would go and seek it where it is to be had. As the Israelites persisted in rebellion and idolatry, the Lord was coming against them as an adversary. Ere long, we must meet our God in judgment; but we shall not be able to stand before him, if he tries us according to our doings. If we would prepare to meet our God with comfort, at the awful period of his coming, we must now meet him in Christ Jesus, the eternal Son of the Father, who came to save lost sinners. We must seek him while he is to be found.

Chapter 5

Chapter Outline

Israel is called to seek the Lord.	(1–6)
Earnest exhortations to repentance.	(7–17)

Threatenings respecting idolatries.

(18–27)

Verses 1-6

The convincing, awakening word must be heard and heeded, as well as words of comfort and peace; for whether we hear or forbear, the word of God shall take effect. The Lord still proclaims mercy to men, but they often expect deliverance from such self-invented forms as make their condemnation sure. While they refuse to come to Christ and to seek mercy in and by him, that they may live, the fire of Divine wrath breaks forth upon them. Men may make an idol of the world, but will find it cannot protect.

Verses 7-17

The same almighty power can, for repenting sinners, easily turn affliction and sorrow into prosperity and joy, and as easily turn the prosperity of daring sinners into utter darkness. Evil times will not bear plain dealing; that is, evil men will not. And these men were evil men indeed, when wise and good men thought it in vain even to speak to them. Those who will seek and love that which is good, may help to save the land from ruin. It behoves us to plead God's spiritual promises, to beseech him to create in us a clean heart, and to renew a right spirit within us. The Lord is ever ready to be gracious to the souls that seek him; and then piety and every duty will be attended to. But as for sinful Israel, God's judgments had often passed by them, now they shall pass through them.

Verses 18-27

Woe unto those that desire the day of the Lord's judgments, that wish for times of war and confusion; as some who long for changes, hoping to rise upon the ruins of their country! but this should be so great a desolation, that nobody could gain by it. The day of the Lord will be a dark, dismal, gloomy day to all impenitent sinners. When God makes a day dark, all the world cannot make it light. Those who are not reformed by the judgments of God, will be pursued by them; if they escape one, another stands ready to seize them. A pretence of piety is double iniquity, and so it will be found. The people of Israel copied the crimes of their forefathers. The law of worshipping the Lord our God, is, Him only we must serve. Professors thrive so little, because they have little or no communion with God in their duties. They were led captive by Satan into idolatry, therefore God caused them to go into captivity among idolaters.

Chapter 6

Chapter Outline

Verses 1-7

Those are looked upon as doing well for themselves, who do well for their bodies; but we are here told what their ease is, and what their woe is. Here is a description of the pride, security, and sensuality, for which God would reckon. Careless sinners are every where in danger; but those at ease in Zion, who are stupid, vainly confident, and abusing their privileges, are in the greatest danger. Yet many fancy themselves the people of God, who are living in sin, and in conformity to the world. But the examples of others' ruin forbid us to be secure. Those who are set upon their pleasures are commonly careless of the troubles of others, but this is great offence to God. Those who placed their happiness in the pleasures of sense, and set their hearts upon them, shall be deprived of those pleasures. Those who try to put the evil day far from them, find it nearest to them.

Verses 8-14

How dreadful, how miserable, is the case of those whose eternal ruin the Lord himself has sworn; for he can execute his purpose, and none can alter it! Those hearts are wretchedly hardened that will not be brought to mention God's name, and to worship him, when the hand of God is gone out against them, when sickness and death are in their families. Those that will not be tilled as fields, shall be abandoned as rocks. When our services of God are soured with sin, his providences will justly be made bitter to us. Men should take warning not to harden their hearts, for those who walk in pride, God will destroy.

Chapter 7

Chapter Outline

Visions of judgments to come upon Israel. (1–9)

Amaziah threatens Amos. (10–17)

Verses 1-9

God bears long, but he will not bear always with a provoking people. The remembrance of the mercies we formerly received, like the produce of the earth of the former growth, should make us submissive to the will of God, when we meet with disappointments in the latter growth. The Lord has many ways of humbling a sinful nation. Whatever trouble we are under, we should be most earnest with God for the forgiveness of sin. Sin will soon make a great people small. What will become of Israel, if the hand that should raise him be stretched out against him? See the power of prayer. See what a blessing praying people are to a land. See how ready, how swift God is to show mercy; how he waits to be gracious. Israel was a wall, a strong wall, which God himself reared as a defence to his sanctuary. The Lord now seems to stand upon this wall. He measures it; it appears to be a bowing, bulging wall. Thus God would bring the people of Israel to the trial, would discover their wickedness; and the time will come, when those who have been spared often, shall be spared no longer. But the Lord still calls Israel his people. The repeated prayer and success of the prophet should lead us to seek the Saviour.

Verses 10-17

It is no new thing for the accusers of the brethren, to misrepresent them as enemies to the king and kingdom, as traitors to their prince, and troublers of the land, when they are the best friends to both. Those who make gain their godliness, and are governed by the hopes of wealth and preferment, are ready to think these the most powerful motives with others also. But those who have a warrant from God, like Amos, ought not to fear the face of man. If God, that sent him, had not strengthened him, he could not thus have set his face as a flint. The Lord often chooses the weak and foolish things of the world to confound the wise and mighty. But no fervent prayers, or self-denying labours, can bring proud sinners to bear faithful reproofs and warnings. And all who oppose or despise the Divine word, must expect fatal effects to their souls, unless they repent.

Chapter 8

Chapter Outline

Verses 1-3

Amos saw a basket of summer fruit gathered, and ready to be eaten; which signified, that the people were ripe for destruction, that the year of God's patience was drawing towards a conclusion. Such summer fruits will not keep till winter, but must be used at once. Yet these judgments shall not draw from them any acknowledgement, either of God's righteousness or their own unrighteousness. Sinners put off repentance from day to day, because they think the Lord thus delays his judgments.

Verses 4-10

The rich and powerful of the land were the most guilty of oppression, as well as the foremost in idolatry. They were weary of the restraints of the sabbaths and the new moons, and wished them over, because no common work might be done therein. This is the character of many who are called Christians. The sabbath day and sabbath work are a burden to carnal hearts. It will either be profaned or be accounted a dull day. But can we spend our time better than in communion with God? When employed in religious services, they were thinking of marketings. They were weary of holy duties, because their worldly business stood still the while. Those are strangers to God, and enemies to themselves, who love market days better than sabbath days, who would rather be selling corn than worshipping God. They have no regard to man: those who have lost the savour of piety, will not long keep the sense of common honesty. They cheat those they deal with. They take advantage of their neighbour's ignorance or necessity, in a traffic which nearly concerns the labouring poor. Could we witness the fraud and covetousness, which, in such numerous forms, render trading an abomination to the Lord, we should not wonder to see many dealers backward in the service of God. But he who thus despises the poor, reproaches his Maker; as it regards Him, rich and poor meet together. Riches that are got by the ruin of the poor, will bring ruin on those that get them. God will remember their sin against them. This speaks the case of such unjust, unmerciful men, to be miserable indeed, miserable for ever. There shall be terror and desolation every where. It shall come upon them when they little think of it. Thus uncertain are all our creature-comforts and enjoyments, even life itself; in the midst of life we are in death. What will be the wailing in the bitter day which follows sinful and sensual pleasures!

Verses 11-14

Here was a token of God's highest displeasure. At any time, and most in a time of trouble, a famine of the word of God is the heaviest judgment. To many this is no affliction, yet some will feel it very much, and will travel far to hear a good sermon; they feel the loss of the mercies others foolishly sin away. But when God visits a backsliding church, their own plans and endeavours to find out a way of salvation, will stand them in no stead. And the most amiable and zealous would perish, for want of the water of life, which Christ only can bestow. Let us value our advantages, seek to profit by them, and fear sinning them away.

Chapter 9

Chapter Outline

The ruin of Israel. (1–10)

The restoration of the Jews and the gospel blessing. (11–15)

Verses 1-10

The prophet, in vision, saw the Lord standing upon the idolatrous altar at Bethel. Wherever sinners flee from God's justice, it will overtake them. Those whom God brings to heaven by his grace, shall never be cast down; but those who seek to climb thither by vain confidence in themselves, will be cast down and filled with shame. That which makes escape impossible and ruin sure, is, that God will set his eyes upon them for evil, not for good. Wretched must those be on whom the Lord looks for evil, and not for good. The Lord would scatter the Jews, and visit them with calamities, as the corn is shaken in a sieve; but he would save some from among them. The astonishing preservation of the Jews as a distinct people, seems here foretold. If professors make themselves like the world, God will level them with the world. The sinners who thus flatter themselves, shall find that their profession will not protect them.

Verses 11-15

Christ died to gather together the children of God that were scattered abroad, here said to be those who were called by his name. The Lord saith this, who doeth this, who can do it, who has determined to do it, the power of whose grace is engaged for doing it. Verses #(13–15) may refer to the early times of Christianity, but will receive a more glorious fulfilment in the events which all the prophets more or less foretold, and may be understood of the happy state when the fulness both of the Jews and the Gentiles come into the church. Let us continue earnest in prayer for the fulfilment of these prophecies, in the peace, purity, and the beauty of the church. God marvellously preserves his elect amidst the most fearful confusions and miseries. When all seems desperate, he wonderfully revives his church, and blesses her with all spiritual blessings in Christ Jesus. And great shall be the glory of that period, in which not one good thing promised shall remain unfulfilled.

Obadiah

The first part denounces the destruction of Edom, dwelling upon the injuries they inflicted upon the Jews. The second foretells the restoration of the Jews, and the latter glories of the church.

Chapter 1

Chapter Outline

Destruction to come upon Edom. Their offences against Jacob. (1–16)

The restoration of the Jews, and their flourishing state in the latter times. (17–21)

Verses 1-16

This prophecy is against Edom. Its destruction seems to have been typical, as their father Esau's rejection; and to refer to the destruction of the enemies of the gospel church. See the prediction of the success of that war; Edom shall be spoiled, and brought down. All the enemies of God's church shall be disappointed in the things they stay themselves on. God can easily lay those low who magnify and exalt themselves; and will do it. Carnal security ripens men for ruin, and makes the ruin worse when it comes. Treasures on earth cannot be so safely laid up but that thieves may break through and steal; it is therefore our wisdom to lay up for ourselves treasures in heaven. Those that make flesh their trust, arm it against themselves. The God of our covenant will never deceive us: but if we trust men with whom we join ourselves, it may prove to us a wound and dishonour. God will justly deny those understanding to keep out of danger, who will not use their understandings to keep out of sin. All violence, all unrighteousness, is sin; but it makes the violence far worse, if it be done against any of God's people. Their barbarous conduct towards Judah and Jerusalem, is charged upon them. In reflecting on ourselves, it is good to consider what we should have done; to compare our practice with the Scripture rule. Sin, thus looked upon in the glass of the commandment, will appear exceedingly sinful. Those have a great deal to answer for, who are idle spectators of the troubles of their neighbours, when able to be active helpers. Those make themselves poor, who think to make themselves rich by the ruin of the people of God; and those deceive themselves, who call all that their own on which they can lay their hands in a day of calamity. Though judgment begins at the house of God, it shall not end there. Let sorrowful believers and insolent oppressors know, that the troubles of the righteous will soon end, but those of the wicked will be eternal.

Verses 17-21

There should be deliverance and holiness at Jerusalem, and the house of Jacob would again occupy their possessions. Much of this prophecy was fulfilled when the Jews returned to their own land. But the salvation and holiness of the gospel, its spread, and the conversion of the Gentiles, seem also to be intended, especially the restoration of Israel, the destruction of antichrist, and the prosperous state of the church, to which all the prophets bear witness. When Christ is come, and not till then, shall the kingdom be the Lord's in the full sense of the term. As none that exalt themselves against the Lord shall prosper, and all shall be brought down; so none that wait upon the Lord, and put their trust in him, shall ever be dismayed. Blessed be the Divine Saviour and Judge on Mount Zion! His word shall be a savour of life unto life unto numbers, while it judges and condemns obstinate unbelievers.

Jonah

Jonah was a native of Galilee, 2Ki 14:25. His miraculous deliverance from out of the fish, rendered him a type of our blessed Lord, who mentions it, so as to show the certain truth of the narrative. All that was done was easy to the almighty power of the Author and Sustainer of life. This book shows us, by the example of the Ninevites, how great are the Divine forbearance and long-suffering towards sinners. It shows a most striking contrast between the goodness and mercy of God, and the rebellion, impatience, and peevishness of his servant; and it will be best understood by those who are most acquainted with their own hearts.

Chapter 1

Chapter Outline

Verses 1-3

It is sad to think how much sin is committed in great cities. Their wickedness, as that of Nineveh, is a bold and open affront to God. Jonah must go at once to Nineveh, and there, on the spot, cry against the wickedness of it. Jonah would not go. Probably there are few among us who would not have tried to decline such a mission. Providence seemed to give him an opportunity to escape; we may be out of the way of duty, and yet may meet with a favourable gale. The ready way is not always the right way. See what the best of men are, when God leaves them to themselves; and what need we have, when the word of the Lord comes to us, to have the Spirit of the Lord to bring every thought within us into obedience.

Verses 4-7

God sent a pursuer after Jonah, even a mighty tempest. Sin brings storms and tempests into the soul, into the family, into churches and nations; it is a disquieting, disturbing thing. Having called upon their gods for help, the sailors did what they could to help themselves. Oh that men would be thus wise for their souls, and would be willing to part with that wealth, pleasure, and honour, which they cannot keep without making shipwreck of faith and a good conscience, and ruining their souls for ever! Jonah was fast asleep. Sin is stupifying, and we are to take heed lest at any time our hearts are hardened by the deceitfulness of it. What do men mean by sleeping on in sin, when the word of God and the convictions of their own consciences, warn them to arise and call on the Lord, if they would escape everlasting misery? Should not we warn each other to awake, to arise, to call upon our God, if so be he will deliver us? The sailors concluded the storm was a messenger of Divine justice sent to some one in that ship. Whatever evil is upon us at any time, there is a cause for it; and each must pray, Lord, show me wherefore thou contendest with me. The lot fell upon Jonah. God has many ways of bringing to light hidden sins and sinners, and making manifest that folly which was thought to be hid from the eyes of all living.

Verses 8-12

Jonah gave an account of his religion, for that was his business. We may hope that he told with sorrow and shame, justifying God, condemning himself, and explaining to the mariners what a great God Jehovah is. They said to him, Why hast thou done this? If thou fearest the God that made the sea and the dry land, why wast thou such a fool as to think thou couldst flee from his presence? If the professors of religion do wrong, they will hear it from those who make no such profession. When sin has raised a storm, and laid us under the tokens of God's displeasure, we must consider what is to be done to the sin that raised the storm. Jonah uses the language of true penitents, who desire that none but themselves may fare the worse for their sins and follies. Jonah sees this to be the punishment of his iniquity, he accepts it, and justifies God in it. When conscience is awakened, and a storm raised, nothing will turn it into a calm but parting with the sin that caused the disturbance. Parting with our money will not pacify the conscience, the Jonah must be thrown overboard.

Verses 13-17

The mariners rowed against wind and tide, the wind of God's displeasure, the tide of his counsel; but it is in vain to think of saving ourselves any other way than by destroying our sins. Even natural conscience cannot but dread blood-guiltiness. And when we are led by Providence God does what he pleases, and we ought to be satisfied, though it may not please us. Throwing Jonah into the sea put an end to the storm. God will not afflict for ever, He will only contend till we submit and turn from our sins. Surely these heathen mariners will rise up in judgment against many called Christians, who neither offer prayers when in distress, nor thanksgiving for signal deliverances. The Lord commands all creatures, and can make any of them serve his designs of mercy to his people. Let us see this salvation of the Lord, and admire his power, that he could thus save a drowning man, and his pity, that he would thus save one who was running from him, and had offended him. It was of the Lord's mercies that Jonah was not consumed. Jonah was alive in the fish three days and nights: to nature this was impossible, but to the God of nature all things are possible. Jonah, by this miraculous preservation, was made a type of Christ; as our blessed Lord himself declared, Mt 12:40.

Chapter 2

Chapter Outline

The prayer of Jonah.   (1–9)

He is delivered from the fish.   (10)

Verses 1-9

Observe when Jonah prayed. When he was in trouble, under the tokens of God's displeasure against him for sin: when we are in affliction we must pray. Being kept alive by miracle, he prayed. A sense of God's good-will to us, notwithstanding our offences, opens the lips in prayer, which were closed with the dread of wrath. Also, where he prayed; in the belly of the fish. No place is amiss for prayer. Men may shut us from communion with one another, but not from communion with God. To whom he prayed; to the Lord his God. This encourages even backsliders to return. What his prayer was. This seems to relate his experience and reflections, then and afterwards, rather than to be the form or substance of his prayer. Jonah reflects on the earnestness of his prayer, and God's readiness to hear and answer. If we would get good by our troubles, we must notice the hand of God in them. He had wickedly fled from the presence of the Lord, who might justly take his Holy Spirit from him, never to visit him more. Those only are miserable, whom God will no longer own and favour. But though he was perplexed, yet not in despair. Jonah reflects on the favour of God to him, when he sought to God, and trusted in him in his distress. He warns others, and tells them to keep close to God. Those who forsake their own duty, forsake their own mercy; those who run away from the work of their place and day, run away from the comfort of it. As far as a believer copies those who observe lying vanities, he forsakes his own mercy, and lives below his privileges.

But Jonah's experience encourages others, in all ages, to trust in God, as the God of salvation.

Verse 10

Jonah's deliverance may be considered as an instance of God's power over all the creatures. As an instance of God's mercy to a poor penitent, who in distress prays to him: and as a type and figure of Christ's resurrection. Amidst all our varying experiences, and the changing scenes of life; we should look by faith, fixedly, upon our once suffering and dying, but now risen and ascended Redeemer. Let us confess our sins, consider Christ's resurrection as an earnest of our own, and thankfully receive every temporal and spiritual deliverance, as the pledge of our eternal redemption.

Chapter 3

Chapter Outline

Verses 1-4

God employs Jonah again in his service. His making use of us is an evidence of his being at peace with us. Jonah was not disobedient, as he had been. He neither endeavoured to avoid hearing the command, nor declined to obey it. See here the nature of repentance; it is the change of our mind and way, and a return to our work and duty. Also, the benefit of affliction; it brings those back to their place who had deserted it. See the power of Divine grace, for affliction of itself would rather drive men from God, than draw them to him. God's servants must go where he sends them, come when he calls them, and do what he bids them; we must do whatever the word of the Lord commands. Jonah faithfully and boldly delivered his errand. Whether Jonah said more, to show the anger of God against them, or whether he only repeated these words again and again, is not certain, but this was the purport of his message. Forty days is a long time for a righteous God to delay judgments, yet it is but a little time for an unrighteous people to repent and reform in. And should it not awaken us to get ready for death, to consider that we cannot be so sure that we shall live forty days, as Nineveh then was that it should stand forty days? We should be alarmed if we were sure not to live a month, yet we are careless though we are not sure to live a day.

Verses 5-10

There was a wonder of Divine grace in the repentance and reformation of Nineveh. It condemns the men of the gospel generation, Mt 12:41. A very small degree of light may convince men that humbling themselves before God, confessing their sins with prayer, and turning from sin, are means of escaping wrath and obtaining mercy. The people followed the example of the king. It became a national act, and it was necessary it should be so, when it was to prevent a national ruin. Let even the brute creatures' cries and moans for want of food remind their owners to cry to God. In prayer we must cry mightily, with fixedness of thought, firmness of faith, and devout affections. It concerns us in prayer to stir up all that is within us. It is not enough to fast for sin, but we must fast from sin; and, in order to the success of our prayers, we must no more regard iniquity in our hearts, Ps 66:18. The work of a fast-day is not done with the day. The Ninevites hoped that God would turn from his fierce anger; and that thus their ruin would be prevented. They could not be so confident of finding mercy upon their repentance, as we may be, who have the death and merits of Christ, to which we may trust for pardon upon repentance. They dared not presume, but they did not despair. Hope of mercy is the great encouragement to repentance and reformation. Let us boldly cast ourselves down at the footstool of free grace, and God will look upon us with compassion. God sees who turn from their evil ways, and who do not. Thus he spared Nineveh. We read of no sacrifices offered to God to make atonement for sin; but a broken and a contrite heart, such as the Ninevites then had, he will not despise.

Chapter 4

Chapter Outline

Verses 1-4

What all the saints make matter of joy and praise, Jonah makes the subject of reflection upon God; as if showing mercy were an imperfection of the Divine nature, which is the greatest glory of it. It is to his sparing, pardoning mercy, we all owe it that we are out of hell. He wishes for death: this was the language of folly, passion, and strong corruption. There appeared in Jonah remains of a proud, uncharitable spirit; and that he neither expected nor desired the welfare of the Ninevites, but had only come to declare and witness their destruction. He was not duly humbled for his own sins, and was not willing to trust the Lord with his credit and safety. In this frame of mind, he overlooked the good of which he had been an instrument, and the glory of the Divine mercy. We should often ask ourselves, Is it well to say thus, to do thus? Can I justify it? Do I well to be so soon angry, so often angry, so long angry, and to give others ill language in my anger? Do I well to be angry at the mercy of God to repenting sinners? That was Jonah's crime. Do we do well to be angry at that which is for the glory of God, and the advancement of his kingdom? Let the conversion of sinners, which is the joy of heaven, be our joy, and never our grief.

Verses 5-11

Jonah went out of the city, yet remained near at hand, as if he expected and desired its overthrow. Those who have fretful, uneasy spirits, often make troubles for themselves, that they may still have something to complain of. See how tender God is of his people in their afflictions, even though they are foolish and froward. A thing small in itself, yet coming seasonably, may be a valuable blessing. A gourd in the right place may do us more service than a cedar. The least creatures may be great plagues, or great comforts, as God is pleased to make them. Persons of strong passions are apt to be cast down with any trifle that crosses them, or to be lifted up with a trifle that pleases them. See what our creature-comforts are, and what we may expect them to be; they are withering things. A small worm at the root destroys a large gourd: our gourds wither, and we know not what is the cause. Perhaps creature-comforts are continued to us, but are made bitter; the creature is continued, but the comfort is gone. God prepared a wind to make Jonah feel the want of the gourd. It is just that those who love to complain, should never be left without something to complain of. When afflicting providences take away relations, possessions, and enjoyments, we must not be angry at God. What should especially silence discontent, is, that when our gourd is gone, our God is not gone. Sin and death are very dreadful, yet Jonah, in his heat, makes light of both. One soul is of more value than the whole world; surely then one soul is of more value than many gourds: we should have more concern for our own and others' precious souls, than for the riches and enjoyments of this world. It is a great encouragement to hope we shall find mercy with the Lord, that he is ready to show mercy. And murmurers shall be made to understand, that how willing soever they are to keep the Divine grace to themselves and those of their own way, there is one Lord over all, who is rich in mercy to all that call upon him. Do we wonder at the forbearance of God towards his perverse servant? Let us study our own hearts and ways; let us not forget our own ingratitude and obstinacy; and let us be astonished at God's patience towards us.

Micah

Micah was raised up to support Isaiah, and to confirm his predictions, while he invited to repentance, both by threatened judgments and promised mercies. A very remarkable passage, Mic 5 contains a summary of prophecies concerning the Messiah.

Chapter 1

Chapter Outline

The wrath of God against Israel.	(1–7)
Also against Jerusalem and other cities, Their precautions vain.	(8–16)

Verses 1-7

The earth is called upon, with all that are therein, to hear the prophet. God's holy temple will not protect false professors. Neither men of high degree, as the mountains, nor men of low degree, as the valleys, can secure themselves or the land from the judgments of God. If sin be found in God's people he will not spare them; and their sins are most provoking to him, for they are most reproaching. When we feel the smart of sin, it behoves us to seek what is the sin we smart for. Persons and places most exalted, are most exposed to spiritual diseases. The vices of leaders and rulers shall be surely and sorely punished. The punishment answers the sin. What they gave to idols, never shall prosper, nor do them any good. What is got by one lust, is wasted on another.

Verses 8-16

The prophet laments that Israel's case is desperate; but declare it not in Gath. Gratify not those that make merry with the sins or with the sorrows of God's Israel. Roll thyself in the dust, as mourners used to do; let every house in Jerusalem become a house of Aphrah, "a house of dust." When God makes the house dust it becomes us to humble ourselves to the dust under his mighty hand. Many places should share this mourning. The names have meanings which pointed out the miseries coming upon them; thereby to awaken the people to a holy fear of Divine wrath. All refuges but Christ, must be refuges of lies to those who trust in them; other heirs will succeed to every inheritance but that of heaven; and all glory will be turned into shame, except that honour which cometh from God only. Sinners may now disregard their neighbours' sufferings, yet their turn to be punished will some come.

Chapter 2

Chapter Outline

Verses 1-5

Woe to the people that devise evil during the night, and rise early to carry it into execution! It is bad to do mischief on a sudden thought, much worse to do it with design and forethought. It is of great moment to improve and employ hours of retirement and solitude in a proper manner. If covetousness reigns in the heart, compassion is banished; and when the heart is thus engaged, violence and fraud commonly occupy the hands. The most haughty and secure in prosperity, are commonly most ready to despair in adversity. Woe to those from whom God turns away! Those are the sorest calamities which cut us off from the congregation of the Lord, or cut us short in the enjoyment of its privileges.

Verses 6-11

Since they say, "Prophesy not," God will take them at their word, and their sin shall be their punishment. Let the physician no longer attend the patient that will not be healed. Those are enemies, not only to God, but to their country, who silence good ministers, and stop the means of grace. What bonds will hold those who have no reverence for God's word? Sinners cannot expect to rest in a land they have polluted. You shall not only be obliged to depart out of this land, but it shall destroy you. Apply this to our state in this present world. There is corruption in the world through lust, and we should keep at a distance from it. It is not our rest: it was designed for our passage, but not for our portion; our inn, but not our home; here we have no continuing city; let us therefore arise and depart, let us seek a continuing city above. Since they will be deceived, let them be deceived. Teachers who recommend self-indulgence by their doctrine and example, best suit such sinners.

Verses 12, 13

These verses may refer to the captivity of Israel and Judah. But the passage is also a prophecy of the conversion of the Jews to Christ. The Lord would not only bring them from captivity, and multiply them, but the Lord Jesus would open their way to God, by taking upon him the nature of man, and by the work of his Spirit in their hearts, breaking the fetters of Satan. Thus he has gone before, and the people follow, breaking, in his strength, through the enemies that would stop their way to heaven.

Chapter 3

Chapter Outline

The cruelty of the princes, and the falsehood   (1–8)
of the prophets.

Their false security.   (9–12)

Verses 1-8

Men cannot expect to do ill, and fare well; but to find that done to them which they did to others. How seldom do wholesome truths reach the ears of those in high stations or in authority! Those who deceive others are preparing confusion for their own faces. The prophet had ardent love to God and to the souls of men; deep concern for his glory and their salvation, and zeal against sin. The difficulties he met with did not drive him from his work. He had this strength; not from and of himself, but he was full of power by the Spirit of the Lord. Those who act honestly, may act boldly. And those who come to hear the word of God, must be willing to be told of their faults, must take it kindly, and be thankful.

Verses 9-12

Zion's walls owe no thanks to those that build them up with blood and iniquity. The sin of man works not the righteousness of God. Even when men do that which in itself is good, but do it for filthy lucre, it becomes abomination both to God and man. Faith rests in the Lord as the soul's foundation: presumption only leans upon the Lord as a prop, and would use him to serve a turn. If men's having the Lord among them will not keep them from doing evil, it never can secure them from suffering evil for so doing. See the doom of wicked Jacob; Therefore shall Zion for your sake be ploughed as a field. This was exactly fulfilled at the destruction of Jerusalem by the Romans, and is so at this day. If sacred places are polluted by sin, they will be wasted and ruined by the judgments of God.

Chapter 4

Chapter Outline

The peace of the kingdom of Christ.   (1–8)

The judgments to come upon Jerusalem, but   (9–13)
the final triumph of Israel.

Verses 1-8

The nations have not yet so submitted to the Prince of Peace, as to beat their swords into ploughshares, nor has war ceased. But very precious promises these are, relating to the gospel church, which will be more and more fulfilled, for He is faithful that has promised. There shall be a glorious church for God set up in the world, in the last days, in the days of the Messiah. Christ himself will build it upon a rock. The Gentiles worshipped their idol gods; but in the period spoken of, the people will cleave to the Lord with full purpose of heart, and delight in doing his will. The word "halteth," describes those who walk not according to the Divine word. The collecting the captives from Babylon was an earnest of healing, purifying, and prospering the church; and the reign of Christ shall continue till succeeded by the everlasting kingdom of heaven. Let us stir up each other to attend the ordinances of God, that we may learn his holy ways, and walk in them, receiving the law from his hands, which, being written in our hearts by his Spirit, may show our interest in the Redeemer's righteousness.

Verses 9-13

Many nations would assemble against Zion to rejoice in her calamities. They would not understand that the Lord had collected them as sheaves are gathered to be threshed; and that Zion would be strengthened to beat them to pieces. Nothing has yet taken place in the history of the Jewish church agreeing with this prediction. When God has conquering work for his people to do, he will furnish them with strength and ability for it. Believers should cry aloud under distresses, with the prayer of faith, not with despondency.

Chapter 5

Chapter Outline

The birth of Christ and conversion of the Gentiles.	(1–6)
The triumphs of Israel.	(7–15)

Verses 1-6

Having showed how low the house of David would be brought, a prediction of the Messiah and his kingdom is added to encourage the faith of God's people. His existence from eternity as God, and his office as Mediator, are noticed. Here is foretold that Bethlehem should be his birthplace. Hence it was universally known among the Jews, Mt 2:5. Christ's government shall be very happy for his subjects; they shall be safe and easy. Under the shadow of protection from the Assyrians, is a promise of protection to the gospel church and all believers, from the designs and attempts of the powers of darkness. Christ is our Peace as a Priest, making atonement for sin, and reconciling us to God; and he is our Peace as a King, conquering our enemies: hence our souls may dwell at ease in him. Christ will find instruments to protect and deliver. Those that threaten ruin to the church of God, soon bring ruin on themselves. This may include the past powerful effects of the preached gospel, its future spread, and the ruin of all antichristian powers. This is, perhaps, the most important single prophecy in the Old Testament: it respects the personal character of the Messiah, and the discoveries of himself to the world. It distinguishes his human birth from his existing from eternity;

it foretells the rejection of the Israelites and Jews for a season, their final restoration, and the universal peace to prevail through the whole earth in the latter days. In the mean time let us trust our Shepherd's care and power. If he permits the assault of our enemies, he will supply helpers and assistance for us.

Verses 7-15

The remnant of Israel, converted to Christ in the primitive times, were among many nations as the drops of dew, and were made instruments in calling a large increase of spiritual worshippers. But to those who neglected or opposed this salvation, they would, as lions, cause terror, their doctrine condemning them. The Lord also declares that he would cause not only the reformation of the Jews, but the purification of the Christian church. In like manner shall we be assured of victory in our personal conflicts, as we simply depend upon the Lord our salvation, worship him, and serve him with diligence.

Chapter 6

Chapter Outline

God's controversy with Israel.	(1–5)
The duties God requires.	(6–8)
The wickedness of Israel.	(9–16)

Verses 1-5

The people are called upon to declare why they were weary of God's worship, and prone to idolatry. Sin causes the controversy between God and man. God reasons with us, to teach us to reason with ourselves. Let them remember God's many favours to them and their fathers, and compare with them their unworthy, ungrateful conduct toward him.

Verses 6-8

These verses seem to contain the substance of Balak's consultation with Balaam how to obtain the favour of Israel's God. Deep conviction of guilt and wrath will put men upon careful inquiries after peace and pardon, and then there begins to be some ground for hope of them. In order to God's being pleased with us, our care must be for an interest in the atonement of Christ, and that the sin by which we displease him may be taken away. What will be a satisfaction to God's justice? In whose name must we come, as we have nothing to plead as our own? In what righteousness shall we appear before him? The proposals betray ignorance, though they show zeal. They offer that which is very rich and costly. Those who are fully convinced of sin, and of their misery and danger by reason of it, would give all the world, if they had it, for peace and pardon. Yet they do not offer aright. The sacrifices had value from their reference to Christ; it was impossible that the blood of bulls and goats should take away sin. And all proposals of peace, except those according to the gospel, are absurd. They could not answer the demands of Divine justice, nor satisfy the wrong done to the honour of God by sin, nor would they serve at all in place of holiness of the heart and reformation of the life. Men will part with any thing rather than their sins; but they part with nothing so as to be accepted of God, unless they do part with their sins. Moral duties are commanded because they are good for man. In keeping God's commandments there is a great reward, as well as after keeping them. God has not only made it known, but made it plain. The good which God requires of us is, not the paying a price for the pardon of sin and acceptance with God, but love to himself; and what is there unreasonable, or hard, in this? Every thought within us must be brought down, to be brought into obedience to God, if we would walk comfortably with him. We must do this as penitent sinners, in dependence on the Redeemer and his atonement. Blessed be the Lord that he is ever ready to give his grace to the humble, waiting penitent.

Verses 9-16

God, having showed how necessary it was that they should do justly, here shows how plain it was that they had done unjustly. This voice of the Lord says to all, Hear the rod when it is coming, before you see it, and feel it. Hear the rod when it is come, and you are sensible of the smart; hear what counsels, what cautions it speaks. The voice of God is to be heard in the rod of God. Those who are dishonest in their dealings shall never be reckoned pure, whatever shows of devotion they may make. What is got by fraud and oppression, cannot be kept or enjoyed with satisfaction. What we hold closest we commonly lose soonest. Sin is a root of bitterness, soon planted, but not soon plucked up again. Their being the people of God in name and profession, while they kept themselves in his love, was an honour to them; but now, being backsliders, their having been once the people of God turns to their reproach.

Chapter 7

Chapter Outline

The general prevalence of wickedness.   (1–7)

Reliance on God, and triumph over enemies.   (8–13)

Promises and encouragements for Israel.   (14–20)

Verses 1-7

The prophet bemoans himself that he lived among a people ripening apace for ruin, in which many good persons would suffer. Men had no comfort, no satisfaction in their own families or in their nearest relations. Contempt and violation of domestic duties are a sad symptom of universal corruption. Those are never likely to come to good who are undutiful to their parents. The prophet saw no safety or comfort but in looking to the Lord, and waiting on God his salvation. When under trials, we should look continually to our Divine Redeemer, that we may have strength and grace to trust in him, and to be examples to those around us.

Verses 8-13

Those truly penitent for sin, will see great reason to be patient under affliction. When we complain to the Lord of the badness of the times, we ought to complain against ourselves for the badness of our hearts. We must depend upon God to work deliverance for us in due time. We must not only look to him, but look for him. In our greatest distresses, we shall see no reason to despair of salvation, if by faith we look to the Lord as the God of our salvation. Though enemies triumph and insult, they shall be silenced and put to shame. Though Zion's walls may long be in ruins, there will come a day when they shall be repaired. Israel shall come from all the remote parts, not turning back for discouragements. Though our enemies may seem to prevail against us, and to rejoice over us, we should not despond. Though cast down, we are not destroyed; we may join hope in God's mercy, with submission to his correction. No hinderances can prevent the favours the Lord intends for his church.

Verses 14-20

When God is about to deliver his people, he stirs up their friends to pray for them. Apply spiritually the prophet's prayer to Christ, to take care of his church, as the great Shepherd of the sheep, and to go before them, while they are here in this world as in a wood, in this world but not of it. God promises in answer to this prayer, he will do that for them which shall be repeating the miracles of former ages. As their sin brought them into bondage, so God's pardoning their sin brought them out. All who find pardoning mercy, cannot but wonder at that mercy; we have reason to stand amazed, if we know what it is. When the Lord takes away the guilt of sin, that it may not condemn us, he will break the power of sin, that it may not have dominion over us. If left to ourselves, our sins will be too hard for us; but God's grace shall be sufficient to subdue them, so that they shall not rule us, and then they shall not ruin us. When God forgives sin, he takes care that it never shall be remembered any more against the sinner. He casts their sins into the sea; not near the shore-side, where they may appear again, but into the depth of the sea, never to rise again. All their sins shall be cast there, for when God forgives sin, he forgives all. He will perfect that which concerns us, and with this good work will do all for us which our case requires, and which he has promised. These engagements relate to Christ, and the success of the gospel to the end of time, the future restoration of Israel, and the final prevailing of true religion in all lands. The Lord will perform his truth and mercy, not one jot or tittle of it shall fall to the ground: faithful is He that has promised, who also will do it. Let us remember that the Lord has given the security of his covenant, for strong consolation to all who flee for refuge to lay hold on the hope set before them in Christ Jesus.

Nahum

This prophet denounces the certain and approaching destruction of the Assyrian empire, particularly of Nineveh, which is described very minutely. Together with this is consolation for his countrymen, encouraging them to trust in God.

Chapter 1

Chapter Outline

The justice and power of the Lord. (1–8)

The overthrow of the Assyrians. (9–15)

Verses 1-8

About a hundred years before, at Jonah's preaching, the Ninevites repented, and were spared, yet, soon after, they became worse than ever. Nineveh knows not that God who contends with her, but is told what a God he is. It is good for all to mix faith with what is here said concerning Him, which speaks great terror to the wicked, and comfort to believers. Let each take his portion from it: let sinners read it and tremble; and let saints read it and triumph. The anger of the Lord is contrasted with his goodness to his people. Perhaps they are obscure and little regarded in the world, but the Lord knows them. The Scripture character of Jehovah agrees not with the views of proud reasoners. The God and Father of our Lord Jesus Christ is slow to wrath and ready to forgive, but he will by no means acquit the wicked; and there is tribulation and anguish for every soul that doeth evil: but who duly regards the power of his wrath?

Verses 9-15

There is a great deal plotted against the Lord by the gates of hell, and against his kingdom in the world; but it will prove in vain. With some sinners God makes quick despatch; and one way or other, he will make an utter end of all his enemies. Though they are quiet, and many very secure, and not in fear, they shall be cut down as grass and corn, when the destroying angel passes through. God would hereby work great deliverance for his own people. But those who make themselves vile by scandalous sins, God will make vile by shameful punishments. The tidings of this great deliverance shall be welcomed with abundant joy. These words are applied to the great redemption wrought out by our Lord Jesus and the everlasting gospel, Ro 10:15. Christ's ministers are messengers of good tidings, that preach peace by Jesus Christ. How welcome to those who see their misery and danger by sin! And the promise they made in the day of trouble must be made good. Let us be thankful for God's ordinances, and gladly attend them. Let us look forward with cheerful hope to a world where the wicked never can enter, and sin and temptation will no more be known.

Chapter 2

Chapter Outline

Nineveh's destruction foretold. (1–10)

The true cause, their sinning against God, and his appearing against them. (11–13)

Verses 1-10

Nineveh shall not put aside this judgment; there is no counsel or strength against the Lord. God looks upon proud cities, and brings them down. Particular account is given of the terrors wherein the invading enemy shall appear against Nineveh. The empire of Assyria is represented as a queen, about to be led captive to Babylon. Guilt in the conscience fills men with terror in an evil day; and what will treasures or glory do for us in times of distress, or in the day of wrath? Yet for such things how many lose their souls!

Verses 11-13

The kings of Assyria had long been terrible and cruel to their neighbours, but the Lord would destroy their power. Many plead as an excuse for rapine and fraud, that they have families to provide for; but what is thus obtained will never do them any good. Those that fear the Lord, and get honestly what they have, shall not want for themselves and theirs. It is just with God to deprive those of children, or of comfort in them, who take sinful courses to enrich them. Those are not worthy to be heard again, that have spoken reproachfully of God. Let us then come to God upon his mercy-seat, that having peace with him through our Lord Jesus Christ, we may know that he is for us, and that all things shall work together for our everlasting good.

Chapter 3

Chapter Outline

The sins and judgments of Nineveh. (1–7)

Its utter destruction. (8–19)

Verses 1-7

When proud sinners are brought down, others should learn not to lift themselves up. The fall of this great city should be a lesson to private persons, who increase wealth by fraud and oppression. They are preparing enemies for themselves; and if the Lord sees good to punish them in this world, they will have none to pity them. Every man who seeks his own prosperity, safety, and peace, should not only act in an upright, honourable manner, but with kindness to all.

Verses 8-19

Strong-holds, even the strongest, are no defence against the judgments of God. They shall be unable to do any thing for themselves. The Chaldeans and Medes would devour the land like canker-worms. The Assyrians also would be eaten up by their own numerous hired troops, which seem to be meant by the word rendered "merchants." Those that have done evil to their neighbours, will find it come home to them. Nineveh, and many other cities, states, and empires, have been ruined, and should be a warning to us. Are we better, except as there are some true Christians amongst us, who are a greater security, and a stronger defence, than all the advantages of situation or strength? When the Lord shows himself against a people, every thing they trust in must fail, or prove a disadvantage; but he continues good to Israel. He is a strong-hold for every believer in time of trouble, that cannot be stormed or taken; and he knoweth those that trust in Him.

Habakkuk

The subject of this prophecy is the destruction of Judea and Jerusalem for the sins of the people, and the consolation of the faithful under national calamities.

Chapter 1

Chapter Outline

The wickedness of the land. The fearful   (1–11)
vengeance to be executed.

These judgments to be inflicted by a nation   (12–17)
more wicked than themselves.

Verses 1-11

The servants of the Lord are deeply afflicted by seeing ungodliness and violence prevail; especially among those who profess the truth. No man scrupled doing wrong to his neighbour. We should long to remove to the world where holiness and love reign for ever, and no violence shall be before us. God has good reasons for his long-suffering towards bad men, and the rebukes of good men. The day will come when the cry of sin will be heard against those that do wrong, and the cry of prayer for those that suffer wrong. They were to notice what was going forward among the heathen by the Chaldeans, and to consider themselves a nation to be scourged by them. But most men presume on continued prosperity, or that calamities will not come in their days. They are a bitter and hasty nation, fierce, cruel, and bearing down all before them. They shall overcome all that oppose them. But it is a great offence, and the common offence of proud people, to take glory to themselves. The closing words give a glimpse of comfort.

Verses 12-17

However matters may be, yet God is the Lord our God, our Holy One. We are an offending people, he is an offended God, yet we will not entertain hard thoughts of him, or of his service. It is great comfort that, whatever mischief men design, the Lord designs good, and we are sure that his counsel shall stand. Though wickedness may prosper a while, yet God is holy, and does not approve the wickedness. As he cannot do iniquity himself, so he is of purer eyes than to behold it with any approval. By this principle we must abide, though the dispensations of his providence may for a time, in some cases, seem to us not to agree with it. The prophet complains that God's patience was abused; and because sentence against these evil works and workers was not executed speedily, their hearts were the more fully set in them to do evil. Some they take up as with the angle, one by one; others they catch in shoals, as in their net, and gather them in their drag, their enclosing net. They admire their own cleverness and contrivance: there is great proneness in us to take the glory of outward prosperity to ourselves. This is idolizing ourselves, sacrificing to the drag-net because it is our own. God will soon end successful and splendid robberies. Death and judgment shall make men cease to prey on others, and they shall be preyed on themselves. Let us remember, whatever advantages we possess, we must give all the glory to God.

Chapter 2

Chapter Outline

Verses 1-4

When tossed and perplexed with doubts about the methods of Providence, we must watch against temptations to be impatient. When we have poured out complaints and requests before God, we must observe the answers God gives by his word, his Spirit, and providences; what the Lord will say to our case. God will not disappoint the believing expectations of those who wait to hear what he will say unto them. All are concerned in the truths of God's word. Though the promised favour be deferred long, it will come at last, and abundantly recompense us for waiting. The humble, broken-hearted, repenting sinner, alone seeks to obtain an interest in this salvation. He will rest his soul on the promise, and on Christ, in and through whom it is given. Thus he walks and works, as well as lives by faith, perseveres to the end, and is exalted to glory; while those who distrust or despise God's all-sufficiency will not walk uprightly with him. The just shall live by faith in these precious promises, while the performance of them is deferred. Only those made just by faith, shall live, shall be happy here and for ever.

Verses 5-14

The prophet reads the doom of all proud and oppressive powers that bear hard upon God's people. The lusts of the flesh, the lust of the eye, and the pride of life, are the entangling snares of men; and we find him that led Israel captive, himself led captive by each of these. No more of what we have is to be reckoned ours, than what we come honestly by. Riches are but clay, thick clay; what are gold and silver but white and yellow earth? Those who travel through thick clay, are hindered and dirtied in their journey; so are those who go through the world in the midst of abundance of wealth. And what fools are those that burden themselves with continual care about it; with a great deal of guilt in getting, saving, and spending it, and with a heavy account which they must give another day! They overload themselves with this thick clay, and so sink themselves down into destruction and perdition. See what will be the end hereof; what is gotten by violence from others, others shall take away by violence. Covetousness brings disquiet and uneasiness into a family; he that is greedy of gain troubles his own house; what is worse, it brings the curse of God upon all the affairs of it. There is a lawful gain, which, by the blessing of God, may be a comfort to a house; but what is got by fraud and injustice, will bring poverty and ruin upon a family. Yet that is not the worst; Thou hast sinned against thine own soul, hast endangered it. Those who wrong their neighbours, do much greater wrong to their own souls. If the sinner thinks he has managed his frauds and violence with art and contrivance, the riches and possessions he heaped together will witness against him. There are not greater drudges in the world than those who are slaves to mere wordly pursuits. And what comes of it? They find themselves disappointed of it, and disappointed in it; they will own it is worse than vanity, it is vexation of spirit. By staining and sinking earthly glory, God manifests and magnifies his own glory, and fills the earth with the knowledge of it, as plentifully as waters cover the sea, which are deep, and spread far and wide.

Verses 15-20

A severe woe is pronounced against drunkenness; it is very fearful against all who are guilty of drunkenness at any time, and in any place, from the stately palace to the paltry ale-house. To give one drink who is in want, who is thirsty and poor, or a weary traveller, or ready to perish, is charity; but to give a neighbour drink, that he may expose himself, may disclose secret concerns, or be drawn into a bad bargain, or for any such purpose, this is wickedness. To be guilty of this sin, to take pleasure in it, is to do what we can towards the murder both of soul and body. There is woe to him, and punishment answering to the sin. The folly of worshipping idols is exposed. The Lord is in his holy temple in heaven, where we have access to him in the way he has appointed. May we welcome his salvation, and worship him in his earthly temples, through Christ Jesus, and by the influence of the Holy Spirit.

Chapter 3

Chapter Outline

The prophet beseeches God for his people.	(1, 2)
He calls to mind former deliverances.	(3–15)
His firm trust in the Divine mercy.	(16–19)

Verses 1, 2

The word prayer seems used here for an act of devotion. The Lord would revive his work among the people in the midst of the years of adversity. This may be applied to every season when the church, or believers, suffer under afflictions and trials. Mercy is what we must flee to for refuge, and rely upon as our only plea. We must not say, Remember our merit, but, Lord, remember thy own mercy.

Verses 3-15

God's people, when in distress, and ready to despair, seek help by considering the days of old, and the years of ancient times, and by pleading them with God in prayer. The resemblance between the Babylonish and Egyptian captivities, naturally presents itself to the mind, as well as the possibility of a like deliverance through the power of Jehovah. God appeared in his glory. All the powers of nature are shaken, and the course of nature changed, but all is for the salvation of God's own people. Even what seems least likely, shall be made to work for their salvation. Hereby is given a type and figure of the redemption of the world by Jesus Christ. It is for salvation with thine anointed. Joshua who led the armies of Israel, was a figure of Him whose name he bare, even Jesus, our Joshua. In all the salvations wrought for them, God looked upon Christ the Anointed, and brought deliverances to pass by him. All the wonders done for Israel of old, were nothing to that which was done when the Son of God suffered on the cross for the sins of his people. How glorious his resurrection and ascension! And how much more glorious will be his second coming, to put an end to all that opposes him, and all that causes suffering to his people!

Verses 16-19

When we see a day of trouble approach, it concerns us to prepare. A good hope through grace is founded in holy fear. The prophet looked back upon the experiences of the church in former ages, and observed what great things God had done for them, and so was not only recovered, but filled with holy joy. He resolved to delight and triumph in the Lord; for when all is gone, his God is not gone. Destroy the vines and the fig-trees, and you make all the mirth of a carnal heart to cease. But those who, when full, enjoyed God in all, when emptied and poor, can enjoy all in God. They can sit down upon the heap of the ruins of their creature-comforts, and even then praise the Lord, as the God of their salvation, the salvation of the soul, and rejoice in him as such, in their greatest distresses. Joy in the Lord is especially seasonable when we meet with losses and crosses in the world. Even when provisions are cut off, to make it appear that man lives not by bread alone, we may be supplied by the graces and comforts of God's Spirit. Then we shall be strong for spiritual warfare and work, and with enlargement of heart may run the way of his commandments, and outrun our troubles. And we shall be successful in spiritual undertakings. Thus the prophet, who began his prayer with fear and trembling, ends it with joy and triumph. And thus faith in Christ prepares for every event. The name of Jesus, when we can speak of Him as ours, is balm for every wound, a cordial for every care. It is as ointment poured forth, shedding fragrance through the whole soul. In the hope of a heavenly crown, let us sit loose to earthly possessions and comforts, and cheerfully bear up under crosses. Yet a little while, and He that shall come will come, and will not tarry; and where he is, we shall be also.

Zephaniah

Zephaniah excites to repentance, foretells the destruction of the enemies of the Jews, and comforts the pious among them with promises of future blessings, the restoration of their nation, and the prosperity of the church in the latter days.

Chapter 1

Chapter Outline

Threatenings against sinners.	(1–6)
More threatenings.	(7–13)
Distress from the approaching judgments.	(14–18)

Verses 1-6

Ruin is coming, utter ruin; destruction from the Almighty. The servants of God all proclaim, There is no peace for the wicked. The expressions are figurative, speaking every where desolation; the land shall be left without inhabitants. The sinners to be consumed are, the professed idolaters, and those that worship Jehovah and idols, or swear to the Lord, and to Malcham. Those that think to divide their affections and worship between God and idols, will come short of acceptance with God; for what communion can there be between light and darkness? If Satan have half, he will have all; if the Lord have but half, he will have none. Neglect of God shows impiety and contempt. May none of us be among those who draw back unto perdition, but of those who believe to the saving of the soul.

Verses 7-13

God's day is at hand; the punishment of presumptuous sinners is a sacrifice to the justice of God. The Jewish royal family shall be reckoned with for their pride and vanity; and those that leap on the threshold, invading their neighbours' rights, and seizing their possessions. The trading people and the rich merchants are called to account. Secure and careless people are reckoned with. They are secure and easy; they say in their heart, the Lord will not do good, neither will he do evil; that is, they deny his dispensing rewards and punishments. But in the day of the Lord's judgment, it will clearly appear that those who perish, fall a sacrifice to Divine justice for breaking God's law, and because they have no interest by faith in the Redeemer's atoning sacrifice.

Verses 14-18

This warning of approaching destruction, is enough to make the sinners in Zion tremble; it refers to the great day of the Lord, the day in which he will show himself by taking vengeance on them. This day of the Lord is very near; it is a day of God's wrath, wrath to the utmost. It will be a day of trouble and distress to sinners. Let them not be laid asleep by the patience of God. What is a man profited if he gain the whole world, and lose his own soul? And what shall a man give in exchange for his soul? Let us flee from the wrath to come, and choose the good part that shall never be taken from us; then we shall be prepared for every event; nothing shall separate us from the love of God in Christ Jesus our Lord.

Chapter 2

Chapter Outline

An exhortation to repentance.	(1–3)
Judgments upon other nations.	(4–15)

Verses 1-3

The prophet calls to national repentance, as the only way to prevent national ruin. A nation not desiring, that has not desires toward God, is not desirous of his favour and grace, has no mind to repent and reform. Or, not desirable, not having any thing to recommend them to God; to whom God might justly say, Depart from me; but he says, Gather together to me that you may seek my face. We know what God's decree will bring against impenitent sinners, therefore it highly concerns all to repent in the accepted time. How careful should we all be to seek peace with God, before the Holy Spirit withdraws from us, or ceases to strive with us; before the day of grace is over, or the day of life; before our everlasting state is determined! Let the poor, despised, and afflicted, seek the Lord, and seek to understand and keep his commandments better, that they may be more humbled for their sins. The chief hope of deliverance from national judgments rests upon prayer.

Verses 4-15

Those are really in a woful condition who have the word of the Lord against them, for no word of his shall fall to the ground. God will restore his people to their rights, though long kept from them. It has been the common lot of God's people, in all ages, to be reproached and reviled. God shall be worshipped, not only by all Israel, and the strangers who join them, but by the heathen. Remote nations must be reckoned with for the wrongs done to God's people. The sufferings of the insolent and haughty in prosperity, are unpitied and unlamented. But all the desolations of flourishing nations will make way for the overturning Satan's kingdom. Let us improve our advantages, and expect the performance of every promise, praying that our Father's name may be hallowed every where, over all the earth.

Chapter 3

Chapter Outline

Verses 1-7

The holy God hates sin most in those nearest to him. A sinful state is, and will be, a woful state. Yet they had the tokens of God's presence, and all the advantages of knowing his will, with the strongest reasons to do it; still they persisted in disobedience. Alas, that men often are more active in doing wickedness than believers are in doing good.

Verses 8-13

The preaching of the gospel is predicted, when vengeance would be executed on the Jewish nation. The purifying doctrines of the gospel, or the pure language of the grace of the Lord, would teach men to use the language of humility, repentance, and faith. Purity and piety in common conversation is good. The pure and happy state of the church in the latter days seems intended. The Lord will shut out boasting, and leave men nothing to glory in, save the Lord Jesus, as made of God to them wisdom, righteousness, sanctification, and redemption. Humiliation for sin, and obligations to the Redeemer, will make true believers upright and sincere, whatever may be the case among mere professors.

Verses 14-20

After the promises of taking away sin, follow promises of taking away trouble. When the cause is removed, the effect will cease. What makes a people holy, will make them happy. The precious promises made to the purified people, were to have full accomplishment in the gospel. These verses appear chiefly to relate to the future conversion and restoration of Israel, and the glorious times which are to follow. They show the abundant peace, comfort, and prosperity of the church, in the happy times yet to come. He will save; he will be Jesus; he will answer the name, for he will save his people from their sins. Before the glorious times foretold, believers would be sorrowful, and objects of reproach. But the Lord will save the weakest believer, and cause true Christians to be greatly honoured where they had been treated with contempt. One act of mercy and grace shall serve, both to gather Israel out of their dispersions and to lead them to their own land. Then will God's Israel be made a name and a praise to eternity. The events alone can fully answer the language of this prophecy. Many are the troubles of the righteous, but they may rejoice in God's love. Surely our hearts should honour the Lord, and rejoice in him, when we hear such words of condescension and grace. If now kept from his ordinances, it is our trial and grief; but in due time we shall be gathered into his temple above. The glory and happiness of the believer will be perfect, unchangeable, and eternal, when he is freed from earthly sorrows, and brought to heavenly bliss.

Haggai

After the return from captivity, Haggai was sent to encourage the people to rebuild the temple, and to reprove their neglect. To encourage their undertaking, the people are assured that the glory of the second temple shall far exceed that of the first, by the appearing therein of Christ, the Desire of all nations.

Chapter 1

Chapter Outline

Haggai reproves the Jews for neglecting the temple.   (1–11)

He promises God's assistance to them.   (12–15)

Verses 1-11

Observe the sin of the Jews, after their return from captivity in Babylon. Those employed for God may be driven from their work by a storm, yet they must go back to it. They did not say that they would not build a temple, but, Not yet. Thus men do not say they will never repent and reform, and be religious, but, Not yet. And so the great business we were sent into the world to do, is not done. There is a proneness in us to think wrongly of discouragements in our duty, as if they were a discharge from our duty, when they are only for the trial of our courage and faith. They neglected the building of God's house, that they might have more time and money for worldly affairs. That the punishment might answer to the sin, the poverty they thought to prevent by not building the temple, God brought upon them for not building it. Many good works have been intended, but not done, because men supposed the proper time was not come. Thus believers let slip opportunities of usefulness, and sinners delay the concerns of their souls, till too late. If we labour only for the meat that perishes, as the Jews here, we are in danger of losing our labour; but we are sure it shall not be in vain in the Lord, if we labour for the meat which lasts to eternal life. If we would have the comfort and continuance of temporal enjoyments, we must have God as our Friend. See also Lu 12:33. When God crosses our temporal affairs, and we meet with trouble and disappointment, we shall find the cause is, that the work we have to do for God and our own souls is left undone, and we seek our own things more than the things of Christ. How many, who plead that they cannot afford to give to pious or charitable designs, often lavish ten times as much in needless expenses on their houses and themselves! But those are strangers to their own interests, who are full of care to adorn and enrich their own houses, while God's temple in their hearts lies waste. It is the great concern of every one, to apply to the necessary duty of self-examination and communion with our own hearts concerning our spiritual state. Sin is what we must answer for; duty is what we must do. But many are quick-sighted to pry into other people's ways, who are careless of their own. If any duty has been neglected, that is no reason why it should still be so. Whatever God will take pleasure in when done, we ought to take pleasure in doing. Let those who have put off their return to God, return with all their heart, while there is time.

Verses 12-15

The people returned to God in the way of duty. In attending to God's ministers, we must have respect to him that sent them. The word of the Lord has success, when by his grace he stirs up our spirits to comply with it. It is in the day of Divine power we are made willing. When God has work to be done, he will either find or make men fit to do it. Every one helped, as his ability was; and this they did with a regard to the Lord as their God. Those who have lost time, need to redeem time; and the longer we have loitered in folly, the more haste we should make. God met them in a way of mercy. Those who work for him, have him with them; and if he be for us, who can be against us? This should stir us up to be diligent.

Chapter 2

Chapter Outline

Greater glory promised to the second temple than to the first.	(1–9)
Their sins hindered the work.	(10–19)
The kingdom of Christ foretold.	(20–23)

Verses 1-9

Those who are hearty in the Lord's service shall receive encouragement to proceed. But they could not build such a temple then, as Solomon built. Though our gracious God is pleased if we do as well as we can in his service, yet our proud hearts will scarcely let us be pleased, unless we do as well as others, whose abilities are far beyond ours. Encouragement is given the Jews to go on in the work notwithstanding. They have God with them, his Spirit and his special presence. Though he chastens their transgressions, his faithfulness does not fail. The Spirit still remained among them. And they shall have the Messiah among them shortly; "He that should come." Convulsions and changes would take place in the Jewish church and state, but first should come great revolutions and commotions among the nations. He shall come, as the Desire of all nations; desirable to all nations, for in him shall all the earth be blessed with the best of blessings; long expected and desired by all believers. The house they were building should be filled with glory, very far beyond Solomon's temple. This house shall be filled with glory of another nature. If we have silver and gold, we must serve and honour God with it, for the property is his. If we have not silver and gold, we must honour him with such as we have, and he will accept us. Let them be comforted that the glory of this latter house shall be greater than that of the former, in what would be beyond all the glories of the first house, the presence of the Messiah, the Son of God, the Lord of glory, personally, and in human nature. Nothing but the presence of the Son of God, in human form and nature, could fulfil this. Jesus is the Christ, is He that should come, and we are to look for no other. This prophecy alone is enough to silence the Jews, and condemn their obstinate rejection of Him, concerning whom all their prophets spake. If God be with us, peace is with us. But the Jews under the latter temple had much trouble; but this promise is fulfilled in that spiritual peace which Jesus Christ has by his blood purchased for all believers. All changes shall make way for Christ to be desired and valued by all nations. And the Jews shall have their eyes opened to behold how precious He is, whom they have hitherto rejected.

Verses 10-19

Many spoiled this good work, by going about it with unholy hearts and hands, and were likely to gain no advantage by it. The sum of these two rules of the law is, that sin is more easily learned from others than holiness. The impurity of their hearts and lives shall make the work of their hands, and all their offerings, unclean before God. The case is the same with us. When employed in any good work, we should watch over ourselves, lest we render it unclean by our corruptions. When we begin to make conscience of duty to God, we may expect his blessing; and whoso is wise will understand the loving-kindness of the Lord. God will curse the blessings of the wicked, and make bitter the prosperity of the careless; but he will sweeten the cup of affliction to those who diligently serve him.

Verses 20-23

The Lord will preserve Zerubbabel and the people of Judah, amidst their enemies. Here is also foretold the establishment and continuance of the kingdom of Christ; by union with whom his people are sealed with the Holy Ghost, sealed with his image, thus distinguished from all others. Here also is foretold the changes, even to that time when the kingdom of Christ shall overthrow and occupy the place of all the empires which opposed his cause. The promise has special reference to Christ, who descended from Zerubbabel in a direct line, and is the sole Builder of the gospel temple. Our Lord Jesus is the Signet on God's right hand, for all power is given to him, and derived from him. By him, and in him, all the promises of God are yea and amen. Whatever changes take place on earth, all will promote the comfort, honour, and happiness of his servants.

Zechariah

This prophecy is suitable to all, as the scope is to reprove for sin, and threaten God's judgments against the impenitent, and to encourage those that feared God, with assurances of the mercy God had in store for his church, and especially of the coming of the Messiah, and the setting up his kingdom in the world.

Chapter 1

Chapter Outline

An exhortation to repentance.	(1–6)
A vision of the ministry of angels.	(7–17)
The security of the Jews and the destruction of their enemies.	(18–21)

Verses 1-6

God's almighty power and sovereign dominion, should engage and encourage sinners to repent and turn to Him. It is very desirable to have the Lord of hosts for our friend, and very dreadful to have him for our enemy. Review what is past, and observe the message God sent by his servants, the prophets, to your fathers. Turn ye now from your evil ways, and from your evil doings. Be persuaded to leave your sins, as the only way to prevent approaching ruin. What is become of our fathers, and of the prophets that preached to them? They are all dead and gone. Here they were, in the towns and countries where we live, passing and repassing in the same streets, dwelling in the same houses, trading in the same shops and exchanges, worshipping God in the same places. But where are they? When they died, there was not an end of them; they are in eternity, in the world of spirits, the unchangeable world to which we hasten apace. Where are they? Those of them who lived and died in sin, are in torment. Those who lived and died in Christ, are in heaven; and if we live and die as they did, we shall be with them shortly and eternally. If they minded not their own souls, is that a reason why their posterity should ruin theirs also? The prophets are gone. Christ is a Prophet that lives for ever, but all other prophets have a period put to their office. Oh that this consideration had its due weight; that dying ministers are dealing with dying people about their never-dying souls, and an awful eternity, upon the brink of which both are standing! In another world, both we and our prophets shall live for ever: to prepare for that world ought to be our great care in this. The preachers died, and the hearers died, but the word of God died not; not one jot or title of it fell to the ground; for he is righteous.

Verses 7-17

The prophet saw a dark, shady grove, hidden by hills. This represented the low, melancholy condition of the Jewish church. A man like a warrior sat on a red horse, in the midst of this shady myrtle-grove. Though the church was in a low condition, Christ was present in the midst, ready to appear for the relief of his people. Behind him were angels ready to be employed by him, some in acts of judgment, others of mercy, others in mixed events. Would we know something of the mysteries of the kingdom of heaven, we must apply, not to angels, for they are themselves learners, but to Christ himself. He is ready to teach those humbly desirous to learn the things of God. The nations near Judea enjoyed peace at that time, but the state of the Jews was unsettled, which gave rise to the pleading that followed; but mercy must only be hoped for through Christ. His intercession for his church prevails. The Lord answered the Angel, this Angel of the covenant, with promises of mercy and deliverance. All the good words and comfortable words of the gospel we receive from Jesus Christ, as he received them from the Father, in answer to the prayer of his blood; and his ministers are to preach them to all the world. The earth sat still, and was at rest. It is not uncommon for the enemies of God to be at rest in sin, while his people are enduring correction, harassed by temptation, disquieted by fears of wrath, or groaning under oppression and persecution. Here are predictions which had reference to the revival of the Jews after the captivity, but those events were shadows of what shall take place in the church, after the oppression of the New Testament Babylon is ended.

Verses 18-21

The enemies of the church threaten to cut off the name of Israel. They are horns, emblems of power, strength, and violence. The prophet saw them so formidable that he began to despair of the safety of every good man, and the success of every good work; but the Lord showed him four workmen empowered to cut off these horns. With an eye of sense we see the power of the enemies of the church; look which way we will, the world shows us that; but it is only with an eye of faith that we see it safe. The Lord shows us that. When God has work to do, he will raise up some to do it, and others to defend it, and to protect those employed in doing it. What cause there is to look up in love and praise to the holy and eternal Spirit, who has the same care over the present and eternal interests of believers, by the holy word bringing the church to know the wonderful things of salvation!

Chapter 2

Chapter Outline

The prosperity of Jerusalem.	(1–5)
The Jews called to return to their own land.	(6–9)
A promise of God's presence.	(10–13)

Verses 1-5

The Son of David, even the Man Christ Jesus, whom the prophet sees with a measuring line in his hand, is the Master-Builder of his church. God notices the extent of his church, and will take care that whatever number of guests are brought to the wedding-supper, there shall be room. This vision means well to Jerusalem. The walls of a city, as they defend it, so they straiten its inhabitants; but Jerusalem shall be extended as freely as if it had no walls at all, yet shall be as safe as if it had the strongest walls. In the church of God there yet is room for other multitudes, more than man can number. None shall be refused who trust in Christ; and He never shuts out from heaven one true member of the church on earth. God will be a Wall of fire round them, which can neither be broken through nor undermined, nor can it be assailed without danger to those who attack. This vision was to have its full accomplishment in the gospel church, which is extended by admitting the Gentiles into it; and which has the Son of God for its Prince and Protector; especially in the glorious times yet to come.

Verses 6-9

If God will build Jerusalem for the people and their comfort, they must inhabit it for him and his glory. The promises and privileges with which God's people are blessed, should engage us to join them, whatever it costs us. When Zion is enlarged to make room for all God's Israel, it is the greatest madness for any of them to stay in Babylon. The captivity of a sinful state is by no means to be continued in, though a man may be easy in worldly matters. Escape for thy life, look not behind thee. Christ has proclaimed that deliverance to the captives, which he has himself wrought out, and it concerns every one to resolve that sin shall not have dominion over him. Those who would be found among God's children, must save themselves from this world, see Ac 2:40. What Christ will do for his church, shall be an evident proof of God's care and affection. He that touches you, touches the apple of his eye. This is a strong expression of God's love to his church. He takes what is done against her as done against the tenderest part of the eye, to which the least touch is a great offence. Christ is sent to be the Protector of his church.

Verses 10-13

Here is a prediction of the coming of Christ in human nature. Many nations in that day would renounce idolatry, and God will own those for his people who join him with purpose of heart. Glorious times are foretold as a prophecy of our Lord's coming and kingdom. God is about to do something unexpected, and very surprising, and to plead his people's cause, which had long seemed neglected. Silently submit to his holy will, and patiently wait the event; assured that God will complete all his work. He will ere long come to judgment, to complete the salvation of his people, and to punish the inhabitants of the earth for their sins.

Chapter 3

Chapter Outline

Verses 1-5

The angel showed Joshua, the high priest, to Zechariah, in a vision. Guilt and corruption are great discouragements when we stand before God. By the guilt of the sins committed by us, we are liable to the justice of God; by the power of sin that dwells in us, we are hateful to the holiness of God. Even God's Israel are in danger on these accounts; but they have relief from Jesus Christ, who is made of God to us both righteousness and sanctification. Joshua, the high priest, is accused as a criminal, but is justified. When we stand before God, to minister to him, or stand up for God, we must expect to meet all the resistance Satan's subtlety and malice can give. Satan is checked by one that has conquered him, and many times silenced him. Those who belong to Christ, will find him ready to appear for them, when Satan appears most strongly against them. A converted soul is a brand plucked out of the fire by a miracle of free grace, therefore shall not be left a prey to Satan. Joshua appears as one polluted, but is purified; he represents the Israel of God, who are all as an unclean thing, till they are washed and sanctified in the name of the Lord Jesus, and by the Spirit of our God. Israel now were free from idolatry, but there were many things amiss in them. There were spiritual enemies warring against them, more dangerous than any neighbouring nations. Christ loathed the filthiness of Joshua's garments, yet did not put him away. Thus God by his grace does with those whom he chooses to be priests to himself. The guilt of sin is taken away by pardoning mercy, and the power of it is broken by renewing grace. Thus Christ washes those from their sins in his own blood, whom he makes kings and priests to our God. Those whom Christ makes spiritual priests, are clothed with the spotless robe of his righteousness, and appear before God in that; and with the graces of his Spirit, which are ornaments to them. The righteousness of saints, both imputed and implanted, is the fine linen, clean and white, with which the bride, the Lamb's wife, is arrayed, Re 19:8. Joshua is restored to former honours and trusts. The crown of the priesthood is put on him. When the Lord designs to restore and revive religion, he stirs up prophets and people to pray for it.

Verses 6-10

All whom God calls to any office he finds fit, or makes so. The Lord will cause the sins of the believer to pass away by his sanctifying grace, and will enable him to walk in newness of life. As the promises made to David often pass into promises of the Messiah, so the promises to Joshua look forward to Christ, of whose priesthood Joshua's was a shadow. Whatever trials we pass through, whatever services we perform, our whole dependence must rest on Christ, the Branch of righteousness. He is God's servant, employed in his work, obedient to his will, devoted to his honour and glory. He is the Branch from which all our fruit must be gathered. The eye of his Father was upon him, especially in his sufferings, and when he was buried in the grave, as the foundation-stones are under ground, out of men's sight. But the prophecy rather denotes the attention paid to this precious Corner-stone. All believers, from the beginning, had looked forward to it in the types and predictions. All believers, after Christ's coming, would look to it with faith, hope, and love. Christ shall appear for all his chosen, as the high priest when before the Lord, with the names of all Israel graven in the precious stones of his breastplate. When God gave a remnant to Christ, to be brought through grace to glory, then he engraved this precious stone. By him sin shall be taken away, both the guilt and the dominion of it; he did it in one day, that day in which he suffered and died. What should terrify when sin is taken away? Then nothing can hurt, and we sit down under Christ's shadow with delight, and are sheltered by it. And gospel grace, coming with power, makes men forward to draw others to it.

Chapter 4

Chapter Outline

A vision of a candlestick, with two olive trees.	(1–7)
Further encouragement.	(8–10)
An explanation respecting the olive trees.	(11–14)

Verses 1-7

The prophet's spirit was willing to attend, but the flesh was weak. We should beg of God that, whenever he speaks to us, he would awaken us, and we should then stir up ourselves. The church is a golden candlestick, or lamp-bearer, set up for enlightening this dark world, and holding forth the light of Divine revelation. Two olive trees were seen, one on each side the candlestick, from which oil flowed into the bowl without ceasing. God brings to pass his gracious purposes concerning his church, without any art or labour of man; sometimes he makes use of his instruments, yet he needs them not. This represented the abundance of Divine grace, for the enlightening and making holy the ministers and members of the church, and which cannot be procured or prevented by any human power. The vision assures us that the good work of building the temple, should be brought to a happy end. The difficulty is represented as a great mountain. But all difficulties shall vanish, and all the objections be got over. Faith will remove mountains, and make them plains. Christ is our Zerubbabel; mountains of difficulty were in the way of his undertaking, but nothing is too hard for him. What comes from the grace of God, may, in faith, be committed to the grace of God, for he will not forsake the work of his own hands.

Verses 8-10

The exact fulfilment of Scripture prophecies is a convincing proof of their Divine original. Though the instruments be weak and unlikely, yet God often chooses such, to bring about great things by them. Let not the dawning light be despised; it will shine more and more to the perfect day. Those who despaired of finishing the work, shall rejoice when they see Zerubbabel giving directions what to do, and taking care that the work be done. It is a comfort to us that the same all-wise, almighty Providence, which governs the earth, is in particular conversant about the church. All that have the plummet in their hands, must look up to the eyes of the Lord, have constant regard to Divine Providence, act in dependence on its guidance and submission to its disposals. Let us fix our faith on Christ, and view Him carrying on his work according to his own glorious plan, and daily bringing his spiritual building nearer to completion. (Zec 4:11-14)

Verses 11-14

Zechariah desires to know what are the two olive trees. Zerubbabel and Joshua, this prince and this priest, were endued with the gifts and graces of God's Spirit. They lived at the same time, and both were instruments in the work and service of God. Christ's offices of King and Priest were shadowed forth by them. From the union of these two offices in his person, both God and man, the fullness of grace is received and imparted. They built the temple, the church of God. So does Christ spiritually. Christ is not only the Messiah, the Anointed One himself, but he is the Good Olive to his church; and from his fulness we receive. And the Holy Spirit is the unction or anointing which we have received. From Christ the Olive Tree, by the Spirit the Olive Branch, all the golden oil of grace flows to believers, which keeps their lamps burning. Let us seek, through the intercession and bounty of the Saviour, supplies from that fulness which has hitherto sufficed for all his saints, according to their trials and employments. Let us wait on him in his ordinances, desiring to be sanctified wholly in body, soul, and spirit.

Chapter 5

Chapter Outline

Verses 1-4

The Scriptures of the Old and New Testament are rolls, in which God has written the great things of his law and gospel; they are flying rolls. God's word runs very swiftly, Ps 147:15. This flying roll contains a declaration of the righteous wrath of God against sinners. Oh that we saw with an eye of faith the flying roll of God's curse hanging over the guilty world as a thick cloud, not only keeping off the sunbeams of God's favour, but big with thunders, lightnings, and storms, ready to destroy them! How welcome then would the tidings of a Saviour be, who came to redeem us from the curse of the law, being himself made a curse for us! Sin is the ruin of houses and families; especially the doing hurt to others and false witness. Who knows the power of God's anger? God's curse cannot be kept out by bars or locks. While one part of the curse of God ruins the substance of the sinner, another part will rest on the soul, and sink it to everlasting punishment. All are transgressors of the law, so we cannot escape this wrath of God, except we flee for refuge to lay hold on the hope set before us in the gospel.

Verses 5-11

In this vision the prophet sees an ephah, something in the shape of a corn measure. This betokened the Jewish nation. They are filling the measure of their iniquity; and when it is full, they shall be delivered into the hands of those to whom God sold them for their sins. The woman sitting in the midst of the ephah represents the sinful church and nation of the Jews, in their latter and corrupt age. Guilt is upon the sinner as a weight of lead, to sink him to the lowest hell. This seems to mean the condemnation of the Jews, after they filled the measure of their iniquities by crucifying Christ and rejecting his gospel. Zechariah sees the ephah, with the woman thus pressed in it, carried away to some far country. This intimates that the Jews should be hurried out of their own land, and forced to dwell in far countries, as they had been in Babylon. There the ephah shall be firmly placed, and their sufferings shall continue far longer than in their late captivity. Blindness is happened unto Israel, and they are settled upon their own unbelief. Let sinners fear to treasure up wrath against the day of wrath; for the more they multiply crimes, the faster the measure fills.

Chapter 6

Chapter Outline

The vision of the chariots. (1–8)

Joshua, the high priest, crowned as a type of Christ. (9–15)

Verses 1-8

This vision may represent the ways of Providence in the government of this lower world. Whatever the providences of God about us are, as to public or private affairs, we should see them all as coming from between the mountains of brass, the immoveable counsels and decrees of God; and therefore reckon it as much our folly to quarrel with them, as it is our duty to submit to them. His providences move swiftly and strongly as chariots, but all are directed and governed by his infinite wisdom and sovereign will. The red horses signify war and bloodshed. The black, signify the dismal consequences of war, famines, pestilences, and desolations. The white, signify the return of comfort, peace, and prosperity. The mixed colour, signify events of different complexions, a day of prosperity and a day of adversity. The angels go forth as messengers of God's counsels, and ministers of his justice and mercy. And the secret motions and impulses upon the spirits of men, by which the designs of Providence are carried on, are these four spirits of the heavens, which go forth from God, and fulfil what the God of the spirits of all flesh appoints. All the events which take place in the world spring from the unchangeable counsels of the Lord, which are formed in unerring wisdom, perfect justice, truth, and goodness; and from history it is found that events happened about the period when this vision was sent to the prophet, which seem referred to therein.

Verses 9-15

Some Jews from Babylon brought an offering to the house of God. Those who cannot forward a good work by their persons, must, as they are able, forward it by their purses: if some find hands, let others fill them. Crowns are to be made, and put upon the head of Joshua. The sign was used, to make the promise more noticed, that God will, in the fulness of time, raise up a great High Priest, like Joshua, who is but the figure of one that is to come. Christ is not only the Foundation, but the Founder of this temple, by his Spirit and grace. Glory is a burden, but not too heavy for Him to bear who upholds all things. The cross was His glory, and he bore that; so is the crown an exceeding weight of glory, and he bears that. The counsel of peace should be between the priest and the throne, between the priestly and kingly offices of Jesus Christ. The peace and welfare of the gospel church, and of all believers, shall be wrought, though not by two several persons, yet by two several offices meeting in one; Christ, purchasing all peace by his priesthood, maintaining and defending it by his kingdom. The crowns used in this solemnity must be kept in the temple, as evidence of this promise of the Messiah. Let us not think of separating what God has joined in his counsel of peace. We cannot come to God by Christ as our Priest, if we refuse to have him rule over us as our King. We have no real ground to think our peace is made with God, unless we try to keep his commandments.

Chapter 7

Chapter Outline

Verses 1-7

If we truly desire to know the will of God in doubtful matters, we must not only consult his word and ministers, but seek his direction by fervent prayer. Those who would know God's mind should consult God's ministers; and, in doubtful cases, ask advice of those whose special business it is to search the Scriptures. The Jews seemed to question whether they ought to continue their fasts, seeing that the city and temple were likely to be finished. The first answer to their inquiry is a sharp reproof of hypocrisy. These fasts were not acceptable to God, unless observed in a better manner, and to better purpose. There was the form of duty, but no life, or soul, or power in it. Holy exercises are to be done to God, looking to his word as our rule, and his glory as our end, seeking to please him and obtain his favour; but self was the centre of all their actions. And it was not enough to weep on fast days; they should have searched the Scriptures of the prophets, that they might have seen what was the ground of God's controversy with their fathers. Whether people are in prosperity or adversity, they must be called upon to leave their sins, and to do their duty.

Verses 8-14

God's judgements upon Israel of old for their sins, were written to warn Christians. The duties required are, not keeping fasts and offering sacrifices, but doing justly and loving mercy, which tend to the public welfare and peace. The law of God lays restraint upon the heart. But they filled their minds with prejudices against the word of God. Nothing is harder than the heart of a presumptuous sinner. See the fatal consequences of this to their fathers. Great sins against the Lord of hosts, bring great wrath from his power, which cannot be resisted. Sin, if regarded in the heart, will certainly spoil the success of prayer. The Lord always hears the cry of the broken-hearted penitent; yet all who die impenitent and unbelieving, will find no remedy or refuge from miseries which while here they despised and defied, but which they then will not be able to bear.

Chapter 8

Chapter Outline

Verses 1-8

The sins of Zion were her worst enemies. God will take away her sins, and then no other enemies shall hurt her. Those who profess religion must adorn their profession by godliness and honesty. When become a city of truth and a mountain of holiness, Jerusalem is peaceable and prosperous. Verses #(4, 5), beautifully describe a state of great outward peace, attended with plenty, temperance, and contentment. The scattered Israelites shall be brought together from all parts. God will never leave nor forsake them in a way of mercy, for this he has promised them; and they shall never leave nor forsake him in a way of duty, as they have promised him. These promises were partly fulfilled in the Jewish church, betwixt the captivity and the time of Christ's coming; and they had fuller accomplishment in the gospel church; but the full import must be as to the future times of the Christian church, or the future restoration of the Jews. With men this is impossible, but with God all things are possible; so far are God's thoughts and ways above ours. In the present low state of vital godliness, we can hardly conceive that so complete a change can be made; but a change thus extensive and glorious, can be brought to pass by the almighty power of the new-creating Spirit, in less time than he was pleased to employ in creating the world. Let the hands of all who labour in the cause of the gospel be strong, serving the Lord in true holiness, assured that their labour shall not be in vain.

Verses 9-17

Those only who lay their hands to the plough of duty, shall have them strengthened with the promises of mercy: those who avoid their fathers' faults have the curse turned into a blessing. Those who believed the promises, were to show their faith by their works, and to wait the fulfilment. When God is displeased, he can cause trade to decay, and set every man against his neighbour; but when he returns in mercy, all is happy and prosperous. Surely believers in Christ must not trifle with the exhortation to put away lying, and to speak every man peace with his neighbour, to hate what the Lord hates, and to love that wherein he delights.

Verses 18-23

When God comes towards us in ways of mercy, we must meet him with joy and thankfulness. Therefore be faithful and honest in all your dealings; and let it be a pleasure to you to be so, though thereby you come short of the gains others get dishonestly; and, as much as in you lies, live peaceably with all men. Let the truths of God rule in your heads, and let the peace of God rule in your hearts. Thus the ancient servants of God drew the notice of heathen neighbours, whose prejudices were softened. A great increase to the church shall be made. Hitherto the Jews had been prone to learn the idolatries of other nations: what more unlikely than that they should teach religion to their conquerors, and to all the principal nations of the earth! Yet this is expressly foretold, and it came to pass. Hitherto the prophecy has been wonderfully fulfilled, and no doubt future events will explain it further. It is good to be with those who have God with them; if we take God for our God, we must take his people for our people, and be willing to take our lot with them. But let not any one think that mere zeal, either for Jews or Gentiles, will stand in the place of personal religion. Let us be living epistles of Christ, known and read of all men, so that others may wish to go with us, and to have their portion with us in the realms of bliss.

Chapter 9

Chapter Outline

God's defence of his church.	(1–8)
Christ's coming and his kingdom.	(9–11)
Promises to the church.	(12–17)

Verses 1-8

Here are judgements foretold on several nations. While the Macedonians and Alexander's successors were in warfare in these countries, the Lord promised to protect his people. God's house lies in the midst of an enemy's country; his church is as a lily among thorns. God's power and goodness are seen in her special preservation. The Lord encamps about his church, and while armies of proud opposers shall pass by and return, his eyes watch over her, so that they cannot prevail, and shortly the time will come when no exactor shall pass by her any more.

Verses 9-17

The prophet breaks forth into a joyful representation of the coming of the Messiah, of whom the ancient Jews explained this prophecy. He took the character of their King, when he entered

Jerusalem amidst the hosannas of the multitude. But his kingdom is a spiritual kingdom. It shall not be advanced by outward force or carnal weapons. His gospel shall be preached to the world, and be received among the heathen. A sinful state is a state of bondage; it is a pit, or dungeon, in which there is no water, no comfort; and we are all by nature prisoners in this pit. Through the precious blood of Christ, many prisoners of Satan have been set at liberty from the horrible pit in which they must otherwise have perished, without hope or comfort. While we admire Him, let us seek that his holiness and truth may be shown in our own spirits and conduct. These promises have accomplishment in the spiritual blessings of the gospel which we enjoy by Jesus Christ. As the deliverance of the Jews was typical of redemption by Christ, so this invitation speaks to all the language of the gospel call. Sinners are prisoners, but prisoners of hope; their case is sad, but not desperate; for there is hope in Israel concerning them. Christ is a Strong-hold, a strong Tower, in whom believers are safe from the fear of the wrath of God, the curse of the law, and the assaults of spiritual enemies. To him we must turn with lively faith; to him we must flee, and trust in his name under all trials and sufferings. It is here promised that the Lord would deliver his people. This passage also refers to the apostles, and the preachers of the gospel in the early ages. God was evidently with them; his words from their lips pierced the hearts and consciences of the hearers. They were wondrously defended in persecution, and were filled with the influences of the Holy Spirit. They were saved by the Good Shepherd as his flock, and honoured as jewels of his crown. The gifts, graces, and consolations of the Spirit, poured forth on the day of Pentecost, Ac 2 and in succeeding times, are represented. Sharp have been, and still will be, the conflicts of Zion's sons, but their God will give them success. The more we are employed, and satisfied with his goodness, the more we shall admire the beauty revealed in the Redeemer. Whatever gifts God bestows on us, we must serve him cheerfully with them; and, when refreshed with blessings, we must say, How great is his goodness!

Chapter 10

Chapter Outline

Verses 1-5

Spiritual blessings had been promised under figurative allusions to earthly plenty. Seasonable rain is a great mercy, which we may ask of God when there is most need of it, and we may look for it to come. We must in our prayers ask for mercies in their proper time. The Lord would make bright clouds, and give showers of rain. This may be an exhortation to seek the influences of the Holy Spirit, in faith and by prayer, through which the blessings held forth in the promises are obtained and enjoyed. The prophet shows the folly of making addresses to idols, as their fathers had done. The Lord visited the remnant of his flock in mercy, and was about to renew their courage and strength for conflict and victory. Every creature is to us what God makes it to be. Every one raised to support the nation, as a corner-stone does the building, or to unite those that differ, as nails join the different timbers, must come from the Lord; and those employed to overcome their enemies, must have strength and success from him. This may be applied to Christ; to him we must look to raise up persons to unite, support, and defend his people. He never will say, Seek ye me in vain.

Verses 6-12

Here are precious promises to the people of God, which look to the state of the Jews, and even to the latter days of the church. Preaching the gospel is God's call for souls to come to Jesus Christ. Those whom Christ redeemed by his blood, God will gather by his grace. Difficulties shall be got over easily, and effectually, as those in the way of the deliverance out of Egypt. God himself will be their strength, and their song. When we resist, and so overcome our spiritual enemies, then our hearts shall rejoice. If God strengthen us, we must bestir ourselves in all the duties of the Christian life, must be active in the work of God; and we must do all in the name of the Lord Jesus.

Chapter 11

Chapter Outline

Verses 1-3

In figurative expressions, that destruction of Jerusalem, and of the Jewish church and nation, is foretold, which our Lord Jesus, when the time was at hand, prophesied plainly and expressly. How can the fir trees stand, if the cedars fall? The falls of the wise and good into sin, and the falls of the rich and great into trouble, are loud alarms to those every way their inferiors. It is sad with a people, when those who should be as shepherds to them, are as young lions. The pride of Jordan was the thickets on the banks; and when the river overflowed the banks, the lions came up from them roaring. Thus the doom of Jerusalem may alarm other churches.

Verses 4-14

Christ came into this world for judgment to the Jewish church and nation, which were wretchedly corrupt and degenerate. Those have their minds wofully blinded, who do ill, and justify themselves in it; but God will not hold those guiltless who hold themselves so. How can we go to God to beg a blessing on unlawful methods of getting wealth, or to return thanks for success in them? There was a general decay of religion among them, and they regarded it not. The Good Shepherd would feed his flock, but his attention would chiefly be directed to the poor. As an emblem, the prophet seems to have taken two staves; Beauty, denoted the privileges of the Jewish nation, in their national covenant; the other he called Bands, denoting the harmony which hitherto united them as the flock of God. But they chose to cleave to false teachers. The carnal mind and the friendship of the world are enmity to God; and God hates all the workers of iniquity: it is easy to foresee what this will end in. The prophet demanded wages, or a reward, and received thirty pieces of silver. By Divine direction he cast it to the potter, as in disdain for the smallness of the sum. This shadowed forth the bargain of Judas to betray Christ, and the final method of applying it. Nothing ruins a people so certainly, as weakening the brotherhood among them. This follows the dissolving of the covenant between God and them: when sin abounds, love waxes cold, and civil contests follow. No wonder if those fall out among themselves, who have provoked God to fall out with them. Wilful contempt of Christ is the great cause of men's ruin. And if professors rightly valued Christ, they would not contend about little matters.

Verses 15-17

God, having showed the misery of this people in their being justly left by the Good Shepherd, shows their further misery in being abused by foolish shepherds. The description suits the character Christ gives of the scribes and Pharisees. They never do any thing to support the weak, or comfort the feeble-minded; but seek their own ease, while they are barbarous to the flock. The idol shepherd has the garb and appearance of a shepherd, receives submission, and is supported at much expense; but he leaves the flock to perish through neglect, or leads them to ruin by his example. This suits many in different churches and nations, but the warning had an awful fulfilment in the Jewish teachers. And while such deceive others to their ruin, they will themselves have the deepest condemnation.

Chapter 12

Chapter Outline

Punishment of the enemies of Judah.   (1–8)

Repentance and sorrow of the Jews.   (9–14)

Verses 1-8

Here is a Divine prediction, which will be a heavy burden to all the enemies of the church. But it is for Israel; for their comfort and benefit. It is promised that God will make foolish the counsels, and weaken the courage of the enemies of the church. The exact meaning is not clear; but God often begins by calling the poor and despised; and in that day even the feeblest will resemble David, and be as eminent in courage and every thing good. Desirable indeed is it that the examples and labours of Christians should render them as fire among wood, as a torch in a sheaf, to kindle the flame of Divine love, to spread religion on the right hand and on the left.

Verses 9-14

The day here spoken of, is the day of Jerusalem's defence and deliverance, that glorious day when God will appear for the salvation of his people. In Christ's first coming he bruised the serpent's head, and broke all the powers of darkness that fought against God's kingdom among men. In his second coming he will complete their destruction, when he shall put down all opposing rule, principality, and power; and death itself shall be swallowed up in that victory. The Holy Spirit is gracious and merciful, and is the Author of all grace or holiness. He, also, is the Spirit of supplications, and shows men their ignorance, want, guilt, misery, and danger. At the time here foretold, the Jews will know who the crucified Jesus was; then they shall look by faith to him, and mourn with the deepest sorrow, not only in public, but in private, even each one separately. There is a holy mourning, the effect of the pouring out of the Spirit; a mourning for sin, which quickens faith in Christ, and qualifies for joy in God. This mourning is a fruit of the Spirit of grace, a proof of a work of grace in the soul, and of the Spirit of supplications. It is fulfilled in all who sorrow for sin after a godly sort; they look to Christ crucified, and mourn for him. Looking by faith upon the cross of Christ will cause us to mourn for sin after a godly sort.

Chapter 13

Chapter Outline

Verses 1-6

In the time mentioned at the close of the foregoing chapter, a fountain would be opened to the rulers and people of the Jews, in which to wash away their sins. Even the atoning blood of Christ, united with his sanctifying grace. It has hitherto been closed to the unbelieving nation of Israel; but when the Spirit of grace shall humble and soften their hearts, he will open it to them also. This fountain opened is the pierced side of Christ. We are all as an unclean thing. Behold a fountain opened for us to wash in, and streams flowing to us from that fountain. The blood of Christ, and God's pardoning mercy in that blood, made known in the new covenant, are a fountain always flowing, that never can be emptied. It is opened for all believers, who as the spiritual seed of Christ, are of the house of David, and, as living members of the church, are inhabitants of Jerusalem. Christ, by the power of his grace, takes away the dominion of sin, even of beloved sins. Those who are washed in the fountain opened, as they are justified, so they are sanctified. Souls are brought off from the world and the flesh, those two great idols, that they may cleave to God only. The thorough reformation which will take place on the conversion of Israel to Christ, is here foretold. False prophets shall be convinced of their sin and folly, and return to their proper employments. When convinced that we are gone out of the way of duty, we must show the truth of our repentance by returning to it again. It is well to acknowledge those to be friends, who by severe discipline are instrumental in bringing us to a sight of error; for faithful are the wounds of a friend, Pr 27:6. And it is always well for us to recollect the wounds of our Saviour. Often has he been wounded by professed friends, nay, even by his real disciples, when they act contrary to his word.

Verses 7-9

Here is a prophecy of the sufferings of Christ. God the Father gave order to the sword of his justice to awake against his Son, when he freely made his soul an offering for sin. As God, he is called "my Fellow." Christ and the Father are one. He is the Shepherd who was to lay down his life for the sheep. If a Sacrifice, he must be slain, for without shedding of the life-blood there was no remission. This sword must awake against him, yet he had no sin of his own to answer for. It may refer to the whole of Christ's sufferings, especially his agonies in the garden and on the cross, when he endured unspeakable anguish till Divine justice was fully satisfied. Smite the Shepherd, and the sheep shall be scattered. This passage our Lord Jesus declares was fulfilled, when all his disciples, in the night wherein he was betrayed, forsook him and fled. It has, and shall have its accomplishment, in the destruction of the corrupt and hypocritical part of the professed church. Because of the sin of the Jews in rejecting and crucifying Christ, and in opposing his gospel, the Romans would destroy the greater part. But a remnant would be saved. And if we are his people, we shall be refined as gold; he will be God, and the end of all our trials and sufferings will be praise, and honour, and glory, at the appearing of our Lord Jesus Christ.

Chapter 14

Chapter Outline

Verses 1-7

The Lord Jesus often stood upon the Mount of Olives when on earth. He ascended from thence to heaven, and then desolations and distresses came upon the Jewish nation. Such is the view taken of this figuratively; but many consider it as a notice of events yet unfulfilled, and that it relates to troubles of which we cannot now form a full idea. Every believer, being related to God as his God, may triumph in the expectation of Christ's coming in power, and speak of it with pleasure. During a long season, the state of the church would be deformed by sin; there would be a mixture of truth and error, of happiness and misery. Such is the experience of God's people, a mingled state of grace and corruption. But, when the season is at the worst, and most unpromising, the Lord will turn darkness into light; deliverance comes when God's people have done looking for it.

Verses 8-15

Some consider that the progress of the gospel, beginning from Jerusalem, is referred to by the living waters flowing from that city. Neither shall the gospel and means of grace, nor the graces of the Spirit wrought in the hearts of believers by those means, ever fail, by reason either of the heat of persecution, or storms of temptation, or the blasts of any other affliction. Tremendous judgments appear to be foretold, to be sent upon those who should oppose the settlement of the Jews in their own land. How far they are to be understood literally, events alone can determine. The furious rage and malice which stir up men against each other, are faint shadows of the enmity which reigns among those who have perished in their sins. Even the inferior creatures often suffer for the sin of man, and in his plagues. Thus God will show his displeasure against sin.

Verses 16-21

As it is impossible for all nations literally to come to Jerusalem once a year, to keep a feast, it is evident that a figurative meaning must here be applied. Gospel worship is represented by the keeping of the feast of tabernacles. Every day of a Christian's life is a day of the feast of tabernacles; every Lord's day especially is the great day of the feast; therefore every day let us worship the Lord of hosts, and keep every Lord's day with peculiar solemnity. It is just for God to withhold the blessings of grace from those who do not attend the means of grace. It is a sin that is its own punishment; those who forsake the duty, forfeit the privilege of communion with God. A time of complete peace and purity of the church will arrive. Men will carry on their common affairs, and their sacred services, upon the same holy principles of faith, love and obedience. Real holiness shall be more diffused, because there shall be a more plentiful pouring forth of the Spirit of holiness than ever before. There shall be holiness even in common things. Every action and every enjoyment of the believer, should be so regulated according to the will of God, that it may be directed to his glory. Our whole lives should be as one constant sacrifice, or act of devotion; no selfish motive should prevail in any of our actions. But how far is the Christian church from this state of purity! Other times, however, are at hand, and the Lord will reform and enlarge his church, as he has promised. Yet in heaven alone will perfect holiness and happiness be found.

Malachi

Malachi was the last of the prophets, and is supposed to have prophesied B.C. 420. He reproves the priests and the people for the evil practices into which they had fallen, and invites them to repentance and reformation, with promises of the blessings to be bestowed at the coming of the Messiah. And now that prophecy was to cease, he speaks clearly of the Messiah, as nigh at hand, and directs the people of God to keep in remembrance the law of Moses, while they were in expectation of the gospel of Christ.

Chapter 1

Chapter Outline

The ingratitude of Israel.   (1–5)

They are careless in God's institutions.   (6–14)

Verses 1-5

All advantages, either as to outward circumstances, or spiritual privileges, come from the free love of God, who makes one to differ from another. All the evils sinners feel and fear, are the just recompence of their crimes, while all their hopes and comforts are from the unmerited mercy of the Lord. He chose his people that they might be holy. If we love him, it is because he has first loved us; yet we all are prone to undervalue the mercies of God, and to excuse our own offences.

Verses 6-14

We may each charge upon ourselves what is here charged upon the priests. Our relation to God, as our Father and Master, strongly obliges us to fear and honour him. But they were so scornful that they derided reproof. Sinners ruin themselves by trying to baffle their convictions. Those who live in careless neglect of holy ordinances, who attend on them without reverence, and go from them under no concern, in effect say, The table of the Lord is contemptible. They despised God's name in what they did. It is evident that these understood not the meaning of the sacrifices, as shadowing forth the unblemished Lamb of God; they grudged the expense, thinking all thrown away which did not turn to their profit. If we worship God ignorantly, and without understanding, we bring the blind for sacrifice; if we do it carelessly, if we are cold, dull, and dead in it, we bring the sick; if we rest in the bodily exercise, and do not make heart-work of it, we bring the lame; and if we suffer vain thoughts and distractions to lodge within us, we bring the torn. And is not this evil? Is it not a great affront to God, and a great wrong and injury to our own souls? In order to the acceptance of our actions with God, it is not enough to do that which, for the matter of it, is good; but we must do it from a right principle, in a right manner, and for a right end. Our constant mercies from God, make worse our slothfulness and niggardliness, in our returns of duty to God. A spiritual worship shall be established. Incense shall be offered to God's name, which signifies prayer and praise. And it shall be a pure offering. When the hour came, in which the true worshippers worshipped the Father in Spirit and in truth, then this incense was offered, even this pure offering. We may rely on God's mercy for pardon as to the past, but not for indulgence to sin in future. If there be a willing mind, it will be accepted, though defective; but if any be a deceiver, devoting his best to Satan and to his lusts, he is under a curse. Men now, though in a different way, profane the name of the Lord, pollute his table, and show contempt for his worship.

Chapter 2

Chapter Outline

Verses 1-9

What is here said of the covenant of priesthood, is true of the covenant of grace made with all believers, as spiritual priests. It is a covenant of life and peace; it assures all believers of all happiness, both in this world and in that to come. It is an honour to God's servants to be employed as his messengers. The priest's lips should not keep knowledge from his people, but keep it for them. The people are all concerned to know the will of the Lord. We must not only consult the written word, but desire instruction and advice from God's messengers, in the affairs of our souls. Ministers must exert themselves to the utmost for the conversion of sinners; and even among those called Israelites, there are many to be turned from iniquity. Those ministers, and those only, are likely to turn men from sin, who preach sound doctrine, and live holy lives according to the Scripture. Many departed from this way; thus they misled the people. Such as walk with God in peace and righteousness, and turn others from sin, honour God; he will honour them, while those who despise him shall be lightly esteemed.

Verses 10-17

Corrupt practices are the fruit of corrupt principles; and he who is false to his God, will not be true to his fellow mortals. In contempt of the marriage covenant, which God instituted, the Jews put away the wives they had of their own nation, probably to make room for strange wives. They made their lives bitter to them; yet, in the sight of others, they pretend to be tender of them. Consider she is thy wife; thy own; the nearest relation thou hast in the world. The wife is to be looked on, not as a servant, but as a companion to the husband. There is an oath of God between them, which is not to be trifled with. Man and wife should continue to their lives' end, in holy love and peace. Did not God make one, one Eve for one Adam? Yet God could have made another Eve. Wherefore did he make but one woman for one man? It was that the children might be made a seed to serve him. Husbands and wives must live in the fear of God, that their seed may be a godly seed. The God of Israel saith that he hateth putting away. Those who would be kept from sin, must take heed to their spirits, for there all sin begins. Men will find that their wrong conduct in their families springs from selfishness, which disregards the welfare and happiness of others, when opposed to their own passions and fancies. It is wearisome to God to hear people justify themselves in wicked practices. Those who think God can be a friend to sin, affront him, and deceive themselves. The scoffers said, Where is the God of judgement? but the day of the Lord will come.

Chapter 3

Chapter Outline

Verses 1-6

The first words of this chapter seem an answer to the scoffers of those days. Here is a prophecy of the appearing of John the Baptist. He is Christ's harbinger. He shall prepare the way before him, by calling men to repentance. The Messiah had been long called, "He that should come," and now shortly he will come. He is the Messenger of the covenant. Those who seek Jesus, shall find pleasure in him, often when not looked for. The Lord Jesus, prepares the sinner's heart to be his temple, by the ministry of his word and the convictions of his Spirit, and he enters it as the Messenger of peace and consolation. No hypocrite or formalist can endure his doctrine, or stand before his tribunal. Christ came to distinguish men, to separate between the precious and the vile. He shall sit as a Refiner. Christ, by his gospel, shall purify and reform his church, and by his Spirit working with it, shall regenerate and cleanse souls. He will take away the dross found in them. He will separate their corruptions, which render their faculties worthless and useless. The believer needs not fear the fiery trial of afflictions and temptations, by which the Saviour refines his gold. He will take care it is not more intense or longer than is needful for his good; and this trial will end far otherwise than that of the wicked. Christ will, by interceding for them, make them accepted. Where no fear of God is, no good is to be expected. Evil pursues sinners. God is unchangeable. And though the sentence against evil works be not executed speedily, yet it will be executed; the Lord is as much an enemy to sin as ever. We may all apply this to ourselves. Because we have to do with a God that changes not, therefore it is that we are not consumed; because his compassions fail not.

Verses 7-12

The men of that generation turned away from God, they had not kept his ordinances. God gives them a gracious call. But they said, Wherein shall we return? God notices what returns our hearts make to the calls of his word. It shows great perverseness in sin, when men make afflictions excuses for sin, which are sent to part between them and their sins. Here is an earnest exhortation to reform.

God must be served in the first place; and the interest of our souls ought to be preferred before that of our bodies. Let them trust God to provide for their comfort. God has blessings ready for us, but through the weakness of our faith and the narrowness of our desires, we have not room to receive them. He who makes trial will find nothing is lost by honouring the Lord with his substance.

Verses 13-18

Among the Jews at this time, some plainly discovered themselves to be children of the wicked one. The yoke of Christ is easy. But those who work wickedness, tempt God by presumptuous sins. Judge of things as they will appear when the doom of these proud sinners comes to be executed. Those that feared the Lord, spake kindly, for preserving and promoting mutual love, when sin thus abounded. They spake one to another, in the language of those that fear the Lord, and think on his name. As evil communications corrupt good minds and manners, so good communications confirm them. A book of remembrance was written before God. He will take care that his children perish not with those that believe not. They shall be vessels of mercy and honour, when the rest are made vessels of wrath and dishonour. The saints are God's jewels; they are dear to him. He will preserve them as his jewels, when the earth is burned up like dross. Those who now own God for theirs, he will then own for his. It is our duty to serve God with the disposition of children; and he will not have his children trained up in idleness; they must do him service from a principle of love. Even God's children stand in need of sparing mercy. All are righteous or wicked, such as serve God, or such as serve him not: all are going to heaven or to hell. We are often deceived in our opinions concerning both the one and the other; but at the bar of Christ, every man's character will be known. As to ourselves, we have need to think among which we shall have our lot; and, as to others, we must judge nothing before the time. But in the end all the world will confess that those alone were wise and happy, who served the Lord and trusted in Him.

Chapter 4

Chapter Outline

The judgements on the wicked, and the   (1–3)
happiness of the righteous.

Regard to be had to the law; John the Baptist   (4–6)
promised as the forerunner of Messiah.

Verses 1-3

Here is a reference to the first and to the second coming of Christ: God has fixed the day of both. Those who do wickedly, who do not fear God's anger, shall feel it. It is certainly to be applied to the day of judgment, when Christ shall be revealed in flaming fire; to execute judgment on the proud, and all that do wickedly. In both, Christ is a rejoicing Light to those who serve him faithfully. By the Sun of Righteousness we understand Jesus Christ. Through him believers are justified and sanctified, and so are brought to see light. His influences render the sinner holy, joyful, and fruitful. It is applicable to the graces and comforts of the Holy Spirit, brought into the souls of men. Christ gave the Spirit to those who are his, to shine in their hearts, and to be a Comforter to them, a Sun and a Shield. That day which to the wicked will burn as an oven, will to the righteous be bright as the morning; it is what they wait for, more than those that wait for the morning. Christ came as the Sun, to bring, not only light to a dark world, but health to a distempered world. Souls shall increase in knowledge and spiritual strength. Their growth is as that of calves of the stall, not as the flower of the field, which is slender and weak, and soon withers. The saints' triumphs are all owing to God's victories; it is not they that do this, but God who does it for them. Behold another day is coming, far more dreadful to all that work wickedness than any which is gone before. How great then the happiness of the believer, when he goes from the darkness and misery of this world, to rejoice in the Lord for evermore!

Verses 4-6

Here is a solemn conclusion, not only of this prophecy, but of the Old Testament. Conscience bids us remember the law. Though we have not prophets, yet, as long as we have Bibles, we may keep up our communion with God. Let others boast in their proud reasoning, and call it enlightening, but let us keep near to that sacred word, through which this Sun of Righteousness shines upon the souls of his people. They must keep up a believing expectation of the gospel of Christ, and must look for the beginning of it. John the Baptist preached repentance and reformation, as Elijah had done. The turning of souls to God and their duty, is the best preparation of them for the great and dreadful day of the Lord. John shall preach a doctrine that shall reach men's hearts, and work a change in them. Thus he shall prepare the way for the kingdom of heaven. The Jewish nation, by wickedness, laid themselves open to the curse. God was ready to bring ruin upon them; but he will once more try whether they will repent and return; therefore he sent John the Baptist to preach repentance to them. Let the believer wait with patience for his release, and cheerfully expect the great day, when Christ shall come the second time to complete our salvation. But those must expect to be smitten with a sword, with a curse, who turn not to Him that smites them with a rod. None can expect to escape the curse of God's broken law, nor to enjoy the happiness of his chosen and redeemed people, unless their hearts are turned from sin and the world, to Christ and holiness. The grace of our Lord Jesus Christ be with us all. Amen.

Matthew

Matthew, surnamed Levi, before his conversion was a publican, or tax-gatherer under the Romans at Capernaum. He is generally allowed to have written his Gospel before any other of the evangelists. The contents of this Gospel, and the evidence of ancient writers, show that it was written primarily for the use of the Jewish nation. The fulfilment of prophecy was regarded by the Jews as strong evidence, therefore this is especially dwelt upon by St. Matthew. Here are particularly selected such parts of our Saviour's history and discourses as were best suited to awaken the Jewish nation to a sense of their sins; to remove their erroneous expectations of an earthly kingdom; to abate their pride and self-conceit; to teach them the spiritual nature and extent of the gospel; and to prepare them for the admission of the Gentiles into the church.

Chapter 1

Chapter Outline

The genealogy of Jesus.   (1–17)

An angel appears to Joseph.   (18–25)

Verses 1-17

Concerning this genealogy of our Saviour, observe the chief intention. It is not a needless genealogy. It is not a vain-glorious one, as those of great men often are. It proves that our Lord Jesus is of the nation and family out of which the Messiah was to arise. The promise of the blessing was made to Abraham and his seed; of the dominion, to David and his seed. It was promised to Abraham that Christ should descend from him, Ge 12:3; 22:18; and to David that he should descend from him, 2Sa 7:12; Ps 89:3, &c.; 132:11; and, therefore, unless Jesus is a son of David, and a son of Abraham, he is not the Messiah. Now this is here proved from well-known records. When the Son of God was pleased to take our nature, he came near to us, in our fallen, wretched condition; but he was perfectly free from sin: and while we read the names in his genealogy, we should not forget how low the Lord of glory stooped to save the human race.

Verses 18-25

Let us look to the circumstances under which the Son of God entered into this lower world, till we learn to despise the vain honours of this world, when compared with piety and holiness. The mystery of Christ's becoming man is to be adored, not curiously inquired into. It was so ordered that Christ should partake of our nature, yet that he should be pure from the defilement of original sin, which has been communicated to all the race of Adam. Observe, it is the thoughtful, not the unthinking, whom God will guide. God's time to come with instruction to his people, is when they are at a loss. Divine comforts most delight the soul when under the pressure of perplexed thoughts. Joseph is told that Mary should bring forth the Saviour of the world. He was to call his name Jesus, a Saviour. Jesus is the same name with Joshua. And the reason of that name is clear, for those whom

Christ saves, he saves from their sins; from the guilt of sin by the merit of his death, and from the power of sin by the Spirit of his grace. In saving them from sin, he saves them from wrath and the curse, and all misery, here and hereafter. Christ came to save his people, not in their sins, but from their sins; and so to redeem them from among men, to himself, who is separate from sinners. Joseph did as the angel of the Lord had bidden him, speedily, without delay, and cheerfully, without dispute. By applying the general rules of the written word, we should in all the steps of our lives, particularly the great turns of them, take direction from God, and we shall find this safe and comfortable.

Chapter 2

Chapter Outline

Verses 1-8

Those who live at the greatest distance from the means of grace often use most diligence, and learn to know the most of Christ and his salvation. But no curious arts, or mere human learning, can direct men unto him. We must learn of Christ by attending to the word of God, as a light that shineth in a dark place, and by seeking the teaching of the Holy Spirit. And those in whose hearts the day-star is risen, to give them any thing of the knowledge of Christ, make it their business to worship him. Though Herod was very old, and never had shown affection for his family, and was not himself likely to live till a new-born infant had grown up to manhood, he began to be troubled with the dread of a rival. He understood not the spiritual nature of the Messiah's kingdom. Let us beware of a dead faith. A man may be persuaded of many truths, and yet may hate them, because they interfere with his ambition, or sinful indulgences. Such a belief will make him uneasy, and the more resolved to oppose the truth and the cause of God; and he may be foolish enough to hope for success therein.

Verses 9-12

What joy these wise men felt upon this sight of the star, none know so well as those who, after a long and melancholy night of temptation and desertion, under the power of a spirit of bondage, at length receive the Spirit of adoption, witnessing with their spirits that they are the children of God. We may well think what a disappointment it was to them, when they found a cottage was his palace, and his own poor mother the only attendant he had. However, these wise men did not think themselves baffled; but having found the King they sought, they presented their gifts to him. The humble inquirer after Christ will not be stumbled at finding him and his disciples in obscure cottages, after having in vain sought them in palaces and populous cities. Is a soul busy, seeking after Christ? Would it worship him, and does it say, Alas! I am a foolish and poor creature, and have nothing to offer? Nothing! Hast thou not a heart, though unworthy of him, dark, hard, and foul? Give it to him as it is, and be willing that he use and dispose of it as it pleases him; he will take it, and will make it better, and thou shalt never repent having given it to him. He shall frame it to his own likeness, and will give thee himself, and be thine for ever. The gifts the wise men presented were gold, frankincense, and myrrh. Providence sent these as a seasonable relief to Joseph and Mary in their present poor condition. Thus our heavenly Father, who knows what his children need, uses some as stewards to supply the wants of others, and can provide for them, even from the ends of the earth.

Verses 13-15

Egypt had been a house of bondage to Israel, and particularly cruel to the infants of Israel; yet it is to be a place of refuge to the holy Child Jesus. God, when he pleases, can make the worst of places serve the best of purposes. This was a trial of the faith of Joseph and Mary. But their faith, being tried, was found firm. If we and our infants are at any time in trouble, let us remember the straits in which Christ was when an infant.

Verses 16-18

Herod killed all the male children, not only in Bethlehem, but in all the villages of that city. Unbridled wrath, armed with an unlawful power, often carries men to absurd cruelties. It was no unrighteous thing with God to permit this; every life is forfeited to his justice as soon as it begins. The diseases and deaths of little children are proofs of original sin. But the murder of these infants was their martyrdom. How early did persecution against Christ and his kingdom begin! Herod now thought that he had baffled the Old Testament prophecies, and the efforts of the wise men in finding Christ; but whatever crafty, cruel devices are in men's hearts, the counsel of the Lord shall stand.

Verses 19-23

Egypt may serve to sojourn in, or take shelter in, for awhile, but not to abide in. Christ was sent to the lost sheep of the house of Israel, to them he must return. Did we but look upon the world as our Egypt, the place of our bondage and banishment, and heaven only as our Canaan, our home, our rest, we should as readily arise and depart thither, when we are called for, as Joseph did out of Egypt. The family must settle in Galilee. Nazareth was a place held in bad esteem, and Christ was crucified with this accusation, Jesus the Nazarene. Wherever Providence allots the bounds of our habitation, we must expect to share the reproach of Christ; yet we may glory in being called by his name, sure that if we suffer with him, we shall also be glorified with him.

Chapter 3

Chapter Outline

Verses 1-6

After Malachi there was no prophet until John the Baptist came. He appeared first in the wilderness of Judea. This was not an uninhabited desert, but a part of the country not thickly peopled, nor much enclosed. No place is so remote as to shut us out from the visits of Divine grace. The doctrine he preached was repentance; "Repent ye." The word here used, implies a total alteration in the mind, a change in the judgment, disposition, and affections, another and a better bias of the soul. Consider your ways, change your minds: you have thought amiss; think again, and think aright. True penitents have other thoughts of God and Christ, sin and holiness, of this world and the other, than they had. The change of the mind produces a change of the way. That is gospel repentance, which flows from a sight of Christ, from a sense of his love, and from hopes of pardon and forgiveness through him. It is a great encouragement to us to repent; repent, for your sins shall be pardoned upon your repentance. Return to God in a way of duty, and he will, through Christ, return unto you in the way of mercy. It is still as necessary to repent and humble ourselves, to prepare the way of the Lord, as it then was. There is a great deal to be done, to make way for Christ into a soul, and nothing is more needful than the discovery of sin, and a conviction that we cannot be saved by our own righteousness. The way of sin and Satan is a crooked way; but to prepare a way for Christ, the paths must be made straight, Heb 12:13. Those whose business it is to call others to mourn for sin, and to mortify it, ought themselves to live a serious life, a life of self-denial, and contempt of the world. By giving others this example, John made way for Christ. Many came to John's baptism, but few kept to the profession they made. There may be many forward hearers, where there are few true believers. Curiosity, and love for novelty and variety, may bring many to attend on good preaching, and to be affected for a while, who never are subject to the power of it. Those who received John's doctrine, testified their repentance by confessing their sins. Those only are ready to receive Jesus Christ as their righteousness, who are brought with sorrow and shame to own their guilt. The benefits of the kingdom of heaven, now at hand, were thereupon sealed to them by baptism. John washed them with water, in token that God would cleanse them from all their iniquities, thereby intimating, that by nature and practice all were polluted, and could not be admitted among the people of God, unless washed from their sins in the fountain Christ was to open, Zec 13:1.

Verses 7-12

To make application to the souls of the hearers, is the life of preaching; so it was of John's preaching. The Pharisees laid their chief stress on outward observances, neglecting the weightier matters of the moral law, and the spiritual meaning of their legal ceremonies. Others of them were detestable hypocrites, making their pretences to holiness a cloak for iniquity. The Sadducees ran into the opposite extreme, denying the existence of spirits, and a future state. They were the scornful infidels of that time and country. There is a wrath to come. It is the great concern of every one to flee from that wrath. God, who delights not in our ruin, has warned us; he warns by the written word, by ministers, by conscience. And those are not worthy of the name of penitents, or their privileges, who say they are sorry for their sins, yet persist in them. It becomes penitents to be humble and low in their own eyes, to be thankful for the least mercy, patient under the greatest affliction, to be watchful against all appearances of sin, to abound in every duty, and to be charitable in judging others. Here is a word of caution, not to trust in outward privileges. There is a great deal which carnal hearts are apt to say within themselves, to put aside the convincing, commanding power of the word of God. Multitudes, by resting in the honours and mere advantages of their being members of an outward church, come short of heaven. Here is a word of terror to the careless and secure. Our corrupt hearts cannot be made to produce good fruit, unless the regenerating Spirit of Christ graft the good word of God upon them. And every tree, however high in gifts and honours, however green in outward professions and performances, if it bring not forth good fruit, the fruits meet for repentance, is hewn down and cast into the fire of God's wrath, the fittest place for barren trees: what else are they good for? If not fit for fruit, they are fit for fuel. John shows the design and intention of Christ's appearing, which they were now speedily to expect. No outward forms can make us clean. No ordinances, by whomsoever administered, or after whatever mode, can supply the want of the baptism of the Holy Ghost and of fire. The purifying and cleansing power of the Holy Spirit alone can produce that purity of heart, and those holy affections, which accompany salvation. It is Christ who baptizes with the Holy Ghost. This he did in the extraordinary gifts of the Spirit sent upon the apostles, Ac 2:4. This he does in the graces and comforts of the Spirit, given to those that ask him, Lu 11:13; Joh 7:38, 39; see Ac 11:16. Observe here, the outward church is Christ's floor, Isa 21:10. True believers are as wheat, substantial, useful, and valuable; hypocrites are as chaff, light and empty, useless and worthless, carried about with every wind; these are mixed, good and bad, in the same outward communion. There is a day coming when the wheat and chaff shall be separated. The last judgment will be the distinguishing day, when saints and sinners shall be parted for ever. In heaven the saints are brought together, and no longer scattered; they are safe, and no longer exposed; separated from corrupt neighbours without, and corrupt affections within, and there is no chaff among them. Hell is the unquenchable fire, which will certainly be the portion and punishment of hypocrites and unbelievers. Here life and death, good and evil, are set before us: according as we now are in the field, we shall be then in the floor.

Verses 13-17

Christ's gracious condescensions are so surprising, that even the strongest believers at first can hardly believe them; so deep and mysterious, that even those who know his mind well, are apt to start objections against the will of Christ. And those who have much of the Spirit of God while here, see that they need to apply to Christ for more. Christ does not deny that John had need to be baptized of him, yet declares he will now be baptized of John. Christ is now in a state of humiliation.

Our Lord Jesus looked upon it as well becoming him to fulfil all righteousness, to own every Divine institution, and to show his readiness to comply with all God's righteous precepts. In and through Christ, the heavens are opened to the children of men. This descent of the Spirit upon Christ, showed that he was endued with his sacred influences without measure. The fruit of the Spirit is love, joy, peace, long-suffering, gentleness, goodness, faith, meekness, temperance. At Christ's baptism there was a manifestation of the three Persons in the sacred Trinity. The Father confirming the Son to be Mediator; the Son solemnly entering upon the work; the Holy Spirit descending on him, to be through his mediation communicated to his people. In Him our spiritual sacrifices are acceptable, for He is the altar that sanctifies every gift, 1Pe 2:5. Out of Christ, God is a consuming fire, but in Christ, a reconciled Father. This is the sum of the gospel, which we must by faith cheerfully embrace.

Chapter 4

Chapter Outline

Verses 1-11

Concerning Christ's temptation, observe, that directly after he was declared to be the Son of God, and the Saviour of the world, he was tempted; great privileges, and special tokens of Divine favour, will not secure any from being tempted. But if the Holy Spirit witness to our being adopted as children of God, that will answer all the suggestions of the evil spirit. Christ was directed to the combat. If we presume upon our own strength, and tempt the devil to tempt us, we provoke God to leave us to ourselves. Others are tempted, when drawn aside of their own lust, and enticed, Jas 1:14; but our Lord Jesus had no corrupt nature, therefore he was tempted only by the devil. In the temptation of Christ it appears that our enemy is subtle, spiteful, and very daring; but he can be resisted. It is a comfort to us that Christ suffered, being tempted; for thus it appears that our temptations, if not yielded to, are not sins, they are afflictions only. Satan aimed in all his temptations, to bring Christ to sin against God. 1. He tempted him to despair of his Father's goodness, and to distrust his Father's care concerning him. It is one of the wiles of Satan to take advantage of our outward condition; and those who are brought into straits have need to double their guard. Christ answered all the temptations of Satan with "It is written;" to set us an example, he appealed to what was written in the Scriptures. This method we must take, when at any time we are tempted to sin. Let us learn not to take any wrong courses for our supply, when our wants are ever so pressing: in some way or other the Lord will provide. 2. Satan tempted Christ to presume upon his Father's power and protection, in a point of safety. Nor are any extremes more dangerous than despair and presumption, especially in the affairs of our souls. Satan has no objection to holy places as the scene of his assaults. Let us not, in any place, be off our watch. The holy city is the place, where he does, with the greatest advantage, tempt men to pride and presumption. All high places are slippery places; advancements in the world makes a man a mark for Satan to shoot his fiery darts at. Is Satan so well versed in Scripture as to be able to quote it readily? He is so. It is possible for a man to have his head full of Scripture notions, and his mouth full of Scripture expressions, while his heart is full of bitter enmity to God and to all goodness. Satan misquoted the words. If we go out of our way, out of the way of our duty, we forfeit the promise, and put ourselves out of God's protection. This passage, De 8:3, made against the tempter, therefore he left out part. This promise is firm and stands good. But shall we continue in sin, that grace may abound? No. 3. Satan tempted Christ to idolatry with the offer of the kingdoms of the world, and the glory of them. The glory of the world is the most charming temptation to the unthinking and unwary; by that men are most easily imposed upon. Christ was tempted to worship Satan. He rejected the proposal with abhorrence. "Get thee hence, Satan!" Some temptations are openly wicked; and they are not merely to be opposed, but rejected at once. It is good to be quick and firm in resisting temptation. If we resist the devil he will flee from us. But the soul that deliberates is almost overcome. We find but few who can decidedly reject such baits as Satan offers; yet what is a man profited if he gain the whole world, and lose his own soul? Christ was succoured after the temptation, for his encouragement to go on in his undertaking, and for our encouragement to trust in him; for as he knew, by experience, what it was to suffer, being tempted, so he knew what it was to be succoured, being tempted; therefore we may expect, not only that he will feel for his tempted people, but that he will come to them with seasonable relief.

Verses 12-17

It is just with God to take the gospel and the means of grace, from those that slight them and thrust them away. Christ will not stay long where he is not welcome. Those who are without Christ, are in the dark. They were sitting in this condition, a contented posture; they chose it rather than light; they were willingly ignorant. When the gospel comes, light comes; when it comes to any place, when it comes to any soul, it makes day there. Light discovers and directs; so does the gospel. The doctrine of repentance is right gospel doctrine. Not only the austere John Baptist, but the gracious Jesus, preached repentance. There is still the same reason to do so. The kingdom of heaven was not reckoned to be fully come, till the pouring out of the Holy Spirit after Christ's ascension.

Verses 18-22

When Christ began to preach, he began to gather disciples, who should be hearers, and afterwards preachers of his doctrine, who should be witnesses of his miracles, and afterwards testify concerning them. He went not to Herod's court, not to Jerusalem, among the chief priests and the elders, but to the sea of Galilee, among the fishermen. The same power which called Peter and Andrew, could have wrought upon Annas and Caiaphas, for with God nothing is impossible. But Christ chooses the foolish things of the world to confound the wise. Diligence in an honest calling is pleasing to Christ, and it is no hinderance to a holy life. Idle people are more open to the temptations of Satan than to the calls of God. It is a happy and hopeful thing to see children careful of their parents, and dutiful. When Christ comes, it is good to be found doing. Am I in Christ? is a very needful question to ask ourselves; and, next to that, Am I in my calling? They had followed Christ before, as common disciples, Joh 1:37; now they must leave their calling. Those who would follow Christ aright, must, at his command, leave all things to follow him, must be ready to part with them. This instance of the power of the Lord Jesus encourages us to depend upon his grace. He speaks, and it is done.

Verses 23-25

Wherever Christ went, he confirmed his Divine mission by miracles, which were emblems of the healing power of his doctrine, and the influences of the Spirit which accompanied it. We do not now find the Saviour's miraculous healing power in our bodies; but if we are cured by medicine, the praise is equally his. Three general words are here used. He healed every sickness or disease; none was too bad; none too hard, for Christ to heal with a word. Three diseases are named; the palsy, which is the greatest weakness of the body; lunacy, which is the greatest malady of the mind; and possession of the devil, which is the greatest misery and calamity of both; yet Christ healed all, and by thus curing bodily diseases, showed that his great errand into the world was to cure spiritual maladies. Sin is the sickness, disease, and torment of the soul: Christ came to take away sin, and so to heal the soul.

Chapter 5

Chapter Outline

Verses 1, 2

None will find happiness in this world or the next, who do not seek it from Christ by the rule of his word. He taught them what was the evil they should abhor, and what the good they should seek and abound in.

Verses 3-12

beholden to the mercy of God for their daily bread. We pray, Give it to us. This teaches us a compassion for the poor. Also that we ought to pray with our families. We pray that God would give it us this day; which teaches us to renew the desires of our souls toward God, as the wants of our bodies are renewed. As the day comes we must pray to our heavenly Father, and reckon we could as well go a day without food, as without prayer. We are taught to hate and dread sin while we hope for mercy, to distrust ourselves, to rely on the providence and grace of God to keep us from it, to be prepared to resist the tempter, and not to become tempters of others. Here is a promise, If you forgive, your heavenly Father will also forgive. We must forgive, as we hope to be forgiven. Those who desire to find mercy with God, must show mercy to their brethren. Christ came into the world as the great Peace-maker, not only to reconcile us to God, but one to another.

Verses 16-18

Religious fasting is a duty required of the disciples of Christ, but it is not so much a duty itself, as a means to dispose us for other duties. Fasting is the humbling of the soul, Ps 35:13; that is the inside of the duty; let that, therefore, be thy principal care, and as to the outside of it, covet not to let it be seen. God sees in secret, and will reward openly.

Verses 19-24

Worldly-mindedness is a common and fatal symptom of hypocrisy, for by no sin can Satan have a surer and faster hold of the soul, under the cloak of a profession of religion. Something the soul will have, which it looks upon as the best thing; in which it has pleasure and confidence above other things. Christ counsels to make our best things the joys and glories of the other world, those things not seen which are eternal, and to place our happiness in them. There are treasures in heaven. It is our wisdom to give all diligence to make our title to eternal life sure through Jesus Christ, and to look on all things here below, as not worthy to be compared with it, and to be content with nothing short of it. It is happiness above and beyond the changes and chances of time, an inheritance incorruptible. The worldly man is wrong in his first principle; therefore all his reasonings and actions therefrom must be wrong. It is equally to be applied to false religion; that which is deemed light is thick darkness. This is an awful, but a common case; we should therefore carefully examine our leading principles by the word of God, with earnest prayer for the teaching of his Spirit. A man may do some service to two masters, but he can devote himself to the service of no more than one. God requires the whole heart, and will not share it with the world. When two masters oppose each other, no man can serve both. He who holds to the world and loves it, must despise God; he who loves God, must give up the friendship of the world.

Verses 25-34

There is scarcely any sin against which our Lord Jesus more warns his disciples, than disquieting, distracting, distrustful cares about the things of this life. This often insnares the poor as much as the love of wealth does the rich. But there is a carefulness about temporal things which is a duty, though we must not carry these lawful cares too far. Take no thought for your life. Not about the length of it; but refer it to God to lengthen or shorten it as he pleases; our times are in his hand, and they are in a good hand. Not about the comforts of this life; but leave it to God to make it bitter or sweet as he pleases. Food and raiment God has promised, therefore we may expect them. Take no thought for the morrow, for the time to come. Be not anxious for the future, how you shall live next year, or when you are old, or what you shall leave behind you. As we must not boast of tomorrow, so we must not care for to-morrow, or the events of it. God has given us life, and has given us the body. And what can he not do for us, who did that? If we take care about our souls and for eternity, which are more than the body and its life, we may leave it to God to provide for us food and raiment, which are less. Improve this as an encouragement to trust in God. We must reconcile ourselves to our worldly estate, as we do to our stature. We cannot alter the disposals of Providence, therefore we must submit and resign ourselves to them. Thoughtfulness for our souls is the best cure of thoughtfulness for the world. Seek first the kingdom of God, and make religion your business: say not that this is the way to starve; no, it is the way to be well provided for, even in this world. The conclusion of the whole matter is, that it is the will and command of the Lord Jesus, that by daily prayers we may get strength to bear us up under our daily troubles, and to arm us against the temptations that attend them, and then let none of these things move us. Happy are those who take the Lord for their God, and make full proof of it by trusting themselves wholly to his wise disposal. Let thy Spirit convince us of sin in the want of this disposition, and take away the worldliness of our hearts.

Chapter 7

Chapter Outline

Christ reproves rash judgment.	(1–6)
Encouragements to prayer.	(7–11)
The broad and narrow way.	(12–14)
Against false prophets.	(15–20)
To be doers of the word, not hearers only.	(21–29)

Verses 1-6

We must judge ourselves, and judge of our own acts, but not make our word a law to everybody. We must not judge rashly, nor pass judgment upon our brother without any ground. We must not make the worst of people. Here is a just reproof to those who quarrel with their brethren for small faults, while they allow themselves in greater ones. Some sins are as motes, while others are as beams; some as a gnat, others as a camel. Not that there is any sin little; if it be a mote, or splinter, it is in the eye; if a gnat, it is in the throat; both are painful and dangerous, and we cannot be easy or well till they are got out. That which charity teaches us to call but a splinter in our brother's eye, true repentance and godly sorrow will teach us to call a beam in our own. It is as strange that a man can be in a sinful, miserable condition, and not be aware of it, as that a man should have a beam in his eye, and not consider it; but the god of this world blinds their minds. Here is a good rule for reprovers; first reform thyself.

Verses 7-11

Prayer is the appointed means for obtaining what we need. Pray; pray often; make a business of prayer, and be serious and earnest in it. Ask, as a beggar asks alms. Ask, as a traveller asks the way. Seek, as for a thing of value that we have lost; or as the merchantman that seeks goodly pearls. Knock, as he that desires to enter into the house knocks at the door. Sin has shut and barred the door against us; by prayer we knock. Whatever you pray for, according to the promise, shall be given you, if God see it fit for you, and what would you have more? This is made to apply to all that pray aright; every one that asketh receiveth, whether Jew or Gentile, young or old, rich or poor, high or low, master or servant, learned or unlearned, all are alike welcome to the throne of grace, if they come in faith. It is explained by a comparison taken from earthly parents, and their readiness to give their children what they ask. Parents are often foolishly fond, but God is all-wise; he knows what we need, what we desire, and what is fit for us. Let us never suppose our heavenly Father would bid us pray, and then refuse to hear, or give us what would be hurtful.

Verses 12-14

Christ came to teach us, not only what we are to know and believe, but what we are to do; not only toward God, but toward men; not only toward those of our party and persuasion, but toward men in general, all with whom we have to do. We must do that to our neighbour which we ourselves acknowledge to be fit and reasonable. We must, in our dealings with men, suppose ourselves in the same case and circumstances with those we have to do with, and act accordingly. There are but two ways right and wrong, good and evil; the way to heaven and the way to hell; in the one or other of these all are walking: there is no middle place hereafter, no middle way now. All the children of men are saints or sinners, godly or ungodly. See concerning the way of sin and sinners, that the gate is wide, and stands open. You may go in at this gate with all your lusts about you; it gives no check to appetites or passions. It is a broad way; there are many paths in it; there is choice of sinful ways. There is a large company in this way. But what profit is there in being willing to go to hell with others, because they will not go to heaven with us? The way to eternal life is narrow. We are not in heaven as soon as we are got through the strait gate. Self must be denied, the body kept under, and corruptions mortified. Daily temptations must be resisted; duties must be done. We must watch in all things, and walk with care; and we must go through much tribulation. And yet this way should invite us all; it leads to life: to present comfort in the favour of God, which is the life of the soul; to eternal bliss, the hope of which at the end of our way, should make all the difficulties of the road easy to us. This plain declaration of Christ has been disregarded by many who have taken pains to explain it away; but in all ages the real disciple of Christ has been looked on as a singular, unfashionable character; and all that have sided with the greater number, have gone on in the broad road to destruction. If we would serve God, we must be firm in our religion. Can we often hear of the strait gate and the narrow way, and how few there are that find it, without being in pain for ourselves, or considering whether we are entered on the narrow way, and what progress we are making in it?

Verses 15-20

Nothing so much prevents men from entering the strait gate, and becoming true followers of Christ, as the carnal, soothing, flattering doctrines of those who oppose the truth. They may be known by the drift and effects of their doctrines. Some part of their temper and conduct is contrary to the mind of Christ. Those opinions come not from God that lead to sin.

Verses 21-29

Christ here shows that it will not be enough to own him for our Master, only in word and tongue. It is necessary to our happiness that we believe in Christ, that we repent of sin, that we live a holy life, that we love one another. This is his will, even our sanctification. Let us take heed of resting in outward privileges and doings, lest we deceive ourselves, and perish eternally, as multitudes do, with a lie in our right hand. Let every one that names the name of Christ, depart from all sin. There are others, whose religion rests in bare hearing, and it goes no further; their heads are filled with empty notions. These two sorts of hearers are represented as two builders. This parable teaches us to hear and do the sayings of the Lord Jesus: some may seem hard to flesh and blood, but they must be done. Christ is laid for a foundation, and every thing besides Christ is sand. Some build their hopes upon worldly prosperity; others upon an outward profession of religion. Upon these they venture; but they are all sand, too weak to bear such a fabric as our hopes of heaven. There is a storm coming that will try every man's work. When God takes away the soul, where is the hope of the hypocrite? The house fell in the storm, when the builder had most need of it, and expected it would be a shelter to him. It fell when it was too late to build another. May the Lord make us wise builders for eternity. Then nothing shall separate us from the love of Christ Jesus. The multitudes were astonished at the wisdom and power of Christ's doctrine. And this sermon, ever so often read over, is always new. Every word proves its Author to be Divine. Let us be more and more decided and earnest, making some one or other of these blessednesses and Christian graces the main subject of our thoughts, even for weeks together. Let us not rest in general and confused desires after them, whereby we grasp at all, but catch nothing.

Chapter 8

Chapter Outline

He heals two possessed with devils.   (28–34)

Verse 1

This verse refers to the close of the foregoing sermon. Those to whom Christ has made himself known, desire to know more of him.

Verses 2-4

In these verses we have an account of Christ's cleansing a leper, who came and worshipped him, as one clothed with Divine power. This cleansing directs us, not only to apply to Christ, who has power over bodily diseases, for the cure of them, but it also teaches us in what manner to apply to him. When we cannot be sure of God's will, we may be sure of his wisdom and mercy. No guilt is so great, but there is that in Christ's blood which atones for it; no corruption so strong, but there is that in his grace which can subdue it. To be made clean we must commend ourselves to his pity; we cannot demand it as a debt, but we must humbly request it as a favour. Those who by faith apply to Christ for mercy and grace, may be sure that he is freely willing to give them the mercy and grace they thus seek. And those afflictions are blessed that bring us to know Christ, and cause us to seek help and salvation from him. Let those who are cleansed from their spiritual leprosy, go to Christ's ministers and open their case, that they may advise, comfort, and pray for them.

Verses 5-13

This centurion was a heathen, a Roman soldier. Though he was a soldier, yet he was a godly man. No man's calling or place will be an excuse for unbelief and sin. See how he states his servant's case. We should concern ourselves for the souls of our children and servants, who are spiritually sick, who feel not spiritual evils, who know not that which is spiritually good; and we should bring them to Christ by faith and prayers. Observe his self-abasement. Humble souls are made more humble by Christ's gracious dealings with them. Observe his great faith. The more diffident we are of ourselves, the stronger will be our confidence in Christ. Herein the centurion owns him to have Divine power, and a full command of all the creatures and powers of nature, as a master over his servants. Such servants we all should be to God; we must go and come, according to the directions of his word and the disposals of his providence. But when the Son of man comes he finds little faith, therefore he finds little fruit. An outward profession may cause us to be called children of the kingdom; but if we rest in that, and have nothing else to show, we shall be cast out. The servant got a cure of his disease, and the master got the approval of his faith. What was said to him, is said to all, Believe, and ye shall receive; only believe. See the power of Christ, and the power of faith. The healing of our souls is at once the effect and evidence of our interest in the blood of Christ.

Verses 14-17

Peter had a wife, yet was an apostle of Christ, who showed that he approved of the married state, by being thus kind to Peter's wife's relations. The church of Rome, which forbids ministers to marry, goes contrary to that apostle upon whom they rest so much. He had his wife's mother with him in his family, which is an example to be kind to our relations. In spiritual healing, the Scripture speaks the word, the Spirit gives the touch, touches the heart, touches the hand. Those who recover from fevers, commonly are weak and feeble some time after; but to show that this cure was above the power of nature, the woman was at once so well as to go about the business of the house. The miracles which Jesus did being noised abroad, many thronged to him. He healed all that were sick, though the patient was ever so mean, and the case ever so bad. Many are the diseases and calamities to which we are liable in the body; and there is more, in those words of the gospel, that Jesus Christ bore our sicknesses and carried our sorrows, to support and comfort us under them, than in all the writings of the philosophers. Let us not grudge labour, trouble, or expense in doing good to others.

Verses 18-22

One of the scribes was too hasty in promising; he proffers himself to be a close follower of Christ. He seems to be very resolute. Many resolutions for religion are produced by sudden conviction, and taken up without due consideration; these come to nothing. When this scribe offered to follow Christ, one would think he should have been encouraged; one scribe might do more credit and service than twelve fishermen; but Christ saw his heart, and answered to its thoughts, and therein teaches all how to come to Christ. His resolve seems to have been from a worldly, covetous principle; but Christ had not a place to lay his head on, and if he follows him, he must not expect to fare better than he fared. We have reason to think this scribe went away. Another was too slow. Delay in doing is as bad on the one hand, as hastiness in resolving is on the other. He asked leave to attend his father to his grave, and then he would be at Christ's service. This seemed reasonable, yet it was not right. He had not true zeal for the work. Burying the dead, especially a dead father, is a good work, but it is not thy work at this time. If Christ requires our service, affection even for the nearest and dearest relatives, and for things otherwise our duty, must give way. An unwilling mind never wants an excuse. Jesus said to him, Follow me; and, no doubt, power went with this word to him as to others; he did follow Christ, and cleaved to him. The scribe said, I will follow thee; to this man Christ said, Follow me; comparing them together, it shows that we are brought to Christ by the force of his call to us, Ro 9:16.

Verses 23-27

It is a comfort to those who go down to the sea in ships, and are often in perils there, to reflect that they have a Saviour to trust in and pray to, who knows what it is to be on the water, and to be in storms there. Those who are passing with Christ over the ocean of this world, must expect storms. His human nature, like to ours in every thing but sin, was wearied, and he slept at this time to try the faith of his disciples. They, in their fear, came to their Master. Thus is it in a soul; when lusts and temptations are swelling and raging, and God is, as it were, asleep to it, this brings it to the brink of despair. Then it cries for a word from his mouth, Lord Jesus, keep not silence to me, or I am undone. Many that have true faith, are weak in it. Christ's disciples are apt to be disquieted with fears in a stormy day; to torment themselves that things are bad with them, and with dismal thoughts that they will be worse. Great storms of doubt and fear in the soul, under the power of the spirit of bondage, sometimes end in a wonderful calm, created and spoken by the Spirit of adoption. They were astonished. They never saw a storm so turned at once into a perfect calm. He that can do this, can do any thing, which encourages confidence and comfort in him, in the most stormy day, within or without, Isa 26:4.

Verses 28-34

The devils have nothing to do with Christ as a Saviour; they neither have, nor hope for any benefit from him. Oh the depth of this mystery of Divine love; that fallen man has so much to do with Christ, when fallen angels have nothing to do with him! Heb 2:16. Surely here was torment, to be forced to own the excellence that is in Christ, and yet they had no part in him. The devils desire not to have any thing to do with Christ as a Ruler. See whose language those speak, who will have nothing to do with the gospel of Christ. But it is not true that the devils have nothing to do with Christ as a Judge; for they have, and they know it, and thus it is with all the children of men. Satan and his instruments can go no further than he permits; they must quit possession when he commands. They cannot break his hedge of protection about his people; they cannot enter even a swine without his leave. They had leave. God often, for wise and holy ends, permits the efforts of Satan's rage. Thus the devil hurries people to sin; hurries them to what they have resolved against, which they know will be shame and grief to them: miserable is the condition of those who are led captive by him at his will. There are a great many who prefer their swine before the Saviour, and so come short of Christ and salvation by him. They desire Christ to depart out of their hearts, and will not suffer his word to have place in them, because he and his word would destroy their brutish lusts, those swine which they give themselves up to feed. And justly will Christ forsake all that are weary of him; and say hereafter, Depart, ye cursed, to those who now say to the Almighty, Depart from us.

Chapter 9

Chapter Outline

Verses 1-8

The faith of the friends of the paralytic in bringing him to Christ, was a strong faith; they firmly believed that Jesus Christ both could and would heal him. A strong faith regards no obstacles in pressing after Christ. It was a humble faith; they brought him to attend on Christ. It was an active faith. Sin may be pardoned, yet the sickness not be removed; the sickness may be removed, yet the sin not pardoned: but if we have the comfort of peace with God, with the comfort of recovery from sickness, this makes the healing a mercy indeed. This is no encouragement to sin. If thou bring thy sins to Jesus Christ, as thy malady and misery to be cured of, and delivered from, it is well; but to come with them, as thy darlings and delight, thinking still to retain them and receive him, is a gross mistake, a miserable delusion. The great intention of the blessed Jesus in the redemption he wrought, is to separate our hearts from sin. Our Lord Jesus has perfect knowledge of all that we say within ourselves. There is a great deal of evil in sinful thoughts, which is very offensive to the Lord Jesus. Christ designed to show that his great errand to the world was, to save his people from their sins. He turned from disputing with the scribes, and spake healing to the sick man. Not only he had no more need to be carried upon his bed, but he had strength to carry it. God must be glorified in all the power that is given to do good.

Verse 9

Matthew was in his calling, as the rest of those whom Christ called. As Satan comes with his temptations to the idle, so Christ comes with his calls to those who are employed. We are all naturally averse from thee, O God; do thou bid us to follow thee; draw us by thy powerful word, and we shall run after thee. Speak by the word of the Spirit to our hearts, the world cannot hold us down, Satan cannot stop our way, we shall arise and follow thee. A saving change is wrought in the soul, by Christ as the author, and his word as the means. Neither Matthew's place, nor his gains by it, could detain him, when Christ called him. He left it, and though we find the disciples, who were fishers, occasionally fishing again afterwards, we never more find Matthew at his sinful gain.

Verses 10-13

Some time after his call, Matthew sought to bring his old associates to hear Christ. He knew by experience what the grace of Christ could do, and would not despair concerning them. Those who are effectually brought to Christ, cannot but desire that others also may be brought to him. Those who suppose their souls to be without disease will not welcome the spiritual Physician. This was the case with the Pharisees; they despised Christ, because they thought themselves whole; but the poor publicans and sinners felt that they wanted instruction and amendment. It is easy, and too common, to put the worst constructions upon the best words and actions. It may justly be suspected that those have not the grace of God themselves, who are not pleased with others' obtaining it. Christ's conversing with sinners is here called mercy; for to promote the conversion of souls is the greatest act of mercy. The gospel call is a call to repentance; a call to us to change our minds, and to change our ways. If the children of men had not been sinners, there had been no need for Christ to come among them. Let us examine whether we have found out our sickness, and have learned to follow the directions of our great Physician.

Verses 14-17

John was at this time in prison; his circumstances, his character, and the nature of the message he was sent to deliver, led those who were peculiarly attached to him, to keep frequent fasts. Christ referred them to John's testimony of him, Joh 3:29. Though there is no doubt that Jesus and his disciples lived in a spare and frugal manner, it would be improper for his disciples to fast while they had the comfort of his presence. When he is with them, all is well. The presence of the sun makes day, and its absence produces night. Our Lord further reminded them of common rules of prudence. It was not usual to take a piece of rough woolen cloth, which had never been prepared, to join to an old garment, for it would not join well with the soft, old garment, but would tear it further, and the rent would be made worse. Nor would men put new wine into old leathern bottles, which were going to decay, and would be liable to burst from the fermenting of the wine; but putting the new wine into strong, new, skin bottles, both would be preserved. Great caution and prudence are necessary, that young converts may not receive gloomy and forbidding ideas of the service of our Lord; but duties are to be urged as they are able to bear them.

Verses 18-26

The death of our relations should drive us to Christ, who is our life. And it is high honour to the greatest rulers to attend on the Lord Jesus; and those who would receive mercy from Christ, must honour him. The variety of methods Christ took in working his miracles, perhaps was because of the different frames and tempers of mind, which those were in who came to him, and which He who searches the heart perfectly knew. A poor woman applied herself to Christ, and received mercy from him by the way. If we do but touch, as it were, the hem of Christ's garment by living faith, our worst evils will be healed; there is no other real cure, nor need we fear his knowing things which are a grief and burden to us, but which we would not tell to any earthly friend. When Christ entered the ruler's house, he said, Give place. Sometimes, when the sorrow of the world prevails, it is difficult for Christ and his comforts to enter. The ruler's daughter was really dead, but not so to Christ. The death of the righteous is in a special manner to be looked on as only a sleep. The words and works of Christ may not at first be understood, yet they are not therefore to be despised. The people were put forth. Scorners who laugh at what they do not understand, are not proper witnesses of the wonderful works of Christ. Dead souls are not raised to spiritual life, unless Christ take them by the hand: it is done in the day of his power. If this single instance of Christ's raising one newly dead so increased his fame, what will be his glory when all that are in their graves shall hear his voice, and come forth; those that have done good to the resurrection of life, and those that have done evil to the resurrection of damnation!

Verses 27-31

At this time the Jews expected Messiah would appear; these blind men knew and proclaimed in the streets of Capernaum that he was come, and that Jesus was he. Those who, by the providence of God, have lost their bodily sight, may, by the grace of God, have the eyes of their understanding fully enlightened. And whatever our wants and burdens are, we need no more for supply and support, than to share in the mercy of our Lord Jesus. In Christ is enough for all. They followed him crying aloud. He would try their faith, and would teach us always to pray, and not to faint, though the answer does not come at once. They followed Christ, and followed him crying; but the great question is, Do ye believe? Nature may make us earnest, but it is only grace that can work faith. Christ touched their eyes. He gives sight to blind souls by the power of his grace going with his word, and he puts the cure upon their faith. Those who apply to Jesus Christ, shall be dealt with, not according to their fancies, nor according to their profession, but according to their faith. Christ sometimes concealed his miracles, because he would not indulge the conceit which prevailed among the Jews, that their Messiah should be a temporal prince, and so give occasion to the people to attempt tumults and seditions.

Verses 32-34

Of the two, better a dumb devil than a blaspheming one. Christ's cures strike at the root, and remove the effect by taking away the cause; they open the lips, by breaking Satan's power in the soul. Nothing can convince those who are under the power of pride. They will believe anything, however false or absurd, rather than the Holy Scriptures; thus they show the enmity of their hearts against a holy God.

Verses 35-38

Jesus visited not only the great and wealthy cities, but the poor, obscure villages; and there he preached, there he healed. The souls of the meanest in the world are as precious to Christ, and should be so to us, as the souls of those who make the greatest figure. There were priests, Levites, and scribes, all over the land; but they were idol shepherds, Zec 11:17; therefore Christ had compassion on the people as sheep scattered, as men perishing for lack of knowledge. To this day vast multitudes are as sheep not having a shepherd, and we should have compassion and do all we can to help them. The multitudes desirous of spiritual instruction formed a plenteous harvest, needing many active labourers; but few deserved that character. Christ is the Lord of the harvest. Let us pray that many may be raised up and sent forth, who will labour in bringing souls to Christ. It is a sign that God is about to bestow some special mercy upon a people, when he stirs them up to pray for it. And commissions given to labourers in answer to prayer, are most likely to be successful.

Chapter 10

Chapter Outline

Directions to the apostles.   (16–42)

Verses 1-4

The word "apostle" signifies messenger; they were Christ's messengers, sent forth to proclaim his kingdom. Christ gave them power to heal all manner of sickness. In the grace of the gospel there is a slave for every sore, a remedy for every malady. There is no spiritual disease, but there is power in Christ for the cure of it. There names are recorded, and it is their honour; yet they had more reason to rejoice that their names were written in heaven, while the high and mighty names of the great ones of the earth are buried in the dust.

Verses 5-15

The Gentiles must not have the gospel brought them, till the Jews have refused it. This restraint on the apostles was only in their first mission. Wherever they went they must proclaim, The kingdom of heaven is at hand. They preached, to establish the faith; the kingdom, to animate the hope; of heaven, to inspire the love of heavenly things, and the contempt of earthly; which is at hand, that men may prepare for it without delay. Christ gave power to work miracles for the confirming of their doctrine. This is not necessary now that the kingdom of God is come. It showed that the intent of the doctrine they preached, was to heal sick souls, and to raise those that were dead in sin. In proclaiming the gospel of free grace for the healing and saving of men's souls, we must above all avoid the appearance of the spirit of an hireling. They are directed what to do in strange towns and cities. The servant of Christ is the ambassador of peace to whatever place he is sent. His message is even to the vilest sinners, yet it behoves him to find out the best persons in every place. It becomes us to pray heartily for all, and to conduct ourselves courteously to all. They are directed how to act as to those that refused them. The whole counsel of God must be declared, and those who will not attend to the gracious message, must be shown that their state is dangerous. This should be seriously laid to heart by all that hear the gospel, lest their privileges only serve to increase their condemnation.

Verses 16-42

Our Lord warned his disciples to prepare for persecution. They were to avoid all things which gave advantage to their enemies, all meddling with worldly or political concerns, all appearance of evil or selfishness, and all underhand measures. Christ foretold troubles, not only that the troubles might not be a surprise, but that they might confirm their faith. He tells them what they should suffer, and from whom. Thus Christ has dealt fairly and faithfully with us, in telling us the worst we can meet with in his service; and he would have us deal so with ourselves, in sitting down and counting the cost. Persecutors are worse than beasts, in that they prey upon those of their own kind. The strongest bonds of love and duty, have often been broken through from enmity against Christ. Sufferings from friends and relations are very grievous; nothing cuts more. It appears plainly, that all who will live godly in Christ Jesus must suffer persecution; and we must expect to enter into the kingdom of God through many tribulations. With these predictions of trouble, are counsels and comforts for a time of trial. The disciples of Christ are hated and persecuted as serpents, and their ruin is sought, and they need the serpent's wisdom. Be ye harmless as doves. Not only, do nobody any hurt, but bear nobody any ill-will. Prudent care there must be, but not an anxious, perplexing thought; let this care be cast upon God. The disciples of Christ must think more how to do well, than how to speak well. In case of great peril, the disciples of Christ may go out of the way of danger, though they must not go out of the way of duty. No sinful, unlawful means may be used to escape; for then it is not a door of God's opening. The fear of man brings a snare, a perplexing snare, that disturbs our peace; an entangling snare, by which we are drawn into sin; and, therefore, it must be striven and prayed against. Tribulation, distress, and persecution cannot take away God's love to them, or theirs to him. Fear Him, who is able to destroy both soul and body in hell. They must deliver their message publicly, for all are deeply concerned in the doctrine of the gospel. The whole counsel of God must be made known, Ac 20:27. Christ shows them why they should be of good cheer. Their sufferings witnessed against those who oppose his gospel. When God calls us to speak for him, we may depend on him to teach us what to say. A believing prospect of the end of our troubles, will be of great use to support us under them. They may be borne to the end, because the sufferers shall be borne up under them. The strength shall be according to the day. And it is great encouragement to those who are doing Christ's work, that it is a work which shall certainly be done. See how the care of Providence extends to all creatures, even to the sparrows. This should silence all the fears of God's people; Ye are of more value than many sparrows. And the very hairs of your head are all numbered. This denotes the account God takes and keeps of his people. It is our duty, not only to believe in Christ, but to profess that faith, in suffering for him, when we are called to it, as well as in serving him. That denial of Christ only is here meant which is persisted in, and that confession only can have the blessed recompence here promised, which is the real and constant language of faith and love. Religion is worth every thing; all who believe the truth of it, will come up to the price, and make every thing else yield to it. Christ will lead us through sufferings, to glory with him. Those are best prepared for the life to come, that sit most loose to this present life. Though the kindness done to Christ's disciples be ever so small, yet if there be occasion for it, and ability to do no more, it shall be accepted. Christ does not say that they deserve a reward; for we cannot merit any thing from the hand of God; but they shall receive a reward from the free gift of God. Let us boldly confess Christ, and show love to him in all things.

Chapter 11

Chapter Outline

Verse 1

Our Divine Redeemer never was weary of his labour of love; and we should not be weary of well-doing, for in due season we shall reap, if we faint not.

Verses 2-6

Some think that John sent this inquiry for his own satisfaction. Where there is true faith, yet there may be a mixture of unbelief. The remaining unbelief of good men may sometimes, in an hour of temptation; call in question the most important truths. But we hope that John's faith did not fail in this matter, and that he only desired to have it strengthened and confirmed. Others think that John sent his disciples to Christ for their satisfaction. Christ points them to what they heard and saw. Christ's gracious condescensions and compassions to the poor, show that it was he that should bring to the world the tender mercies of our God. Those things which men see and hear, if compared with the Scriptures, direct in what way salvation is to be found. It is difficult to conquer prejudices, and dangerous not to conquer them; but those who believe in Christ, their faith will be found so much the more to praise, and honour, and glory.

Verses 7-15

What Christ said concerning John, was not only for his praise, but for the people's profit. Those who attend on the word will be called to give an account of their improvements. Do we think when the sermon is done, the care is over? No, then the greatest of the care begins. John was a self-denying man, dead to all the pomps of the world and the pleasures of sense. It becomes people, in all their appearances, to be consistent with their character and their situation. John was a great and good man, yet not perfect; therefore he came short of glorified saints. The least in heaven knows more, loves more, and does more in praising God, and receives more from him, than the greatest in this world. But by the kingdom of heaven here, is rather to be understood the kingdom of grace, the gospel dispensation in its power and purity. What reason we have to be thankful that our lot is cast in the days of the kingdom of heaven, under such advantages of light and love! Multitudes were wrought upon by the ministry of John, and became his disciples. And those strove for a place in this kingdom, that one would think had no right nor title to it, and so seemed to be intruders. It shows us what fervency and zeal are required of all. Self must be denied; the bent, the frame and temper of the mind must be altered. Those who will have an interest in the great salvation, will have it upon any terms, and not think them hard, nor quit their hold without a blessing. The things of God are of great and common concern. God requires no more from us than the right use of the faculties he has given us. People are ignorant, because they will not learn.

Verses 16-24

Christ reflects on the scribes and Pharisees, who had a proud conceit of themselves. He likens their behaviour to children's play, who being out of temper without reason, quarrel with all the attempts of their fellows to please them, or to get them to join in the plays for which they used to assemble. The cavils of worldly men are often very trifling and show great malice. Something they have to urge against every one, however excellent and holy. Christ, who was undefiled, and separate from sinners, is here represented as in league with them, and polluted by them. The most unspotted innocence will not always be a defence against reproach. Christ knew that the hearts of the Jews were more bitter and hardened against his miracles and doctrines, than those of Tyre and Sidon would have been; therefore their condemnation would be the greater. The Lord exercises his almighty power, yet he punishes none more than they deserve, and never withholds the knowledge of the truth from those who long after it.

Verses 25-30

It becomes children to be grateful. When we come to God as a Father, we must remember that he is Lord of heaven and earth, which obliges us to come to him with reverence as to the sovereign Lord of all; yet with confidence, as one able to defend us from evil, and to supply us with all good. Our blessed Lord added a remarkable declaration, that the Father had delivered into his hands all power, authority, and judgment. We are indebted to Christ for all the revelation we have of God the Father's will and love, ever since Adam sinned. Our Saviour has invited all that labour and are heavy-laden, to come unto him. In some senses all men are so. Worldly men burden themselves with fruitless cares for wealth and honours; the gay and the sensual labour in pursuit of pleasures; the slave of Satan and his own lusts, is the merest drudge on earth. Those who labour to establish their own righteousness also labour in vain. The convinced sinner is heavy-laden with guilt and terror; and the tempted and afflicted believer has labours and burdens. Christ invites all to come to him for rest to their souls. He alone gives this invitation; men come to him, when, feeling their guilt and misery, and believing his love and power to help, they seek him in fervent prayer. Thus it is the duty and interest of weary and heavy-laden sinners, to come to Jesus Christ. This is the gospel call; Whoever will, let him come. All who thus come will receive rest as Christ's gift, and obtain peace and comfort in their hearts. But in coming to him they must take his yoke, and submit to his authority. They must learn of him all things, as to their comfort and obedience. He accepts the willing servant, however imperfect the services. Here we may find rest for our souls, and here only. Nor need we fear his yoke. His commandments are holy, just, and good. It requires self-denial, and exposes to difficulties, but this is abundantly repaid, even in this world, by inward peace and joy. It is a yoke that is lined with love. So powerful are the assistances he gives us, so suitable the encouragements, and so strong the consolations to be found in the way of duty, that we may truly say, it is a yoke of pleasantness. The way of duty is the way of rest. The truths Christ teaches are such as we may venture our souls upon. Such is the Redeemer's mercy; and why should the labouring and burdened sinner seek for rest from any other quarter? Let us come to him daily, for deliverance from wrath and guilt, from sin and Satan, from all our cares, fears, and sorrows. But forced obedience, far from being easy and light, is a heavy burden. In vain do we draw near to Jesus with our lips, while the heart is far from him. Then come to Jesus to find rest for your souls.

Chapter 12

Chapter Outline

Verses 1-8

Being in the corn-fields, the disciples began to pluck the ears of corn: the law of God allowed it, De 23:25. This was slender provision for Christ and his disciples; but they were content with it. The Pharisees did not quarrel with them for taking another man's corn, but for doing it on the sabbath day. Christ came to free his followers, not only from the corruptions of the Pharisees, but from their unscriptural rules, and justified what they did. The greatest shall not have their lusts indulged, but the meanest shall have their wants considered. Those labours are lawful on the sabbath day which are necessary, and sabbath rest is to froward, not to hinder sabbath worship. Needful provision for health and food is to be made; but when servants are kept at home, and families become a scene of hurry and confusion on the Lord's day, to furnish a feast for visitors, or for indulgence, the case is very different. Such things as these, and many others common among professors, are to be blamed. The resting on the sabbath was ordained for man's good, De 5:14. No law must be understood so as to contradict its own end. And as Christ is the Lord of the sabbath, it is fit the day and the work of it should be dedicated to him.

Verses 9-13

Christ shows that works of mercy are lawful and proper to be done on the Lord's day. There are more ways of doing well upon sabbath days, than by the duties of worship: attending the sick, relieving the poor, helping those who need speedy relief, teaching the young to care for their souls; these are doing good: and these must be done from love and charity, with humility and self-denial, and shall be accepted, Ge 4:7. This, like other cures which Christ wrought, had a spiritual meaning. By nature our hands are withered, and we are unable of ourselves to do any thing that is good. Christ only, by the power of his grace, cures us; he heals the withered hand by putting life into the dead soul, works in us both to will and to do: for, with the command, there is a promise of grace given by the word.

Verses 14-21

The Pharisees took counsel to find some accusation, that Jesus might be condemned to death. Aware of their design, as his time was not come, he retired from that place. Face does not more exactly answer to face in water, than the character of Christ drawn by the prophet, to his temper and conduct as described by the evangelists. Let us with cheerful confidence commit our souls to so kind and faithful a Friend. Far from breaking, he will strengthen the bruised reed; far from quenching the smoking flax, or wick nearly out, he will rather blow it up into a flame. Let us lay aside contentious and angry debates; let us receive one another as Christ receives us. And while encouraged by the gracious kindness of our Lord, we should pray that his Spirit may rest upon us, and make us able to copy his example.

Verses 22-30

A soul under Satan's power, and led captive by him, is blind in the things of God, and dumb at the throne of grace; sees nothing, and says nothing to the purpose. Satan blinds the eyes by unbelief, and seals up the lips from prayer. The more people magnified Christ, the more desirous the Pharisees were to vilify him. It was evident that if Satan aided Jesus in casting out devils, the kingdom of hell was divided against itself; how then could it stand! And if they said that Jesus cast out devils by the prince of the devils, they could not prove that their children cast them out by any other power. There are two great interests in the world; and when unclean spirits are cast out by the Holy Spirit, in the conversion of sinners to a life of faith and obedience, the kingdom of God is come unto us. All who do not aid or rejoice in such a change are against Christ.

Verses 31, 32

Here is a gracious assurance of the pardon of all sin upon gospel terms. Christ herein has set an example to the sons of men, to be ready to forgive words spoken against them. But humble and conscientious believers, at times are tempted to think they have committed the unpardonable sin, while those who have come the nearest to it, seldom have any fear about it. We may be sure that those who indeed repent and believe the gospel, have not committed this sin, or any other of the same kind; for repentance and faith are the special gifts of God, which he would not bestow on any man, if he were determined never to pardon him; and those who fear they have committed this sin, give a good sign that they have not. The trembling, contrite sinner, has the witness in himself that this is not his case.

Verses 33-37

Men's language discovers what country they are of, likewise what manner of spirit they are of. The heart is the fountain, words are the streams. A troubled fountain, and a corrupt spring, must send forth muddy and unpleasant streams. Nothing but the salt of grace, cast into the spring, will heal the waters, season the speech, and purify the corrupt communication. An evil man has an evil treasure in his heart, and out of it brings forth evil things. Lusts and corruptions, dwelling and reigning in the heart, are an evil treasure, out of which the sinner brings forth bad words and actions, to dishonour God, and hurt others. Let us keep constant watch over ourselves, that we may speak words agreeable to the Christian character.

Verses 38-45

Though Christ is always ready to hear and answer holy desires and prayers, yet those who ask amiss, ask and have not. Signs were granted to those who desired them to confirm their faith, as Abraham and Gideon; but denied to those who demanded them to excuse their unbelief. The resurrection of Christ from the dead by his own power, called here the sign of the prophet Jonah, was the great proof of Christ's being the Messiah. As Jonah was three days and three nights in the whale, and then came out again alive, thus Christ would be so long in the grave, and then rise again. The Ninevites would shame the Jews for not repenting; the queen of Sheba, for not believing in Christ. And we have no such cares to hinder us, we come not to Christ upon such uncertainties. This parable represents the case of the Jewish church and nation. It is also applicable to all those who hear the word of God, and are in part reformed, but not truly converted. The unclean spirit leaves for a time, but when he returns, he finds Christ is not there to shut him out; the heart is swept by outward reformation, but garnished by preparation to comply with evil suggestions, and the man becomes a more decided enemy of the truth. Every heart is the residence of unclean spirits, except those which are temples of the Holy Ghost, by faith in Christ.

Verses 46-50

Christ's preaching was plain, easy, and familiar, and suited to his hearers. His mother and brethren stood without, desiring to speak with him, when they should have been standing within, desiring to hear him. Frequently, those who are nearest to the means of knowledge and grace are most negligent. We are apt to neglect that which we think we may have any day, forgetting that to-morrow is not ours. We often meet with hinderances in our work from friends about us, and are taken off by care for the things of this life, from the concerns of our souls. Christ was so intent on his work, that no natural or other duty took him from it. Not that, under pretence of religion, we may be disrespectful to parents, or unkind to relations; but the lesser duty must stand by, while the greater is done. Let us cease from men, and cleave to Christ; let us look upon every Christian, in whatever condition of life, as the brother, sister, or mother of the Lord of glory; let us love, respect, and be kind to them, for his sake, and after his example.

Chapter 13

Chapter Outline

Verses 1-23

Jesus entered into a boat that he might be the less pressed, and be the better heard by the people. By this he teaches us in the outward circumstances of worship not to covet that which is stately, but to make the best of the conveniences God in his providence allots to us. Christ taught in parables. Thereby the things of God were made more plain and easy to those willing to be taught, and at the same time more difficult and obscure to those who were willingly ignorant. The parable of the sower is plain. The seed sown is the word of God. The sower is our Lord Jesus Christ, by himself, or by his ministers. Preaching to a multitude is sowing the corn; we know not where it will light. Some sort of ground, though we take ever so much pains with it, brings forth no fruit to purpose, while the good soil brings forth plentifully. So it is with the hearts of men, whose different characters are here described by four sorts of ground. Careless, trifling hearers, are an easy prey to Satan; who, as he is the great murderer of souls, so he is the great thief of sermons, and will be sure to rob us of the word, if we take not care to keep it. Hypocrites, like the stony ground, often get the start of true Christians in the shows of profession. Many are glad to hear a good sermon, who do not profit by it. They are told of free salvation, of the believer's privileges, and the happiness of heaven; and, without any change of heart, without any abiding conviction of their own depravity, their need of a Saviour, or the excellence of holiness, they soon profess an unwarranted assurance. But when some heavy trial threatens them, or some sinful advantage may be had, they give up or disguise their profession, or turn to some easier system. Worldly cares are fitly compared to thorns, for they came in with sin, and are a fruit of the curse; they are good in their place to stop a gap, but a man must be well armed that has much to do with them; they are entangling, vexing, scratching, and their end is to be burned, Heb 6:8. Worldly cares are great hinderances to our profiting by the word of God. The deceitfulness of riches does the mischief; they cannot be said to deceive us unless we put our trust in them, then they choke the good seed. What distinguished the good ground was fruitfulness. By this true Christians are distinguished from hypocrites. Christ does not say that this good ground has no stones in it, or no thorns; but none that could hinder its fruitfulness. All are not alike; we should aim at the highest, to bring forth most fruit. The sense of hearing cannot be better employed than in hearing God's word; and let us look to ourselves that we may know what sort of hearers we are.

Verses 24-30

, 36–43 This parable represents the present and future state of the gospel church; Christ's care of it, the devil's enmity against it, the mixture there is in it of good and bad in this world, and the separation between them in the other world. So prone is fallen man to sin, that if the enemy sow the tares, he may go his way, they will spring up, and do hurt; whereas, when good seed is sown, it must be tended, watered, and fenced. The servants complained to their master; Sir, didst thou not sow good seed in thy field? No doubt he did; whatever is amiss in the church, we are sure it is not from Christ. Though gross transgressors, and such as openly oppose the gospel, ought to be separated from the society of the faithful, yet no human skill can make an exact separation. Those who oppose must not be cut off, but instructed, and that with meekness. And though good and bad are together in this world, yet at the great day they shall be parted; then the righteous and the wicked shall be plainly known; here sometimes it is hard to distinguish between them. Let us, knowing the terrors of the Lord, not do iniquity. At death, believers shall shine forth to themselves; at the great day they shall shine forth before all the world. They shall shine by reflection, with light borrowed from the Fountain of light. Their sanctification will be made perfect, and their justification published. May we be found of that happy number.

Verses 31-35

The scope of the parable of the seed sown, is to show that the beginnings of the gospel would be small, but its latter end would greatly increase; in this way the work of grace in the heart, the kingdom of God within us, would be carried on. In the soul where grace truly is, it will grow really; though perhaps at first not to be discerned, it will at last come to great strength and usefulness. The preaching of the gospel works like leaven in the hearts of those who receive it. The leaven works certainly, so does the word, yet gradually. It works silently, and without being seen, Mr 4:26–29, yet strongly; without noise, for so is the way of the Spirit, but without fail. Thus it was in the world. The apostles, by preaching the gospel, hid a handful of leaven in the great mass of mankind. It was made powerful by the Spirit of the Lord of hosts, who works, and none can hinder. Thus it is in the heart. When the gospel comes into the soul, it works a thorough change; it spreads itself into all the powers and faculties of the soul, and alters the property even of the members of the body, Ro 6:13. From these parables we are taught to expect a gradual progress; therefore let us inquire, Are we growing in grace? and in holy principles and habits?

Verses 44-52

Here are four parables. 1. That of the treasure hid in the field. Many slight the gospel, because they look only upon the surface of the field. But all who search the Scriptures, so as in them to find Christ and eternal life, Joh 5:39, will discover such treasure in this field as makes it unspeakably valuable; they make it their own upon any terms. Though nothing can be given as a price for this salvation, yet much must be given up for the sake of it. 2. All the children of men are busy; one would be rich, another would be honourable, another would be learned; but most are deceived, and take up with counterfeits for pearls. Jesus Christ is a Pearl of great price; in having him, we have enough to make us happy here and for ever. A man may buy gold too dear, but not this Pearl of great price. When the convinced sinner sees Christ as the gracious Saviour, all things else become worthless to his thoughts. 3. The world is a vast sea, and men, in their natural state, are like the fishes. Preaching the gospel is casting a net into this sea, to catch something out of it, for His glory who has the sovereignty of this sea. Hypocrites and true Christians shall be parted: miserable is the condition of those that shall then be cast away. 4. A skilful, faithful minister of the gospel, is a scribe, well versed in the things of the gospel, and able to teach them. Christ compares him to a good householder, who brings forth fruits of last year's growth and this year's gathering, abundance and variety, to entertain his friends. Old experiences and new observations, all have their use. Our place is at Christ's feet, and we must daily learn old lessons over again, and new ones also.

Verses 53-58

Christ repeats his offer to those who have repulsed them. They upbraid him, Is not this the carpenter's son? Yes, it is true he was reputed to be so; and no disgrace to be the son of an honest tradesman; they should have respected him the more because he was one of themselves, but therefore they despised him. He did not many mighty works there, because of their unbelief. Unbelief is the great hinderance to Christ's favours. Let us keep faithful to him as the Saviour who has made our peace with God.

Chapter 14

Chapter Outline

Death of John the Baptist.	(1–12)
Five thousand people miraculously fed.	(13–21)
Jesus walks upon the sea.	(22–33)
Jesus healing the sick.	(34–36)

Verses 1-12

The terror and reproach of conscience, which Herod, like other daring offenders, could not shake off, are proofs and warnings of a future judgment, and of future misery to them. But there may be the terror of convictions, where there is not the truth of conversion. When men pretend to favour the gospel, yet live in evil, we must not favour their self-delusion, but must deliver our consciences as John did. The world may call this rudeness and blind zeal. False professors, or timid Christians, may censure it as want of civility; but the most powerful enemies can go no further than the Lord sees good to permit. Herod feared that the putting of John to death might raise a rebellion among the people, which it did not; but he never feared it might stir up his own conscience against him, which it did. Men fear being hanged for what they do not fear being damned for. And times of carnal mirth and jollity are convenient times for carrying on bad designs against God's people. Herod would profusely reward a worthless dance, while imprisonment and death were the recompence of the man of God who sought the salvation of his soul. But there was real malice to John beneath his consent, or else Herod would have found ways to get clear of his promise. When the under shepherds are smitten, the sheep need not be scattered while they have the Great Shepherd to go to. And it is better to be drawn to Christ by want and loss, than not to come to him at all.

Verses 13-21

When Christ and his word withdraw, it is best for us to follow, seeking the means of grace for our souls before any worldly advantages. The presence of Christ and his gospel, makes a desert not only tolerable, but desirable. This little supply of bread was increased by Christ's creating power, till the whole multitude were satisfied. In seeking the welfare of men's souls, we should have compassion on their bodies likewise. Let us also remember always to crave a blessing on our meals, and learn to avoid all waste, as frugality is the proper source of liberality. See in this miracle an emblem of the Bread of life, which came down from heaven to sustain our perishing souls. The provisions of Christ's gospel appear mean and scanty to the world, yet they satisfy all that feed on him in their hearts by faith with thanksgiving.

Verses 22-33

Those are not Christ's followers who cannot enjoy being alone with God and their own hearts. It is good, upon special occasions, and when we find our hearts enlarged, to continue long in secret prayer, and in pouring out our hearts before the Lord. It is no new thing for Christ's disciples to meet with storms in the way of duty, but he thereby shows himself with the more grace to them and for them. He can take what way he pleases to save his people. But even appearances of deliverance sometimes occasion trouble and perplexity to God's people, from mistakes about Christ. Nothing ought to affright those that have Christ near them, and know he is theirs; not death itself. Peter walked upon the water, not for diversion or to boast of it, but to go to Jesus; and in that he was thus wonderfully borne up. Special supports are promised, and are to be expected, but only in spiritual pursuits; nor can we ever come to Jesus, unless we are upheld by his power. Christ bade Peter come, not only that he might walk upon the water, and so know his Lord's power, but that he might know his own weakness. And the Lord often lets his servants have their choice, to humble and prove them, and to show the greatness of his power and grace. When we look off from Christ, and look at the greatness of opposing difficulties, we shall begin to fall; but when we call to him, he will stretch out his arm, and save us. Christ is the great Saviour; those who would be saved, must come to him, and cry to him, for salvation; we are never brought to this, till we find ourselves sinking: the sense of need drives us to him. He rebuked Peter. Could we but believe more, we should suffer less. The weakness of faith, and the prevailing of our doubts, displease our Lord Jesus, for there is no good reason why Christ's disciples should be of a doubtful mind. Even in a stormy day he is to them a very present help. None but the world's Creator could multiply the loaves, none but its Governor could tread upon the waters of the sea: the disciples yield to the evidence, and confess their faith. They were suitably affected, and worshipped Christ. He that comes to God, must believe; and he that believes in God, will come, Heb 11:6.

Verses 34-36

Whithersoever Christ went, he was doing good. They brought unto him all that were diseased. They came humbly beseeching him to help them. The experiences of others may direct and encourage us in seeking for Christ. As many as touched, were made perfectly whole. Those whom Christ heals, he heals perfectly. Were men more acquainted with Christ, and with the diseased state of their souls, they would flock to receive his healing influences. The healing virtue was not in the finger, but in their faith; or rather, it was in Christ, whom their faith took hold upon.

Chapter 15

Chapter Outline

Jesus discourses about human traditions.	(1–9)
He warns against things which really defile.	(10–20)
He heals the daughter of a Syrophenician woman.	(21–28)
Jesus heals the sick, and miraculously feeds four thousand.	(29–39)

Verses 1-9

Additions to God's laws reflect upon his wisdom, as if he had left out something which was needed, and which man could supply; in one way or other they always lead men to disobey God. How thankful ought we to be for the written word of God! Never let us think that the religion of the Bible can be improved by any human addition, either in doctrine or practice. Our blessed Lord spoke of their traditions as inventions of their own, and pointed out one instance in which this was very clear, that of their transgressing the fifth commandment. When a parent's wants called for assistance, they pleaded, that they had devoted to the temple all they could spare, even though they did not part with it, and therefore their parents must expect nothing from them. This was making the command of God of no effect. The doom of hypocrites is put in a little compass; "In vain do they worship me." It will neither please God, nor profit themselves; they trust in vanity, and vanity will be their recompence.

Verses 10-20

Christ shows that the defilement they ought to fear, was not from what entered their mouths as food, but from what came out of their mouths, which showed the wickedness of their hearts. Nothing will last in the soul but the regenerating graces of the Holy Spirit; and nothing should be admitted into the church but what is from above; therefore, whoever is offended by a plain, seasonable declaration of the truth, we should not be troubled at it. The disciples ask to be better taught as to this matter. Where a weak head doubts concerning any word of Christ, an upright heart and a willing mind seek for instruction. It is the heart that is desperately wicked, Jer 17:9, for there is no sin in word or deed, which was not first in the heart. They all come out of the man, and are fruits of that wickedness which is in the heart, and is wrought there. When Christ teaches, he will show men the deceitfulness and wickedness of their own hearts; he will teach them to humble themselves, and to seek to be cleansed in the Fountain opened for sin and uncleanness.

Verses 21-28

The dark corners of the country, the most remote, shall share Christ's influences; afterwards the ends of the earth shall see his salvation. The distress and trouble of her family brought a woman to Christ; and though it is need that drives us to Christ, yet we shall not therefore be driven from him. She did not limit Christ to any particular instance of mercy, but mercy, mercy, is what she begged for: she pleads not merit, but depends upon mercy. It is the duty of parents to pray for their children, and to be earnest in prayer for them, especially for their souls. Have you a son, a daughter, grievously vexed with a proud devil, an unclean devil, a malicious devil, led captive by him at his will? this is a case more deplorable than that of bodily possession, and you must bring them by faith and prayer to Christ, who alone is able to heal them. Many methods of Christ's providence, especially of his grace, in dealing with his people, which are dark and perplexing, may be explained by this story, which teaches that there may be love in Christ's heart while there are frowns in his face; and it encourages us, though he seems ready to slay us, yet to trust in him. Those whom Christ intends most to honour, he humbles to feel their own unworthiness. A proud, unhumbled heart would not have borne this; but she turned it into an argument to support her request. The state of this woman is an emblem of the state of a sinner, deeply conscious of the misery of his soul. The least of Christ is precious to a believer, even the very crumbs of the Bread of life. Of all graces, faith honours Christ most; therefore of all graces Christ honours faith most. He cured her daughter. He spake, and it was done. From hence let such as seek help from the Lord, and receive no gracious answer, learn to turn even their unworthiness and discouragements into pleas for mercy.

Verses 29-39

Whatever our case is, the only way to find ease and relief, is to lay it at Christ's feet, to submit it to him, and refer it to his disposal. Those who would have spiritual healing from Christ, must be ruled as he pleases. See what work sin has made; what various diseases human bodies are subject to. Here were such diseases as fancy could neither guess the cause nor the cure of, yet these were subject to the command of Christ. The spiritual cures that Christ works are wonderful. When blind souls are made to see by faith, the dumb to speak in prayer, the maimed and the lame to walk in holy obedience, it is to be wondered at. His power was also shown to the multitude, in the plentiful provision he made for them: the manner is much the same as before. All did eat, and were filled. Those whom Christ feeds, he fills. With Christ there is bread enough, and to spare; supplies of grace for more than seek it, and for those that seek for more. Christ sent away the people. Though he had fed them twice, they must not look for miracles to find their daily bread. Let them go home to their callings and their own tables. Lord, increase our faith, and pardon our unbelief, teaching us to live upon thy fulness and bounty, for all things pertaining to this life, and that which is to come.

Chapter 16

Chapter Outline

Verses 1-4

The Pharisees and Sadducees were opposed to each other in principles and in conduct; yet they joined against Christ. But they desired a sign of their own choosing: they despised those signs which relieved the necessity of the sick and sorrowful, and called for something else which would gratify the curiosity of the proud. It is great hypocrisy, when we slight the signs of God's ordaining, to seek for signs of our own devising.

Verses 5-12

Christ speaks of spiritual things under a similitude, and the disciples misunderstand him of carnal things. He took it ill that they should think him as thoughtful about bread as they were; that they should be so little acquainted with his way of preaching. Then understood they what he meant. Christ teaches by the Spirit of wisdom in the heart, opening the understanding to the Spirit of revelation in the word.

Verses 13-20

Peter, for himself and his brethren, said that they were assured of our Lord's being the promised Messiah, the Son of the living God. This showed that they believed Jesus to be more than man. Our Lord declared Peter to be blessed, as the teaching of God made him differ from his unbelieving countrymen. Christ added that he had named him Peter, in allusion to his stability or firmness in professing the truth. The word translated "rock," is not the same word as Peter, but is of a similar meaning. Nothing can be more wrong than to suppose that Christ meant the person of Peter was the rock. Without doubt Christ himself is the Rock, the tried foundation of the church; and woe to him that attempts to lay any other! Peter's confession is this rock as to doctrine. If Jesus be not the Christ, those that own him are not of the church, but deceivers and deceived. Our Lord next declared the authority with which Peter would be invested. He spoke in the name of his brethren, and this related to them as well as to him. They had no certain knowledge of the characters of men, and were liable to mistakes and sins in their own conduct; but they were kept from error in stating the way of acceptance and salvation, the rule of obedience, the believer's character and experience, and the final doom of unbelievers and hypocrites. In such matters their decision was right, and it was confirmed in heaven. But all pretensions of any man, either to absolve or retain men's sins, are blasphemous and absurd. None can forgive sins but God only. And this binding and loosing, in the common language of the Jews, signified to forbid and to allow, or to teach what is lawful or unlawful.

Verses 21-23

Christ reveals his mind to his people gradually. From that time, when the apostles had made the full confession of Christ, that he was the Son of God, he began to show them of his sufferings. He spake this to set right the mistakes of his disciples about the outward pomp and power of his kingdom. Those that follow Christ, must not expect great or high things in this world. Peter would have Christ to dread suffering as much as he did; but we mistake, if we measure Christ's love and patience by our own. We do not read of any thing said or done by any of his disciples, at any time, that Christ resented so much as this. Whoever takes us from that which is good, and would make us fear to do too much for God, speaks Satan's language. Whatever appears to be a temptation to sin, must be resisted with abhorrence, and not be parleyed with. Those that decline suffering for Christ, savour more of the things of man than of the things of God.

Verses 24-28

A true disciple of Christ is one that does follow him in duty, and shall follow him to glory. He is one that walks in the same way Christ walked in, is led by his Spirit, and treads in his steps, whithersoever he goes. "Let him deny himself." If self-denial be a hard lesson, it is no more than what our Master learned and practised, to redeem us, and to teach us. "Let him take up his cross." The cross is here put for every trouble that befalls us. We are apt to think we could bear another's cross better than our own; but that is best which is appointed us, and we ought to make the best of it. We must not by our rashness and folly pull crosses down upon our own heads, but must take them up when they are in our way. If any man will have the name and credit of a disciple, let him follow Christ in the work and duty of a disciple. If all worldly things are worthless when compared with the life of the body, how forcible the same argument with respect to the soul and its state of never-ending happiness or misery! Thousands lose their souls for the most trifling gain, or the most worthless indulgence, nay, often from mere sloth and negligence. Whatever is the object for which men forsake Christ, that is the price at which Satan buys their souls. Yet one soul is worth more than all the world. This is Christ's judgment upon the matter; he knew the price of souls, for he redeemed them; nor would he underrate the world, for he made it. The dying transgressor cannot purchase one hour's respite to seek mercy for his perishing soul. Let us then learn rightly to value our souls, and Christ as the only Saviour of them.

Chapter 17

Chapter Outline

Verses 1-13

Now the disciples beheld somewhat of Christ's glory, as of the only begotten of the Father. It was intended to support their faith, when they would have to witness his crucifixion; and would give them an idea of the glory prepared for them, when changed by his power and made like him. The apostles were overcome by the glorious sight. Peter thought that it was most desirable to continue there, and to go no more down to meet the sufferings of which he was so unwilling to hear. In this he knew not what he said. We are wrong, if we look for a heaven here upon earth. Whatever tabernacles we propose to make for ourselves in this world, we must always remember to ask Christ's leave. That sacrifice was not yet offered, without which the souls of sinful men could not have been saved; and important services were to be done by Peter and his brethren. While Peter spoke, a bright cloud overshadowed them, an emblem of the Divine presence and glory. Ever since man sinned, and heard God's voice in the garden, unusual appearances of God have been terrible to man. They fell prostrate to the earth, till Jesus encouraged them; when looking round, they beheld only their Lord as they commonly saw him. We must pass through varied experiences in our way to glory; and when we return to the world after an ordinance, it must be our care to take Christ with us, and then it may be our comfort that he is with us.

Verses 14-21

The case of afflicted children should be presented to God by faithful and fervent prayer. Christ cured the child. Though the people were perverse, and Christ was provoked, yet care was taken of the child. When all other helps and succours fail, we are welcome to Christ, may trust in him, and in his power and goodness. See here an emblem of Christ's undertaking as our Redeemer. It encourages parents to bring children to Christ, whose souls are under Satan's power; he is able to heal them, and as willing as he is able. Not only bring them to Christ by prayer, but bring them to the word of Christ; to means by which Satan's strong-holds in the soul are beaten down. It is good for us to distrust ourselves and our own strength; but it is displeasing to Christ when we distrust any power derived from him, or granted by him. There was also something in the malady which rendered the cure difficult. The extraordinary power of Satan must not discourage our faith, but quicken us to more earnestness in praying to God for the increase of it. Do we wonder to see Satan's bodily possession of this young man from a child, when we see his spiritual possession of every son of Adam from the fall!

Verses 22, 23

Christ perfectly knew all things that should befall him, yet undertook the work of our redemption, which strongly shows his love. What outward debasement and Divine glory was the life of the Redeemer! And all his humiliation ended in his exaltation. Let us learn to endure the cross, to despise riches and worldly honours, and to be content with his will.

Verses 24-27

Peter felt sure that his Master was ready to do what was right. Christ spoke first to give him proof that no thought can be withholden from him. We must never decline our duty for fear of giving offence; but we must sometimes deny ourselves in our worldly interests, rather than give offence. However the money was lodged in the fish, He who knows all things alone could know it, and only almighty power could bring it to Peter's hook. The power and the poverty of Christ should be mentioned together. If called by providence to be poor, like our Lord, let us trust in his power, and our God shall supply all our need, according to his riches in glory by Christ Jesus. In the way of obedience, in the course, perhaps, of our usual calling, as he helped Peter, so he will help us. And if any sudden call should occur, which we are not prepared to meet, let us not apply to others, till we first seek Christ.

Chapter 18

Chapter Outline

Verses 1-6

Christ spoke many words of his sufferings, but only one of his glory; yet the disciples fasten upon that, and overlook the others. Many love to hear and speak of privileges and glory, who are willing to pass by the thoughts of work and trouble. Our Lord set a little child before them, solemnly assuring them, that unless they were converted and made like little children, they could not enter his kingdom. Children, when very young, do not desire authority, do not regard outward distinctions, are free from malice, are teachable, and willingly dependent on their parents. It is true that they soon begin to show other dispositions, and other ideas are taught them at an early age; but these are marks of childhood, and render them proper emblems of the lowly minds of true Christians. Surely we need to be daily renewed in the spirit of our minds, that we may become simple and humble, as little children, and willing to be the least of all. Let us daily study this subject, and examine our own spirits.

Verses 7-14

Considering the cunning and malice of Satan, and the weakness and depravity of men's hearts, it is not possible but that there should be offences. God permits them for wise and holy ends, that those who are sincere, and those who are not, may be made known. Being told before, that there will be seducers, tempters, persecutors, and bad examples, let us stand on our guard. We must, as far as lawfully we may, part with what we cannot keep without being entangled by it in sin. The outward occasions of sin must be avoided. If we live after the flesh, we must die. If we, through the Spirit, mortify the deeds of the body, we shall live. Christ came into the world to save souls, and he will reckon severely with those who hinder the progress of others who are setting their faces heavenward. And shall any of us refuse attention to those whom the Son of God came to seek and to save? A father takes care of all his children, but is particularly tender of the little ones.

Verses 15-20

If a professed Christian is wronged by another, he ought not to complain of it to others, as is often done merely upon report, but to go to the offender privately, state the matter kindly, and show him his conduct. This would generally have all the desired effect with a true Christian, and the parties would be reconciled. The principles of these rules may be practised every where, and under all circumstances, though they are too much neglected by all. But how few try the method which Christ has expressly enjoined to all his disciples! In all our proceedings we should seek direction in prayer; we cannot too highly prize the promises of God. Wherever and whenever we meet in the name of Christ, we should consider him as present in the midst of us.

Verses 21-35

Though we live wholly on mercy and forgiveness, we are backward to forgive the offences of our brethren. This parable shows how much provocation God has from his family on earth, and how untoward his servants are. There are three things in the parable: 1. The master's wonderful clemency. The debt of sin is so great, that we are not able to pay it. See here what every sin deserves; this is the wages of sin, to be sold as a slave. It is the folly of many who are under strong convictions of their sins, to fancy they can make God satisfaction for the wrong they have done him. 2. The servant's unreasonable severity toward his fellow-servant, notwithstanding his lord's clemency toward him. Not that we may make light of wronging our neighbour, for that is also a sin against God; but we should not aggravate our neighbour's wronging us, nor study revenge. Let our complaints, both of the wickedness of the wicked, and of the afflictions of the afflicted, be brought to God, and left with him. 3. The master reproved his servant's cruelty. The greatness of sin magnifies the riches of pardoning mercy; and the comfortable sense of pardoning mercy, does much to dispose our hearts to forgive our brethren. We are not to suppose that God actually forgives men, and afterwards reckons their guilt to them to condemn them; but this latter part of the parable shows the false conclusions many draw as to their sins being pardoned, though their after-conduct shows that they never entered into the spirit, or experienced the sanctifying grace of the gospel. We do not forgive our offending brother aright, if we do not forgive from the heart. Yet this is not enough;

we must seek the welfare even of those who offend us. How justly will those be condemned, who, though they bear the Christian name, persist in unmerciful treatment of their brethren! The humbled sinner relies only on free, abounding mercy, through the ransom of the death of Christ. Let us seek more and more for the renewing grace of God, to teach us to forgive others as we hope for forgiveness from him.

Chapter 19

Chapter Outline

Verses 1, 2

Great multitudes followed Christ. When Christ departs, it is best for us to follow him. They found him as able and ready to help elsewhere, as he had been in Galilee; wherever the Sun of Righteousness arose, it was with healing in his wings.

Verses 3-12

The Pharisees were desirous of drawing something from Jesus which they might represent as contrary to the law of Moses. Cases about marriage have been numerous, and sometimes perplexed; made so, not by the law of God, but by the lusts and follies of men; and often people fix what they will do, before they ask for advice. Jesus replied by asking whether they had not read the account of the creation, and the first example of marriage; thus pointing out that every departure therefrom was wrong. That condition is best for us, and to be chosen and kept to accordingly, which is best for our souls, and tends most to prepare us for, and preserve us to, the kingdom of heaven. When the gospel is really embraced, it makes men kind relatives and faithful friends; it teaches them to bear the burdens, and to bear with the infirmities of those with whom they are connected, to consider their peace and happiness more than their own. As to ungodly persons, it is proper that they should be restrained by laws, from breaking the peace of society. And we learn that the married state should be entered upon with great seriousness and earnest prayer.

Verses 13-15

It is well when we come to Christ ourselves, and bring our children. Little children may be brought to Christ as needing, and being capable of receiving blessings from him, and having an interest in his intercession. We can but beg a blessing for them: Christ only can command the blessing. It is well for us, that Christ has more love and tenderness in him than the best of his disciples have. And let us learn of him not to discountenance any willing, well-meaning souls, in their seeking after Christ, though they are but weak. Those who are given to Christ, as part of his purchase, he will in no wise cast out. Therefore he takes it ill of all who forbid, and try to shut out those whom he has received. And all Christians should bring their children to the Saviour that he may bless them with spiritual blessings.

Verses 16-22

Christ knew that covetousness was the sin which most easily beset this young man; though he had got honestly what he possessed, yet he could not cheerfully part with it, and by this his want of sincerity was shown. Christ's promises make his precepts easy, and his yoke pleasant and very comfortable; yet this promise was as much a trial of the young man's faith, as the precept was of his charity and contempt of the world. It is required of us in following Christ, that we duly attend his ordinances, strictly follow his pattern, and cheerfully submit to his disposals; and this from love to him, and in dependence on him. To sell all, and give to the poor, will not serve, but we are to follow Christ. The gospel is the only remedy for lost sinners. Many abstain from gross vices who do not attend to their obligations to God. Thousands of instances of disobedience in thought, word, and deed, are marked against them in the book of God. Thus numbers forsake Christ, loving this present world: they feel convictions and desires, but they depart sorrowful, perhaps trembling. It behoves us to try ourselves in these matters, for the Lord will try us.

Verses 23-30

Though Christ spoke so strongly, few that have riches do not trust in them. How few that are poor are not tempted to envy! But men's earnestness in this matter is like their toiling to build a high wall to shut themselves and their children out of heaven. It should be satisfaction to those who are in a low condition, that they are not exposed to the temptations of a high and prosperous condition. If they live more hardly in this world than the rich, yet, if they get more easily to a better world, they have no reason to complain. Christ's words show that it is hard for a rich man to be a good Christian, and to be saved. The way to heaven is a narrow way to all, and the gate that leads into it, a strait gate; particularly so to rich people. More duties are expected from them than from others, and more sins easily beset them. It is hard not to be charmed with a smiling world. Rich people have a great account to make up for their opportunities above others. It is utterly impossible for a man that sets his heart upon his riches, to get to heaven. Christ used an expression, denoting a difficulty altogether unconquerable by the power of man. Nothing less than the almighty grace of God will enable a rich man to get over this difficulty. Who then can be saved? If riches hinder rich people, are not pride and sinful lusts found in those not rich, and as dangerous to them? Who can be saved? say the disciples. None, saith Christ, by any created power. The beginning, progress, and perfecting the work of salvation, depend wholly on the almighty power of God, to which all things are possible. Not that rich people can be saved in their worldliness, but that they should be saved from it. Peter said, We have forsaken all. Alas! it was but a poor all, only a few boats and nets; yet observe how Peter speaks, as if it had been some mighty thing. We are too apt to make the most of our services and sufferings, our expenses and losses, for Christ. However, Christ does not upbraid them; though it was but little that they had forsaken, yet it was their all, and as dear to them as if it had been more. Christ took it kindly that they left it to follow him; he accepts according to what a man hath. Our Lord's promise to the apostles is, that when the Son of man shall sit on the throne of his glory, he will make all things new, and they shall sit with him in judgement on those who will be judged according to their doctrine. This sets forth the honour, dignity, and authority of their office and ministry. Our Lord added, that every one who had forsaken possessions or comforts, for his sake and the gospel, would be recompensed at last. May God give us faith to rest our hope on this his promise; then we shall be ready for every service or sacrifice. Our Saviour, in the last verse, does away a mistake of some. The heavenly inheritance is not given as earthly ones are, but according to God's pleasure. Let us not trust in promising appearances or outward profession. Others may, for aught we know, become eminent in faith and holiness.

Chapter 20

Chapter Outline

Verses 1-16

The direct object of this parable seems to be, to show that though the Jews were first called into the vineyard, at length the gospel should be preached to the Gentiles, and they should be admitted to equal privileges and advantages with the Jews. The parable may also be applied more generally, and shows, 1. That God is debtor to no man. 2. That many who begin last, and promise little in religion, sometimes, by the blessing of God, arrive at a great deal of knowledge, grace, and usefulness. 3. That the recompense of reward will be given to the saints, but not according to the time of their conversion. It describes the state of the visible church, and explains the declaration that the last shall be first, and the first last, in its various references. Till we are hired into the service of God, we are standing all the day idle: a sinful state, though a state of drudgery to Satan, may be called a state of idleness. The market-place is the world, and from that we are called by the gospel. Come, come from this market-place. Work for God will not admit of trifling. A man may go idle to hell, but he that will go to heaven, must be diligent. The Roman penny was sevenpence halfpenny in our money, wages then enough for the day's support. This does not prove that the reward of our obedience to God is of works, or of debt; when we have done all, we are unprofitable servants; but it signifies that there is a reward set before us, yet let none, upon this presumption, put off repentance till they are old. Some were sent into the vineyard at the eleventh hour; but nobody had hired them before. The Gentiles came in at the eleventh hour; the gospel had not been before preached to them. Those that have had gospel offers made them at the third or sixth hour, and have refused them, will not have to say at the eleventh hour, as these had, No man has hired us. Therefore, not to discourage any, but to awaken all, be it remembered, that now is the accepted time. The riches of Divine grace are loudly murmured at, among proud Pharisees and nominal Christians. There is great proneness in us to think that we have too little, and others too much of the tokens of God's favour; and that we do too much, and others too little in the work of God. But if God gives grace to others, it is kindness to them, and no injustice to us. Carnal worldlings agree with God for their penny in this world; and choose their portion in this life. Obedient believers agree with God for their penny in the other world, and must remember they have so agreed. Didst not thou agree to take up with heaven as thy portion, thy all; wilt thou seek for happiness in the creature? God punishes none more than they deserve, and recompenses every service done for him; he therefore does no wrong to any, by showing extraordinary grace to some. See here the nature of envy. It is an evil eye, which is displeased at the good of others, and desires their hurt. It is a grief to ourselves, displeasing to God, and hurtful to our neighbours: it is a sin that has neither pleasure, profit, nor honour. Let us forego every proud claim, and seek for salvation as a free gift. Let us never envy or grudge, but rejoice and praise God for his mercy to others as well as to ourselves.

Verses 17-19

Christ is more particular here in foretelling his sufferings than before. And here, as before, he adds the mention of his resurrection and his glory, to that of his death and sufferings, to encourage his disciples, and comfort them. A believing view of our once crucified and now glorified Redeemer, is good to humble a proud, self-justifying disposition. When we consider the need of the humiliation and sufferings of the Son of God, in order to the salvation of perishing sinners, surely we must be aware of the freeness and richness ofDivine grace in our salvation.

Verses 20-28

The sons of Zebedee abused what Christ said to comfort the disciples. Some cannot have comforts but they turn them to a wrong purpose. Pride is a sin that most easily besets us; it is sinful ambition to outdo others in pomp and grandeur. To put down the vanity and ambition of their request, Christ leads them to the thoughts of their sufferings. It is a bitter cup that is to be drunk of; a cup of trembling, but not the cup of the wicked. It is but a cup, it is but a draught, bitter perhaps, but soon emptied; it is a cup in the hand of a Father, Joh 18:11. Baptism is an ordinance by which we are joined to the Lord in covenant and communion; and so is suffering for Christ, Eze 20:37; Isa 48:10. Baptism is an outward and visible sign of an inward and spiritual grace; and so is suffering for Christ, for unto us it is given, Php 1:29. But they knew not what Christ's cup was, nor what his baptism. Those are commonly most confident, who are least acquainted with the cross. Nothing makes more mischief among brethren, than desire of greatness. And we never find Christ's disciples quarrelling, but something of this was at the bottom of it. That man who labours most diligently, and suffers most patiently, seeking to do good to his brethren, and to promote the salvation of souls, most resembles Christ, and will be most honoured by him to all eternity. Our Lord speaks of his death in the terms applied to the sacrifices of old. It is a sacrifice for the sins of men, and is that true and substantial sacrifice, which those of the law faintly and imperfectly represented. It was a ransom for many, enough for all, working upon many; and, if for many, then the poor trembling soul may say, Why not for me?

Verses 29-34

It is good for those under the same trial, or infirmity of body or mind, to join in prayer to God for relief, that they may quicken and encourage one another. There is mercy enough in Christ for all that ask. They were earnest in prayer. They cried out as men in earnest. Cold desires beg denials. They were humble in prayer, casting themselves upon, and referring themselves cheerfully to, the Mediator's mercy. They showed faith in prayer, by the title they gave to Christ. Surely it was by the Holy Ghost that they called Jesus, Lord. They persevered in prayer. When they were in pursuit of such mercy, it was no time for timidity or hesitation: they cried earnestly. Christ encouraged them. The wants and burdens of the body we are soon sensible of, and can readily relate. Oh that we did as feelingly complain of our spiritual maladies, especially our spiritual blindness! Many are spiritually blind, yet say they see. Jesus cured these blind men; and when they had received sight, they followed him. None follow Christ blindly. He first by his grace opens men's eyes, and so draws their hearts after him. These miracles are our call to Jesus; may we hear it, and make it our daily prayer to grow in grace and in the knowledge of the Lord and Saviour Jesus Christ.

Chapter 21

Chapter Outline

Verses 1-11

This coming of Christ was described by the prophet Zechariah, Zec 9:9. When Christ would appear in his glory, it is in his meekness, not in his majesty, in mercy to work salvation. As meekness and outward poverty were fully seen in Zion's King, and marked his triumphal entrance to Jerusalem, how wrong covetousness, ambition, and the pride of life must be in Zion's citizens! They brought the ass, but Jesus did not use it without the owner's consent. The trappings were such as came to hand. We must not think the clothes on our backs too dear to part with for the service of Christ. The chief priests and the elders afterwards joined with the multitude that abused him upon the cross;

but none of them joined the multitude that did him honour. Those that take Christ for their King, must lay their all under his feet. Hosanna signifies, Save now, we beseech thee! Blessed is he that cometh in the name of the Lord! But of how little value is the applause of the people! The changing multitude join the cry of the day, whether it be Hosanna, or Crucify him. Multitudes often seem to approve the gospel, but few become consistent disciples. When Jesus was come into Jerusalem all the city was moved; some perhaps were moved with joy, who waited for the Consolation of Israel; others, of the Pharisees, were moved with envy. So various are the motions in the minds of men upon the approach of Christ's kingdom.

Verses 12-17

Christ found some of the courts of the temple turned into a market for cattle and things used in the sacrifices, and partly occupied by the money-changers. Our Lord drove them from the place, as he had done at his entering upon his ministry, Joh 2:13–17. His works testified of him more than the hosannas; and his healing in the temple was the fulfilling the promise, that the glory of the latter house should be greater than the glory of the former. If Christ came now into many parts of his visible church, how many secret evils he would discover and cleanse! And how many things daily practised under the cloak of religion, would he show to be more suitable to a den of thieves than to a house of prayer!

Verses 18-22

This cursing of the barren fig-tree represents the state of hypocrites in general, and so teaches us that Christ looks for the power of religion in those who profess it, and the savour of it from those that have the show of it. His just expectations from flourishing professors are often disappointed; he comes to many, seeking fruit, and finds leaves only. A false profession commonly withers in this world, and it is the effect of Christ's curse. The fig-tree that had no fruit, soon lost its leaves. This represents the state of the nation and people of the Jews in particular. Our Lord Jesus found among them nothing but leaves. And after they rejected Christ, blindness and hardness grew upon them, till they were undone, and their place and nation rooted up. The Lord was righteous in it. Let us greatly fear the doom denounced on the barren fig-tree.

Verses 23-27

As our Lord now openly appeared as the Messiah, the chief priests and scribes were much offended, especially because he exposed and removed the abuses they encouraged. Our Lord asked what they thought of John's ministry and baptism. Many are more afraid of the shame of lying than of the sin, and therefore scruple not to speak what they know to be false, as to their own thoughts, affections, and intentions, or their remembering and forgetting. Our Lord refused to answer their inquiry. It is best to shun needless disputes with wicked opposers.

Verses 28-32

Parables which give reproof, speak plainly to the offenders, and judge them out of their own mouths. The parable of the two sons sent to work in the vineyard, is to show that those who knew not John's baptism to be of God, were shamed by those who knew it, and owned it. The whole human race are like children whom the Lord has brought up, but they have rebelled against him, only some are more plausible in their disobedience than others. And it often happens, that the daring rebel is brought to repentance and becomes the Lord's servant, while the formalist grows hardened in pride and enmity.

Verses 33-46

This parable plainly sets forth the sin and ruin of the Jewish nation; and what is spoken to convict them, is spoken to caution all that enjoy the privileges of the outward church. As men treat God's people, they would treat Christ himself, if he were with them. How can we, if faithful to his cause, expect a favourable reception from a wicked world, or from ungodly professors of Christianity! And let us ask ourselves, whether we who have the vineyard and all its advantages, render fruits in due season, as a people, as a family, or as separate persons. Our Saviour, in his question, declares that the Lord of the vineyard will come, and when he comes he will surely destroy the wicked. The chief priests and the elders were the builders, and they would not admit his doctrine or laws; they threw him aside as a despised stone. But he who was rejected by the Jews, was embraced by the Gentiles. Christ knows who will bring forth gospel fruits in the use of gospel means. The unbelief of sinners will be their ruin. But God has many ways of restraining the remainders of wrath, as he has of making that which breaks out redound to his praise. May Christ become more and more precious to our souls, as the firm Foundation and Cornerstone of his church. May we be willing to follow him, though despised and hated for his sake.

Chapter 22

Chapter Outline

Verses 1-14

The provision made for perishing souls in the gospel, is represented by a royal feast made by a king, with eastern liberality, on the marriage of his son. Our merciful God has not only provided food, but a royal feast, for the perishing souls of his rebellious creatures. There is enough and to spare, of every thing that can add to our present comfort and everlasting happiness, in the salvation of his Son Jesus Christ. The guests first invited were the Jews. When the prophets of the Old Testament prevailed not, nor John the Baptist, nor Christ himself, who told them the kingdom of God was at hand, the apostles and ministers of the gospel were sent, after Christ's resurrection, to tell them it was come, and to persuade them to accept the offer. The reason why sinners come not to Christ and salvation by him, is, not because they cannot, but because they will not. Making light of Christ, and of the great salvation wrought out by him, is the damning sin of the world. They were careless. Multitudes perish for ever through mere carelessness, who show no direct aversion, but are careless as to their souls. Also the business and profit of worldly employments hinder many in closing with the Saviour. Both farmers and merchants must be diligent; but whatever we have of the world in our hands, our care must be to keep it out of our hearts, lest it come between us and Christ. The utter ruin coming upon the Jewish church and nation, is here represented. Persecution of Christ's faithful ministers fills up the measure of guilt of any people. The offer of Christ and salvation to the Gentiles was not expected; it was such a surprise as it would be to wayfaring men, to be invited to a royal wedding-feast. The design of the gospel is to gather souls to Christ; all the children of God scattered abroad, Joh 10:16; 11:52. The case of hypocrites is represented by the guest that had not on a wedding-garment. It concerns all to prepare for the scrutiny; and those, and those only, who put on the Lord Jesus, who have a Christian temper of mind, who live by faith in Christ, and to whom he is all in all, have the wedding-garment. The imputed righteousness of Christ, and the sanctification of the Spirit, are both alike necessary. No man has the wedding-garment by nature, or can form it for himself. The day is coming, when hypocrites will be called to account for all their presumptuous intruding into gospel ordinances, and usurpation of gospel privileges. Take him away. Those that walk unworthy of Christianity, forfeit all the happiness they presumptuously claimed. Our Saviour here passes out of the parable into that which it teaches. Hypocrites go by the light of the gospel itself down to utter darkness. Many are called to the wedding-feast, that is, to salvation, but few have the wedding-garment, the righteousness of Christ, the sanctification of the Spirit. Then let us examine ourselves whether we are in the faith, and seek to be approved by the King.

Verses 15-22

The Pharisees sent their disciples with the Herodians, a party among the Jews, who were for full subjection to the Roman emperor. Though opposed to each other, they joined against Christ. What they said of Christ was right; whether they knew it or not, blessed be God we know it. Jesus Christ was a faithful Teacher, and a bold reprover. Christ saw their wickedness. Whatever mask the hypocrite puts on, our Lord Jesus sees through it. Christ did not interpose as a judge in matters of this nature, for his kingdom is not of this world, but he enjoins peaceable subjection to the powers that be. His adversaries were reproved, and his disciples were taught that the Christian religion is no enemy to civil government. Christ is, and will be, the wonder, not only of his friends, but of his enemies. They admire his wisdom, but will not be guided by it; his power, but will not submit to it.

Verses 23-33

The doctrines of Christ displeased the infidel Sadducees, as well as the Pharisees and Herodians. He carried the great truths of the resurrection and a future state, further than they had yet been reveled. There is no arguing from the state of things in this world, as to what will take place hereafter. Let truth be set in a clear light, and it appears in full strength. Having thus silenced them, our Lord proceeded to show the truth of the doctrine of the resurrection from the books of Moses. God declared to Moses that he was the God of the patriarchs, who had died long before; this shows that they were then in a state of being, capable of enjoying his favour, and proves that the doctrine of the resurrection is clearly taught in the Old Testament as well as in the New. But this doctrine was kept for a more full revelation, after the resurrection of Christ, who was the first-fruits of them that slept. All errors arise from not knowing the Scriptures and the power of God. In this world death takes away one after another, and so ends all earthly hopes, joys, sorrows, and connexions. How wretched are those who look for nothing better beyond the grave!

Verses 34-40

An interpreter of the law asked our Lord a question, to try, not so much his knowledge, as his judgment. The love of God is the first and great commandment, and the sum of all the commands of the first table. Our love of God must be sincere, not in word and tongue only. All our love is too little to bestow upon him, therefore all the powers of the soul must be engaged for him, and carried out toward him. To love our neighbour as ourselves, is the second great commandment. There is a self-love which is corrupt, and the root of the greatest sins, and it must be put off and mortified; but there is a self-love which is the rule of the greatest duty: we must have a due concern for the welfare of our own souls and bodies. And we must love our neighbour as truly and sincerely as we love ourselves; in many cases we must deny ourselves for the good of others. By these two commandments let our hearts be formed as by a mould.

Verses 41-46

When Christ baffled his enemies, he asked what thoughts they had of the promised Messiah? How he could be the Son of David and yet his Lord? He quotes Ps 110:1. If the Christ was to be a mere man, who would not exist till many ages after David's death, how could his forefather call him Lord? The Pharisees could not answer it. Nor can any solve the difficulty except he allows the Messiah to be the Son of God, and David's Lord equally with the Father. He took upon him human nature, and so became God manifested in the flesh; in this sense he is the Son of man and the Son of David. It behoves us above all things seriously to inquire, "What think we of Christ?" Is he altogether glorious in our eyes, and precious to our hearts? May Christ be our joy, our confidence, our all. May we daily be made more like to him, and more devoted to his service.

Chapter 23

Chapter Outline

Verses 1-12

The scribes and Pharisees explained the law of Moses, and enforced obedience to it. They are charged with hypocrisy in religion. We can only judge according to outward appearance; but God searches the heart. They made phylacteries. These were scrolls of paper or parchment, wherein were written four paragraphs of the law, to be worn on their foreheads and left arms, Ex 13:2–10; 13:11–16; De 6:4–9; 11:13–21. They made these phylacteries broad, that they might be thought more zealous for the law than others. God appointed the Jews to make fringes upon their garments, Nu 15:38, to remind them of their being a peculiar people; but the Pharisees made them larger than common, as if they were thereby more religious than others. Pride was the darling, reigning sin of the Pharisees, the sin that most easily beset them, and which our Lord Jesus takes all occasions to speak against. For him that is taught in the word to give respect to him that teaches, is commendable; but for him that teaches, to demand it, to be puffed up with it, is sinful. How much is all this against the spirit of Christianity! The consistent disciple of Christ is pained by being put into chief places. But who that looks around on the visible church, would think this was the spirit required? It is plain that some measure of this antichristian spirit prevails in every religious society, and in every one of our hearts.

Verses 13-33

The scribes and Pharisees were enemies to the gospel of Christ, and therefore to the salvation of the souls of men. It is bad to keep away from Christ ourselves, but worse also to keep others from him. Yet it is no new thing for the show and form of godliness to be made a cloak to the greatest enormities. But dissembled piety will be reckoned double iniquity. They were very busy to turn souls to be of their party. Not for the glory of God and the good of souls, but that they might have the credit and advantage of making converts. Gain being their godliness, by a thousand devices they made religion give way to their worldly interests. They were very strict and precise in smaller matters of the law, but careless and loose in weightier matters. It is not the scrupling a little sin that Christ here reproves; if it be a sin, though but a gnat, it must be strained out; but the doing that, and then swallowing a camel, or, committing a greater sin. While they would seem to be godly, they were neither sober nor righteous. We are really, what we are inwardly. Outward motives may keep the outside clean, while the inside is filthy; but if the heart and spirit be made new, there will be newness of life; here we must begin with ourselves. The righteousness of the scribes and Pharisees was like the ornaments of a grave, or dressing up a dead body, only for show. The deceitfulness of sinners' hearts appears in that they go down the streams of the sins of their own day, while they fancy that they should have opposed the sins of former days. We sometimes think, if we had lived when Christ was upon earth, that we should not have despised and rejected him, as men then did; yet Christ in his Spirit, in his word, in his ministers, is still no better treated. And it is just with God to give those up to their hearts' lusts, who obstinately persist in gratifying them. Christ gives men their true characters.

Verses 34-39

Our Lord declares the miseries the inhabitants of Jerusalem were about to bring upon themselves, but he does not notice the sufferings he was to undergo. A hen gathering her chickens under her wings, is an apt emblem of the Saviour's tender love to those who trust in him, and his faithful care of them. He calls sinners to take refuge under his tender protection, keeps them safe, and nourishes them to eternal life. The present dispersion and unbelief of the Jews, and their future conversion to Christ, were here foretold. Jerusalem and her children had a large share of guilt, and their punishment has been signal. But ere long, deserved vengeance will fall on every church which is Christian in name only. In the mean time the Saviour stands ready to receive all who come to him. There is nothing between sinners and eternal happiness, but their proud and unbelieving unwillingness.

Chapter 24

Chapter Outline

Christ foretells the destruction of the temple.	(1–3)
The troubles before the destruction of Jerusalem.	(4–28)
Christ foretells other signs and miseries, to the end of the world.	(29–41)
Exhortations to watchfulness.	(42–51)

Verses 1-3

Christ foretells the utter ruin and destruction coming upon the temple. A believing foresight of the defacing of all worldly glory, will help to keep us from admiring it, and overvaluing it. The most beautiful body soon will be food for worms, and the most magnificent building a ruinous heap. See ye not all these things? It will do us good so to see them as to see through them, and see to the end of them. Our Lord having gone with his disciples to the Mount of Olives, he set before them the order of the times concerning the Jews, till the destruction of Jerusalem; and as to men in general till the end of the world.

Verses 4-28

The disciples had asked concerning the times, When these things should be? Christ gave them no answer to that; but they had also asked, What shall be the sign? This question he answers fully. The prophecy first respects events near at hand, the destruction of Jerusalem, the end of the Jewish church and state, the calling of the Gentiles, and the setting up of Christ's kingdom in the world; but it also looks to the general judgment; and toward the close, points more particularly to the latter. What Christ here said to his disciples, tended more to promote caution than to satisfy their curiosity; more to prepare them for the events that should happen, than to give a distinct idea of the events. This is that good understanding of the times which all should covet, thence to infer what Israel ought to do. Our Saviour cautions his disciples to stand on their guard against false teachers. And he foretells wars and great commotions among nations. From the time that the Jews rejected Christ, and he left their house desolate, the sword never departed from them. See what comes of refusing the gospel. Those who will not hear the messengers of peace, shall be made to hear the messengers of war. But where the heart is fixed, trusting in God, it is kept in peace, and is not afraid. It is against the mind of Christ, that his people should have troubled hearts, even in troublous times. When we looked forward to the eternity of misery that is before the obstinate refusers of Christ and his gospel, we may truly say, The greatest earthly judgments are but the beginning of sorrows. It is comforting that some shall endure even to the end. Our Lord foretells the preaching of the gospel in all the world. The end of the world shall not be till the gospel has done its work. Christ foretells the ruin coming upon the people of the Jews; and what he said here, would be of use to his disciples, for their conduct and for their comfort. If God opens a door of escape, we ought to make our escape, otherwise we do not trust God, but tempt him. It becomes Christ's disciples, in times of public trouble, to be much in prayer: that is never out of season, but in a special manner seasonable when we are distressed on every side. Though we must take what God sends, yet we may pray against sufferings; and it is very trying to a good man, to be taken by any work of necessity from the solemn service and worship of God on the sabbath day. But here is one word of comfort, that for the elect's sake these days shall be made shorter than their enemies designed, who would have cut all off, if God, who used these foes to serve his own purpose, had not set bounds to their wrath. Christ foretells the rapid spreading of the gospel in the world. It is plainly seen as the lightning. Christ preached his gospel openly. The Romans were like an eagle, and the ensign of their armies was an eagle. When a people, by their sin, make themselves as loathsome carcasses, nothing can be expected but that God should send enemies to destroy them. It is very applicable to the day of judgment, the coming of our Lord Jesus Christ in that day, 2Th 2:1. Let us give diligence to make our calling and election sure; then may we know that no enemy or deceiver shall ever prevail against us.

Verses 29-41

Christ foretells his second coming. It is usual for prophets to speak of things as near and just at hand, to express the greatness and certainty of them. Concerning Christ's second coming, it is foretold that there shall be a great change, in order to the making all things new. Then they shall see the Son of man coming in the clouds. At his first coming, he was set for a sign that should be spoken against, but at his second coming, a sign that should be admired. Sooner or later, all sinners will be mourners; but repenting sinners look to Christ, and mourn after a godly sort; and those who sow in those tears shall shortly reap in joy. Impenitent sinners shall see Him whom they have pierced, and, though they laugh now, shall mourn and weep in endless horror and despair. The elect of God are scattered abroad; there are some in all places, and all nations; but when that great gathering day comes, there shall not one of them be missing. Distance of place shall keep none out of heaven. Our Lord declares that the Jews should never cease to be a distinct people, until all things he had been predicting were fulfilled. His prophecy reaches to the day of final judgment; therefore he here, ver. 34, foretells that Judah shall never cease to exist as a distinct people, so long as this world shall endure. Men of the world scheme and plan for generation upon generation here, but they plan not with reference to the overwhelming, approaching, and most certain event of Christ's second coming, which shall do away every human scheme, and set aside for ever all that God forbids. That will be as surprising a day, as the deluge to the old world. Apply this, first, to temporal judgments, particularly that which was then hastening upon the nation and people of the Jews. Secondly, to the eternal judgment. Christ here shows the state of the old world when the deluge came. They were secure and careless; they knew not, until the flood came; and they believed not. Did we know aright that all earthly things must shortly pass away, we should not set our eyes and hearts so much upon them as we do. The evil day is not the further off for men's putting it far from them. What words can more strongly describe the suddenness of our Saviour's coming! Men will be at their respective businesses, and suddenly the Lord of glory will appear. Women will be in their house employments, but in that moment every other work will be laid aside, and every heart will turn inward and say, It is the Lord! Am I prepared to meet him? Can I stand before him? And what, in fact, is the day of judgment to the whole world, but the day of death to every one?

Verses 42-51

To watch for Christ's coming, is to maintain that temper of mind which we would be willing that our Lord should find us in. We know we have but a little time to live, we cannot know that we have a long time to live; much less do we know the time fixed for the judgment. Our Lord's coming will be happy to those that shall be found ready, but very dreadful to those that are not. If a man, professing to be the servant of Christ, be an unbeliever, covetous, ambitious, or a lover of pleasure, he will be cut off. Those who choose the world for their portion in this life, will have hell for their portion in the other life. May our Lord, when he cometh, pronounce us blessed, and present us to the Father, washed in his blood, purified by his Spirit, and fit to be partakers of the inheritance of the saints in light.

Chapter 25

Chapter Outline

The judgment.   (31–46)

Verses 1-13

The circumstances of the parable of the ten virgins were taken from the marriage customs among the Jews, and explain the great day of Christ's coming. See the nature of Christianity. As Christians we profess to attend upon Christ, to honour him, also to be waiting for his coming. Sincere Christians are the wise virgins, and hypocrites the foolish ones. Those are the truly wise or foolish that are so in the affairs of their souls. Many have a lamp of profession in their hands, but have not, in their hearts, sound knowledge and settled resolution, which are needed to carry them through the services and trials of the present state. Their hearts are not stored with holy dispositions, by the new-creating Spirit of God. Our light must shine before men in good works; but this is not likely to be long done, unless there is a fixed, active principle in the heart, of faith in Christ, and love to God and our brethren. They all slumbered and slept. The delay represents the space between the real or apparent conversion of these professors, and the coming of Christ, to take them away by death, or to judge the world. But though Christ tarry past our time, he will not tarry past the due time. The wise virgins kept their lamps burning, but they did not keep themselves awake. Too many real Christians grow remiss, and one degree of carelessness makes way for another. Those that allow themselves to slumber, will scarcely keep from sleeping; therefore dread the beginning of spiritual decays. A startling summons was given. Go ye forth to meet Him, is a call to those prepared. The notice of Christ's approach, and the call to meet him, will awaken. Even those best prepared for death have work to do to get actually ready, 2Pe 3:14. It will be a day of search and inquiry; and it concerns us to think how we shall then be found. Some wanted oil to supply their lamps when going out. Those that take up short of true grace, will certainly find the want of it one time or other. An outward profession may light a man along this world, but the damps of the valley of the shadow of death will put out such a light. Those who care not to live the life, yet would die the death of the righteous. But those that would be saved, must have grace of their own; and those that have most grace, have none to spare. The best need more from Christ. And while the poor alarmed soul addresses itself, upon a sick-bed, to repentance and prayer, in awful confusion, death comes, judgment comes, the work is undone, and the poor sinner is undone for ever. This comes of having oil to buy when we should burn it, grace to get when we should use it. Those, and those only, shall go to heaven hereafter, that are made ready for heaven here. The suddenness of death and of Christ's coming to us then, will not hinder our happiness, if we have been prepared. The door was shut. Many will seek admission into heaven when it is too late. The vain confidence of hypocrites will carry them far in expectations of happiness. The unexpected summons of death may alarm the Christian; but, proceeding without delay to trim his lamp, his graces often shine more bright; while the mere professor's conduct shows that his lamp is going out. Watch therefore, attend to the business of your souls. Be in the fear of the Lord all the day long.

Verses 14-30

Christ keeps no servants to be idle: they have received their all from him, and have nothing they can call their own but sin. Our receiving from Christ is in order to our working for him. The manifestation of the Spirit is given to every man to profit withal. The day of account comes at last.

We must all be reckoned with as to what good we have got to our own souls, and have done to others, by the advantages we have enjoyed. It is not meant that the improving of natural powers can entitle a man to Divine grace. It is the real Christian's liberty and privilege to be employed as his Redeemer's servant, in promoting his glory, and the good of his people: the love of Christ constrains him to live no longer to himself, but to Him that died for him, and rose again. Those who think it impossible to please God, and in vain to serve him, will do nothing to purpose in religion. They complain that He requires of them more than they are capable of, and punishes them for what they cannot help. Whatever they may pretend, the fact is, they dislike the character and work of the Lord. The slothful servant is sentenced to be deprived of his talent. This may be applied to the blessings of this life; but rather to the means of grace. Those who know not the day of their visitation, shall have the things that belong to their peace hid from their eyes. His doom is, to be cast into outer darkness. It is a usual way of expressing the miseries of the damned in hell. Here, as in what was said to the faithful servants, our Saviour goes out of the parable into the thing intended by it, and this serves as a key to the whole. Let us not envy sinners, or covet any of their perishing possessions.

Verses 31-46

This is a description of the last judgment. It is as an explanation of the former parables. There is a judgment to come, in which every man shall be sentenced to a state of everlasting happiness, or misery. Christ shall come, not only in the glory of his Father, but in his own glory, as Mediator. The wicked and godly here dwell together, in the same cities, churches, families, and are not always to be known the one from the other; such are the weaknesses of saints, such the hypocrisies of sinners; and death takes both: but in that day they will be parted for ever. Jesus Christ is the great Shepherd; he will shortly distinguish between those that are his, and those that are not. All other distinctions will be done away; but the great one between saints and sinners, holy and unholy, will remain for ever. The happiness the saints shall possess is very great. It is a kingdom; the most valuable possession on earth; yet this is but a faint resemblance of the blessed state of the saints in heaven. It is a kingdom prepared. The Father provided it for them in the greatness of his wisdom and power; the Son purchased it for them; and the blessed Spirit, in preparing them for the kingdom, is preparing it for them. It is prepared for them: it is in all points adapted to the new nature of a sanctified soul. It is prepared from the foundation of the world. This happiness was for the saints, and they for it, from all eternity. They shall come and inherit it. What we inherit is not got by ourselves. It is God that makes heirs of heaven. We are not to suppose that acts of bounty will entitle to eternal happiness. Good works done for God's sake, through Jesus Christ, are here noticed as marking the character of believers made holy by the Spirit of Christ, and as the effects of grace bestowed on those who do them. The wicked in this world were often called to come to Christ for life and rest, but they turned from his calls; and justly are those bid to depart from Christ, that would not come to him. Condemned sinners will in vain offer excuses. The punishment of the wicked will be an everlasting punishment; their state cannot be altered. Thus life and death, good and evil, the blessing and the curse, are set before us, that we may choose our way, and as our way so shall our end be.

Chapter 26

Chapter Outline

Verses 1-5

Our Lord had often told of his sufferings as at a distance, now he speaks of them as at hand. At the same time the Jewish council consulted how they might put him to death secretly. But it pleased God to defeat their intention. Jesus, the true paschal Lamb, was to be sacrificed for us at that very time, and his death and resurrection rendered public.

Verses 6-13

The pouring ointment upon the head of Christ was a token of the highest respect. Where there is true love in the heart to Jesus Christ, nothing will be thought too good to bestow upon him. The more Christ's servants and their services are cavilled at, the more he manifests his acceptance. This act of faith and love was so remarkable, that it would be reported, as a memorial of Mary's faith and love, to all future ages, and in all places where the gospel should be preached. This prophecy is fulfilled.

Verses 14-16

There were but twelve called apostles, and one of them was like a devil; surely we must never expect any society to be quite pure on this side heaven. The greater profession men make of religion, the greater opportunity they have of doing mischief, if their hearts be not right with God. Observe, that Christ's own disciple, who knew so well his doctrine and manner of his life, and was false to him, could not charge him with any thing criminal, though it would have served to justify his treachery. What did Judas want? Was not he welcome wherever his Master was? Did he not fare as Christ fared? It is not the lack, but the love of money, that is the root of all evil. After he had made that wicked bargain, Judas had time to repent, and to revoke it; but when lesser acts of dishonesty have hardened the conscience men do without hesitation that which is more shameful.

Verses 17-25

Observe, the place for their eating the passover was pointed out by Christ to the disciples. He knows those hidden ones who favour his cause, and will graciously visit all who are willing to receive him. The disciples did as Jesus had appointed. Those who would have Christ's presence in the gospel passover, must do what he says. It well becomes the disciples of Christ always to be jealous over themselves, especially in trying times. We know not how strongly we may be tempted, nor how far God may leave us to ourselves, therefore we have reason not to be high-minded, but to fear. Heart-searching examination and fervent prayer are especially proper before the Lord's supper, that, as Christ our Passover is now sacrificed for us, we may keep this feast, renewing our repentance, our faith in his blood, and surrendering ourselves to his service.

Verses 26-30

This ordinance of the Lord's supper is to us the passover supper, by which we commemorate a much greater deliverance than that of Israel out of Egypt. Take, eat; accept of Christ as he is offered to you; receive the atonement, approve of it, submit to his grace and his government. Meat looked upon, be the dish ever so well garnished, will not nourish; it must be fed upon: so must the doctrine of Christ. This is my body; that is, spiritually, it signifies and represents his body. We partake of the sun, not by having the sun put into our hands, but the beams of it darted down upon us; so we partake of Christ by partaking of his grace, and the blessed fruits of the breaking of his body. The blood of Christ is signified and represented by the wine. He gave thanks, to teach us to look to God in every part of the ordinance. This cup he gave to the disciples with a command, Drink ye all of it. The pardon of sin is that great blessing which is, in the Lord's supper, conferred on all true believers; it is the foundation of all other blessings. He takes leave of such communion; and assures them of a happy meeting again at last; "Until that day when I drink it new with you\rdblquote , may be understood of the joys and glories of the future state, which the saints shall partake with the Lord Jesus. That will be the kingdom of his Father; the wine of consolation will there be always new. While we look at the outward signs of Christ's body broken and his blood shed for the remission of our sins, let us recollect that the feast cost him as much as though he had literally given his flesh to be eaten and his blood for us to drink.

Verses 31-35

Improper self-confidence, like that of Peter, is the first step to a fall. There is a proneness in all of us to be over-confident. But those fall soonest and foulest, who are the most confident in themselves. Those are least safe, who think themselves most secure. Satan is active to lead such astray; they are most off their guard: God leaves them to themselves, to humble them.

Verses 36-46

He who made atonement for the sins of mankind, submitted himself in a garden of suffering, to the will of God, from which man had revolted in a garden of pleasure. Christ took with him into that part of the garden where he suffered his agony, only those who had witnessed his glory in his transfiguration. Those are best prepared to suffer with Christ, who have by faith beheld his glory. The words used denote the most entire dejection, amazement, anguish, and horror of mind; the state of one surrounded with sorrows, overwhelmed with miseries, and almost swallowed up with terror and dismay. He now began to be sorrowful, and never ceased to be so till he said, It is finished. He prayed that, if possible, the cup might pass from him. But he also showed his perfect readiness to bear the load of his sufferings; he was willing to submit to all for our redemption and salvation. According to this example of Christ, we must drink of the bitterest cup which God puts into our hands; though nature struggle, it must submit. It should be more our care to get troubles sanctified, and our hearts satisfied under them, than to get them taken away. It is well for us that our salvation is in the hand of One who neither slumbers nor sleeps. All are tempted, but we should be much afraid of entering into temptation. To be secured from this, we should watch and pray, and continually look unto the Lord to hold us up that we may be safe. Doubtless our Lord had a clear and full view of the sufferings he was to endure, yet he spoke with the greatest calmness till this time. Christ was a Surety, who undertook to be answerable for our sins. Accordingly he was made sin for us, and suffered for our sins, the Just for the unjust; and Scripture ascribes his heaviest sufferings to the hand of God. He had full knowledge of the infinite evil of sin, and of the immense extent of that guilt for which he was to atone; with awful views of the Divine justice and holiness, and the punishment deserved by the sins of men, such as no tongue can express, or mind conceive. At the same time, Christ suffered being tempted; probably horrible thoughts were suggested by Satan that tended to gloom and every dreadful conclusion: these would be the more hard to bear from his perfect holiness. And did the load of imputed guilt so weigh down the soul of Him of whom it is said, He upholdeth all things by the word of his power? into what misery then must those sink whose sins are left upon their own heads! How will those escape who neglect so great salvation?

Verses 47-56

No enemies are so much to be abhorred as those professed disciples that betray Christ with a kiss. God has no need of our services, much less of our sins, to bring about his purposes. Though Christ was crucified through weakness, it was voluntary weakness; he submitted to death. If he had not been willing to suffer, they could not conquer him. It was a great sin for those who had left all to follow Jesus; now to leave him for they knew not what. What folly, for fear of death to flee from Him, whom they knew and acknowledged to be the Fountain of life!

Verses 57-68

Jesus was hurried into Jerusalem. It looks ill, and bodes worse, when those who are willing to be Christ's disciples, are not willing to be known to be so. Here began Peter's denying him: for to follow Christ afar off, is to begin to go back from him. It is more our concern to prepare for the end, whatever it may be, than curiously to ask what the end will be. The event is God's, but the duty is ours. Now the Scriptures were fulfilled, which said, False witnesses are risen up against me. Christ was accused, that we might not be condemned; and if at any time we suffer thus, let us remember we cannot expect to fare better than our Master. When Christ was made sin for us, he was silent, and left it to his blood to speak. Hitherto Jesus had seldom professed expressly to be the Christ, the Son of God; the tenor of his doctrine spoke it, and his miracles proved it; but now he would not omit to make an open confession of it. It would have looked like declining his sufferings. He thus confessed, as an example and encouragement to his followers, to confess him before men, whatever hazard they ran. Disdain, cruel mocking, and abhorrence, are the sure portion of the disciple as they were of the Master, from such as would buffet and deride the Lord of glory. These things were exactly foretold in the fiftieth chapter of Isaiah. Let us confess Christ's name, and bear the reproach, and he will confess us before his Father's throne.

Verses 69-75

Peter's sin is truly related, for the Scriptures deal faithfully. Bad company leads to sin: those who needlessly thrust themselves into it, may expect to be tempted and insnared, as Peter. They scarcely can come out of such company without guilt or grief, or both. It is a great fault to be shy of Christ; and to dissemble our knowledge of him, when we are called to own him, is, in effect, to deny him. Peter's sin was aggravated; but he fell into the sin by surprise, not as Judas, with design. But conscience should be to us as the crowing of the cock, to put us in mind of the sins we had forgotten. Peter was thus left to fall, to abate his self-confidence, and render him more modest, humble, compassionate, and useful to others. The event has taught believers many things ever since, and if infidels, Pharisees, and hypocrites stumble at it or abuse it, it is at their peril. Little do we know how we should act in very difficult situations, if we were left to ourselves. Let him, therefore, that thinketh he standeth, take heed lest he fall; let us all distrust our own hearts, and rely wholly on the Lord. Peter wept bitterly. Sorrow for sin must not be slight, but great and deep. Peter, who wept so bitterly for denying Christ, never denied him again, but confessed him often in the face of danger. True repentance for any sin will be shown by the contrary grace and duty; that is a sign of our sorrowing not only bitterly, but sincerely.

Chapter 27

Chapter Outline

The burial of Christ.   (57–61)

The sepulchre secured.   (62–66)

Verses 1-10

Wicked men see little of the consequences of their crimes when they commit them, but they must answer for them all. In the fullest manner Judas acknowledged to the chief priests that he had sinned, and betrayed an innocent person. This was full testimony to the character of Christ; but the rulers were hardened. Casting down the money, Judas departed, and went and hanged himself, not being able to bear the terror of Divine wrath, and the anguish of despair. There is little doubt but that the death of Judas was before that of our blessed Lord. But was it nothing to them that they had thirsted after this blood, and hired Judas to betray it, and had condemned it to be shed unjustly? Thus do fools make a mock at sin. Thus many make light of Christ crucified. And it is a common instance of the deceitfulness of our hearts, to make light of our own sin by dwelling upon other people's sins. But the judgment of God is according to truth. Many apply this passage of the buying the piece of ground, with the money Judas brought back, to signify the favour intended by the blood of Christ to strangers, and sinners of the Gentiles. It fulfilled a prophecy, Zec 11:12. Judas went far toward repentance, yet it was not to salvation. He confessed, but not to God; he did not go to him, and say, I have sinned, Father, against heaven. Let none be satisfied with such partial convictions as a man may have, and yet remain full of pride, enmity, and rebellion.

Verses 11-25

Having no malice against Jesus, Pilate urged him to clear himself, and laboured to get him discharged. The message from his wife was a warning. God has many ways of giving checks to sinners, in their sinful pursuits, and it is a great mercy to have such checks from Providence, from faithful friends, and from our own consciences. O do not this abominable thing which the Lord hates! is what we may hear said to us, when we are entering into temptation, if we will but regard it. Being overruled by the priests, the people made choice of Barabbas. Multitudes who choose the world, rather than God, for their ruler and portion, thus choose their own delusions. The Jews were so bent upon the death of Christ, that Pilate thought it would be dangerous to refuse. And this struggle shows the power of conscience even on the worst men. Yet all was so ordered to make it evident that Christ suffered for no fault of his own, but for the sins of his people. How vain for Pilate to expect to free himself from the guilt of the innocent blood of a righteous person, whom he was by his office bound to protect! The Jews' curse upon themselves has been awfully answered in the sufferings of their nation. None could bear the sin of others, except Him that had no sin of his own to answer for. And are we not all concerned? Is not Barabbas preferred to Jesus, when sinners reject salvation that they may retain their darling sins, which rob God of his glory, and murder their souls? The blood of Christ is now upon us for good, through mercy, by the Jews' rejection of it. O let us flee to it for refuge!

Verses 26-30

Crucifixion was a death used only among the Romans; it was very terrible and miserable. A cross was laid on the ground, to which the hands and feet were nailed, it was then lifted up and fixed upright, so that the weight of the body hung on the nails, till the sufferer died in agony. Christ thus answered the type of the brazen serpent raised on a pole. Christ underwent all the misery and shame here related, that he might purchase for us everlasting life, and joy, and glory.

Verses 31-34

Christ was led as a Lamb to the slaughter, as a Sacrifice to the altar. Even the mercies of the wicked are really cruel. Taking the cross from him, they compelled one Simon to bear it. Make us ready, O Lord, to bear the cross thou hast appointed us, and daily to take it up with cheerfulness, following thee. Was ever sorrow like unto his sorrow? And when we behold what manner of death he died, let us in that behold with what manner of love he loved us. As if death, so painful a death, were not enough, they added to its bitterness and terror in several ways.

Verses 35-44

It was usual to put shame upon malefactors, by a writing to notify the crime for which they suffered. So they set up one over Christ's head. This they designed for his reproach, but God so overruled it, that even his accusation was to his honour. There were crucified with him at the same time, two robbers. He was, at his death, numbered among the transgressors, that we, at our death, might be numbered among the saints. The taunts and jeers he received are here recorded. The enemies of Christ labour to make others believe that of religion and of the people of God, which they themselves know to be false. The chief priests and scribes, and the elders, upbraid Jesus with being the King of Israel. Many people could like the King of Israel well enough, if he would but come down from the cross; if they could but have his kingdom without the tribulation through which they must enter into it. But if no cross, then no Christ, no crown. Those that would reign with him, must be willing to suffer with him. Thus our Lord Jesus, having undertaken to satisfy the justice of God, did it, by submitting to the punishment of the worst of men. And in every minute particular recorded about the sufferings of Christ, we find some prediction in the Prophets or the Psalms fulfilled.

Verses 45-50

During the three hours which the darkness continued, Jesus was in agony, wrestling with the powers of darkness, and suffering his Father's displeasure against the sin of man, for which he was now making his soul an offering. Never were there three such hours since the day God created man upon the earth, never such a dark and awful scene; it was the turning point of that great affair, man's redemption and salvation. Jesus uttered a complaint from Ps 22:1. Hereby he teaches of what use the word of God is to direct us in prayer, and recommends the use of Scripture expressions in prayer. The believer may have tasted some drops of bitterness, but he can only form a very feeble idea of the greatness of Christ's sufferings. Yet, hence he learns something of the Saviour's love to sinners; hence he gets deeper conviction of the vileness and evil of sin, and of what he owes to Christ, who delivers him from the wrath to come. His enemies wickedly ridiculed his complaint. Many of the reproaches cast upon the word of God and the people of God, arise, as here, from gross mistakes. Christ, just before he expired, spake in his full strength, to show that his life was not forced from him, but was freely delivered into his Father's hands. He had strength to bid defiance to the powers of death: and to show that by the eternal Spirit he offered himself, being the Priest as well as the Sacrifice, he cried with a loud voice. Then he yielded up the ghost. The Son of God upon the cross, did die by the violence of the pain he was put to. His soul was separated from his body, and so his body was left really and truly dead. It was certain that Christ did die, for it was needful that he should die. He had undertaken to make himself an offering for sin, and he did it when he willingly gave up his life.

Verses 51-56

The rending of the veil signified that Christ, by his death, opened a way to God. We have an open way through Christ to the throne of grace, or mercy-seat now, and to the throne of glory hereafter. When we duly consider Christ's death, our hard and rocky hearts should be rent; the heart, and not the garments. That heart is harder than a rock that will not yield, that will not melt, where Jesus Christ is plainly set forth crucified. The graves were opened, and many bodies of saints which slept, arose. To whom they appeared, in what manner, and how they disappeared, we are not told; and we must not desire to be wise above what is written. The dreadful appearances of God in his providence, sometimes work strangely for the conviction and awakening of sinners. This was expressed in the terror that fell upon the centurion and the Roman soldiers. We may reflect with comfort on the abundant testimonies given to the character of Jesus; and, seeking to give no just cause of offence, we may leave it to the Lord to clear our characters, if we live to Him. Let us, with an eye of faith, behold Christ and him crucified, and be affected with that great love wherewith he loved us. But his friends could give no more than a look; they beheld him, but could not help him. Never were the horrid nature and effects of sin so tremendously displayed, as on that day when the beloved Son of the Father hung upon the cross, suffering for sin, the Just for the unjust, that he might bring us to God. Let us yield ourselves willingly to his service.

Verses 57-61

In the burial of Christ was nothing of pomp or solemnity. As Christ had not a house of his own, wherein to lay his head, while he lived, so he had not a grave of his own, wherein to lay his body, when he was dead. Our Lord Jesus, who had no sin of his own, had no grave of his own. The Jews designed that he should have made his grave with the wicked, should have been buried with the thieves with whom he was crucified, but God overruled it, so that he should make it with the rich in his death, Isa 53:9. And although to the eye of man the beholding a funeral may cause terror, yet if we remember how Christ by his burial has changed the nature of the grave to believers, it should make us rejoice. And we are ever to imitate Christ's burial in being continually occupied in the spiritual burial of our sins.

Verses 62-66

On the Jewish sabbath, the chief priests and Pharisees, when they should have been at their devotions, were dealing with Pilate about securing the sepulchre. This was permitted that there might be certain proof of our Lord's resurrection. Pilate told them that they might secure the sepulchre as carefully as they could. They sealed the stone, and set a guard, and were satisfied that all needful care was taken. But to guard the sepulchre against the poor weak disciples was folly, because needless; while to think to guard it against the power of God, was folly, because fruitless, and to no purpose; yet they thought they dealt wisely. But the Lord took the wise in their own craftiness. Thus shall all the rage and the plans of Christ's enemies be made to promote his glory.

Chapter 28

Chapter Outline

Christ's resurrection.	(1–8)
He appears to the women.	(9, 10)
Confession of the soldiers.	(11–15)
Christ's commission to his disciples.	(16–20)

Verses 1-8

Christ rose the third day after his death; that was the time he had often spoken of. On the first day of the first week God commanded the light to shine out of darkness. On this day did He who is the Light of the world, shine out of the darkness of the grave; and this day is from henceforward often mentioned in the New Testament, as the day which Christians religiously observed in solemn assemblies, to the honour of Christ. Our Lord Jesus could have rolled back the stone by his own power, but he chose to have it done by an angel. The resurrection of Christ, as it is the joy of his friends, so it is the terror and confusion of his enemies. The angel encouraged the women against their fears. Let the sinners in Zion be afraid. Fear not ye, for his resurrection will be your consolation. Our communion with him must be spiritual, by faith in his word. When we are ready to make this world our home, and to say, It is good to be here, then let us remember our Lord Jesus is not here, he is risen; therefore let our hearts rise, and seek the things that are above. He is risen, as he said. Let us never think that strange which the word of Christ has told us to expect; whether the sufferings of this present time, or the glory that is to be revealed. It may have a good effect upon us, by faith to view the place where the Lord lay. Go quickly. It was good to be there, but the servants of God have other work appointed. Public usefulness must be chosen before the pleasure of secret communion with God. Tell the disciples, that they may be comforted under their present sorrows. Christ knows where his disciples dwell, and will visit them. Even to those at a distance from the plenty of the means of grace, he will graciously manifest himself. The fear and the joy together quickened their pace. The disciples of Christ should be forward to make known to each other their experiences of communion with their Lord; and should tell others what God has done for their souls.

Verses 9, 10

God's gracious visits usually meet us in the way of duty; and to those who use what they have for others' benefit, more shall be given. This interview with Christ was unexpected; but Christ was nigh them, and still is nigh us in the word. The salutation speaks the good-will of Christ to man, even since he entered upon his state of exaltation. It is the will of Christ that his people should be a cheerful, joyful people, and his resurrection furnishes abundant matter for joy. Be not afraid. Christ rose from the dead, to silence his people's fears, and there is enough in that to silence them. The disciples had just before shamefully deserted him in his sufferings; but, to show that he could forgive, and to teach us to do so, he calls them brethren. Notwithstanding his majesty and purity, and our meanness and unworthiness, he still condescends to call believers his brethren.

Verses 11-15

What wickedness is it which men will not be brought to by the love of money! Here was large money given to the soldiers for advancing that which they knew to be a lie, yet many grudge a little money for advancing what they know to be the truth. Let us never starve a good cause, when we see bad ones so liberally supported. The priests undertook to secure them from the sword of Pilate, but could not secure these soldiers from the sword of God's justice, which hangs over the heads of those that love and make a lie. Those men promise more than they can perform, who undertake to save a man harmless in doing a wilful sin. But this falsehood disproved itself. Had the soldiers been all asleep, they could not have known what passed. If any had been awake, they would have roused the others and prevented the removal; and certainly if they had been asleep, they never would have dared to confess it; while the Jewish rulers would have been the first to call for their punishment. Again, had there been any truth in the report, the rulers would have prosecuted the apostles with severity for it. The whole shows that the story was entirely false. And we must not charge such things to the weakness of the understanding, but to the wickedness of the heart. God left them to expose their own course. The great argument to prove Christ to be the Son of God, is his resurrection; and none could have more convincing proofs of the truth of that than these soldiers; yet they took bribes to hinder others from believing. The plainest evidence will not affect men, without the work of the Holy Spirit.

Verses 16-20

This evangelist passes over other appearances of Christ, recorded by Luke and John, and hastens to the most solemn; one appointed before his death, and after his resurrection. All that see the Lord Jesus with an eye of faith, will worship him. Yet the faith of the sincere may be very weak and wavering. But Christ gave such convincing proofs of his resurrection, as made their faith to triumph over doubts. He now solemnly commissioned the apostles and his ministers to go forth among all nations. The salvation they were to preach, is a common salvation; whoever will, let him come, and take the benefit; all are welcome to Christ Jesus. Christianity is the religion of a sinner who applies for salvation from deserved wrath and from sin; he applies to the mercy of the Father, through the atonement of the incarnate Son, and by the sanctification of the Holy Spirit, and gives up himself to be the worshipper and servant of God, as the Father, Son, and Holy Ghost, three Persons but one God, in all his ordinances and commandments. Baptism is an outward sign of that inward washing, or sanctification of the Spirit, which seals and evidences the believer's justification. Let us examine ourselves, whether we really possess the inward and spiritual grace of a death unto sin, and a new birth unto righteousness, by which those who were the children of wrath become the children of God. Believers shall have the constant presence of their Lord always; all days, every day. There is no day, no hour of the day, in which our Lord Jesus is not present with his churches and with his ministers; if there were, in that day, that hour, they would be undone. The God of Israel, the Saviour, is sometimes a God that hideth himself, but never a God at a distance. To these precious words Amen is added. Even so, Lord Jesus, be thou with us and all thy people; cause thy face to shine upon us, that thy way may be known upon earth, thy saving health among all nations.

Mark

Mark was a sister's son to Barnabas, Col 4:10; and Ac 12:12 shows that he was the son of Mary, a pious woman of Jerusalem, at whose house the apostles and first Christians assembled. From Peter's styling him his son, 1Pe 5:13, the evangelist is supposed to have been converted by that apostle. Thus Mark was closely united with the followers of our Lord, if not himself one of the number. Mark wrote at Rome; some suppose that Peter dictated to him, though the general testimony is, that the apostle having preached at Rome, Mark, who was the apostle's companion, and had a clear understanding of what Peter delivered, was desired to commit the particulars to writing. And we may remark, that the great humility of Peter is very plain where any thing is said about himself. Scarcely an action or a work of Christ is mentioned, at which this apostle was not present, and the minuteness shows that the facts were related by an eye-witness. This Gospel records more of the miracles than of the discourses of our Lord, and though in many things it relates the same things as the Gospel according to St. Matthew, we may reap advantages from reviewing the same events, placed by each of the evangelists in that point of view which most affected his own mind.

Chapter 1

Chapter Outline

The office of John the Baptist.	(1–8)
The baptism and temptation of Christ.	(9–13)
Christ preaches and calls disciples.	(14–22)
He casts out an unclean spirit.	(23–28)
He heals many diseased.	(29–39)
He heals a leper.	(40–45)

Verses 1-8

Isaiah and Malachi each spake concerning the beginning of the gospel of Jesus Christ, in the ministry of John. From these prophets we may observe, that Christ, in his gospel, comes among us, bringing with him a treasure of grace, and a sceptre of government. Such is the corruption of the world, that there is great opposition to his progress. When God sent his Son into the world, he took care, and when he sends him into the heart, he takes care, to prepare his way before him. John thinks himself unworthy of the meanest office about Christ. The most eminent saints have always been the most humble. They feel their need of Christ's atoning blood and sanctifying Spirit, more than others. The great promise Christ makes in his gospel to those who have repented, and have had their sins forgiven them, is, they shall be baptized with the Holy Ghost; shall be purified by his graces, and refreshed by his comforts. We use the ordinances, word, and sacraments without profit and comfort, for the most part, because we have not of that Divine light within us; and we have it not because we ask it not; for we have his word that cannot fail, that our heavenly Father will give this light, his Holy Spirit, to those that ask it.

Verses 9-13

Christ's baptism was his first public appearance, after he had long lived unknown. How much hidden worth is there, which in this world is not known! But sooner or later it shall be known, as Christ was. He took upon himself the likeness of sinful flesh; and thus, for our sakes, he sanctified himself, that we also might be sanctified, and be baptized with him, Joh 17:19. See how honourably God owned him, when he submitted to John's baptism. He saw the Spirit descending upon him like a dove. We may see heaven opened to us, when we perceive the Spirit descending and working upon us. God's good work in us, is sure evidence of his good will towards us, and preparations for us. As to Christ's temptation, Mark notices his being in the wilderness and that he was with the wild beasts. It was an instance of his Father's care of him, which encouraged him the more that his Father would provide for him. Special protections are earnests of seasonable supplies. The serpent tempted the first Adam in the garden, the Second Adam in the wilderness; with different success indeed; and ever since he still tempts the children of both, in all places and conditions. Company and conversation have their temptations; and being alone, even in a wilderness, has its own also. No place or state exempts, no business, not lawful labouring, eating, or drinking, not even fasting and praying; often in these duties there are the most assaults, but in them is the sweetest victory. The ministration of the good angels is matter of great comfort in reference to the malignant designs of the evil angels; but much more does it comfort us, to have the indwelling of God the Holy Spirit in our hearts.

Verses 14-22

Jesus began to preach in Galilee, after that John was put in prison. If some be laid aside, others shall be raised up, to carry on the same work. Observe the great truths Christ preached. By repentance we give glory to our Creator whom we have offended; by faith we give glory to our Redeemer who came to save us from our sins. Christ has joined these two together, and let no man think to put them asunder. Christ puts honour upon those who, though mean in this world, are diligent in their business and kind to one another. Industry and unity are good and pleasant, and the Lord Jesus commands a blessing on them. Those whom Christ calls, must leave all to follow him; and by his grace he makes them willing to do so. Not that we must needs go out of the world, but we must sit loose to the world; forsake every thing that is against our duty to Christ, and that cannot be kept without hurt to our souls. Jesus strictly kept the sabbath day, by applying himself unto, and abounding in the sabbath work, in order to which the sabbath rest was appointed. There is much in the doctrine of Christ that is astonishing; and the more we hear it, the more cause we see to admire it.

Verses 23-28

The devil is an unclean spirit, because he has lost all the purity of his nature, because he acts in direct opposition to the Holy Spirit of God, and by his suggestions defiles the spirits of men. There are many in our assemblies who quietly attend under merely formal teachers; but if the Lord come with faithful ministers and holy doctrine, and by his convincing Spirit, they are ready to say, like this man, What have we to do with thee, Jesus of Nazareth! No disorder could enable a man to know Jesus to be the Holy One of God. He desires to have nothing to do with Jesus, for he despairs of being saved by him, and dreads being destroyed by him. See whose language those speak, that say to the Almighty, Depart from us. This unclean spirit hated and dreaded Christ, because he knew him to be a Holy One; for the carnal mind is enmity against God, especially against his holiness. When Christ by his grace delivers souls out of the hands of Satan, it is not without tumult in the soul; for that spiteful enemy will disquiet those whom he cannot destroy. This put all who saw it upon considering, What is this new doctrine? A work as great often is wrought now, yet men treat it with contempt and neglect. If this were not so, the conversion of a notorious wicked man to a sober, righteous, and godly life, by the preaching of a crucified Saviour, would cause many to ask, What doctrine is this?

Verses 29-39

Wherever Christ comes, he comes to do good. He cures, that we may minister to him, and to others who are his, and for his sake. Those kept from public ordinances by sickness or other real hinderances, may expect the Saviour's gracious presence; he will soothe their sorrows, and abate their pains. Observe how numerous the patients were. When others speed well with Christ, it should quicken us in seeking after him. Christ departed into a solitary place. Though he was in no danger of distraction, or of temptation to vain-glory, yet he retired. Those who have the most business in public, and of the best kind, must yet sometimes be alone with God.

Verses 40-45

We have here Christ's cleansing of a leper. It teaches us to apply to the Saviour with great humility, and with full submission to his will, saying, "Lord, if thou wilt," without any doubt of Christ's readiness to help the distressed. See also what to expect from Christ; that according to our faith it shall be to us. The poor leper said, If thou wilt. Christ readily wills favours to those who readily refer themselves to his will. Christ would have nothing done that looked like seeking praise of the people. But no reasons now exist why we should hesitate to spread the praises of Christ.

Chapter 2

Chapter Outline

Christ heals one sick of the palsy.	(1–12)
Levi's call, and the entertainment given to Jesus.	(13–17)
Why Christ's disciples did not fast.	(18–22)
He justifies his disciples for plucking corn on the sabbath.	(23–28)

Verses 1-12

It was this man's misery that he needed to be so carried, and shows the suffering state of human life; it was kind of those who so carried him, and teaches the compassion that should be in men, toward their fellow-creatures in distress. True faith and strong faith may work in various ways; but it shall be accepted and approved by Jesus Christ. Sin is the cause of all our pains and sicknesses. The way to remove the effect, is to take away the cause. Pardon of sin strikes at the root of all diseases. Christ proved his power to forgive sin, by showing his power to cure the man sick of the palsy. And his curing diseases was a figure of his pardoning sin, for sin is the disease of the soul; when it is pardoned, it is healed. When we see what Christ does in healing souls, we must own that we never saw the like. Most men think themselves whole; they feel no need of a physician, therefore despise or neglect Christ and his gospel. But the convinced, humbled sinner, who despairs of all help, excepting from the Saviour, will show his faith by applying to him without delay.

Verses 13-17

Matthew was not a good character, or else, being a Jew, he would never have been a publican, that is, a tax-gatherer for the Romans. However, Christ called this publican to follow him. With God, through Christ, there is mercy to pardon the greatest sins, and grace to change the greatest sinners, and make them holy. A faithful, fair-dealing publican was rare. And because the Jews had a particular hatred to an office which proved that they were subject to the Romans, they gave these tax-gatherers an ill name. But such as these our blessed Lord did not hesitate to converse with, when he appeared in the likeness of sinful flesh. And it is no new thing for that which is both well done and well designed, to be slandered, and turned to the reproach of the wisest and best of men. Christ would not withdraw, though the Pharisees were offended. If the world had been righteous, there had been no occasion for his coming, either to preach repentance, or to purchase forgiveness. We must not keep company with ungodly men out of love to their vain conversation; but we are to show love to their souls, remembering that our good Physician had the power of healing in himself, and was in no danger of taking the disease; but it is not so with us. In trying to do good to others, let us be careful we do not get harm to ourselves.

Verses 18-22

Strict professors are apt to blame all that do not fully come up to their own views. Christ did not escape slanders; we should be willing to bear them, as well as careful not to deserve them; but should attend to every part of our duty in its proper order and season.

Verses 23-28

The sabbath is a sacred and Divine institution; a privilege and benefit, not a task and drudgery. God never designed it to be a burden to us, therefore we must not make it so to ourselves. The sabbath was instituted for the good of mankind, as living in society, having many wants and troubles, preparing for a state of happiness or misery. Man was not made for the sabbath, as if his keeping it could be of service to God, nor was he commanded to keep it outward observances to his real hurt. Every observance respecting it, is to be interpreted by the rule of mercy.

Chapter 3

Chapter Outline

Verses 1-5

This man's case was piteous; he had a withered hand, which disabled him from working for his living; and those that are so, are the most proper objects of charity. Let those be helped that cannot help themselves. But stubborn infidels, when they can say nothing against the truth, yet will not yield. We hear what is said amiss, and see what is done amiss; but Christ looks at the root of bitterness in the heart, the blindness and hardness of that, and is grieved. Let hard-hearted sinners tremble to think of the anger with which he will look upon them shortly, when the day of his wrath comes. The great healing day now is the sabbath, and the healing place the house of prayer; but the healing power is of Christ. The gospel command is like that recorded here: though our hands are withered, yet, if we will not stretch them out, it is our own fault that we are not healed. But if we are healed, Christ, his power and grace, must have all the glory.

Verses 6-12

All our sicknesses and calamities spring from the anger of God against our sins. Their removal, or the making them blessings to us, was purchased to us by the blood of Christ. But the plagues and diseases of our souls, of our hearts, are chiefly to be dreaded; and He can heal them also by a word. May more and more press to Christ to be healed of these plagues, and to be delivered from the enemies of their souls.

Verses 13-21

Christ calls whom he will; for his grace is his own. He had called the apostles to separate themselves from the crowd, and they came unto him. He now gave them power to heal sicknesses, and to cast out devils. May the Lord send forth more and more of those who have been with him, and have learned of him to preach his gospel, to be instruments in his blessed work. Those whose hearts are enlarged in the work of God, can easily bear with what is inconvenient to themselves, and will rather lose a meal than an opportunity of doing good. Those who go on with zeal in the work of God, must expect hinderances, both from the hatred of enemies, and mistaken affections of friends, and need to guard against both.

Verses 22-30

It was plain that the doctrine of Christ had a direct tendency to break the devil's power; and it was as plain, that casting of him out of the bodies of people, confirmed that doctrine; therefore Satan could not support such a design. Christ gave an awful warning against speaking such dangerous words. It is true the gospel promises, because Christ has purchased, forgiveness for the greatest sins and sinners; but by this sin, they would oppose the gifts of the Holy Ghost after Christ's ascension. Such is the enmity of the heart, that unconverted men pretend believers are doing Satan's work, when sinners are brought to repentance and newness of life.

Verses 31-35

It is a great comfort to all true Christians, that they are dearer to Christ than mother, brother, or sister as such, merely as relations in the flesh would have been, even had they been holy. Blessed be God, this great and gracious privilege is ours even now; for though Christ's bodily presence cannot be enjoyed by us, his spiritual presence is not denied us.

Chapter 4

Chapter Outline

Verses 1-20

This parable contained instruction so important, that all capable of hearing were bound to attend to it. There are many things we are concerned to know; and if we understand not the plain truths of the gospel, how shall we learn those more difficult! It will help us to value the privileges we enjoy as disciples of Christ, if we seriously consider the deplorable state of all who have not such privileges. In the great field of the church, the word of God is dispensed to all. Of the many that hear the word of the gospel, but few receive it, so as to bring forth fruit. Many are much affected with the word for the present, who yet receive no abiding benefit. The word does not leave abiding impressions upon the minds of men, because their hearts are not duly disposed to receive it. The devil is very busy about careless hearers, as the fowls of the air go about the seed that lies above ground. Many continue in a barren, false profession, and go down to hell. Impressions that are not deep, will not last. Many do not mind heart-work, without which religion is nothing. Others are hindered from profiting by the word of God, by abundance of the world. And those who have but little of the world, may yet be ruined by indulging the body. God expects and requires fruit from those who enjoy the gospel, a temper of mind and Christian graces daily exercised, Christian duties duly performed. Let us look to the Lord, that by his new-creating grace our hearts may become good ground, and that the good seed of the word may produce in our lives those good words and works which are through Jesus Christ, to the praise and glory of God the Father.

Verses 21-34

These declarations were intended to call the attention of the disciples to the word of Christ. By his thus instructing them, they were made able to instruct others; as candles are lighted, not to be covered, but to be placed on a candlestick, that they may give light to a room. This parable of the good seed, shows the manner in which the kingdom of God makes progress in the world. Let but the word of Christ have the place it ought to have in a soul, and it will show itself in a good conversation. It grows gradually: first the blade; then the ear; after that the full corn in the ear. When it is sprung up, it will go forward. The work of grace in the soul is, at first, but the day of small things; yet it has mighty products even now, while it is in its growth; but what will there be when it is perfected in heaven!

Verses 35-41

Christ was asleep in the storm, to try the faith of his disciples, and to stir them up to pray. Their faith appeared weak, and their prayers strong. When our wicked hearts are like the troubled sea which cannot rest, when our passions are unruly, let us think we hear the law of Christ, saying, Be silent, be dumb. When without are fightings, and within are fears, and the spirits are in a tumult, if he say, "Peace, be still," there is a great calm at once. Why are ye so fearful? Though there may be cause for some fear, yet not for such fear as this. Those may suspect their faith, who can have such a thought as that Jesus careth not though his people perish. How imperfect are the best of saints! Faith and fear take their turns while we are in this world; but ere long, fear will be overcome, and faith will be lost in sight.

Chapter 5

Chapter Outline

The demoniac healed.	(1–20)
A woman healed.	(21–34)
The daughter of Jairus raised.	(35–43)

Verses 1-20

Some openly wilful sinners are like this madman. The commands of the law are as chains and fetters, to restrain sinners from their wicked courses; but they break those bands in sunder; and it is an evidence of the power of the devil in them. A legion of soldiers consisted of six thousand men, or more. What multitudes of fallen spirits there must be, and all enemies to God and man, when here was a legion in one poor wretched creature! Many there are that rise up against us. We are not a match for our spiritual enemies, in our own strength; but in the Lord, and in the power of his might, we shall be able to stand against them, though there are legions of them. When the vilest transgressor is delivered by the power of Jesus from the bondage of Satan, he will gladly sit at the feet of his Deliverer, and hear his word, who delivers the wretched slaves of Satan, and numbers them among his saints and servants. When the people found that their swine were lost, they had a dislike to Christ. Long-suffering and mercy may be seen, even in the corrections by which men lose their property while their lives are saved, and warning given them to seek the salvation of their souls. The man joyfully proclaimed what great things Jesus had done for him. All men marvelled, but few followed him. Many who cannot but wonder at the works of Christ, yet do not, as they ought, wonder after him.

Verses 21-34

A despised gospel will go where it will be better received. One of the rulers of a synagogue earnestly besought Christ for a little daughter, about twelve years old, who was dying. Another cure was wrought by the way. We should do good, not only when in the house, but when we walk by the way, De 6:7. It is common with people not to apply to Christ till they have tried in vain all other helpers, and find them, as certainly they will, physicians of no value. Some run to diversions and gay company; others plunge into business, or even into intemperance; others go about to establish their own righteousness, or torment themselves by vain superstitions. Many perish in these ways; but none will ever find rest to the soul by such devices; while those whom Christ heals of the disease of sin, find in themselves an entire change for the better. As secret acts of sin, so secret acts of faith, are known to the Lord Jesus. The woman told all the truth. It is the will of Christ that his people should be comforted, and he has power to command comfort to troubled spirits. The more simply we depend on Him, and expect great things from him, the more we shall find in ourselves that he is become our salvation. Those who, by faith, are healed of their spiritual diseases, have reason to go in peace.

Verses 35-43

We may suppose Jairus hesitating whether he should ask Christ to go on or not, when told that his daughter was dead. But have we not as much occasion for the grace of God, and the comfort of his Spirit, for the prayers of our ministers and Christian friends, when death is in the house, as when sickness is there? Faith is the only remedy against grief and fear at such a time. Believe the resurrection, then fear not. He raised the dead child to life by a word of power. Such is the gospel call to those who are by nature dead in trespasses and sins. It is by the word of Christ that spiritual life is given. All who saw it, and heard of it, admired the miracle, and Him that wrought it. Though we cannot now expect to have our dead children or relatives restored, we may hope to find comfort under our trials.

Chapter 6

Chapter Outline

Verses 1-6

Our Lord's countrymen tried to prejudice the minds of people against him. Is not this the carpenter? Our Lord Jesus probably had worked in that business with his father. He thus put honour upon mechanics, and encouraged all persons who eat by the labour of their hands. It becomes the followers of Christ to content themselves with the satisfaction of doing good, although they are denied the praise of it. How much did these Nazarenes lose by obstinate prejudices against Jesus! May Divine grace deliver us from that unbelief, which renders Christ a savour of death, rather than of life to the soul. Let us, like our Master, go and teach cottages and peasants the way of salvation.

Verses 7-13

Though the apostles were conscious to themselves of great weakness, and expected no wordly advantage, yet, in obedience to their Master, and in dependence upon his strength, they went out. They did not amuse people with curious matters, but told them they must repent of their sins, and turn to God. The servants of Christ may hope to turn many from darkness unto God, and to heal souls by the power of the Holy Ghost.

Verses 14-29

Herod feared John while he lived, and feared him still more when he was dead. Herod did many of those things which John in his preaching taught him; but it is not enough to do many things, we must have respect to all the commandments. Herod respected John, till he touched him in his Herodias. Thus many love good preaching, if it keep far away from their beloved sin. But it is better that sinners persecute ministers now for faithfulness, than curse them eternally for unfaithfulness. The ways of God are unsearchable; but we may be sure he never can be at a loss to repay his servants for what they endure or lose for his sake. Death could not come so as to surprise this holy man; and the triumph of the wicked was short.

Verses 30-44

Let not ministers do any thing or teach any thing, but what they are willing should be told to their Lord. Christ notices the frights of some, and the toils of others of his disciples, and provides rest for those that are tired, and refuge for those that are terrified. The people sought the spiritual food of Christ's word, and then he took care that they should not want bodily food. If Christ and his disciples put up with mean things, surely we may. And this miracle shows that Christ came into the world, not only to restore, but to preserve and nourish spiritual life; in him there is enough for all that come. None are sent empty away from Christ but those who come to him full of themselves. Though Christ had bread enough at command, he teaches us not to waste any of God's bounties, remembering how many are in want. We may, some time, need the fragments that we now throw away.

Verses 45-56

The church is often like a ship at sea, tossed with tempests, and not comforted: we may have Christ for us, yet wind and tide against us; but it is a comfort to Christ's disciples in a storm, that their Master is in the heavenly mount, interceding for them. And no difficulties can hinder Christ's appearance for his people, when the set time is come. He silenced their fears, by making himself known to them. Our fears are soon satisfied, if our mistakes are set right, especially our mistakes as to Christ. Let the disciples have their Master with them, and all is well. It is for want of rightly understanding Christ's former works, that we view his present works as if there never were the like before. If Christ's ministers now could cure people's bodily diseases, what multitudes would flock after them! It is sad to think how much more most care about their bodies than about their souls.

Chapter 7

Chapter Outline

The traditions of the elders.	(1–13)
What defiles the man.	(14–23)
The woman of Canaan's daughter cured.	(24–30)
Christ restores a man to hearing and speech.	(31–37)

Verses 1-13

One great design of Christ's coming was, to set aside the ceremonial law; and to make way for this, he rejects the ceremonies men added to the law of God's making. Those clean hands and that pure heart which Christ bestows on his disciples, and requires of them, are very different from the outward and superstitious forms of Pharisees of every age. Jesus reproves them for rejecting the commandment of God. It is clear that it is the duty of children, if their parents are poor, to relieve them as far as they are able; and if children deserve to die that curse their parents, much more those that starve them. But if a man conformed to the traditions of the Pharisees, they found a device to free him from the claim of this duty.

Verses 14-23

Our wicked thoughts and affections, words and actions, defile us, and these only. As a corrupt fountain sends forth corrupt streams, so does a corrupt heart send forth corrupt reasonings, corrupt appetites and passions, and all the wicked words and actions that come from them. A spiritual understanding of the law of God, and a sense of the evil of sin, will cause a man to seek for the grace of the Holy Spirit, to keep down the evil thoughts and affections that work within.

Verses 24-30

Christ never put any from him that fell at his feet, which a poor trembling soul may do. As she was a good woman, so a good mother. This sent her to Christ. His saying, Let the children first be filled, shows that there was mercy for the Gentiles, and not far off. She spoke, not as making light of the mercy, but magnifying the abundance of miraculous cures among the Jews, in comparison with which a single cure was but as a crumb. Thus, while proud Pharisees are left by the blessed Saviour, he manifests his compassion to poor humbled sinners, who look to him for children's bread. He still goes about to seek and save the lost.

Verses 31-37

Here is a cure of one that was deaf and dumb. Those who brought this poor man to Christ, besought him to observe the case, and put forth his power. Our Lord used more outward actions in the doing of this cure than usual. These were only signs of Christ's power to cure the man, to encourage his faith, and theirs that brought him. Though we find great variety in the cases and manner of relief of those who applied to Christ, yet all obtained the relief they sought. Thus it still is in the great concerns of our souls.

Chapter 8

Chapter Outline

Verses 1-10

Our Lord Jesus encouraged the meanest to come to him for life and grace. Christ knows and considers our frames. The bounty of Christ is always ready; to show that, he repeated this miracle. His favours are renewed, as our wants and necessities are. And those need not fear want, who have Christ to live upon by faith, and do so with thanksgiving.

Verses 11-21

Obstinate unbelief will have something to say, though ever so unreasonable. Christ refused to answer their demand. If they will not be convinced, they shall not. Alas! what cause we have to lament for those around us, who destroy themselves and others by their perverse and obstinate unbelief, and enmity to the gospel! When we forget the works of God, and distrust him, we should chide ourselves severely, as Christ here reproves his disciples. How is it that we so often mistake his meaning, disregard his warnings, and distrust his providence?

Verses 22-26

Here is a blind man brought to Christ by his friends. Therein appeared the faith of those that brought him. If those who are spiritually blind, do not pray for themselves, yet their friends and relations should pray for them, that Christ would be pleased to touch them. The cure was wrought gradually, which was not usual in our Lord's miracles. Christ showed in what method those commonly are healed by his grace, who by nature are spiritually blind. At first, their knowledge is confused; but, like the light of the morning, it shines more and more to the perfect day, and then they see all things clearly. Slighting Christ's favours is forfeiting them; and he will make those who do so know the worth of privileges by the want of them.

Verses 27-33

These things are written, that we may believe that Jesus is the Christ, the Son of God. These miracles of our Lord assure us that he was not conquered, but a Conqueror. Now the disciples are convinced that Jesus is the Christ; they may bear to hear of his sufferings, of which Christ here begins to give them notice. He sees that amiss in what we say and do, of which we ourselves are not aware, and knows what manner of spirit we are of, when we ourselves do not. The wisdom of man is folly, when it pretends to limit the Divine counsels. Peter did not rightly understand the nature of Christ's kingdom.

Verses 34-38

Frequent notice is taken of the great flocking there was to Christ for help in various cases. All are concerned to know this, if they expect him to heal their souls. They must not indulge the ease of the body. As the happiness of heaven with Christ, is enough to make up for the loss of life itself for him, so the gain of all the world in sin, will not make up for the ruin of the soul by sin. And there is a day coming, when the cause of Christ will appear as glorious, as some now think it mean and contemptible. May we think of that season, and view every earthly object as we shall do at that great day.

Chapter 9

Chapter Outline

Verses 1-13

Here is a prediction of the near approach Christ's kingdom. A glimpse of that kingdom was given in the transfiguration of Christ. It is good to be away from the world, and alone with Christ: and how good to be with Christ glorified in heaven with all the saints! But when it is well with us, we are apt not to care for others, and in the fulness of our enjoyments, we forget the many wants of our brethren. God owns Jesus, and accepts him as his beloved Son, and is ready to accept us in him. Therefore we must own and accept him as our beloved Saviour, and must give up ourselves to be ruled by him. Christ does not leave the soul, when joys and comforts leave it. Jesus explained to the disciples the prophecy about Elias. This was very suitable to the ill usage of John Baptist.

Verses 14-29

The father of the suffering youth reflected on the want of power in the disciples; but Christ will have him reckon the disappointment to the want of faith. Very much is promised to our believing. If thou canst believe, it is possible that thy hard heart may be softened, thy spiritual diseases may be cured; and, weak as thou art, thou mayest be able to hold out to the end. Those that complain of unbelief, must look up to Christ for grace to help them against it, and his grace will be sufficient for them. Whom Christ cures, he cures effectually. But Satan is unwilling to be driven from those that have been long his slaves, and, when he cannot deceive or destroy the sinner, he will cause him all the terror that he can. The disciples must not think to do their work always with the same ease; some services call for more than ordinary pains.

Verses 30-40

The time of Christ's suffering drew nigh. Had he been delivered into the hands of devils, and they had done this, it had not been so strange; but that men should thus shamefully treat the Son of man, who came to redeem and save them, is wonderful. Still observe that when Christ spake of his death, he always spake of his resurrection, which took the reproach of it from himself, and should have taken the grief of it from his disciples. Many remain ignorant because they are ashamed to inquire. Alas! that while the Saviour teaches so plainly the things which belong to his love and grace, men are so blinded that they understand not his sayings. We shall be called to account about our discourses, and to account for our disputes, especially about being greater than others. Those who are most humble and self-denying, most resemble Christ, and shall be most tenderly owned by him. This Jesus taught them by a sign; whoever shall receive one like this child, receives me. Many have been like the disciples, ready to silence men who have success in preaching to sinners repentance in Christ's name, because they follow not with them. Our Lord blamed the apostles, reminding them that he who wrought miracles in his name would not be likely to hurt his cause. If sinners are brought to repent, to believe in the Saviour, and to live sober, righteous, and godly lives, we then see that the Lord works by the preacher.

Verses 41-50

It is repeatedly said of the wicked, Their worm dieth not, as well as, The fire is never quenched. Doubtless, remorse of conscience and keen self-reflection are this never-dying worm. Surely it is beyond compare better to undergo all possible pain, hardship, and self-denial here, and to be happy for ever hereafter, than to enjoy all kinds of worldly pleasure for a season, and to be miserable for ever. Like the sacrifices, we must be salted with salt; our corrupt affections must be subdued and mortified by the Holy Spirit. Those that have the salt of grace, must show they have a living principle of grace in their hearts, which works out corrupt dispositions in the soul that would offend God, or our own consciences.

Chapter 10

Chapter Outline

Verses 1-12

Wherever Jesus was, the people flocked after him in crowds, and he taught them. Preaching was Christ's constant practice. He here shows that the reason why Moses' law allowed divorce, was such that they ought not to use the permission; it was only for the hardness of their hearts. God himself joined man and wife together; he has fitted them to be comforts and helps for each other.

The bond which God has tied, is not to be lightly untied. Let those who are for putting away their wives consider what would become of themselves, if God should deal with them in like manner.

Verses 13-16

Some parents or nurses brought little children to Christ, that he should touch them, in token of his blessing them. It does not appear that they needed bodily cures, nor were they capable of being taught: but those who had the care of them believed that Christ's blessing would do their souls good; therefore they brought them to him. Jesus ordered that they should be brought to him, and that nothing should be said or done to hinder it. Children should be directed to the Saviour as soon as they are able to understand his words. Also, we must receive the kingdom of God as little children; we must stand affected to Christ and his grace, as little children to their parents, nurses, and teachers.

Verses 17-22

This young ruler showed great earnestness. He asked what he should do now, that he might be happy for ever. Most ask for good to be had in this world; any good, Ps 4:6; he asks for good to be done in this world, in order to enjoy the greatest good in the other world. Christ encouraged this address by assisting his faith, and by directing his practice. But here is a sorrowful parting between Jesus and this young man. He asks Christ what he shall do more than he has done, to obtain eternal life; and Christ puts it to him, whether he has indeed that firm belief of, and that high value for eternal life which he seems to have. Is he willing to bear a present cross, in expectation of future crown? The young man was sorry he could not be a follower of Christ upon easier terms; that he could not lay hold on eternal life, and keep hold of his worldly possessions too. He went away grieved. See Mt 6:24, Ye cannot serve God and mammon.

Verses 23-31

Christ took this occasion to speak to his disciples about the difficulty of the salvation of those who have abundance of this world. Those who thus eagerly seek the wealth of the world, will never rightly prize Christ and his grace. Also, as to the greatness of the salvation of those who have but little of this world, and leave it for Christ. The greatest trial of a good man's constancy is, when love to Jesus calls him to give up love to friends and relatives. Even when gainers by Christ, let them still expect to suffer for him, till they reach heaven. Let us learn contentment in a low state, and to watch against the love of riches in a high one. Let us pray to be enabled to part with all, if required, in Christ's service, and to use all we are allowed to keep in his service.

Verses 32-45

Christ's going on with his undertaking for the salvation of mankind, was, is, and will be, the wonder of all his disciples. Worldly honour is a glittering thing, with which the eyes of Christ's own disciples have many times been dazzled. Our care must be, that we may have wisdom and grace to know how to suffer with him; and we may trust him to provide what the degrees of our glory shall be. Christ shows them that dominion was generally abused in the world. If Jesus would gratify all our desires, it would soon appear that we desire fame or authority, and are unwilling to taste of his cup, or to have his baptism; and should often be ruined by having our prayers answered. But he loves us, and will only give his people what is good for them.

Verses 46-52

Bartimeus had heard of Jesus and his miracles, and learning that he was passing by, hoped to recover his eyesight. In coming to Christ for help and healing, we should look to him as the promised Messiah. The gracious calls Christ gives us to come to him, encourage our hope, that if we come to him we shall have what we come for. Those who would come to Jesus, must cast away the garment of their own sufficiency, must free themselves from every weight, and the sin that, like long garments, most easily besets them, Heb 12:1. He begged that his eyes might be opened. It is very desirable to be able to earn our bread; and where God has given men limbs and senses, it is a shame, by foolishness and slothfulness, to make themselves, in effect, blind and lame. His eyes were opened. Thy faith has made thee whole: faith in Christ as the Son of David, and in his pity and power; not thy repeated words, but thy faith; Christ setting thy faith to work. Let sinners be exhorted to imitate blind Bartimeus. Where the gospel is preached, or the written words of truth circulated, Jesus is passing by, and this is the opportunity. It is not enough to come to Christ for spiritual healing, but, when we are healed, we must continue to follow him; that we may honour him, and receive instruction from him. Those who have spiritual eyesight, see that beauty in Christ which will draw them to run after him.

Chapter 11

Chapter Outline

Christ's triumphant entry into Jerusalem.	(1–11)
The barren fig-tree cursed, The temple cleansed.	(12–18)
Prayer in faith.	(19–26)
The priests and elders questioned concerning John the Baptist.	(27–33)

Verses 1-11

Christ's coming into Jerusalem thus remarkably, shows that he was not afraid of the power and malice of his enemies. This would encourage his disciples who were full of fear. Also, that he was not disquieted at the thoughts of his approaching sufferings. But all marked his humiliation; and these matters teach us not to mind high things, but to condescend to those of low estate. How ill it becomes Christians to take state, when Christ was so far from claiming it! They welcomed his person; Blessed is he that cometh, the "He that should come," so often promised, so long expected;

he comes in the name of the Lord. Let him have our best affections; he is a blessed Saviour, and brings blessings to us, and blessed be He that sent him. Praises be to our God, who is in the highest heavens, over all, God blessed for ever.

Verses 12-18

Christ looked to find some fruit, for the time of gathering figs, though it was near, was not yet come; but he found none. He made this fig-tree an example, not to the trees, but to the men of that generation. It was a figure of the doom upon the Jewish church, to which he came seeking fruit, but found none. Christ went to the temple, and began to reform the abuses in its courts, to show that when the Redeemer came to Zion, it was to turn away ungodliness from Jacob. The scribes and the chief priests sought, not how they might make their peace with him, but how they might destroy him. A desperate attempt, which they could not but fear was fighting against God.

Verses 19-26

The disciples could not think why that fig-tree should so soon wither away; but all wither who reject Christ; it represented the state of the Jewish church. We should rest in no religion that does not make us fruitful in good works. Christ taught them from hence to pray in faith. It may be applied to that mighty faith with which all true Christians are endued, and which does wonders in spiritual things. It justifies us, and so removes mountains of guilt, never to rise up in judgment against us. It purifies the heart, and so removes mountains of corruption, and makes them plain before the grace of God. One great errand to the throne of grace is to pray for the pardon of our sins; and care about this ought to be our daily concern.

Verses 27-33

Our Saviour shows how near akin his doctrine and baptism were to those of John; they had the same design and tendency, to bring in the gospel kingdom. These elders did not deserve to be taught; for it was plain that they contended not for truth, but victory: nor did he need to tell them; for the works he did, told them plainly he had authority from God; since no man could do the miracles which he did, unless God were with him.

Chapter 12

Chapter Outline

Verses 1-12

Christ showed in parables, that he would lay aside the Jewish church. It is sad to think what base usage God's faithful ministers have met with in all ages, from those who have enjoyed the privileges of the church, but have not brought forth fruit answerable. God at length sent his Son, his Well-beloved; and it might be expected that he whom their Master loved, they also should respect and love; but instead of honouring him because he was the Son and Heir, they therefore hated him. But the exaltation of Christ was the Lord's doing; and it is his doing to exalt him in our hearts, and to set up his throne there; and if this be done, it cannot but be marvellous in our eyes. The Scriptures, and faithful preachers, and the coming of Christ in the flesh, call on us to render due praise to God in our lives. Let sinners beware of a proud, carnal spirit; if they revile or despise the preachers of Christ, they would have done so their Master, had they lived when he was upon earth.

Verses 13-17

The enemies of Christ would be thought desirous to know their duty, when really they hoped that which soever side he took of the question, they might find occasion to accuse him. Nothing is more likely to insnare the followers of Christ, than bringing them to meddle with disputes about worldly politics. Jesus avoided the snare, by referring to the submission they had already made as a nation; and all that heard him, marvelled at the great wisdom of his answer. Many will praise the words of a sermon, who will not be commanded by the doctrines of it.

Verses 18-27

A right knowledge of the Scripture, as the fountain whence all revealed religion now flows, and the foundation on which it is built, is the best preservative against error. Christ put aside the objection of the Sadducees, who were the scoffing infidels of that day, by setting the doctrine of the future state in a true light. The relation between husband and wife, though appointed in the earthly paradise, will not be known in the heavenly one. It is no wonder if we confuse ourselves with foolish errors, when we form our ideas of the world of spirits by the affairs of this world of sense. It is absurd to think that the living God should be the portion and happiness of a man if he is for ever dead; and therefore it is certain that Abraham's soul exists and acts, though now for a time separate from the body. Those that deny the resurrection greatly err, and ought to be told so. Let us seek to pass through this dying world, with a joyful hope of eternal happiness, and of a glorious resurrection.

Verses 28-34

Those who sincerely desire to be taught their duty, Christ will guide in judgment, and teach his way. He tells the scribe that the great commandment, which indeed includes all, is, that of loving God with all our hearts. Wherever this is the ruling principle in the soul, there is a disposition to every other duty. Loving God with all our heart, will engage us to every thing by which he will be pleased. The sacrifices only represented the atonements for men's transgressions of the moral law; they were of no power except as they expressed repentance and faith in the promised Saviour, and as they led to moral obedience. And because we have not thus loved God and man, but the very reverse, therefore we are condemned sinners; we need repentance, and we need mercy. Christ approved what the scribe said, and encouraged him. He stood fair for further advance; for this knowledge of the law leads to conviction of sin, to repentance, to discovery of our need of mercy, and understanding the way of justification by Christ.

Verses 35-40

When we attend to what the Scriptures declare, as to the person and offices of Christ, we shall be led to confess him as our Lord and God; to obey him as our exalted Redeemer. If the common people hear these things gladly, while the learned and distinguished oppose, the former are happy, and the latter to be pitied. And as sin, disguised with a show of piety, is double iniquity, so its doom will be doubly heavy.

Verses 41-44

Let us not forget that Jesus still sees the treasury. He knows how much, and from what motives, men give to his cause. He looks at the heart, and what our views are, in giving alms; and whether we do it as unto the Lord, or only to be seen of men. It is so rare to find any who would not blame this widow, that we cannot expect to find many who will do like to her; and yet our Saviour commends her, therefore we are sure that she did well and wisely. The feeble efforts of the poor to honour their Saviour, will be commended in that day, when the splendid actions of unbelievers will be exposed to contempt.

Chapter 13

Chapter Outline

Verses 1-4

See how little Christ values outward pomp, where there is not real purity of heart. He looks with pity upon the ruin of precious souls, and weeps over them, but we do not find him look with pity upon the ruin of a fine house. Let us then be reminded how needful it is for us to have a more lasting abode in heaven, and to be prepared for it by the influences of the Holy Spirit, sought in the earnest use of all the means of grace.

Verses 5-13

Our Lord Jesus, in reply to the disciples' question, does not so much satisfy their curiosity as direct their consciences. When many are deceived, we should thereby be awakened to look to ourselves. And the disciples of Christ, if it be not their own fault, may enjoy holy security and peace of mind, when all around is in disorder. But they must take heed that they are not drawn away from Christ and their duty to him, by the sufferings they will meet with for his sake. They shall be hated of all men: trouble enough! Yet the work they were called to should be carried on and prosper. Though they may be crushed and borne down, the gospel cannot be. The salvation promised is more than deliverance from evil, it is everlasting blessedness.

Verses 14-23

The Jews in rebelling against the Romans, and in persecuting the Christians, hastened their own ruin apace. Here we have a prediction of that ruin which came upon them within less than forty years after this. Such destruction and desolation, that the like cannot be found in any history. Promises of power to persevere, and cautions against falling away, well agree with each other. But the more we consider these things, the more we shall see abundant cause to flee without delay for refuge to Christ, and to renounce every earthly object, for the salvation of our souls.

Verses 24-27

The disciples had confounded the destruction of Jerusalem and the end of the world. This mistake Christ set right, and showed that the day of Christ's coming, and the day of judgment, shall be after that tribulation. Here he foretells the final dissolution of the present frame and fabric of the world. Also, the visible appearance of the Lord Jesus coming in the clouds, and the gathering together of all the elect to him.

Verses 28-37

We have the application of this prophetic sermon. As to the destruction of Jerusalem, expect it to come very shortly. As to the end of the world, do not inquire when it will come, for of that day and that hour knoweth no man. Christ, as God, could not be ignorant of anything; but the Divine wisdom which dwelt in our Saviour, communicated itself to his human soul according to the Divine pleasure. As to both, our duty is to watch and pray. Our Lord Jesus, when he ascended on high, left something for all his servants to do. We ought to be always upon our watch, in expectation of his return. This applies to Christ's coming to us at our death, as well as to the general judgment. We know not whether our Master will come in the days of youth, or middle age, or old age; but, as soon as we are born, we begin to die, and therefore we must expect death. Our great care must be, that, whenever our Lord comes, he may not find us secure, indulging in ease and sloth, mindless of our work and duty. He says to all, Watch, that you may be found in peace, without spot, and blameless.

Chapter 14

Chapter Outline

Christ anointed at Bethany.	(1–11)
The passover, Jesus declares that Judas would betray him.	(12–21)
The Lord's supper instituted.	(22–31)
Christ's agony in the garden.	(32–42)
He is betrayed and taken.	(43–52)
Christ before the high priest.	(53–65)
Peter denies Christ.	(66–72)

Verses 1-11

Did Christ pour out his soul unto death for us, and shall we think any thing too precious for him? Do we give him the precious ointment of our best affections? Let us love him with all the heart, though it is common for zeal and affection to be misunderstood and blamed; and remember that charity to the poor will not excuse any from particular acts of piety to the Lord Jesus. Christ commended this woman's pious attention to the notice of believers in all ages. Those who honour Christ he will honour. Covetousness was Judas' master lust, and that betrayed him to the sin of betraying his Master; the devil suited his temptation to that, and so conquered him. And see what wicked contrivances many have in their sinful pursuits; but what appears to forward their plans, will prove curses in the end.

Verses 12-21

Nothing could be less the result of human foresight than the events here related. But our Lord knows all things about us before they come to pass. If we admit him, he will dwell in our hearts. The Son of man goes, as it is written of him, as a lamb to the slaughter; but woe to that man by whom he is betrayed! God's permitting the sins of men, and bringing glory to himself out of them, does not oblige them to sin; nor will this be any excuse for their guilt, or lessen their punishment.

Verses 22-31

The Lord's supper is food for the soul, therefore a very little of that which is for the body, as much as will serve for a sign, is enough. It was instituted by the example and the practice of our Master, to remain in force till his second coming. It was instituted with blessing and giving of thanks, to be a memorial of Christ's death. Frequent mention is made of his precious blood, as the price of our redemption. How comfortable is this to poor repenting sinners, that the blood of Christ is shed for many! If for many, why not for me? It was a sign of the conveyance of the benefits purchased for us by his death. Apply the doctrine of Christ crucified to yourselves; let it be meat and drink to your souls, strengthening and refreshing your spiritual life. It was to be an earnest and foretaste of the happiness of heaven, and thereby to put us out of taste for the pleasures and delights of sense. Every one that has tasted spiritual delights, straightway desires eternal ones. Though the great Shepherd passed through his sufferings without one false step, yet his followers often have been scattered by the small measure of sufferings allotted to them. How very apt we are to think well of ourselves, and to trust our own hearts! It was ill done of Peter thus to answer his Master, and not with fear and trembling. Lord, give me grace to keep me from denying thee.

Verses 32-42

Christ's sufferings began with the sorest of all, those in his soul. He began to be sorely amazed; words not used in St. Matthew, but very full of meaning. The terrors of God set themselves in array against him, and he allowed him to contemplate them. Never was sorrow like unto his at this time. Now he was made a curse for us; the curses of the law were laid upon him as our Surety. He now tasted death, in all the bitterness of it. This was that fear of which the apostle speaks, the natural fear of pain and death, at which human nature startles. Can we ever entertain favourable, or even slight thoughts of sin, when we see the painful sufferings which sin, though but reckoned to him, brought on the Lord Jesus? Shall that sit light upon our souls, which sat so heavy upon his? Was Christ in such agony for our sins, and shall we never be in agony about them? How should we look upon Him whom we have pierced, and mourn! It becomes us to be exceedingly sorrowful for sin, because He was so, and never to mock at it. Christ, as Man, pleaded, that, if it were possible, his sufferings might pass from him. As Mediator, he submitted to the will of God, saying, Nevertheless, not what I will, but what thou wilt; I bid it welcome. See how the sinful weakness of Christ's disciples returns, and overpowers them. What heavy clogs these bodies of ours are to our souls! But when we see trouble at the door, we should get ready for it. Alas, even believers often look at the Redeemer's sufferings in a drowsy manner, and instead of being ready to die with Christ, they are not even prepared to watch with him one hour.

Verses 43-52

Because Christ appeared not as a temporal prince, but preached repentance, reformation, and a holy life, and directed men's thoughts, and affections, and aims to another world, therefore the Jewish rulers sought to destroy him. Peter wounded one of the band. It is easier to fight for Christ than to die for him. But there is a great difference between faulty disciples and hypocrites. The latter rashly and without thought call Christ Master, and express great affection for him, yet betray him to his enemies. Thus they hasten their own destruction.

Verses 53-65

We have here Christ's condemnation before the great council of the Jews. Peter followed; but the high priest's fire-side was no proper place, nor his servants proper company, for Peter: it was an entrance into temptation. Great diligence was used to procure false witnesses against Jesus, yet their testimony was not equal to the charge of a capital crime, by the utmost stretch of their law. He was asked, Art thou the Son of the Blessed? that is, the Son of God. For the proof of his being the Son of God, he refers to his second coming. In these outrages we have proofs of man's enmity to God, and of God's free and unspeakable love to man.

Verses 66-72

Peter's denying Christ began by keeping at a distance from him. Those that are shy of godliness, are far in the way to deny Christ. Those who think it dangerous to be in company with Christ's disciples, because thence they may be drawn in to suffer for him, will find it much more dangerous to be in company with his enemies, because there they may be drawn in to sin against him. When Christ was admired and flocked after, Peter readily owned him; but will own no relation to him now he is deserted and despised. Yet observe, Peter's repentance was very speedy. Let him that thinketh he standeth take heed lest he fall; and let him that has fallen think of these things, and of his own offences, and return to the Lord with weeping and supplication, seeking forgiveness, and to be raised up by the Holy Spirit.

Chapter 15

Chapter Outline

Christ before Pilate.	(1–14)
Christ led to be crucified.	(15–21)
The crucifixion.	(22–32)
The death of Christ.	(33–41)
His body buried.	(42–47)

Verses 1-14

They bound Christ. It is good for us often to remember the bonds of the Lord Jesus, as bound with him who was bound for us. By delivering up the King, they, in effect, delivered up the kingdom of God, which was, therefore, as by their own consent, taken from them, and given to another nation. Christ gave Pilate a direct answer, but would not answer the witnesses, because the things they alleged were known to be false, even Pilate himself was convinced they were so. Pilate thought that he might appeal from the priests to the people, and that they would deliver Jesus out of the priests' hands. But they were more and more urged by the priests, and cried, Crucify him! Crucify him! Let us judge of persons and things by their merits, and the standard of God's word, and not by common report. The thought that no one ever was so shamefully treated, as the only perfectly wise, holy, and excellent Person that ever appeared on earth, leads the serious mind to strong views of man's wickedness and enmity to God. Let us more and more abhor the evil dispositions which marked the conduct of these persecutors.

Verses 15-21

Christ met death in its greatest terror. It was the death of the vilest malefactors. Thus the cross and the shame are put together. God having been dishonoured by the sin of man, Christ made satisfaction by submitting to the greatest disgrace human nature could be loaded with. It was a cursed death; thus it was branded by the Jewish law, De 21:23. The Roman soldiers mocked our Lord Jesus as a King; thus in the high priest's hall the servants had mocked him as a Prophet and Saviour. Shall a purple or scarlet robe be matter of pride to a Christian, which was matter of reproach and shame to Christ? He wore the crown of thorns which we deserved, that we might wear the crown of glory which he merited. We were by sin liable to everlasting shame and contempt; to deliver us, our Lord Jesus submitted to shame and contempt. He was led forth with the workers of iniquity, though he did no sin. The sufferings of the meek and holy Redeemer, are ever a source of instruction to the believer, of which, in his best hours, he cannot be weary. Did Jesus thus suffer, and shall I, a vile sinner, fret or repine? Shall I indulge anger, or utter reproaches and threats because of troubles and injuries?

Verses 22-32

The place where our Lord Jesus was crucified, was called the place of a scull; it was the common place of execution; for he was in all respects numbered with the transgressors. Whenever we look unto Christ crucified, we must remember what was written over his head; he is a King, and we must give up ourselves to be his subjects, as Israelites indeed. They crucified two thieves with him, and him in the midst; they thereby intended him great dishonour. But it was foretold that he should be numbered with the transgressors, because he was made sin for us. Even those who passed by railed at him. They told him to come down from the cross, and they would believe; but they did not believe, though he gave them a more convincing sign when he came up from the grave. With what earnestness will the man who firmly believes the truth, as made known by the sufferings of Christ, seek for salvation! With what gratitude will he receive the dawning hope of forgiveness and eternal life, as purchased for him by the sufferings and death of the Son of God! and with what godly sorrow will he mourn over the sins which crucified the Lord of glory!

Verses 33-41

There was a thick darkness over the land, from noon until three in the afternoon. The Jews were doing their utmost to extinguish the Sun of Righteousness. The darkness signified the cloud which the human soul of Christ was under, when he was making it an offering for sin. He did not complain that his disciples forsook him, but that his Father forsook him. In this especially he was made sin for us. When Paul was to be offered as a sacrifice for the service saints, he could joy and rejoice, Php 2:17; but it is another thing to be offered as a sacrifice for the sin of sinners. At the same instant that Jesus died, the veil of the temple was rent from the top to the bottom. This spake terror to the unbelieving Jews, and was a sign of the destruction of their church and nation. It speaks comfort to all believing Christians, for it signified the laying open a new and living way into the holiest by the blood of Jesus. The confidence with which Christ had openly addressed God as his Father, and committed his soul into his hands, seems greatly to have affected the centurion. Right views of Christ crucified will reconcile the believer to the thought of death; he longs to behold, love, and praise, as he ought, that Saviour who was wounded and pierced to save him from the wrath to come.

Verses 42-47

We are here attending the burial of our Lord Jesus. Oh that we may by grace be planted in the likeness of it! Joseph of Arimathea was one who waited for the kingdom of God. Those who hope for a share in its privileges, must own Christ's cause, when it seems to be crushed. This man God raised up for his service. There was a special providence, that Pilate should be so strict in his inquiry, that there might be no pretence to say Jesus was alive. Pilate gave Joseph leave to take down the body, and do what he pleased with it. Some of the women beheld where Jesus was laid, that they might come after the sabbath to anoint the dead body, because they had not time to do it before. Special notice was taken of Christ's sepulchre, because he was to rise again. And he will not forsake those who trust in him, and call upon him. Death, deprived of its sting, will soon end the believer's sorrows, as it ended those of the Saviour.

Chapter 16

Chapter Outline

Verses 1-8

Nicodemus brought a large quantity of spices, but these good women did not think that enough. The respect others show to Christ, should not hinder us from showing our respect. And those who are carried by holy zeal, to seek Christ diligently, will find the difficulties in their way speedily vanish. When we put ourselves to trouble and expense, from love to Christ, we shall be accepted, though our endeavours are not successful. The sight of the angel might justly have encouraged them, but they were affrighted. Thus many times that which should be matter of comfort to us, through our own mistake, proves a terror to us. He was crucified, but he is glorified. He is risen, he is not here, not dead, but alive again; hereafter you will see him, but you may here see the place where he was laid. Thus seasonable comforts will be sent to those that lament after the Lord Jesus. Peter is particularly named, Tell Peter; it will be most welcome to him, for he is in sorrow for sin. A sight of Christ will be very welcome to a true penitent, and a true penitent is very welcome to a sight of Christ. The men ran with all the haste they could to the disciples; but disquieting fears often hinder us from doing that service to Christ and to the souls of men, which, if faith and the joy of faith were strong, we might do.

Verses 9-13

Better news cannot be brought to disciples in tears, than to tell them of Christ's resurrection. And we should study to comfort disciples that are mourners, by telling them whatever we have seen of Christ. It was a wise providence that the proofs of Christ's resurrection were given gradually, and admitted cautiously, that the assurance with which the apostles preached this doctrine afterwards might the more satisfy. Yet how slowly do we admit the consolations which the word of God holds forth! Therefore while Christ comforts his people, he often sees it needful to rebuke and correct them for hardness of heart in distrusting his promise, as well as in not obeying his holy precepts.

Verses 14-18

The evidences of the truth of the gospel are so full, that those who receive it not, may justly be upbraided with their unbelief. Our blessed Lord renewed his choice of the eleven as his apostles, and commissioned them to go into all the world, to preach his gospel to every creature. Only he that is a true Christian shall be saved through Christ. Simon Magus professed to believe, and was baptized, yet he was declared to be in the bonds of iniquity: see his history in Ac 8:13–25. Doubtless this is a solemn declaration of that true faith which receives Christ in all his characters and offices, and for all the purposes of salvation, and which produces its right effect on the heart and life; not a mere assent, which is a dead faith, and cannot profit. The commission of Christ's ministers extends to every creature throughout the world, and the declarations of the gospel contain not only truths, encouragements, and precepts, but also most awful warnings. Observe what power the apostles should be endued with, for confirming the doctrine they were to preach. These were miracles to confirm the truth of the gospel, and means of spreading the gospel among nations that had not heard it.

Verses 19, 20

After the Lord had spoken he went up into heaven. Sitting is a posture of rest, he had finished his work; and a posture of rule, he took possession of his kingdom. He sat at the right hand of God, which denotes his sovereign dignity and universal power. Whatever God does concerning us, gives to us, or accepts from us, it is by his Son. Now he is glorified with the glory he had before the world. The apostles went forth, and preached every where, far and near. Though the doctrine they preached was spiritual and heavenly, and directly contrary to the spirit and temper of the world; though it met with much opposition, and was wholly destitute of all worldly supports and advantages; yet in a few years the sound went forth unto the ends of the earth. Christ's ministers do not now need to work miracles to prove their message; the Scriptures are proved to be of Divine origin, and this renders those without excuse who reject or neglect them. The effects of the gospel, when faithfully preached, and truly believed, in changing the tempers and characters of mankind, form a constant proof, a miraculous proof, that the gospel is the power of God unto salvation, of all who believe.

Luke

This evangelist is generally supposed to have been a physician, and a companion of the apostle Paul. The style of his writings, and his acquaintance with the Jewish rites and usages, sufficiently show that he was a Jew, while his knowledge of the Greek language and his name, speak his Gentile origin. He is first mentioned Ac 16:10, 11, as with Paul at Troas, whence he attended him to Jerusalem, and was with him in his voyage, and in his imprisonment at Rome. This Gospel appears to be designed to supersede many defective and unauthentic narratives in circulation, and to give a genuine and inspired account of the life, miracles, and doctrines of our Lord, learned from those who heard and witnessed his discourses and miracles.

Chapter 1

Chapter Outline

Verses 1-4

Luke will not write of things about which Christians may safely differ from one another, and hesitate within themselves; but the things which are, and ought to be surely believed. The doctrine of Christ is what the wisest and best of men have ventured their souls upon with confidence and satisfaction. And the great events whereon our hopes depend, have been recorded by those who were from the beginning eye-witnesses and ministers of the word, and who were perfected in their understanding of them through Divine inspiration.

Verses 5-25

The father and mother of John the Baptist were sinners as all are, and were justified and saved in the same way as others; but they were eminent for piety and integrity. They had no children, and it could not be expected that Elisabeth should have any in her old age. While Zacharias was burning incense in the temple, the whole multitude of the people were praying without. All the prayers we offer up to God, are acceptable and successful only by Christ's intercession in the temple of God above. We cannot expect an interest therein if we do not pray, and pray with our spirits, and are not earnest in prayer. Nor can we expect that the best of our prayers should gain acceptance, and bring an answer of peace, but through the mediation of Christ, who ever lives, making intercession. The prayers Zacharias often made, received an answer of peace. Prayers of faith are filed in heaven, and are not forgotten. Prayers made when we were young and entering into the world, may be answered when we are old and going out of the world. Mercies are doubly sweet that are given in answer to prayer. Zacharias shall have a son in his old age, who shall be instrumental in the conversion of many souls to God, and preparing them to receive the gospel of Christ. He shall go before Him with courage, zeal, holiness, and a mind dead to earthly interests and pleasures. The disobedient and rebellious would be brought back to the wisdom of their righteous forefathers, or rather, brought to attend to the wisdom of that Just One who was coming among them. Zacharias heard all that the angel said; but his unbelief spake. In striking him dumb, God dealt justly with him, because he had objected against God's word. We may admire the patience of God towards us. God dealt kindly with him, for thus he prevented his speaking any more distrustful, unbelieving words. Thus also God confirmed his faith. If by the rebukes we are under for our sin, we are brought to give the more credit to the word of God, we have no reason to complain. Even real believers are apt to dishonour God by unbelief; and their mouths are stopped in silence and confusion, when otherwise they would have been praising God with joy and gratitude. In God's gracious dealings with us we ought to observe his gracious regards to us. He has looked on us with compassion and favour, and therefore has thus dealt with us.

Verses 26-38

We have here an account of the mother of our Lord; though we are not to pray to her, yet we ought to praise God for her. Christ must be born miraculously. The angel's address means only, Hail, thou that art the especially chosen and favoured of the Most High, to attain the honour Jewish mothers have so long desired. This wondrous salutation and appearance troubled Mary. The angel then assured her that she had found favour with God, and would become the mother of a son whose name she should call Jesus, the Son of the Highest, one in a nature and perfection with the Lord God. JESUS! the name that refreshes the fainting spirits of humbled sinners; sweet to speak and sweet to hear, Jesus, a Saviour! We know not his riches and our own poverty, therefore we run not to him; we perceive not that we are lost and perishing, therefore a Saviour is a word of little relish. Were we convinced of the huge mass of guilt that lies upon us, and the wrath that hangs over us for it, ready to fall upon us, it would be our continual thought, Is the Saviour mine? And that we might find him so, we should trample on all that hinders our way to him. Mary's reply to the angel was the language of faith and humble admiration, and she asked no sign for the confirming her faith. Without controversy, great was the mystery of godliness, God manifest in the flesh, 1Ti 3:16. Christ's human nature must be produced so, as it was fit that should be which was to be taken into union with the Divine nature. And we must, as Mary here, guide our desires by the word of God. In all conflicts, let us remember that with God nothing is impossible; and as we read and hear his promises, let us turn them into prayers, Behold the willing servant of the Lord; let it be unto me according to thy word.

Verses 39-56

It is very good for those who have the work of grace begun in their souls, to communicate one to another. On Mary's arrival, Elisabeth was conscious of the approach of her who was to be the mother of the great Redeemer. At the same time she was filled with the Holy Ghost, and under his influence declared that Mary and her expected child were most blessed and happy, as peculiarly honoured of and dear to the Most High God. Mary, animated by Elisabeth's address, and being also under the influence of the Holy Ghost, broke out into joy, admiration, and gratitude. She knew herself to be a sinner who needed a Saviour, and that she could no otherwise rejoice in God than as interested in his salvation through the promised Messiah. Those who see their need of Christ, and are desirous of righteousness and life in him, he fills with good things, with the best things; and they are abundantly satisfied with the blessings he gives. He will satisfy the desires of the poor in spirit who long for spiritual blessings, while the self-sufficient shall be sent empty away.

Verses 57-66

In these verses we have an account of the birth of John the Baptist, and the great joy among all the relations of the family. He shall be called Johanan, or "Gracious," because he shall bring in the gospel of Christ, wherein God's grace shines most bright. Zacharias recovered his speech. Unbelief closed his mouth, and believing opened it again: he believers, therefore he speaks. When God opens our lips, our mouths must show forth his praise; and better be without speech, than not use it in praising God. It is said, The hand of the Lord was working with John. God has ways of working on children in their infancy, which we cannot account for. We should observe the dealings of God, and wait the event.

Verses 67-80

Zacharias uttered a prophecy concerning the kingdom and salvation of the Messiah. The gospel brings light with it; in it the day dawns. In John the Baptist it began to break, and increased apace to the perfect day. The gospel is discovering; it shows that about which we were utterly in the dark; it is to give light to those that sit in darkness, the light of the knowledge of the glory of God in the face of Jesus Christ. It is reviving; it brings light to those that sit in the shadow of death, as condemned prisoners in the dungeon. It is directing; it is to guide our feet in the way of peace, into that way which will bring us to peace at last, Ro 3:17. John gave proofs of strong faith, vigorous and holy affections, and of being above the fear and love of the world. Thus he ripened for usefulness; but he lived a retired life, till he came forward openly as the forerunner of the Messiah. Let us follow peace with all men, as well as seek peace with God and our own consciences. And if it be the will of God that we live unknown to the world, still let us diligently seek to grow strong in the grace of Jesus Christ.

Chapter 2

Chapter Outline

Verses 1-7

The fulness of time was now come, when God would send forth his Son, made of a woman, and made under the law. The circumstances of his birth were very mean. Christ was born at an inn; he came into the world to sojourn here for awhile, as at an inn, and to teach us to do likewise. We are become by sin like an outcast infant, helpless and forlorn; and such a one was Christ. He well knew how unwilling we are to be meanly lodged, clothed, or fed; how we desire to have our children decorated and indulged; how apt the poor are to envy the rich, and how prone the rich to disdain the poor. But when we by faith view the Son of God being made man and lying in a manger, our vanity, ambition, and envy are checked. We cannot, with this object rightly before us, seek great things for ourselves or our children.

Verses 8-20

Angels were heralds of the new-born Saviour, but they were only sent to some poor, humble, pious, industrious shepherds, who were in the business of their calling, keeping watch over their flock. We are not out of the way of Divine visits, when we are employed in an honest calling, and abide with God in it. Let God have the honour of this work; Glory to God in the highest. God's good-will to men, manifested in sending the Messiah, redounds to his praise. Other works of God are for his glory, but the redemption of the world is for his glory in the highest. God's goodwill in sending the Messiah, brought peace into this lower world. Peace is here put for all that good which flows to us from Christ's taking our nature upon him. This is a faithful saying, attested by an innumerable company of angels, and well worthy of all acceptation, That the good-will of God toward men, is glory to God in the highest, and peace on the earth. The shepherds lost no time, but came with haste to the place. They were satisfied, and made known abroad concerning this child, that he was the Saviour, even Christ the Lord. Mary carefully observed and thought upon all these things, which were so suited to enliven her holy affections. We should be more delivered from errors in judgment and practice, did we more fully ponder these things in our hearts. It is still proclaimed in our ears that to us is born a Saviour, Christ the Lord. These should be glad tidings to all.

Verses 21-24

Our Lord Jesus was not born in sin, and did not need that mortification of a corrupt nature, or that renewal unto holiness, which were signified by circumcision. This ordinance was, in his case, a pledge of his future perfect obedience to the whole law, in the midst of sufferings and temptations, even unto death for us. At the end of forty days, Mary went up to the temple to offer the appointed sacrifices for her purification. Joseph also presented the holy child Jesus, because, as a first-born son, he was to be presented to the Lord, and redeemed according to the law. Let us present our children to the Lord who gave them to us, beseeching him to redeem them from sin and death, and make them holy to himself.

Verses 25-35

The same Spirit that provided for the support of Simeon's hope, provided for his joy. Those who would see Christ must go to his temple. Here is a confession of his faith, that this Child in his arms was the Saviour, the salvation itself, the salvation of God's appointing. He bids farewell to this world. How poor does this world look to one that has Christ in his arms, and salvation in his view! See here, how comfortable is the death of a good man; he departs in peace with God, peace with his own conscience, in peace with death. Those that have welcomed Christ, may welcome death. Joseph and Mary marvelled at the things which were spoken of this Child. Simeon shows them likewise, what reason they had to rejoice with trembling. And Jesus, his doctrine, and people, are still spoken against; his truth and holiness are still denied and blasphemed; his preached word is still the touchstone of men's characters. The secret good affections in the minds of some, will be revealed by their embracing Christ; the secret corruptions of others will be revealed by their enmity to Christ. Men will be judged by the thoughts of their hearts concerning Christ. He shall be a suffering Jesus; his mother shall suffer with him, because of the nearness of her relation and affection.

Verses 36-40

There was much evil then in the church, yet God left not himself without witness. Anna always dwelt in, or at least attended at, the temple. She was always in a praying spirit; gave herself to prayer, and in all things she served God. Those to whom Christ is made known, have great reason to thank the Lord. She taught others concerning him. Let the example of the venerable saints, Simeon and Anna, give courage to those whose hoary heads are, like theirs, a crown of glory, being found in the way of righteousness. The lips soon to be silent in the grave, should be showing forth the praises of the Redeemer. In all things it became Christ to be made like unto his brethren, therefore he passed through infancy and childhood as other children, yet without sin, and with manifest proofs of the Divine nature in him. By the Spirit of God all his faculties performed their offices in a manner not seen in any one else. Other children have foolishness bound in their hearts, which appears in what they say or do, but he was filled with wisdom, by the influence of the Holy Ghost; every thing he said and did, was wisely said and wisely done, above his years. Other children show the corruption of their nature; nothing but the grace of God was upon him.

Verses 41-52

It is for the honour of Christ that children should attend on public worship. His parents did not return till they had stayed all the seven days of the feast. It is well to stay to the end of an ordinance, as becomes those who say, It is good to be here. Those that have lost their comforts in Christ, and the evidences of their having a part in him, must bethink themselves where, and when, and how they lost them, and must turn back again. Those that would recover their lost acquaintance with Christ, must go to the place in which he has put his name; there they may hope to meet him. They found him in some part of the temple, where the doctors of the law kept their schools; he was sitting there, hearkening to their instructions, proposing questions, and answering inquiries, with such wisdom, that those who heard were delighted with him. Young persons should seek the knowledge of Divine truth, attend the ministry of the gospel, and ask such questions of their elders and teachers as may tend to increase their knowledge. Those who seek Christ in sorrow, shall find him with the greater joy. Know ye not that I ought to be in my Father's house; at my Father's work; I must be about my Father's business. Herein is an example; for it becomes the children of God, in conformity to Christ, to attend their heavenly Father's business, and make all other concerns give way to it. Though he was the Son of God, yet he was subject to his earthly parents; how then will the foolish and weak sons of men answer it, who are disobedient to their parents? However we may neglect men's sayings, because they are obscure, yet we must not think so of God's sayings. That which at first is dark, may afterwards become plain and easy. The greatest and wisest, those most eminent, may learn of this admirable and Divine Child, that it is the truest greatness of soul to know our own place and office; to deny ourselves amusements and pleasures not consistent with our state and calling.

Chapter 3

Chapter Outline

John the Baptist's ministry.	(1–14)
John the Baptist testifies concerning Christ.	(15–20)
The baptism of Christ.	(21, 22)
The genealogy of Christ.	(23–38)

Verses 1-14

The scope and design of John's ministry were, to bring the people from their sins, and to their Saviour. He came preaching, not a sect, or party, but a profession; the sign or ceremony was washing with water. By the words here used John preached the necessity of repentance, in order to the remission of sins, and that the baptism of water was an outward sign of that inward cleansing and renewal of heart, which attend, or are the effects of true repentance, as well as a profession of it. Here is the fulfilling of the Scriptures, Isa 40:3, in the ministry of John. When way is made for the gospel into the heart, by taking down high thoughts, and bringing them into obedience to Christ, by levelling the soul, and removing all that hinders us in the way of Christ and his grace, then preparation is made to welcome the salvation of God. Here are general warnings and exhortations which John gave. The guilty, corrupted race of mankind is become a generation of vipers; hateful to God, and hating one another. There is no way of fleeing from the wrath to come, but by repentance; and by the change of our way the change of our mind must be shown. If we are not really holy, both in heart and life, our profession of religion and relation to God and his church, will stand us in no stead at all; the sorer will our destruction be, if we do not bring forth fruits meet for repentance. John the Baptist gave instructions to several sorts of persons. Those that profess and promise repentance, must show it by reformation, according to their places and conditions. The gospel requires mercy, not sacrifice; and its design is, to engage us to do all the good we can, and to be just to all men. And the same principle which leads men to forego unjust gain, leads to restore that which is gained by wrong. John tells the soldiers their duty. Men should be cautioned against the temptations of their employments. These answers declared the present duty of the inquirers, and at once formed a test of their sincerity. As none can or will accept Christ's salvation without true repentance, so the evidence and effects of this repentance are here marked out.

Verses 15-20

John the Baptist disowned being himself the Christ, but confirmed the people in their expectations of the long-promised Messiah. He could only exhort them to repent, and assure them of forgiveness upon repentance; but he could not work repentance in them, nor confer remission on them. Thus highly does it become us to speak of Christ, and thus humbly of ourselves. John can do no more than baptize with water, in token that they ought to purify and cleanse themselves; but Christ can, and will baptize with the Holy Ghost; he can give the Spirit, to cleanse and purify the heart, not only as water washes off the dirt on the outside, but as fire clears out the dross that is within, and melts down the metal, that it may be cast into a new mould. John was an affectionate preacher; he was beseeching; he pressed things home upon his hearers. He was a practical preacher; quickening them to their duty, and directing them in it. He was a popular preacher; he addressed the people, according to their capacity. He was an evangelical preacher. In all his exhortations, he directed people to Christ. When we press duty upon people, we must direct them to Christ, both for righteousness and strength. He was a copious preacher; he shunned not to declare the whole counsel of God. But a full stop was put to John's preaching when he was in the midst of his usefulness. Herod being reproved by him for many evils, shut up John in prison. Those who injure the faithful servants of God, add still greater guilt to their other sins.

Verses 21, 22

Christ did not confess sin, as others did, for he had none to confess; but he prayed, as others did, and kept up communion with his Father. Observe, all the three voices from heaven, by which the Father bare witness to the Son, were pronounced while he was praying, or soon after, Lu 9:35; Joh 12:28. The Holy Ghost descended in a bodily shape like a dove upon him, and there came a voice from heaven, from God the Father, from the excellent glory. Thus was a proof of the Holy Trinity, of the Three Persons in the Godhead, given at the baptism of Christ.

Verses 23-38

Matthew's list of the forefathers of Jesus showed that Christ was the son of Abraham, in whom all the families of the earth are blessed, and heir to the throne of David; but Luke shows that Jesus was the Seed of the woman that should break the serpent's head, and traces the line up to Adam, beginning with Eli, or Heli, the father, not of Joseph, but of Mary. The seeming differences between the two evangelists in these lists of names have been removed by learned men. But our salvation does not depend upon our being able to solve these difficulties, nor is the Divine authority of the

Gospels at all weakened by them. The list of names ends thus, "Who was the son of Adam, the son of God;" that is, the offspring of God by creation. Christ was both the son of Adam and the Son of God, that he might be a proper Mediator between God and the sons of Adam, and might bring the sons of Adam to be, through him, the sons of God. All flesh, as descended from the first Adam, is as grass, and withers as the flower of the field; but he who partakes of the Holy Spirit of life from the Second Adam, has that eternal happiness, which by the gospel is preached unto us.

Chapter 4

Chapter Outline

Verses 1-13

Christ's being led into the wilderness gave an advantage to the tempter; for there he was alone, none were with him by whose prayers and advice he might be helped in the hour of temptation. He who knew his own strength might give Satan advantage; but we may not, who know our own weakness. Being in all things made like unto his brethren, Jesus would, like the other children of God, live in dependence upon the Divine Providence and promise. The word of God is our sword, and faith in that word is our shield. God has many ways of providing for his people, and therefore is at all times to be depended upon in the way of duty. All Satan's promises are deceitful; and if he is permitted to have any influence in disposing of the kingdoms of the world and the glory of them, he uses them as baits to insnare men to destruction. We should reject at once and with abhorrence, every opportunity of sinful gain or advancement, as a price offered for our souls; we should seek riches, honours, and happiness in the worship and service of God only. Christ will not worship Satan; nor, when he has the kingdoms of the world delivered to him by his Father, will he suffer any remains of the worship of the devil to continue in them. Satan also tempted Jesus to be his own murderer, by unfitting confidence in his Father's protection, such as he had no warrant for. Let not any abuse of Scripture by Satan or by men abate our esteem, or cause us to abandon its use; but let us study it still, seek to know it, and seek our defence from it in all kinds of assaults. Let this word dwell richly in us, for it is our life. Our victorious Redeemer conquered, not for himself only, but for us also. The devil ended all the temptation. Christ let him try all his force, and defeated him. Satan saw it was to no purpose to attack Christ, who had nothing in him for his fiery darts to fasten upon. And if we resist the devil, he will flee from us. Yet he departed but till the season when he was again to be let loose upon Jesus, not as a tempter, to draw him to sin, and so to strike at his head, at which he now aimed and was wholly defeated in; but as a persecutor, to bring Christ to suffer, and so to bruise his heel, which it was told him, he should have to do, and would do, though it would be the breaking of his own head, Ge 3:15. Though Satan depart for a season, we shall never be out of his reach till removed from this present evil world.

Verses 14-30

Christ taught in their synagogues, their places of public worship, where they met to read, expound, and apply the word, to pray and praise. All the gifts and graces of the Spirit were upon him and on him, without measure. By Christ, sinners may be loosed from the bonds of guilt, and by his Spirit and grace from the bondage of corruption. He came by the word of his gospel, to bring light to those that sat in the dark, and by the power of his grace, to give sight to those that were blind. And he preached the acceptable year of the Lord. Let sinners attend to the Saviour's invitation when liberty is thus proclaimed. Christ's name was Wonderful; in nothing was he more so than in the word of his grace, and the power that went along with it. We may well wonder that he should speak such words of grace to such graceless wretches as mankind. Some prejudice often furnishes an objection against the humbling doctrine of the cross; and while it is the word of God that stirs up men's enmity, they will blame the conduct or manner of the speaker. The doctrine of God's sovereignty, his right to do his will, provokes proud men. They will not seek his favour in his own way; and are angry when others have the favours they neglect. Still is Jesus rejected by multitudes who hear the same message from his words. While they crucify him afresh by their sins, may we honour him as the Son of God, the Saviour of men, and seek to show we do so by our obedience.

Verses 31-44

Christ's preaching much affected the people; and a working power went with it to the consciences of men. These miracles showed Christ to be a controller and conqueror of Satan, a healer of diseases. Where Christ gives a new life, in recovery from sickness, it should be a new life, spent more than ever in his service, to his glory. Our business should be to spread abroad Christ's fame in every place, to beseech him in behalf of those diseased in body or mind, and to use our influence in bringing sinners to him, that his hands may be laid upon them for their healing. He cast the devils out of many who were possessed. We were not sent into this world to live to ourselves only, but to glorify God, and to do good in our generation. The people sought him, and came unto him. A desert is no desert, if we are with Christ there. He will continue with us, by his word and Spirit, and extend the same blessings to other nations, till, throughout the earth, the servants and worshippers of Satan are brought to acknowledge him as the Christ, the Son of God, and to find redemption through his blood, even the forgiveness of sins.

Chapter 5

Chapter Outline

Verses 1-11

When Christ had done preaching, he told Peter to apply to the business of his calling. Time spent on week days in public exercises of religion, need be but little hinderance in time, and may be great furtherance to us in temper of mind, as to our worldly business. With what cheerfulness may we go about the duties of our calling, when we have been with God, and thus have our worldly employments sanctified to us by the word and prayer! Though they had taken nothing, yet Christ told them to let down their nets again. We must not abruptly quit our callings because we have not the success in them we desire. We are likely to speed well, when we follow the guidance of Christ's word. The draught of fishes was by a miracle. We must all, like Peter, own ourselves to be sinful men, therefore Jesus Christ might justly depart from us. But we must beseech him that he would not depart; for woe unto us if the Saviour depart from sinners! Rather let us entreat him to come and dwell in our hearts by faith, that he may transform and cleanse them. These fishermen forsook all, and followed Jesus, when their calling prospered. When riches increase, and we are tempted to set our hearts upon them, then to quit them for Christ is thankworthy.

Verses 12-16

This man is said to be full of leprosy; he had that distemper in a high degree, which represents our natural pollution by sin; we are full of that leprosy; from the crown of the head to the sole of the foot there is no soundness in us. Strong confidence and deep humility are united in the words of this leper. And if any sinner, from a deep sense of vileness, says, I know the Lord can cleanse, but will he look upon such a one as me? will he apply his own precious blood for my cleansing and healing? Yes, he will. Speak not as doubting, but as humbly referring the matter to Christ. And being saved from the guilt and power of our sins, let us spread abroad Christ's fame, and bring others to hear him and to be healed.

Verses 17-26

How many are there in our assemblies, where the gospel is preached, who do not sit under the word, but sit by! It is to them as a tale that is told them, not as a message that is sent to them. Observe the duties taught and recommended to us by the history of the paralytic. In applying to Christ, we must be very pressing and urgent; that is an evidence of faith, and is very pleasing to Christ, and prevailing with him. Give us, Lord, the same kind of faith with respect to thy ability and willingness to heal our souls. Give us to desire the pardon of sin more than any earthly blessing, or life itself. Enable us to believe thy power to forgive sins; then will our souls cheerfully arise and go where thou pleasest.

Verses 27-39

It was a wonder of Christ's grace, that he would call a publican to be his disciple and follower. It was a wonder of his grace, that the call was made so effectual. It was a wonder of his grace, that he came to call sinners to repentance, and to assure them of pardon. It was a wonder of his grace, that he so patiently bore the contradiction of sinners against himself and his disciples. It was a wonder of his grace, that he fixed the services of his disciples according to their strength and standing. The Lord trains up his people gradually for the trials allotted them; we should copy his example in dealing with the weak in faith, or the tempted believer.

Chapter 6

Chapter Outline

Verses 1-5

Christ justifies his disciples in a work of necessity for themselves on the sabbath day, and that was plucking the ears of corn when they were hungry. But we must take heed that we mistake not this liberty for leave to commit sin. Christ will have us to know and remember that it is his day, therefore to be spent in his service, and to his honour.

Verses 6-11

Christ was neither ashamed nor afraid to own the purposes of his grace. He healed the poor man, though he knew that his enemies would take advantage against him for it. Let us not be drawn either from our duty or from our usefulness by any opposition. We may well be amazed, that the sons of men should be so wicked.

Verses 12-19

We often think one half hour a great deal to spend in meditation and secret prayer, but Christ was whole nights engaged in these duties. In serving God, our great care should be not to lose time, but to make the end of one good duty the beginning of another. The twelve apostles are here named;

never were men so privileged, yet one of them had a devil, and proved a traitor. Those who have not faithful preaching near them, had better travel far than be without it. It is indeed worth while to go a great way to hear the word of Christ, and to go out of the way of other business for it. They came to be cured by him, and he healed them. There is a fulness of grace in Christ, and healing virtue in him, ready to go out from him, that is enough for all, enough for each. Men regard the diseases of the body as greater evils than those of their souls; but the Scripture teaches us differently.

Verses 20-26

Here begins a discourse of Christ, most of which is also found in Mt 5; 7. But some think that this was preached at another time and place. All believers that take the precepts of the gospel to themselves, and live by them, may take the promises of the gospel to themselves, and live upon them. Woes are denounced against prosperous sinners as miserable people, though the world envies them. Those are blessed indeed whom Christ blesses, but those must be dreadfully miserable who fall under his woe and curse! What a vast advantage will the saint have over the sinner in the other world! and what a wide difference will there be in their rewards, how much soever the sinner may prosper, and the saint be afflicted here!

Verses 27-36

These are hard lessons to flesh and blood. But if we are thoroughly grounded in the faith of Christ's love, this will make his commands easy to us. Every one that comes to him for washing in his blood, and knows the greatness of the mercy and the love there is in him, can say, in truth and sincerity, Lord, what wilt thou have me to do? Let us then aim to be merciful, even according to the mercy of our heavenly Father to us.

Verses 37-49

All these sayings Christ often used; it was easy to apply them. We ought to be very careful when we blame others; for we need allowance ourselves. If we are of a giving and a forgiving spirit, we shall ourselves reap the benefit. Though full and exact returns are made in another world, not in this world, yet Providence does what should encourage us in doing good. Those who follow the multitude to do evil, follow in the broad way that leads to destruction. The tree is known by its fruits; may the word of Christ be so grafted in our hearts, that we may be fruitful in every good word and work. And what the mouth commonly speaks, generally agrees with what is most in the heart. Those only make sure work for their souls and eternity, and take the course that will profit in a trying time, who think, speak, and act according to the words of Christ. Those who take pains in religion, found their hope upon Christ, who is the Rock of Ages, and other foundation can no man lay. In death and judgment they are safe, being kept by the power of Christ through faith unto salvation, and they shall never perish.

Chapter 7

Chapter Outline

Verses 1-10

Servants should study to endear themselves to their masters. Masters ought to take particular care of their servants when they are sick. We may still, by faithful and fervent prayer, apply to Christ, and ought to do so when sickness is in our families. The building places for religious worship is a good work, and an instance of love to God and his people. Our Lord Jesus was pleased with the centurion's faith; and he never fails to answer the expectations of that faith which honours his power and love. The cure soon wrought and perfect.

Verses 11-18

When the Lord saw the poor widow following her son to the grave, he had compassion on her. See Christ's power over death itself. The gospel call to all people, to young people particularly, is, Arise from the dead, and Christ shall give you light and life. When Christ put life into him, it appeared by the youth's sitting up. Have we grace from Christ? Let us show it. He began to speak: whenever Christ gives us spiritual life, he opens the lips in prayer and praise. When dead souls are raised to spiritual life, by Divine power going with the gospel, we must glorify God, and look upon it as a gracious visit to his people. Let us seek for such an interest in our compassionate Saviour, that we may look forward with joy to the time when the Redeemer's voice shall call forth all that are in their graves. May we be called to the resurrection of life, not to that of damnation.

Verses 19-35

To his miracles in the kingdom of nature, Christ adds this in the kingdom of grace, To the poor the gospel is preached. It clearly pointed out the spiritual nature of Christ's kingdom, that the messenger he sent before him to prepare his way, did it by preaching repentance and reformation of heart and life. We have here the just blame of those who were not wrought upon by the ministry of John Baptist or of Jesus Christ himself. They made a jest of the methods God took to do them good. This is the ruin of multitudes; they are not serious in the concerns of their souls. Let us study to prove ourselves children of Wisdom, by attending the instructions of God's word, and adoring those mysteries and glad tidings which infidels and Pharisees deride and blaspheme.

Verses 36-50

None can truly perceive how precious Christ is, and the glory of the gospel, except the broken-hearted. But while they feel they cannot enough express self-abhorrence on account of sin, and admiration of his mercy, the self-sufficient will be disgusted, because the gospel encourages such repenting sinners. The Pharisee, instead of rejoicing in the tokens of the woman's repentance, confined his thoughts to her former bad character. But without free forgiveness none of us can escape the wrath to come; this our gracious Saviour has purchased with his blood, that he may freely bestow it on every one that believes in him. Christ, by a parable, forced Simon to acknowledge that the greater sinner this woman had been, the greater love she ought to show to Him when her sins were pardoned. Learn here, that sin is a debt; and all are sinners, are debtors to Almighty God. Some sinners are greater debtors; but whether our debt be more or less, it is more than we are able to pay. God is ready to forgive; and his Son having purchased pardon for those who believe in him, his gospel promises it to them, and his Spirit seals it to repenting sinners, and gives them the comfort. Let us keep far from the proud spirit of the Pharisee, simply depending upon and rejoicing in Christ alone, and so be prepared to obey him more zealously, and more strongly to recommend him unto all around us. The more we express our sorrow for sin, and our love to Christ, the clearer evidence we have of the forgiveness of our sins. What a wonderful change does grace make upon a sinner's heart and life, as well as upon his state before God, by the full remission of all his sins through faith in the Lord Jesus!

Chapter 8

Chapter Outline

Verses 1-3

We are here told what Christ made the constant business of his life, it was teaching the gospel. Tidings of the kingdom of God are glad tidings, and what Christ came to bring. Certain women attended upon him who ministered to him of their substance. It showed the mean condition to which the Saviour humbled himself, that he needed their kindness, and his great humility, that he accepted it. Though rich, yet for our sakes he became poor.

Verses 4-21

There are many very needful and excellent rules and cautions for hearing the word, in the parable of the sower, and the application of it. Happy are we, and for ever indebted to free grace, if the same thing that is a parable to others, with which they are only amused, is a plain truth to us, by which we are taught and governed. We ought to take heed of the things that will hinder our profiting by the word we hear; to take heed lest we hear carelessly and slightly, lest we entertain prejudices against the word we hear; and to take heed to our spirits after we have heard the word, lest we lose what we have gained. The gifts we have, will be continued to us or not, as we use them for the glory of God, and the good of our brethren. Nor is it enough not to hold the truth in unrighteousness; we should desire to hold forth the word of life, and to shine, giving light to all around. Great encouragement is given to those who prove themselves faithful hearers of the word, by being doers of the work. Christ owns them as his relations.

Verses 22-40

Those that put to sea in a calm, even at Christ's word, must yet prepare for a storm, and for great peril in that storm. There is no relief for souls under a sense of guilt, and fear of wrath, but to go to Christ, and call him Master, and say, I am undone, if thou dost not help me. When our dangers are over, it becomes us to take to ourselves the shame of our own fears, and to give Christ the glory of our deliverance. We may learn much out of this history concerning the world of infernal, malignant spirits, which though not working now exactly in the same way as then, yet all must at all times carefully guard against. And these malignant spirits are very numerous. They have enmity to man and all his comforts. Those under Christ's government are sweetly led with the bands of love; those under the devil's government are furiously driven. Oh what a comfort it is to the believer, that all the powers of darkness are under the control of the Lord Jesus! It is a miracle of mercy, if those whom Satan possesses, are not brought to destruction and eternal ruin. Christ will not stay with those who slight him; perhaps he may no more return to them, while others are waiting for him, and glad to receive him.

Verses 41-56

Let us not complain of a crowd, and a throng, and a hurry, as long as we are in the way of our duty, and doing good; but otherwise every wise man will keep himself out of it as much as he can. And many a poor soul is healed, and helped, and saved by Christ, that is hidden in a crowd, and nobody notices it. This woman came trembling, yet her faith saved her. There may be trembling, where yet there is saving faith. Observe Christ's comfortable words to Jairus, Fear not, believe only, and thy daughter shall be made whole. No less hard was it not to grieve for the loss of an only child, than not to fear the continuance of that grief. But in perfect faith there is no fear; the more we fear, the less we believe. The hand of Christ's grace goes with the calls of his word, to make them effectual. Christ commanded to give her meat. As babes new born, so those newly raised from sin, desire spiritual food, that they may grow thereby.

<h1 style="text-align:center">Chapter 9</h1>

Chapter Outline

Verses 1-9

Christ sent his twelve disciples abroad, who by this time were able to teach others what they had received from the Lord. They must not be anxious to commend themselves to people's esteem by outward appearance. They must go as they were. The Lord Jesus is the fountain of power and authority, to whom all creatures must, in one way or another, be subject; and if he goes with the word of his ministers in power, to deliver sinners from Satan's bondage, they may be sure that he will care for their wants. When truth and love thus go together, and yet the message of God is rejected and despised, it leaves men without excuse, and turns to a testimony against them. Herod's guilty conscience was ready to conclude that John was risen from the dead. He desired to see Jesus; and why did he not go and see him? Probably, because he thought it below him, or because he wished not to have any more reprovers of sin. Delaying it now, his heart was hardened, and when he did see Jesus, he was as much prejudiced against him as others, Lu 23:11.

Verses 10-17

The people followed Jesus, and though they came unseasonably, yet he gave them what they came for. He spake unto them of the kingdom of God. He healed those who had need of healing. And with five loaves of bread and two fishes, Christ fed five thousand men. He will not see those that fear him, and serve him faithfully, want any good thing. When we receive creature-comforts, we must acknowledge that we receive them from God, and that we are unworthy to receive them; that we owe them all, and all the comfort we have in them, to the mediation of Christ, by whom the curse is taken away. The blessing of Christ will make a little go a great way. He fills every hungry soul, abundantly satisfies it with the goodness of his house. Here were fragments taken up: in our Father's house there is bread enough, and to spare. We are not straitened, nor stinted in Christ.

Verses 18-27

It is an unspeakable comfort that our Lord Jesus is God's Anointed; this signifies that he was both appointed to be the Messiah, and qualified for it. Jesus discourses concerning his own sufferings and death. And so far must his disciples be from thinking how to prevent his sufferings, that they must prepare for their own. We often meet with crosses in the way of duty; and though we must not pull them upon our own heads, yet, when they are laid for us, we must take them up, and carry them after Christ. It is well or ill with us, according as it is well or ill with our souls. The body cannot be happy, if the soul be miserable in the other world; but the soul may be happy, though the body is greatly afflicted and oppressed in this world. We must never be ashamed of Christ and his gospel.

Verses 28-36

Christ's transfiguration was a specimen of that glory in which he will come to judge the world; and was an encouragement to his disciples to suffer for him. Prayer is a transfiguring, transforming duty, which makes the face to shine. Our Lord Jesus, even in his transfiguration, was willing to speak concerning his death and sufferings. In our greatest glories on earth, let us remember that in this world we have no continuing city. What need we have to pray to God for quickening grace, to make us lively! Yet that the disciples might be witnesses of this sign from heaven, after awhile they became awake, so that they were able to give a full account of what passed. But those know not what they say, that talk of making tabernacles on earth for glorified saints in heaven.

Verses 37-42

How deplorable the case of this child! He was under the power of an evil spirit. Disease of that nature are more frightful than such as arise merely from natural causes. What mischief Satan does where he gets possession! But happy those that have access to Christ! He can do that for us which his disciples cannot. A word from Christ healed the child; and when our children recover from sickness, it is comfortable to receive them as healed by the hand of Christ.

Verses 43-50

This prediction of Christ's sufferings was plain enough, but the disciples would not understand it, because it agreed not with their notions. A little child is the emblem by which Christ teaches us simplicity and humility. What greater honour can any man attain to in this world, than to be received by men as a messenger of God and Christ; and to have God and Christ own themselves received and welcomed in him! If ever any society of Christians in this world, had reason to silence those not of their own communion, the twelve disciples at this time had; yet Christ warned them not to do the like again. Those may be found faithful followers of Christ, and may be accepted of him, who do not follow with us.

Verses 51-56

The disciples did not consider that the conduct of the Samaritans was rather the effect of national prejudices and bigotry, than of enmity to the word and worship of God; and through they refused to receive Christ and his disciples, they did not ill use or injure them, so that the case was widely different from that of Ahaziah and Elijah. Nor were they aware that the gospel dispensation was to be marked by miracles of mercy. But above all, they were ignorant of the prevailing motives of their own hearts, which were pride and carnal ambition. Of this our Lord warned them. It is easy for us to say, Come, see our zeal for the Lord! and to think we are very faithful in his cause, when we are seeking our own objects, and even doing harm instead of good to others.

Verses 57-62

Here is one that is forward to follow Christ, but seems to have been hasty and rash, and not to have counted the cost. If we mean to follow Christ, we must lay aside the thoughts of great things in the world. Let us not try to join the profession of Christianity, with seeking after worldly advantages. Here is another that seems resolved to follow Christ, but he begs a short delay. To this man Christ first gave the call; he said to him, Follow me. Religion teaches us to be kind and good, to show piety at home, and to requite our parents; but we must not make these an excuse for neglecting our duty to God. Here is another that is willing to follow Christ, but he must have a little time to talk with his friends about it, and to set in order his household affairs, and give directions concerning them. He seemed to have worldly concerns more upon his heart than he ought to have, and he was willing to enter into a temptation leading him from his purpose of following Christ. No one can do any business in a proper manner, if he is attending to other things. Those who begin with the work of God, must resolve to go on, or they will make nothing of it. Looking back, leads to drawing back, and drawing back is to perdition. He only that endures to the end shall be saved.

Chapter 10

Chapter Outline

Verses 1-16

Christ sent the seventy disciples, two and two, that they might strengthen and encourage one another. The ministry of the gospel calls men to receive Christ as a Prince and a Saviour; and he will surely come in the power of his Spirit to all places whither he sends his faithful servants. But the doom of those who receive the grace of God in vain, will be very fearful Those who despise the faithful ministers of Christ, who think meanly of them, and look scornfully upon them, will be reckoned as despisers of God and Christ.

Verses 17-24

All our victories over Satan, are obtained by power derived from Jesus Christ, and he must have all the praise. But let us beware of spiritual pride, which has been the destruction of many. Our Lord rejoiced at the prospect of the salvation of many souls. It was fit that particular notice should be taken of that hour of joy; there were few such, for He was a man of sorrows: in that hour in which he saw Satan fall, and heard of the good success of his ministers, in that hour he rejoiced. He has ever resisted the proud, and given grace to the humble. The more simply dependent we are on the teaching, help, and blessing of the Son of God, the more we shall know both of the Father and of the Son; the more blessed we shall be in seeing the glory, and hearing the words of the Divine Saviour; and the more useful we shall be made in promoting his cause.

Verses 25-37

If we speak of eternal life, and the way to it, in a careless manner, we take the name of God in vain. No one will ever love God and his neighbour with any measure of pure, spiritual love, who is not made a partaker of converting grace. But the proud heart of man strives hard against these convictions. Christ gave an instance of a poor Jew in distress, relieved by a good Samaritan. This poor man fell among thieves, who left him about to die of his wounds. He was slighted by those who should have been his friends, and was cared for by a stranger, a Samaritan, of the nation which the Jews most despised and detested, and would have no dealings with. It is lamentable to observe how selfishness governs all ranks; how many excuses men will make to avoid trouble or expense in relieving others. But the true Christian has the law of love written in his heart. The Spirit of Christ dwells in him; Christ's image is renewed in his soul. The parable is a beautiful explanation of the law of loving our neighbour as ourselves, without regard to nation, party, or any other distinction. It also sets forth the kindness and love of God our Saviour toward sinful, miserable men. We were like this poor, distressed traveller. Satan, our enemy, has robbed us, and wounded us: such is the mischief sin has done us. The blessed Jesus had compassion on us. The believer considers that Jesus loved him, and gave his life for him, when an enemy and a rebel; and having shown him mercy, he bids him go and do likewise. It is the duty of us all , in our places, and according to our ability, to succour, help, and relieve all that are in distress and necessity.

Verses 38-42

A good sermon is not the worse for being preached in a house; and the visits of our friends should be so managed, as to make them turn to the good of their souls. Sitting at Christ's feet, signifies readiness to receive his word, and submission to the guidance of it. Martha was providing for the entertainment of Christ, and those that came with him. Here were respect to our Lord Jesus and right care of her household affairs. But there was something to be blamed. She was for much serving; plenty, variety, and exactness. Worldly business is a snare to us, when it hinders us from serving God, and getting good to our souls. What needless time is wasted, and expense often laid out, even in entertaining professors of the gospel! Though Martha was on this occasion faulty, yet she was a true believer, and in her general conduct did not neglect the one thing needful. The favour of God is needful to our happiness; the salvation of Christ is needful to our safety. Where this is attended to, all other things will be rightly pursued. Christ declared, Mary hath chosen the good part. For one thing is needful, this one thing that she has done, to give up herself to the guidance of Christ. The things of this life will be taken away from us, at the furthest, when we shall be taken away from them; but nothing shall separate from the love of Christ, and a part in that love. Men and devils cannot take it away from us, and God and Christ will not. Let us mind the one thing needful more diligently.

Chapter 11

Chapter Outline

The disciples taught to pray.	(1–4)
Christ encourages being earnest in prayer.	(5–13)
Christ casts out a devil, The blasphemy of the Pharisees.	(14–26)
True happiness.	(27, 28)
Christ reproves the Jews.	(29–36)
He reproves the Pharisees.	(37–54)

Verses 1-4

"Lord, teach us to pray," is a good prayer, and a very needful one, for Jesus Christ only can teach us, by his word and Spirit, how to pray. Lord, teach me what it is to pray; Lord, stir up and quicken me to the duty; Lord, direct me what to pray for; teach me what I should say. Christ taught them a prayer, much the same that he had given before in his sermon upon the mount. There are some differences in the words of the Lord's prayer in Matthew and in Luke, but they are of no moment. Let us in our requests, both for others and for ourselves, come to our heavenly Father, confiding in his power and goodness.

Verses 5-13

Christ encourages fervency and constancy in prayer. We must come for what we need, as a man does to his neighbour or friend, who is kind to him. We must come for bread; for that which is needful. If God does not answer our prayers speedily, yet he will in due time, if we continue to pray. Observe what to pray for; we must ask for the Holy Spirit, not only as necessary in order to our praying well, but as all spiritual blessings are included in that one. For by the influences of the Holy Spirit we are brought to know God and ourselves, to repent, believe in, and love Christ, and so are made comfortable in this world, and meet for happiness in the next. All these blessings our heavenly Father is more ready to bestow on every one that asks for them, than an indulgent parent is to give food to a hungry child. And this is the advantage of the prayer of faith, that it quiets and establishes the heart in God.

Verses 14-26

Christ's thus casting out the devils, was really the destroying of their power. The heart of every unconverted sinner is the devil's palace, where he dwells, and where he rules. There is a kind of peace in the heart of an unconverted soul, while the devil, as a strong man armed, keeps it. The sinner is secure, has no doubt concerning the goodness of his state, nor any dread of the judgment to come. But observe the wonderful change made in conversion. The conversion of a soul to God, is Christ's victory over the devil and his power in that soul, restoring the soul to its liberty, and recovering his own interest in it and power over it. All the endowments of mind of body are now employed for Christ. Here is the condition of a hypocrite. The house is swept from common sins, by a forced confession, as Pharaoh's; by a feigned contrition, as Ahab's; or by a partial reformation, as Herod's. The house is swept, but it is not washed; the heart is not made holy. Sweeping takes off only the loose dirt, while the sin that besets the sinner, the beloved sin, is untouched. The house is garnished with common gifts and graces. It is not furnished with any true grace; it is all paint and varnish, not real nor lasting. It was never given up to Christ, nor dwelt in by the Spirit. Let us take heed of resting in that which a man may have, and yet come short of heaven. The wicked spirits enter in without any difficulty; they are welcomed, and they dwell there; there they work, there they rule. From such an awful state let all earnestly pray to be delivered.

Verses 27, 28

While the scribes and Pharisees despised and blasphemed the discourses of our Lord Jesus, this good woman admired them, and the wisdom and power with which he spake. Christ led the woman to a higher consideration. Though it is a great privilege to hear the word of God, yet those only are truly blessed, that is, blessed of the Lord, that hear it, keep it in memory, and keep to it as their way and rule.

Verses 29-36

Christ promised that there should be one sign more given, even the sign of Jonah the prophet; which in Matthew is explained, as meaning the resurrection of Christ; and he warned them to improve this sign. But though Christ himself were the constant preacher in any congregation, and worked miracles daily among them, yet unless his grace humbled their hearts, they would not profit by his word. Let us not desire more evidence and fuller teaching than the Lord is pleased to afford us. We should pray without ceasing that our hearts and understandings may be opened, that we may profit by the light we enjoy. And especially take heed that the light which is in us be not darkness; for if our leading principles be wrong, our judgment and practice must become more so.

Verses 37-54

We should all look to our hearts, that they may be cleansed and new-created; and while we attend to the great things of the law and of the gospel, we must not neglect the smallest matter God has appointed. When any wait to catch something out of our mouths, that they may insnare us, O Lord, give us thy prudence and thy patience, and disappoint their evil purposes. Furnish us with such meekness and patience that we may glory in reproaches, for Christ's sake, and that thy Holy Spirit may rest upon us.

Chapter 12

Chapter Outline

Christ reproves the interpreters of the law.	(1–12)
A caution against covetousness, The parable of the rich man.	(13–21)
Worldly care reproved.	(22–40)
Watchfulness enforced.	(41–53)
A warning to be reconciled to God.	(54–59)

Verses 1-12

A firm belief of the doctrine of God's universal providence, and the extent of it, would satisfy us when in peril, and encourage us to trust God in the way of duty. Providence takes notice of the meanest creatures, even of the sparrows, and therefore of the smallest interests of the disciples of Christ. Those who confess Christ now, shall be owned by him in the great day, before the angels of God. To deter us from denying Christ, and deserting his truths and ways, we are here assured that those who deny Christ, though they may thus save life itself, and though they may gain a kingdom by it, will be great losers at last; for Christ will not know them, will not own them, nor show them favour. But let no trembling, penitent backslider doubt of obtaining forgiveness. This is far different from the determined enmity that is blasphemy against the Holy Ghost, which shall never be forgiven, because it will never be repented of.

Verses 13-21

Christ's kingdom is spiritual, and not of this world. Christianity does not meddle with politics; it obliges all to do justly, but wordly dominion is not founded in grace. It does not encourage expectations of worldly advantages by religion. The rewards of Christ's disciples are of another nature. Covetousness is a sin we need constantly to be warned against; for happiness and comfort do not depend on the wealth of this world. The things of the world will not satisfy the desires of a soul. Here is a parable, which shows the folly of carnal worldling while they live, and their misery when they die. The character drawn is exactly that of a prudent, worldly man, who has no grateful regard to the providence of God, nor any right thought of the uncertainty of human affairs, the worth of his soul, or the importance of eternity. How many, even among professed Christians, point out similar characters as models for imitation, and proper persons to form connexions with! We mistake if we think that thoughts are hid, and thoughts are free. When he saw a great crop upon his ground, instead of thanking God for it, or rejoicing to be able to do more good, he afflicts himself. What shall I do now? The poorest beggar in the country could not have said a more anxious word. The more men have, the more perplexity they have with it. It was folly for him to think of making no other use of his plenty, than to indulge the flesh and gratify the sensual appetites, without any thought of doing good to others. Carnal worldlings are fools; and the day is coming when God will call them by their own name, and they will call themselves so. The death of such persons is miserable in itself, and terrible to them. Thy soul shall be required. He is loth to part with it; but God shall require it, shall require an account of it, require it as a guilty soul to be punished without delay. It is the folly of most men, to mind and pursue that which is for the body and for time only, more than that for the soul and eternity.

Verses 22-40

Christ largely insisted upon this caution not to give way to disquieting, perplexing cares, Mt 6:25–34. The arguments here used are for our encouragement to cast our care upon God, which is the right way to get ease. As in our stature, so in our state, it is our wisdom to take it as it is. An eager, anxious pursuit of the things of this world, even necessary things, ill becomes the disciples of Christ. Fears must not prevail; when we frighten ourselves with thoughts of evil to come, and put ourselves upon needless cares how to avoid it. If we value the beauty of holiness, we shall not crave the luxuries of life. Let us then examine whether we belong to this little flock. Christ is our Master, and we are his servants; not only working servants, but waiting servants. We must be as men that wait for their lord, that sit up while he stays out late, to be ready to receive him. In this Christ alluded to his own ascension to heaven, his coming to call his people to him by death, and his return to judge the world. We are uncertain as to the time of his coming to us, we should therefore be always ready. If men thus take care of their houses, let us be thus wise for our souls. Be ye therefore ready also; as ready as the good man of the house would be, if he knew at what hour the thief would come.

Verses 41-53

All are to take to themselves what Christ says in his word, and to inquire concerning it. No one is left so ignorant as not to know many things to be wrong which he does, and many things to be right which he neglects; therefore all are without excuse in their sin. The bringing in the gospel dispensation would occasion desolations. Not that this would be the tendency of Christ's religion, which is pure, peaceable, and loving; but the effect of its being contrary to men's pride and lusts. There was to be a wide publication of the gospel. But before that took place, Christ had a baptism to be baptized with, far different from that of water and the Holy Spirit. He must endure sufferings and death. It agreed not with his plan to preach the gospel more widely, till this baptism was completed. We should be zealous in making known the truth, for though divisions will be stirred up, and a man's own household may be his foes, yet sinners will be converted, and God will be glorified.

Verses 54-59

Christ would have the people to be as wise in the concerns of their souls as they are in outward affairs. Let them hasten to obtain peace with God before it is too late. If any man has found that God has set himself against him concerning his sins, let him apply to him as God in Christ reconciling the world to himself. While we are alive, we are in the way, and now is our time.

Chapter 13

Chapter Outline

Verses 1-5

Mention was made to Christ of the death of some Galileans. This tragical story is briefly related here, and is not met with in any historians. In Christ's reply he spoke of another event, which, like it, gave an instance of people taken away by sudden death. Towers, that are built for safety, often prove to be men's destruction. He cautioned his hearers not to blame great sufferers, as if they were therefore to be accounted great sinners. As no place or employment can secure from the stroke of death, we should consider the sudden removals of others as warnings to ourselves. On these accounts Christ founded a call to repentance. The same Jesus that bids us repent, for the kingdom of heaven is at hand, bids us repent, for otherwise we shall perish.

Verses 6-9

This parable of the barren fig-tree is intended to enforce the warning given just before: the barren tree, except it brings forth fruit, will be cut down. This parable in the first place refers to the nation and people of the Jews. Yet it is, without doubt, for awakening all that enjoy the means of grace, and the privileges of the visible church. When God has borne long, we may hope that he will bear with us yet a little longer, but we cannot expect that he will bear always.

Verses 10-17

Our Lord Jesus attended upon public worship on the sabbaths. Even bodily infirmities, unless very grievous, should not keep us from public worship on sabbath days. This woman came to Christ to be taught, and to get good to her soul, and then he relieved her bodily infirmity. This cure represents the work of Christ's grace upon the soul. And when crooked souls are made straight, they will show it by glorifying God. Christ knew that this ruler had a real enmity to him and to his gospel, and that he did but cloak it with a pretended zeal for the sabbath day; he really would not have them be healed any day; but if Jesus speaks the word, and puts forth his healing power, sinners are set free. This deliverance is often wrought on the Lord's day; and whatever labour tends to put men in the way of receiving the blessing, agrees with the design of that day.

Verses 18-22

Here is the progress of the gospel foretold in two parables, as in Mt 13. The kingdom of the Messiah is the kingdom of God. May grace grow in our hearts; may our faith and love grow exceedingly, so as to give undoubted evidence of their reality. May the example of God's saints be blessed to those among whom they live; and may his grace flow from heart to heart, until the little one becomes a thousand.

Verses 23-30

Our Saviour came to guide men's consciences, not to gratify their curiosity. Ask not, How many shall be saved? But, Shall I be one of them? Not, What shall become of such and such? But, What shall I do, and what will become of me? Strive to enter in at the strait gate. This is directed to each of us; it is, Strive ye. All that will be saved, must enter in at the strait gate, must undergo a change of the whole man. Those that would enter in, must strive to enter. Here are awakening considerations, to enforce this exhortation. Oh that we may be all awakened by them! They answer the question, Are there few that shall be saved? But let none despond either as to themselves or others, for there are last who shall be first, and first who shall be last. If we reach heaven, we shall meet many there whom we little thought to meet, and miss many whom we expected to find.

Verses 31-35

Christ, in calling Herod a fox, gave him his true character. The greatest of men were accountable to God, therefore it became him to call this proud king by his own name; but it is not an example for us. I know, said our Lord, that I must die very shortly; when I die, I shall be perfected, I shall have completed my undertaking. It is good for us to look upon the time we have before us as but little, that we may thereby be quickened to do the work of the day in its day. The wickedness of persons and places which more than others profess religion and relation to God, especially displeases and grieves the Lord Jesus. The judgment of the great day will convince unbelievers; but let us learn thankfully to welcome, and to profit by all who come in the name of the Lord, to call us to partake of his great salvation.

Chapter 14

Chapter Outline

Verses 1-6

This Pharisee, as well as others, seems to have had an ill design in entertaining Jesus at his house. But our Lord would not be hindered from healing a man, though he knew a clamour would be raised at his doing it on the sabbath. It requires care to understand the proper connexion between piety and charity in observing the sabbath, and the distinction between works of real necessity and habits of self-indulgence. Wisdom from above, teaches patient perseverance in well-doing.

Verses 7-14

Even in the common actions of life, Christ marks what we do, not only in our religious assemblies, but at our tables. We see in many cases, that a man's pride will bring him low, and before honour is humility. Our Saviour here teaches, that works of charity are better than works of show. But our Lord did not mean that a proud and unbelieving liberality should be rewarded, but that his precept of doing good to the poor and afflicted should be observed from love to him.

Verses 15-24

In this parable observe the free grace and mercy of God shining in the gospel of Christ, which will be food and a feast for the soul of a man that knows its own wants and miseries. All found some pretence to put off their attendance. This reproves the Jewish nation for their neglect of the offers of Christ's grace. It shows also the backwardness there is to close with the gospel call. The want of gratitude in those who slight gospel offers, and the contempt put upon the God of heaven thereby, justly provoke him. The apostles were to turn to the Gentiles, when the Jews refused the offer; and with them the church was filled. The provision made for precious souls in the gospel of Christ, has not been made in vain; for if some reject, others will thankfully accept the offer. The very poor and low in the world, shall be as welcome to Christ as the rich and great; and many times the gospel has the greatest success among those that labour under worldly disadvantages and bodily infirmities. Christ's house shall at last be filled; it will be so when the number of the elect is completed.

Verses 25-35

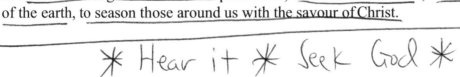

Do not put the created before the Creator

Though the disciples of Christ are not all crucified, yet they all bear their cross, and must bear it in the way of duty. Jesus bids them count upon it, and then consider of it. Our Saviour explains this by two similitudes; the former showing that we must consider the expenses of our religion; the latter, that we must consider the perils of it. Sit down and count the cost; consider it will cost the mortifying of sin, even the most beloved lusts. The proudest and most daring sinner cannot stand against God, for who knows the power of his anger? It is our interest to seek peace with him, and we need not send to ask conditions of peace, they are offered to us, and are highly to our advantage. In some way a disciple of Christ will be put to the trial. May we seek to be disciples indeed, and be careful not to grow slack in our profession, or afraid of the cross; that we may be the good salt of the earth, to season those around us with the savour of Christ.

✳ Hear it ✳ Seek God ✳

Chapter 15

Chapter Outline

Verses 1-10

The parable of the lost sheep is very applicable to the great work of man's redemption. The lost sheep represents the sinner as departed from God, and exposed to certain ruin if not brought back to him, yet not desirous to return. Christ is earnest in bringing sinners home. In the parable of the lost piece of silver, that which is lost, is one piece, of small value compared with the rest. Yet the woman seeks diligently till she finds it. This represents the various means and methods God makes use of to bring lost souls home to himself, and the Saviour's joy on their return to him. How careful then should we be that our repentance is unto salvation!

Verses 11-16

The parable of the prodigal son shows the nature of repentance, and the Lord's readiness to welcome and bless all who return to him. It fully sets forth the riches of gospel grace; and it has been, and will be, while the world stands, of unspeakable use to poor sinners, to direct and to encourage them in repenting and returning to God. It is bad, and the beginning of worse, when men look upon God's gifts as debts due to them. The great folly of sinners, and that which ruins them, is, being content in their life-time to receive their good things. Our first parents ruined themselves and all their race, by a foolish ambition to be independent, and this is at the bottom of sinners' persisting in their sin. We may all discern some features of our own characters in that of the prodigal son. A sinful state is of departure and distance from God. A sinful state is a spending state: wilful sinners misemploy their thoughts and the powers of their souls, mispend their time and all their opportunities. A sinful state is a wanting state. Sinners want necessaries for their souls; they have neither food nor raiment for them, nor any provision for hereafter. A sinful state is a vile, slavish state. The business of the devil's servants is to make provision for the flesh, to fulfil the lusts thereof, and that is no better than feeding swine. A sinful state is a state constant discontent. The wealth of the world and the pleasures of the senses will not even satisfy our bodies; but what are they to precious souls! A sinful state is a state which cannot look for relief from any creature. In vain do we cry to the world and to the flesh; they have that which will poison a soul, but have nothing to give which will feed and nourish it. A sinful state is a state of death. A sinner is dead in trespasses and sins, destitute of spiritual life. A sinful state is a lost state. Souls that are separated from God, if his mercy prevent not, will soon be lost for ever. The prodigal's wretched state, only faintly shadows forth the awful ruin of man by sin. Yet how few are sensible of their own state and character!

Verses 17-24

Having viewed the prodigal in his abject state of misery, we are next to consider his recovery from it. This begins by his coming to himself. That is a turning point in the sinner's conversion. The Lord opens his eyes, and convinces him of sin; then he views himself and every object, in a different light from what he did before. Thus the convinced sinner perceives that the meanest servant of God is happier than he is. To look unto God as a Father, and our Father, will be of great use in our repentance and return to him. The prodigal arose, nor stopped till he reached his home. Thus the repenting sinner resolutely quits the bondage of Satan and his lusts, and returns to God by prayer, notwithstanding fears and discouragements. The Lord meets him with unexpected tokens of his forgiving love. Again; the reception of the humbled sinner is like that of the prodigal. He is clothed in the robe of the Redeemer's righteousness, made partaker of the Spirit of adoption, prepared by peace of conscience and gospel grace to walk in the ways of holiness, and feasted with Divine consolations. Principles of grace and holiness are wrought in him, to do, as well as to will.

Verses 25-32

In the latter part of this parable we have the character of the Pharisees, though not of them alone. It sets forth the kindness of the Lord, and the proud manner in which his gracious kindness is often received. The Jews, in general, showed the same spirit towards the converted Gentiles; and numbers in every age object to the gospel and its preachers, on the same ground. What must that temper be, which stirs up a man to despise and abhor those for whom the Saviour shed his precious blood, who are objects of the Father's choice, and temples of the Holy Ghost! This springs from pride, self-preference, and ignorance of a man's own heart. The mercy and grace of our God in Christ, shine almost as bright in his tender and gentle bearing with peevish saints, as his receiving prodigal sinners upon their repentance. It is the unspeakable happiness of all the children of God, who keep close to their Father's house, that they are, and shall be ever with him. Happy will it be for those who thankfully accept Christ's invitation.

Chapter 16

Chapter Outline

Verses 1-12

Whatever we have, the property of it is God's; we have only the use of it, according to the direction of our great Lord, and for his honour. This steward wasted his lord's goods. And we are all liable to the same charge; we have not made due improvement of what God has trusted us with. The steward cannot deny it; he must make up his accounts, and be gone. This may teach us that death will come, and deprive us of the opportunities we now have. The steward will make friends of his lord's debtors or tenants, by striking off a considerable part of their debt to his lord. The lord referred to in this parable commended not the fraud, but the policy of the steward. In that respect alone is it so noticed. Worldly men, in the choice of their object, are foolish; but in their activity, and perseverance, they are often wiser than believers. The unjust steward is not set before us as an example in cheating his master, or to justify any dishonesty, but to point out the careful ways of worldly men. It would be well if the children of light would learn wisdom from the men of the world, and would as earnestly pursue their better object. The true riches signify spiritual blessings; and if a man spends upon himself, or hoards up what God has trusted to him, as to outward things, what evidence can he have, that he is an heir of God through Christ? The riches of this world are deceitful and uncertain. Let us be convinced that those are truly rich, and very rich, who are rich in faith, and rich toward God, rich in Christ, in the promises; let us then lay up our treasure in heaven, and expect our portion from thence.

Verses 13-18

To this parable our Lord added a solemn warning. Ye cannot serve God and the world, so divided are the two interests. When our Lord spoke thus, the covetous Pharisees treated his instructions with contempt. But he warned them, that what they contended for as the law, was a wresting of its meaning: this our Lord showed in a case respecting divorce. There are many covetous sticklers for the forms of godliness, who are the bitterest enemies to its power, and try to set others against the truth.

Verses 19-31

Here the spiritual things are represented, in a description of the different state of good and bad, in this world and in the other. We are not told that the rich man got his estate by fraud, or oppression; but Christ shows, that a man may have a great deal of the wealth, pomp, and pleasure of this world, yet perish for ever under God's wrath and curse. The sin of this rich man was his providing for himself only. Here is a godly man, and one that will hereafter be happy for ever, in the depth of adversity and distress. It is often the lot of some of the dearest of God's saints and servants to be greatly afflicted in this world. We are not told that the rich man did him any harm, but we do not find that he had any care for him. Here is the different condition of this godly poor man, and this wicked rich man, at and after death. The rich man in hell lifted up his eyes, being in torment. It is not probable that there are discourses between glorified saints and damned sinners, but this dialogue shows the hopeless misery and fruitless desires, to which condemned spirits are brought. There is a day coming, when those who now hate and despise the people of God, would gladly receive kindness from them. But the damned in hell shall not have the least abatement of their torment. Sinners are now called upon to remember; but they do not, they will not, they find ways to avoid it. As wicked people have good things only in this life, and at death are for ever separated from all good, so godly people have evil things only in this life, and at death they are for ever put from them. In this world, blessed be God, there is no gulf between a state of nature and grace, we may pass from sin to God; but if we die in our sins, there is no coming out. The rich man had five brethren, and would have them stopped in their sinful course; their coming to that place of torment, would make his misery the worse, who had helped to show them the way thither. How many would now desire to recall or to undo what they have written or done! Those who would make the rich man's praying to Abraham justify praying to saints departed, go far to seek for proofs, when the mistake of a damned sinner is all they can find for an example. And surely there is no encouragement to follow the example, when all his prayers were made in vain. A messenger from the dead could say no more than what is said in the Scriptures. The same strength of corruption that breaks through the convictions of the written word, would triumph over a witness from the dead. Let us seek to the law and to the testimony, Isa 8:19, 20, for that is the sure word of prophecy, upon which we may rest, 2Pe 1:19. Circumstances in every age show that no terrors, or arguments, can give true repentance without the special grace of God renewing the sinner's heart.

Chapter 17

Chapter Outline

Verses 1-10

It is no abatement of their guilt by whom an offence comes, nor will it lessen their punishment that offences will come. Faith in God's pardoning mercy, will enable us to get over the greatest difficulties in the way of forgiving our brethren. As with God nothing is impossible, so all things are possible to him that can believe. Our Lord showed his disciples their need of deep humility. The Lord has such a property in every creature, as no man can have in another; he cannot be in debt to them for their services, nor do they deserve any return from him.

Verses 11-19

A sense of our spiritual leprosy should make us very humble whenever we draw near to Christ. It is enough to refer ourselves to the compassions of Christ, for they fail not. We may look for God to meet us with mercy, when we are found in the way of obedience. Only one of those who were healed returned to give thanks. It becomes us, like him, to be very humble in thanksgivings, as well as in prayers. Christ noticed the one who thus distinguished himself, he was a Samaritan. The others only got the outward cure, he alone got the spiritual blessing.

Verses 20-37

The kingdom of God was among the Jews, or rather within some of them. It was a spiritual kingdom, set up in the heart by the power of Divine grace. Observe how it had been with sinners formerly, and in what state the judgments of God, which they had been warned of, found them. Here is shown what a dreadful surprise this destruction will be to the secure and sensual. Thus shall it be in the day when the Son of man is revealed. When Christ came to destroy the Jewish nation by the Roman armies, that nation was found in such a state of false security as is here spoken of. In like manner, when Jesus Christ shall come to judge the world, sinners will be found altogether regardless; for in like manner the sinners of every age go on securely in their evil ways, and remember not their latter end. But wherever the wicked are, who are marked for eternal ruin, they shall be found by the judgments of God.

Chapter 18

Chapter Outline

Verses 1-8

All God's people are praying people. Here earnest steadiness in prayer for spiritual mercies is taught. The widow's earnestness prevailed even with the unjust judge: she might fear lest it should set him more against her; but our earnest prayer is pleasing to our God. Even to the end there will still be ground for the same complaint of weakness of faith.

Verses 9-14

This parable was to convince some who trusted in themselves that they were righteous, and despised others. God sees with what disposition and design we come to him in holy ordinances. What the Pharisee said, shows that he trusted to himself that he was righteous. We may suppose he was free from gross and scandalous sins. All this was very well and commendable. Miserable is the condition of those who come short of the righteousness of this Pharisee, yet he was not accepted; and why not? He went up to the temple to pray, but was full of himself and his own goodness; the favour and grace of God he did not think worth asking. Let us beware of presenting proud devotions to the Lord, and of despising others. The publican's address to God was full of humility, and of repentance for sin, and desire toward God. His prayer was short, but to the purpose; God be merciful to me a sinner. Blessed be God, that we have this short prayer upon record, as an answered prayer; and that we are sure that he who prayed it, went to his house justified; for so shall we be, if we pray it, as he did, through Jesus Christ. He owned himself a sinner by nature, by practice, guilty before God. He had no dependence but upon the mercy of God; upon that alone he relied. And God's glory is to resist the proud, and give grace to the humble. Justification is of God in Christ; therefore the self-condemned, and not the self-righteous, are justified before God.

Verses 15-17

None are too little, too young, to be brought to Christ, who knows how to show kindness to those not capable of doing service to him. It is the mind of Christ, that little children should be brought to him. The promise is to us, and to our seed; therefore He will bid them welcome to him with us. And we must receive his kingdom as children, not by purchase, and must call it our Father's gift.

Verses 18-30

Many have a great deal in them very commendable, yet perish for lack of some one thing; so this ruler could not bear Christ's terms, which would part between him and his estate. Many who are loth to leave Christ, yet do leave him. After a long struggle between their convictions and their corruptions, their corruptions carry the day. They are very sorry that they cannot serve both; but if one must be quitted, it shall be their God, not their wordly gain. Their boasted obedience will be found mere outside show; the love of the world in some form or other lies at the root. Men are apt to speak too much of what they have left and lost, of what they have done and suffered for Christ, as Peter did. But we should rather be ashamed that there has been any regret or difficulty in doing it.

Verses 31-34

The Spirit of Christ, in the Old Testament prophets, testified beforehand his sufferings, and the glory that should follow, 1Pe 1:11. The disciples' prejudices were so strong, that they would not understand these things literally. They were so intent upon the prophecies which spake of Christ's glory, that they overlooked those which spake of his sufferings. People run into mistakes, because they read their Bibles by halves, and are only for the smooth things. We are as backward to learn the proper lessons from the sufferings, crucifixion, and resurrection of Christ, as the disciples were to what he told them as to those events; and for the same reason; self-love, and a desire of worldly objects, close our understandings.

Verses 35-43

This poor blind man sat by the wayside, begging. He was not only blind, but poor, the fitter emblem of the world of mankind which Christ came to heal and save. The prayer of faith, guided by Christ's encouraging promises, and grounded on them, shall not be in vain. The grace of Christ ought to be thankfully acknowledged, to the glory of God. It is for the glory of God if we follow Jesus, as those will do whose eyes are opened. We must praise God for his mercies to others, as well as for mercies to ourselves. Would we rightly understand these things, we must come to Christ, like the blind man, earnestly beseeching him to open our eyes, and to show us clearly the excellence of his precepts, and the value of his salvation.

Chapter 19

Chapter Outline

Verses 1-10

Those who sincerely desire a sight of Christ, like Zaccheus, will break through opposition, and take pains to see him. Christ invited himself to Zaccheus' house. Wherever Christ comes he opens the heart, and inclines it to receive him. He that has a mind to know Christ, shall be known of him. Those whom Christ calls, must humble themselves, and come down. We may well receive him joyfully, who brings all good with him. Zaccheus gave proofs publicly that he was become a true convert. He does not look to be justified by his works, as the Pharisee; but by his good works he will, through the grace of God, show the sincerity of his faith and repentance. Zaccheus is declared to be a happy man, now he is turned from sin to God. Now that he is saved from his sins, from the guilt of them, from the power of them, all the benefits of salvation are his. Christ is come to his house, and where Christ comes he brings salvation with him. He came into this lost world to seek and to save it. His design was to save, when there was no salvation in any other. He seeks those that sought him not, and asked not for him.

Verses 11-27

This parable is like that of the talents, Mt 25. Those that are called to Christ, he furnishes with gifts needful for their business; and from those to whom he gives power, he expects service. The manifestation of the Spirit is given to every man to profit withal, 1Co 12:7. And as every one has received the gift, so let him minister the same, 1Pe 4:10. The account required, resembles that in the parable of the talents; and the punishment of the avowed enemies of Christ, as well as of false professors, is shown. The principal difference is, that the pound given to each seems to point out the gift of the gospel, which is the same to all who hear it; but the talents, distributed more or less, seem to mean that God gives different capacities and advantages to men, by which this one gift of the gospel may be differently improved.

Verses 28-40

Christ has dominion over all creatures, and may use them as he pleases. He has all men's hearts both under his eye and in his hand. Christ's triumphs, and his disciples' joyful praises, vex proud Pharisees, who are enemies to him and to his kingdom. But Christ, as he despises the contempt of the proud, so he accepts the praises of the humble. Pharisees would silence the praises of Christ, but they cannot; for as God can out of stones raise up children unto Abraham, and turn the stony heart to himself, so he can bring praise out of the mouths of children. And what will be the feelings of men when the Lord returns in glory to judge the world!

Verses 41-48

Who can behold the holy Jesus, looking forward to the miseries that awaited his murderers, weeping over the city where his precious blood was about to be shed, without seeing that the likeness of God in the believer, consists much in good-will and compassion? Surely those cannot be right who take up any doctrines of truth, so as to be hardened towards their fellow-sinners. But let every one remember, that though Jesus wept over Jerusalem, he executed awful vengeance upon it. Though he delights not in the death of a sinner, yet he will surely bring to pass his awful threatenings on those who neglect his salvation. The Son of God did not weep vain and causeless tears, nor for a light matter, nor for himself. He knows the value of souls, the weight of guilt, and how low it will press and sink mankind. May he then come and cleanse our hearts by his Spirit, from all that defiles. May sinners, on every side, become attentive to the words of truth and salvation.

Chapter 20

Chapter Outline

Verses 1-8

Men often pretend to examine the evidences of revelation, and the truth of the gospel, when only seeking excuses for their own unbelief and disobedience. Christ answered these priests and scribes with a plain question about the baptism of John, which the common people could answer. They all knew it was from heaven, nothing in it had an earthly tendency. Those that bury the knowledge they have, are justly denied further knowledge. It was just with Christ to refuse to give account of his authority, to those who knew the baptism of John to be from heaven, yet would not believe in him, nor own their knowledge.

Verses 9-19

Christ spake this parable against those who resolved not to own his authority, though the evidence of it was so full. How many resemble the Jews who murdered the prophets and crucified Christ, in their enmity to God, and aversion to his service, desiring to live according to their lusts, without control! Let all who are favoured with God's word, look to it that they make proper use of their advantages. Awful will be the doom, both of those who reject the Son, and of those who profess to reverence Him, yet render not the fruits in due season. Though they could not but own that for such a sin, such a punishment was just, yet they could not bear to hear of it. It is the folly of sinners, that they persevere in sinful ways, though they dread the destruction at the end of those ways.

Verses 20-26

Those who are most crafty in their designs against Christ and his gospel, cannot hide them. He did not give a direct answer, but reproved them for offering to impose upon him; and they could not fasten upon any thing wherewith to stir up either the governor or the people against him. The wisdom which is from above, will direct all who teach the way of God truly, to avoid the snares laid for them by wicked men; and will teach our duty to God, to our rulers, and to all men, so clearly, that opposers will have no evil to say of us.

Verses 27-38

It is common for those who design to undermine any truth of God, to load it with difficulties. But we wrong ourselves, and wrong the truth of Christ, when we form our notions of the world of spirits by this world of sense. There are more worlds than one; a present visible world, and a future unseen world; and let every one compare this world and that world, and give the preference in his thoughts and cares to that which deserves them. Believers shall obtain the resurrection from the dead, that is the blessed resurrection. What shall be the happy state of the inhabitants of that world, we cannot express or conceive, 1Co 2:9. Those that are entered into the joy of their Lord, are entirely taken up therewith; when there is perfection of holiness there will be no occasion for preservatives from sin. And when God called himself the God of these patriarchs, he meant that he was a God all-sufficient to them, Ge 17:1, their exceeding great Reward, Ge 15:1. He never did that for them in this world, which answered the full extent of his undertaking; therefore there must be another life, in which he will do that for them, which will completely fulfil the promise.

Verses 39-47

The scribes commended the reply Christ made to the Sadducees about the resurrection, but they were silenced by a question concerning the Messiah. Christ, as God, was David's Lord; but Christ, as man, was David's son. The scribes would receive the severest judgement for defrauding the poor widows, and for their abuse of religion, particularly of prayer, which they used as a pretence for carrying on worldly and wicked plans. Dissembled piety is double sin. Then let us beg of God to keep us from pride, ambition, covetousness, and every evil thing; and to teach us to seek that honour which comes from him alone.

Chapter 21

Chapter Outline

Verses 1-4

From the offering of this poor widow, learn that what we rightly give for the relief of the poor, and the support of God's worship, is given unto God; and our Saviour sees with pleasure whatever we have in our hearts to give for the relief of his members, or for his service. Blessed Lord! the poorest of thy servants have two mites, they have a soul and a body; persuade and enable us to offer both unto thee; how happy shall we be in thine accepting of them!

Verses 5-28

With much curiosity those about Christ ask as to the time when the great desolation should be. He answers with clearness and fulness, as far as was necessary to teach them their duty; for all knowledge is desirable as far as it is in order to practice. Though spiritual judgements are the most common in gospel times, yet God makes use of temporal judgments also. Christ tells them what hard things they should suffer for his name's sake, and encourages them to bear up under their trials, and to go on in their work, notwithstanding the opposition they would meet with. God will stand by you, and own you, and assist you. This was remarkably fulfilled after the pouring out of the Spirit, by whom Christ gave his disciples wisdom and utterance. Though we may be losers for Christ, we shall not, we cannot be losers by him, in the end. It is our duty and interest at all times, especially in perilous, trying times, to secure the safety of our own souls. It is by Christian patience we keep possession of our own souls, and keep out all those impressions which would put us out of temper. We may view the prophecy before us much as those Old Testament prophecies, which, together with their great object, embrace, or glance at some nearer object of importance to the church. Having given an idea of the times for about thirty-eight years next to come, Christ shows what all those things would end in, namely, the destruction of Jerusalem, and the utter dispersion of the Jewish nation; which would be a type and figure of Christ's second coming. The scattered Jews around us preach the truth of Christianity; and prove, that though heaven and earth shall pass away, the words of Jesus shall not pass away. They also remind us to pray for those times when neither the real, nor the spiritual Jerusalem, shall any longer be trodden down by the Gentiles, and when both Jews and Gentiles shall be turned to the Lord. When Christ came to destroy the Jews, he came to redeem the Christians that were persecuted and oppressed by them; and then had the churches rest. When he comes to judge the world, he will redeem all that are his from their troubles. So fully did the Divine judgements come upon the Jews, that their city is set as an example before us, to show that sins will not pass unpunished; and that the terrors of the Lord, and his threatenings against impenitent sinners, will all come to pass, even as his word was true, and his wrath great upon Jerusalem.

Verses 29-38

Christ tells his disciples to observe the signs of the times, which they might judge by. He charges them to look upon the ruin of the Jewish nation as near. Yet this race and family of Abraham shall not be rooted out; it shall survive as a nation, and be found as prophesied, when the Son of man shall be revealed. He cautions them against being secure and sensual. This command is given to all Christ's disciples, Take heed to yourselves, that ye be not overpowered by temptations, nor betrayed by your own corruptions. We cannot be safe, if we are carnally secure. Our danger is, lest the day of death and of judgment should come upon us when we are not prepared. Lest, when we are called to meet our Lord, that be the furthest from our thoughts, which ought to be nearest our hearts. For so it will come upon the most of men, who dwell upon the earth, and mind earthly things only, and have no converse with heaven. It will be a terror and a destruction to them. Here see what should be our aim, that we may be accounted worthy to escape all those things; that when the judgements of God are abroad, we may not be in the common calamity, or it may not be that to us which it is to others. Do you ask how you may be found worthy to stand before Christ at that day? Those who never yet sought Christ, let them now go unto him; those who never yet were humbled for their sins, let them now begin; those who have already begun, let them go forward and be kept humbled. Watch therefore, and pray always. Watch against sin; watch in every duty, and make the most of every opportunity to do good. Pray always: those shall be accounted worthy to live a life of praise in the other world, who live a life of prayer in this world. May we begin, employ, and conclude each day attending to Christ's word, obeying his precepts, and following his example, that whenever he comes we may be found watching.

Chapter 22

Chapter Outline

Verses 1-6

Christ knew all men, and had wise and holy ends in taking Judas to be a disciple. How he who knew Christ so well, came to betray him, we are here told; Satan entered into Judas. It is hard to say whether more mischief is done to Christ's kingdom, by the power of its open enemies, or by the treachery of its pretended friends; but without the latter, its enemies could not do so much evil as they do.

Verses 7-18

Christ kept the ordinances of the law, particularly that of the passover, to teach us to observe his gospel institutions, and most of all that of the Lord's supper. Those who go upon Christ's word, need not fear disappointment. According to the orders given them, the disciples got all ready for the passover. Jesus bids this passover welcome. He desired it, though he knew his sufferings would follow, because it was in order to his Father's glory and man's redemption. He takes his leave of all passovers, signifying thereby his doing away all the ordinances of the ceremonial law, of which the passover was one of the earliest and chief. That type was laid aside, because now in the kingdom of God the substance was come.

Verses 19, 20

The Lord's supper is a sign or memorial of Christ already come, who by dying delivered us; his death is in special manner set before us in that ordinance, by which we are reminded of it. The breaking of Christ's body as a sacrifice for us, is therein brought to our remembrance by the breaking of bread. Nothing can be more nourishing and satisfying to the soul, than the doctrine of Christ's making atonement for sin, and the assurance of an interest in that atonement. Therefore we do this in remembrance of what He did for us, when he died for us; and for a memorial of what we do, in joining ourselves to him in an everlasting covenant. The shedding of Christ's blood, by which the atonement was made, is represented by the wine in the cup.

Verses 21-38

How unbecoming is the worldly ambition of being the greatest, to the character of a follower of Jesus, who took upon him the form of a servant, and humbled himself to the death of the cross! In the way to eternal happiness, we must expect to be assaulted and sifted by Satan. If he cannot destroy, he will try to disgrace or distress us. Nothing more certainly forebodes a fall, in a professed follower of Christ, than self-confidence, with disregard to warnings, and contempt of danger. Unless we watch and pray always, we may be drawn in the course of the day into those sins which we were in the morning most resolved against. If believers were left to themselves, they would fall; but they are kept by the power of God, and the prayer of Christ. Our Lord gave notice of a very great change of circumstances now approaching. The disciples must not expect that their friends would be kind to them as they had been. Therefore, he that has a purse, let him take it, for he may need it. They must now expect that their enemies would be more fierce than they had been, and they would need weapons. At the time the apostles understood Christ to mean real weapons, but he spake only of the weapons of the spiritual warfare. The sword of the Spirit is the sword with which the disciples of Christ must furnish themselves.

Verses 39-46

Every description which the evangelists give of the state of mind in which our Lord entered upon this conflict, proves the tremendous nature of the assault, and the perfect foreknowledge of its terrors possessed by the meek and lowly Jesus. Here are three things not in the other evangelists. 1. When Christ was in his agony, there appeared to him an angel from heaven, strengthening him. It was a part of his humiliation that he was thus strengthened by a ministering spirit. 2. Being in agony, he prayed more earnestly. Prayer, though never out of season, is in a special manner seasonable when we are in an agony. 3. In this agony his sweat was as it were great drops of blood falling down. This showed the travail of his soul. We should pray also to be enabled to resist unto the shedding of our blood, striving against sin, if ever called to it. When next you dwell in imagination upon the delights of some favourite sin, think of its effects as you behold them here! See its fearful effects in the garden of Gethsemane, and desire, by the help of God, deeply to hate and to forsake that enemy, to ransom sinners from whom the Redeemer prayed, agonized, and bled.

Verses 47-53

Nothing can be a greater affront or grief to the Lord Jesus, than to be betrayed by those who profess to be his followers, and say that they love him. Many instances there are, of Christ's being betrayed by those who, under the form of godliness, fight against the power of it. Jesus here gave an illustrious example of his own rule of doing good to those that hate us, as afterwards he did of praying for those that despitefully use us. Corrupt nature warps our conduct to extremes; we should seek for the Lord's direction before we act in difficult circumstances. Christ was willing to wait for his triumphs till his warfare was accomplished, and we must be so too. But the hour and the power of darkness were short, and such the triumphs of the wicked always will be.

Verses 54-62

Peter's fall was his denying that he knew Christ, and was his disciple; disowning him because of distress and danger. He that has once told a lie, is strongly tempted to persist: the beginning of that sin, like strife, is as the letting forth of water. The Lord turned and looked upon Peter. 1. It was a convincing look. Jesus turned and looked upon him, as if he should say, Dost thou not know me, Peter? 2. It was a chiding look. Let us think with what a rebuking countenance Christ may justly look upon us when we have sinned. 3. It was an expostulating look. Thou who wast the most forward to confess me to be the Son of God, and didst solemnly promise thou wouldest never disown me! 4. It was a compassionate look. Peter, how art thou fallen and undone if I do not help thee! 5. It was a directing look, to go and bethink himself. 6. It was a significant look; it signified the conveying of grace to Peter's heart, to enable him to repent. The grace of God works in and by the word of God, brings that to mind, and sets that home upon the conscience, and so gives the soul the happy turn. Christ looked upon the chief priests, and made no impression upon them as he did on Peter. It was not the mere look from Christ, but the Divine grace with it, that restored Peter.

Verses 63-71

Those that condemned Jesus for a blasphemer, were the vilest blasphemers. He referred them to his second coming, for the full proof of his being the Christ, to their confusion, since they would not admit the proof of it to their conviction. He owns himself to be the Son of God, though he knew he should suffer for it. Upon this they ground his condemnation. Their eyes being blinded, they rush on. Let us meditate on this amazing transaction, and consider Him who endured such contradiction of sinners against himself.

Chapter 23

Chapter Outline

The death of Christ.   (44–49)

The burial of Christ.   (50–56)

Verses 1-5

Pilate well understood the difference between armed forces and our Lord's followers. But instead of being softened by Pilate's declaration of his innocence, and considering whether they were not bringing the guilt of innocent blood upon themselves, the Jews were the more angry. The Lord brings his designs to a glorious end, even by means of those who follow the devices of their own hearts. Thus all parties joined, so as to prove the innocence of Jesus, who was the atoning sacrifice for our sins.

Verses 6-12

Herod had heard many things of Jesus in Galilee, and out of curiosity longed to see him. The poorest beggar that asked a miracle for the relief of his necessity, was never denied; but this proud prince, who asked for a miracle only to gratify his curiosity, is refused. He might have seen Christ and his wondrous works in Galilee, and would not, therefore it is justly said, Now he would see them, and shall not. Herod sent Christ again to Pilate: the friendships of wicked men are often formed by union in wickedness. They agree in little, except in enmity to God, and contempt of Christ.

Verses 13-25

The fear of man brings many into this snare, that they will do an unjust thing, against their consciences, rather than get into trouble. Pilate declares Jesus innocent, and has a mind to release him; yet, to please the people, he would punish him as an evil-doer. If no fault be found in him, why chastise him? Pilate yielded at length; he had not courage to go against so strong a stream. He delivered Jesus to their will, to be crucified.

Verses 26-31

We have here the blessed Jesus, the Lamb of God, led as a lamb to the slaughter, to the sacrifice. Though many reproached and reviled him, yet some pitied him. But the death of Christ was his victory and triumph over his enemies: it was our deliverance, the purchase of eternal life for us. Therefore weep not for him, but let us weep for our own sins, and the sins of our children, which caused his death; and weep for fear of the miseries we shall bring upon ourselves, if we slight his love, and reject his grace. If God delivered him up to such sufferings as these, because he was made a sacrifice for sin, what will he do with sinners themselves, who make themselves a dry tree, a corrupt and wicked generation, and good for nothing! The bitter sufferings of our Lord Jesus should make us stand in awe of the justice of God. The best saints, compared with Christ, are dry trees; if he suffer, why may not they expect to suffer? And what then shall the damnation of sinners be! Even the sufferings of Christ preach terror to obstinate transgressors.

Verses 32-43

As soon as Christ was fastened to the cross, he prayed for those who crucified him. The great thing he died to purchase and procure for us, is the forgiveness of sin. This he prays for. Jesus was crucified between two thieves; in them were shown the different effects the cross of Christ would have upon the children of men in the preaching the gospel. One malefactor was hardened to the last. No troubles of themselves will change a wicked heart. The other was softened at the last: he was snatched as a brand out of the burning, and made a monument of Divine mercy. This gives no encouragement to any to put off repentance to their death-beds, or to hope that they shall then find mercy. It is certain that true repentance is never too late; but it is as certain that late repentance is seldom true. None can be sure they shall have time to repent at death, but every man may be sure he cannot have the advantages this penitent thief had. We shall see the case to be singular, if we observe the uncommon effects of God's grace upon this man. He reproved the other for railing on Christ. He owned that he deserved what was done to him. He believed Jesus to have suffered wrongfully. Observe his faith in this prayer. Christ was in the depth of disgrace, suffering as a deceiver, and not delivered by his Father. He made this profession before the wonders were displayed which put honour on Christ's sufferings, and startled the centurion. He believed in a life to come, and desired to be happy in that life; not like the other thief, to be only saved from the cross. Observe his humility in this prayer. All his request is, Lord, remember me; quite referring it to Jesus in what way to remember him. Thus he was humbled in true repentance, and he brought forth all the fruits for repentance his circumstances would admit. Christ upon the cross, is gracious like Christ upon the throne. Though he was in the greatest struggle and agony, yet he had pity for a poor penitent. By this act of grace we are to understand that Jesus Christ died to open the kingdom of heaven to all penitent, obedient believers. It is a single instance in Scripture; it should teach us to despair of none, and that none should despair of themselves; but lest it should be abused, it is contrasted with the awful state of the other thief, who died hardened in unbelief, though a crucified Saviour was so near him. Be sure that in general men die as they live.

Verses 44-49

We have here the death of Christ magnified by the wonders that attended it, and his death explained by the words with which he breathed out his soul. He was willing to offer himself. Let us seek to glorify God by true repentance and conversion; by protesting against those who crucify the Saviour; by a sober, righteous, and godly life; and by employing our talents in the service of Him who died for us and rose again.

Verses 50-56

Many, though they do not make any show in outward profession, yet, like Joseph of Arimathea, will be far more ready to do real service, when there is occasion, than others who make a greater noise. Christ was buried in haste, because the sabbath drew on. Weeping must not hinder sowing. Though they were in tears for the death of their Lord, yet they must prepare to keep holy the sabbath. When the sabbath draws on, there must be preparation. Our worldly affairs must be so ordered, that they may not hinder us from our sabbath work; and our holy affections so stirred up, that they may carry us on in it. In whatever business we engage, or however our hearts may be affected, let us never fail to get ready for, and to keep holy, the day of sacred rest, which is the Lord's day.

Chapter 24

Chapter Outline

Verses 1-12

See the affection and respect the women showed to Christ, after he was dead and buried. Observe their surprise when they found the stone rolled away, and the grave empty. Christians often perplex themselves about that with which they should comfort and encourage themselves. They look rather to find their Master in his grave-clothes, than angels in their shining garments. The angels assure them that he is risen from the dead; is risen by his own power. These angels from heaven bring not any new gospel, but remind the women of Christ's words, and teach them how to apply them. We may wonder that these disciples, who believed Jesus to be the Son of God and the true Messiah, who had been so often told that he must die, and rise again, and then enter into his glory, who had seen him more than once raise the dead, yet should be so backward to believe his raising himself. But all our mistakes in religion spring from ignorance or forgetfulness of the words Christ has spoken. Peter now ran to the sepulchre, who so lately ran from his Master. He was amazed. There are many things puzzling and perplexing to us, which would be plain and profitable, if we rightly understood the words of Christ.

Verses 13-27

This appearance of Jesus to the two disciples going to Emmaus, happened the same day that he rose from the dead. It well becomes the disciples of Christ to talk together of his death and resurrection; thus they may improve one another's knowledge, refresh one another's memory, and stir up each other's devout affections. And where but two together are well employed in work of that kind, he will come to them, and make a third. Those who seek Christ, shall find him: he will manifest himself to those that inquire after him; and give knowledge to those who use the helps for knowledge which they have. No matter how it was, but so it was, they did not know him; he so ordering it, that they might the more freely discourse with him. Christ's disciples are often sad and sorrowful, even when they have reason to rejoice; but through the weakness of their faith, they cannot take the comfort offered to them. Though Christ is entered into his state of exaltation, yet he notices the sorrows of his disciples, and is afflicted in their afflictions. Those are strangers in Jerusalem, that know not of the death and sufferings of Jesus. Those who have the knowledge of Christ crucified, should seek to spread that knowledge. Our Lord Jesus reproved them for the weakness of their faith in the Scriptures of the Old Testament. Did we know more of the Divine counsels as far as they are made known in the Scriptures, we should not be subject to the perplexities we often entangle ourselves in. He shows them that the sufferings of Christ were really the appointed way to his glory; but the cross of Christ was that to which they could not reconcile themselves. Beginning at Moses, the first inspired writer of the Old Testament, Jesus expounded to them the things concerning himself. There are many passages throughout all the Scriptures concerning Christ, which it is of great advantage to put together. We cannot go far in any part, but we meet with something that has reference to Christ, some prophecy, some promise, some prayer, some type or other. A golden thread of gospel grace runs through the whole web of the Old Testament. Christ is the best expositor of Scripture; and even after his resurrection, he led people to know the mystery concerning himself, not by advancing new notions, but by showing how the Scripture was fulfilled, and turning them to the earnest study of it.

Verses 28-35

If we would have Christ dwell with us, we must be earnest with him. Those that have experienced the pleasure and profit of communion with him, cannot but desire more of his company. He took bread, and blessed it, and brake, and gave to them. This he did with his usual authority and affection, with the same manner, perhaps with the same words. He here teaches us to crave a blessing on every meal. See how Christ by his Spirit and grace makes himself known to the souls of his people. He opens the Scriptures to them. He meets them at his table, in the ordinance of the Lord's supper; is known to them in breaking of bread. But the work is completed by the opening of the eyes of their mind; yet it is but short views we have of Christ in this world, but when we enter heaven, we shall see him for ever. They had found the preaching powerful, even when they knew not the preacher. Those Scriptures which speak of Christ, will warm the hearts of his true disciples. That is likely to do most good, which affects us with the love of Jesus in dying for us. It is the duty of those to whom he has shown himself, to let others know what he has done for their souls. It is of great use for the disciples of Christ to compare their experiences, and tell them to each other.

Verses 36-49

Jesus appeared in a miraculous manner, assuring the disciples of his peace, though they had so lately forsaken him, and promising spiritual peace with every blessing. Many troublesome thoughts which disquiet our minds, rise from mistakes concerning Christ. All the troublesome thoughts which rise in our hearts at any time, are known to the Lord Jesus, and are displeasing to him. He spake with them on their unreasonable unbelief. Nothing had passed but what was foretold by the prophets, and necessary for the salvation of sinners. And now all men should be taught the nature and necessity of repentance, in order to the forgiveness of their sins. And these blessings were to be sought for, by faith in the name of Jesus. Christ by his Spirit works on the minds of men. Even good men need to have their understandings opened. But that we may have right thoughts of Christ, there needs no more than to be made to understand the Scriptures.

Verses 50-53

Christ ascended from Bethany, near the Mount of Olives. There was the garden in which his sufferings began; there he was in his agony. Those that would go to heaven, must ascend thither from the house of sufferings and sorrows. The disciples did not see him rise out of the grave; his resurrection could be proved by their seeing him alive afterwards: but they saw him ascend into heaven; they could not otherwise have a proof of his ascension. He lifted up his hands, and blessed them. He did not go away in displeasure, but in love, he left a blessing behind him. As he arose, so he ascended, by his own power. They worshipped him. This fresh display of Christ's glory drew from them fresh acknowledgments. They returned to Jerusalem with great joy. The glory of Christ is the joy of all true believers, even while they are here in this world. While waiting for God's promises, we must go forth to meet them with our praises. And nothing better prepares the mind for receiving the Holy Ghost. Fears are silenced, sorrows sweetened and allayed, and hopes kept up. And this is the ground of a Christian's boldness at the throne of grace; yea, the Father's throne is the throne of grace to us, because it is also the throne of our Mediator, Jesus Christ. Let us rely on his promises, and plead them. Let us attend his ordinances, praise and bless God for his mercies, set our affections on things above, and expect the Redeemer's return to complete our happiness. Amen. Even so, Lord Jesus, come quickly.

John

The apostle and evangelist, John, seems to have been the youngest of the twelve. He was especially favoured with our Lord's regard and confidence, so as to be spoken of as the disciple whom Jesus loved. He was very sincerely attached to his Master. He exercised his ministry at Jerusalem with much success, and outlived the destruction of that city, agreeably to Christ's prediction, ch. 21:22. History relates that after the death of Christ's mother, John resided chiefly at Ephesus. Towards the close of Domitian's reign he was banished to the isle of Patmos, where he wrote his Revelation. On the accession of Nerva, he was set at liberty, and returned to Ephesus, where it is thought he wrote his Gospel and Epistles, about A. D. 97, and died soon after. The design of this Gospel appears to be to convey to the Christian world, just notions of the real nature, office, and character of that Divine Teacher, who came to instruct and to redeem mankind. For this purpose, John was directed to select for his narrative, those passages of our Saviour's life, which most clearly displayed his Divine power and authority; and those of his discourses, in which he spake most plainly of his own nature, and of the power of his death, as an atonement for the sins of the world. By omitting, or only briefly mentioning, the events recorded by the other evangelists, John gave testimony that their narratives are true, and left room for the doctrinal statements already mentioned, and for particulars omitted in the other Gospels, many of which are exceedingly important.

Chapter 1

Chapter Outline

Verses 1-5

The plainest reason why the Son of God is called the Word, seems to be, that as our words explain our minds to others, so was the Son of God sent in order to reveal his Father's mind to the world. What the evangelist says of Christ proves that he is God. He asserts, His existence in the beginning; His coexistence with the Father. The Word was with God. All things were made by him, and not as an instrument. Without him was not any thing made that was made, from the highest angel to the meanest worm. This shows how well qualified he was for the work of our redemption and salvation. The light of reason, as well as the life of sense, is derived from him, and depends upon him. This eternal Word, this true Light shines, but the darkness comprehends it not. Let us pray without ceasing, that our eyes may be opened to behold this Light, that we may walk in it; and thus be made wise unto salvation, by faith in Jesus Christ.

Verses 6-14

John the Baptist came to bear witness concerning Jesus. Nothing more fully shows the darkness of men's minds, than that when the Light had appeared, there needed a witness to call attention to it. Christ was the true Light; that great Light which deserves to be called so. By his Spirit and grace he enlightens all that are enlightened to salvation; and those that are not enlightened by him, perish in darkness. Christ was in the world when he took our nature upon him, and dwelt among us. The Son of the Highest was here in this lower world. He was in the world, but not of it. He came to save a lost world, because it was a world of his own making. Yet the world knew him not. When he comes as a Judge, the world shall know him. Many say that they are Christ's own, yet do not receive him, because they will not part with their sins, nor have him to reign over them. All the children of God are born again. This new birth is through the word of God as the means, 1Pe 1:23, and by the Spirit of God as the Author. By his Divine presence Christ always was in the world. But now that the fulness of time was come, he was, after another manner, God manifested in the flesh. But observe the beams of his Divine glory, which darted through this veil of flesh. Men discover their weaknesses to those most familiar with them, but it was not so with Christ; those most intimate with him saw most of his glory. Although he was in the form of a servant, as to outward circumstances, yet, in respect of graces, his form was like the Son of God His Divine glory appeared in the holiness of his doctrine, and in his miracles. He was full of grace, fully acceptable to his Father, therefore qualified to plead for us; and full of truth, fully aware of the things he was to reveal.

Verses 15-18

As to the order of time and entrance on his work, Christ came after John, but in every other way he was before him. The expression clearly shows that Jesus had existence before he appeared on earth as man. All fulness dwells in him, from which alone fallen sinners have, and shall receive, by faith, all that renders them wise, strong, holy, useful, and happy. Our receivings by Christ are all summed up in this one word, grace; we have received "even grace," a gift so great, so rich, so invaluable; the good will of God towards us, and the good work of God in us. The law of God is holy, just, and good; and we should make the proper use of it. But we cannot derive from it pardon, righteousness, or strength. It teaches us to adorn the doctrine of God our Saviour, but it cannot supply the place of that doctrine. As no mercy comes from God to sinners but through Jesus Christ, no man can come to the Father but by him; no man can know God, except as he is made known in the only begotten and beloved Son.

Verses 19-28

John disowns himself to be the Christ, who was now expected and waited for. He came in the spirit and power of Elias, but he was not the person of Elias. John was not that Prophet whom Moses said the Lord would raise up to them of their brethren, like unto him. He was not such a prophet as they expected, who would rescue them from the Romans. He gave such an account of himself, as might excite and awaken them to hearken to him. He baptized the people with water as a profession of repentance, and as an outward sign of the spiritual blessings to be conferred on them by the Messiah, who was in the midst of them, though they knew him not, and to whom he was unworthy to render the meanest service.

Verses 29-36

John saw Jesus coming to him, and pointed him out as the Lamb of God. The paschal lamb, in the shedding and sprinkling of its blood, the roasting and eating of its flesh, and all the other circumstances of the ordinance, represented the salvation of sinners by faith in Christ. And the lambs sacrificed every morning and evening, can only refer to Christ slain as a sacrifice to redeem us to God by his blood. John came as a preacher of repentance, yet he told his followers that they were to look for the pardon of their sins to Jesus only, and to his death. It agrees with God's glory to pardon all who depend on the atoning sacrifice of Christ. He takes away the sin of the world; purchases pardon for all that repent and believe the gospel. This encourages our faith; if Christ takes away the sin of the world, then why not my sin? He bore sin for us, and so bears it from us. God could have taken away sin, by taking away the sinner, as he took away the sin of the old world; but here is a way of doing away sin, yet sparing the sinner, by making his Son sin, that is, a sin-offering, for us. See Jesus taking away sin, and let that cause hatred of sin, and resolutions against it. Let us not hold that fast, which the Lamb of God came to take away. To confirm his testimony concerning Christ, John declares the appearance at his baptism, in which God himself bore witness to him. He saw and bare record that he is the Son of God. This is the end and object of John's testimony, that Jesus was the promised Messiah. John took every opportunity that offered to lead people to Christ.

Verses 37-42

The strongest and most prevailing argument with an awakened soul to follow Christ, is, that it is he only who takes away sin. Whatever communion there is between our souls and Christ, it is he who begins the discourse. He asked, What seek ye? The question Jesus put to them, we should all put to ourselves when we begin to follow Him, What do we design and desire? In following Christ, do we seek the favour of God and eternal life? He invites them to come without delay. Now is the accepted time, 2Co 6:2. It is good for us to be where Christ is, wherever it be. We ought to labour for the spiritual welfare of those related to us, and seek to bring them to Him. Those who come to Christ, must come with a fixed resolution to be firm and constant to him, like a stone, solid and stedfast; and it is by his grace that they are so.

Verses 43-51

See the nature of true Christianity, it is following Jesus; devoting ourselves to him, and treading in his steps. Observe the objection Nathanael made. All who desire to profit by the word of God, must beware of prejudices against places, or denominations of men. They should examine for themselves, and they will sometimes find good where they looked for none. Many people are kept from the ways of religion by the unreasonable prejudices they conceive. The best way to remove false notions of religion, is to make trial of it. In Nathanael there was no guile. His profession was not hypocritical. He was not a dissembler, nor dishonest; he was a sound character, a really upright, godly man. Christ knows what men are indeed. Does He know us? Let us desire to know him. Let us seek and pray to be Israelites indeed, in whom is no guile; truly Christians, approved of Christ himself. Some things weak, imperfect, and sinful, are found in all, but hypocrisy belongs not to a believer's character. Jesus witnessed what passed when Nathanael was under the fig-tree. Probably he was then in fervent prayer, seeking direction as to the Hope and Consolation of Israel, where no human eye observed him. This showed him that our Lord knew the secrets of his heart. Through Christ we commune with, and benefit by the holy angels; and things in heaven and things on earth are reconciled and united together.

Chapter 2

Chapter Outline

Verses 1-11

It is very desirable when there is a marriage, to have Christ own and bless it. Those that would have Christ with them at their marriage, must invite him by prayer, and he will come. While in this world we sometimes find ourselves in straits, even when we think ourselves in fulness. There was want at a marriage feast. Those who are come to care for the things of the world, must look for trouble, and count upon disappointment. In our addresses to Christ, we must humbly spread our case before him, and then refer ourselves to him to do as he pleases. In Christ's reply to his mother there was no disrespect. He used the same word when speaking to her with affection from the cross; yet it is a standing testimony against the idolatry of after-ages, in giving undue honours to his mother. His hour is come when we know not what to do. Delays of mercy are not denials of prayer. Those that expect Christ's favours, must observe his orders with ready obedience. The way of duty is the way to mercy; and Christ's methods must not be objected against. The beginning of Moses' miracles was turning water into blood, Ex 7:20; the beginning of Christ's miracles was turning water into wine; which may remind us of the difference between the law of Moses and the gospel of Christ. He showed that he improves creature-comforts to all true believers, and make them comforts indeed. And Christ's works are all for use. Has he turned thy water into wine, given thee knowledge and grace? it is to profit withal; therefore draw out now, and use it. It was the best wine. Christ's works commend themselves even to those who know not their Author. What was produced by miracles, always was the best in its kind. Though Christ hereby allows a right use of wine, he does not in the least do away his own caution, which is, that our hearts be not at any time overcharged with surfeiting and drunkenness, Lu 21:34. Though we need not scruple to feast with our friends on proper occasions, yet every social interview should be so conducted, that we might invite the Redeemer to join with us, if he were now on earth; and all levity, luxury, and excess offend him.

Verses 12-22

The first public work in which we find Christ engaged, was driving from the temple the traders whom the covetous priests and rulers encouraged to make a market-place of its courts. Those now make God's house a house of merchandise, whose minds are filled with cares about worldly business when attending religious exercises, or who perform Divine offices for love of gain. Christ, having thus cleansed the temple, gave a sign to those who demanded it, to prove his authority for so doing. He foretells his death by the Jews' malice, Destroy ye this temple; I will permit you to destroy it. He foretells his resurrection by his own power; In three days I will raise it up. Christ took again his own life. Men mistake by understanding that according to the letter, which the Scripture speaks by way of figure. When Jesus was risen from the dead, his disciples remembered he has said this. It helps much in understanding the Divine word, to observe the fulfilling of the Scriptures.

Verses 23-25

Our Lord knew all men, their nature, dispositions, affections, designs, so as we do not know any man, not even ourselves. He knows his crafty enemies, and all their secret projects; his false friends, and their true characters. He knows who are truly his, knows their uprightness, and knows their weaknesses. We know what is done by men; Christ knows what is in them, he tries the heart. Beware of a dead faith, or a formal profession: carnal, empty professors are not to be trusted, and however men impose on others or themselves, they cannot impose on the heart-searching God.

Chapter 3

Chapter Outline

Verses 1-8

Nicodemus was afraid, or ashamed to be seen with Christ, therefore came in the night. When religion is out of fashion, there are many Nicodemites. But though he came by night, Jesus bid him welcome, and hereby taught us to encourage good beginnings, although weak. And though now he came by night, yet afterward he owned Christ publicly. He did not talk with Christ about state affairs, though he was a ruler, but about the concerns of his own soul and its salvation, and went at once to them. Our Saviour spoke of the necessity and nature of regeneration or the new birth, and at once directed Nicodemus to the source of holiness of the heart. Birth is the beginning of life; to be born again, is to begin to live anew, as those who have lived much amiss, or to little purpose. We must have a new nature, new principles, new affections, new aims. By our first birth we were corrupt, shapen in sin; therefore we must be made new creatures. No stronger expression could have been chosen to signify a great and most remarkable change of state and character. We must be entirely different from what we were before, as that which begins to be at any time, is not, and cannot be the same with that which was before. This new birth is from heaven, ch. 1:13, and its tendency is to heaven. It is a great change made in the heart of a sinner, by the power of the Holy Spirit. It means that something is done in us, and for us, which we cannot do for ourselves. Something is wrong, whereby such a life begins as shall last for ever. We cannot otherwise expect any benefit by Christ; it is necessary to our happiness here and hereafter. What Christ speak, Nicodemus misunderstood, as if there had been no other way of regenerating and new-moulding an immortal soul, than by new-framing the body. But he acknowledged his ignorance, which shows a desire to be better informed. It is then further explained by the Lord Jesus. He shows the Author of this blessed change. It is not wrought by any wisdom or power of our own, but by the power of the blessed Spirit. We are shapen in iniquity, which makes it necessary that our nature be changed. We are not to marvel at this; for, when we consider the holiness of God, the depravity of our nature, and the happiness set before us, we shall not think it strange that so much stress is laid upon this. The regenerating work of the Holy Spirit is compared to water. It is also probable that Christ had reference to the ordinance of baptism. Not that all those, and those only, that are baptized, are saved; but without that new birth which is wrought by the Spirit, and signified by baptism, none shall be subjects of the kingdom of heaven. The same word signifies both the wind and the Spirit. The wind bloweth where it listeth for us; God directs it. The Spirit sends his influences where, and when, on whom, and in what measure and degree, he pleases. Though the causes are hidden, the effects are plain, when the soul is brought to mourn for sin, and to breathe after Christ. Christ's stating of the doctrine and the necessity of regeneration, it should seem, made it not clearer to Nicodemus. Thus the things of the Spirit of God are foolishness to the natural man. Many think that cannot be proved, which they cannot believe. Christ's discourse of gospel truths, ver. #(11–13), shows the folly of those who make these things strange unto them; and it recommends us to search them out. Jesus Christ is every way able to reveal the will of God to us; for he came down from heaven, and yet is in heaven. We have here a notice of Christ's two distinct natures in one person, so that while he is the Son of man, yet he is in heaven. God is the "HE THAT IS," and heaven is the dwelling-place of his holiness. The knowledge of this must be from above, and can be received by faith alone. Jesus Christ came to save us by healing us, as the children of Israel, stung with fiery serpents, were cured and lived by looking up to the brazen serpent, Nu 21:6–9. In this observe the deadly and destructive nature of sin. Ask awakened consciences, ask damned sinners, they will tell you, that how charming soever the allurements of sin may be, at the last it bites like a serpent. See the powerful remedy against this fatal malady. Christ is plainly set forth to us in the gospel. He whom we offended is our Peace, and the way of applying for a cure is by believing. If any so far slight either their disease by sin, or the method of cure by Christ, as not to receive Christ upon his own terms, their ruin is upon their own heads. He has said, Look and be saved, look and live; lift up the eyes of your faith to Christ crucified. And until we have grace to do this, we shall not be cured, but still are wounded with the stings of Satan, and in a dying state. Jesus Christ came to save us by pardoning us, that we might not die by the sentence of the law. Here is gospel, good news indeed. Here is God's love in giving his Son for the world. God so loved the world; so really, so richly. Behold and wonder, that the great God should love such a worthless world! Here, also, is the great gospel duty, to believe in Jesus Christ. God having given him to be our Prophet, Priest, and King, we must give up ourselves to be ruled, and taught, and saved by him. And here is the great gospel benefit, that whoever believes in Christ, shall not perish, but shall have everlasting life. God was in Christ reconciling the world to himself, and so saving it. It could not be saved, but through him; there is no salvation in any other. From all this is shown the happiness of true believers; he that believeth in Christ is not condemned. Though he has been a great sinner, yet he is not dealt with according to what his sins deserve. How great is the sin of unbelievers! God sent One to save us, that was dearest to himself; and shall he not be dearest to us? How great is the misery of unbelievers! they are condemned already; which speaks a certain condemnation; a present condemnation. The wrath of God now fastens upon them; and their own hearts condemn them. There is also a condemnation grounded on their former guilt; they are open to the law for all their sins; because they are not by faith interested in the gospel pardon. Unbelief is a sin against the remedy. It springs from the enmity of the heart of man to God, from love of sin in some form. Read also the doom of those that would not know Christ. Sinful works are works of darkness. The wicked world keep as far from this light as they can, lest their deeds should be reproved. Christ is hated, because sin is loved. If they had not hated saving knowledge, they would not sit down contentedly in condemning ignorance. On the other hand, renewed hearts bid this light welcome. A good man acts truly and sincerely in all he does. He desires to know what the will of God is, and to do it, though against his own worldly interest. A change in his whole character and conduct has taken place. The love of God is shed abroad in his heart by the Holy Ghost, and is become the commanding principle of his actions. So long as he continues under a load of unforgiven guilt, there can be little else than slavish fear of God; but when his doubts are done away, when he sees the righteous ground whereon this forgiveness is built, he rests on it as his own, and is united to God by unfeigned love. Our works are good when the will of God is the rule of them, and the glory of God the end of them; when they are done in his strength, and for his sake; to him, and not to men. Regeneration, or the new birth, is a subject to which the world is very averse; it is, however, the grand concern, in comparison with which every thing else is but trifling. What does it signify though we have food to eat in plenty, and variety of raiment to put on, if we are not born again? if after a few mornings and evenings spent in unthinking mirth, carnal pleasure, and riot, we die in our sins, and lie down in sorrow? What does it signify though we are well able to act our parts in life, in every other respect, if at last we hear from the Supreme Judge, "Depart from me, I know you not, ye workers of iniquity?"

Verses 22-36

John was fully satisfied with the place and work assigned him; but Jesus came on a more important work. He also knew that Jesus would increase in honour and influence, for of his government and peace there would be no end, while he himself would be less followed. John knew that Jesus came from heaven as the Son of God, while he was a sinful, mortal man, who could only speak about the more plain subjects of religion. The words of Jesus were the words of God; he had the Spirit, not by measure, as the prophets, but in all fulness. Everlasting life could only be had by faith in Him, and might be thus obtained; whereas all those, who believe not in the Son of God, cannot partake of salvation, but the wrath of God for ever rests upon them.

Chapter 4

Chapter Outline

Verses 1-3

Jesus applied himself more to preaching, which was the more excellent, 1Co 1:17, than to baptism. He would put honour upon his disciples, by employing them to baptize. He teaches us that the benefit of sacraments depends not on the hand that administers them.

Verses 4-26

There was great hatred between the Samaritans and the Jews. Christ's road from Judea to Galilee lay through Samaria. We should not go into places of temptation but when we needs must; and then must not dwell in them, but hasten through them. We have here our Lord Jesus under the common fatigue of travellers. Thus we see that he was truly a man. Toil came in with sin; therefore Christ, having made himself a curse for us, submitted to it. Also, he was a poor man, and went all his journeys on foot. Being wearied, he sat thus on the well; he had no couch to rest upon. He sat thus, as people wearied with travelling sit. Surely, we ought readily to submit to be like the Son of God in such things as these. Christ asked a woman for water. She was surprised because he did not show the anger of his own nation against the Samaritans. Moderate men of all sides are men wondered at. Christ took the occasion to teach her Divine things: he converted this woman, by showing her ignorance and sinfulness, and her need of a Saviour. By this living water is meant the Spirit. Under this comparison the blessing of the Messiah had been promised in the Old Testament. The graces of the Spirit, and his comforts, satisfy the thirsting soul, that knows its own nature and necessity. What Jesus spake figuratively, she took literally. Christ shows that the water of Jacob's well yielded a very short satisfaction. Of whatever waters of comfort we drink, we shall thirst again. But whoever partakes of the Spirit of grace, and the comforts of the gospel, shall never want that which will abundantly satisfy his soul. Carnal hearts look no higher than carnal ends. Give it me, saith she, not that I may have everlasting life, which Christ proposed, but that I come not hither to draw. The carnal mind is very ingenious in shifting off convictions, and keeping them from fastening. But how closely our Lord Jesus brings home the conviction to her conscience! He severely reproved her present state of life. The woman acknowledged Christ to be a prophet. The power of his word in searching the heart, and convincing the conscience of secret things, is a proof of Divine authority. It should cool our contests, to think that the things we are striving about are passing away. The object of worship will continue still the same, God, as a Father; but an end shall be put to all differences about the place of worship. Reason teaches us to consult decency and convenience in the places of our worship; but religion gives no preference to one place above another, in respect of holiness and approval with God. The Jews were certainly in the right. Those who by the Scriptures have obtained some knowledge of God, know whom they worship. The word of salvation was of the Jews. It came to other nations through them. Christ justly preferred the Jewish worship before the Samaritan, yet here he speaks of the former as soon to be done away. God was about to be revealed as the Father of all believers in every nation. The spirit or the soul of man, as influenced by the Holy Spirit, must worship God, and have communion with him. Spiritual affections, as shown in fervent prayers, supplications, and thanksgivings, form the worship of an upright heart, in which God delights and is glorified. The woman was disposed to leave the matter undecided, till the coming of the Messiah. But Christ told her, I that speak to thee, am He. She was an alien and a hostile Samaritan, merely speaking to her was thought to disgrace our Lord Jesus. Yet to this woman did our Lord reveal himself more fully than as yet he had done to any of his disciples. No past sins can bar our acceptance with him, if we humble ourselves before him, believing in him as the Christ, the Saviour of the world.

Verses 27-42

The disciples wondered that Christ talked thus with a Samaritan. Yet they knew it was for some good reason, and for some good end. Thus when particular difficulties occur in the word and providence of God, it is good to satisfy ourselves that all is well that Jesus Christ says and does. Two things affected the woman. The extent of his knowledge. Christ knows all the thoughts, words, and actions, of all the children of men. And the power of his word. He told her secret sins with power. She fastened upon that part of Christ's discourse, many would think she would have been most shy of repeating; but the knowledge of Christ, into which we are led by conviction of sin, is most likely to be sound and saving. They came to him: those who would know Christ, must meet him where he records his name. Our Master has left us an example, that we may learn to do the will of God as he did; with diligence, as those that make a business of it; with delight and pleasure in it. Christ compares his work to harvest-work. The harvest is appointed and looked for before it comes; so was the gospel. Harvest-time is busy time; all must be then at work. Harvest-time is a short time, and harvest-work must be done then, or not at all; so the time of the gospel is a season, which if once past, cannot be recalled. God sometimes uses very weak and unlikely instruments for beginning and carrying on a good work. Our Saviour, by teaching one poor woman, spread knowledge to a whole town. Blessed are those who are not offended at Christ. Those taught of God, are truly desirous to learn more. It adds much to the praise of our love to Christ and his word, if it conquers prejudices. Their faith grew. In the matter of it: they believed him to be the Saviour, not only of the Jews but of the world. In the certainty of it: we know that this is indeed the Christ. And in the ground of it, for we have heard him ourselves.

Verses 43-54

The father was a nobleman, yet the son was sick. Honours and titles are no security from sickness and death. The greatest men must go themselves to God, must become beggars. The nobleman did not stop from his request till he prevailed. But at first he discovered the weakness of his faith in the power of Christ. It is hard to persuade ourselves that distance of time and place, are no hinderance to the knowledge, mercy, and power of our Lord Jesus. Christ gave an answer of peace. Christ's saying that the soul lives, makes it alive. The father went his way, which showed the sincerity of his faith. Being satisfied, he did not hurry home that night, but returned as one easy in his own mind. His servants met him with the news of the child's recovery. Good news will meet those that hope in God's word. Diligent comparing the works of Jesus with his word, will confirm our faith. And the bringing the cure to the family brought salvation to it. Thus an experience of the power of one word of Christ, may settle the authority of Christ in the soul. The whole family believed likewise. The miracle made Jesus dear to them. The knowledge of Christ still spreads through families, and men find health and salvation to their souls.

Chapter 5

Chapter Outline

Verses 1-9

We are all by nature impotent folk in spiritual things, blind, halt, and withered; but full provision is made for our cure, if we attend to it. An angel went down, and troubled the water; and what disease soever it was, this water cured it, but only he that first stepped in had benefit. This teaches us to be careful, that we let not a season slip which may never return. The man had lost the use of his limbs thirty-eight years. Shall we, who perhaps for many years have scarcely known what it has been to be a day sick, complain of one wearisome night, when many others, better than we, have scarcely known what it has been to be a day well? Christ singled this one out from the rest. Those long in affliction, may comfort themselves that God keeps account how long. Observe, this man speaks of the unkindness of those about him, without any peevish reflections. As we should be thankful, so we should be patient. Our Lord Jesus cures him, though he neither asked nor thought of it. Arise, and walk. God's command, Turn and live; Make ye a new heart; no more supposes power in us without the grace of God, his distinguishing grace, than this command supposed such power in the impotent man: it was by the power of Christ, and he must have all the glory. What a joyful surprise to the poor cripple, to find himself of a sudden so easy, so strong, so able to help himself! The proof of spiritual cure, is our rising and walking. Has Christ healed our spiritual diseases, let us go wherever he sends us, and take up whatever he lays upon us; and walk before him.

Verses 10-16

Those eased of the punishment of sin, are in danger of returning to sin, when the terror and restraint are over, unless Divine grace dries up the fountain. The misery believers are made whole from, warns us to sin no more, having felt the smart of sin. This is the voice of every providence, Go, and sin no more. Christ saw it necessary to give this caution; for it is common for people, when sick, to promise much; when newly recovered, to perform only something; but after awhile to forget all. Christ spoke of the wrath to come, which is beyond compare worse than the many hours, nay, weeks and years of pain, some wicked men have to suffer in consequence of their unlawful indulgences. And if such afflictions are severe, how dreadful will be the everlasting punishment of the wicked!

Verses 17-23

The Divine power of the miracle proved Jesus to be the Son of God, and he declared that he worked with, and like unto his Father, as he saw good. These ancient enemies of Christ understood him, and became more violent, charging him not only with sabbath-breaking, but blasphemy, in calling God his own Father, and making himself equal with God. But all things now, and at the final judgment, are committed to the Son, purposely that all men might honour the Son, as they honour the Father; and every one who does not thus honour the Son, whatever he may think or pretend, does not honour the Father who sent him.

Verses 24-29

Our Lord declared his authority and character, as the Messiah. The time was come when the dead should hear his voice, as the Son of God, and live. Our Lord first refers to his raising those who were dead in sin, to newness of life, by the power of the Spirit, and then to his raising the dead in their graves. The office of Judge of all men, can only be exercised by one who has all knowledge, and almighty power. May we believe His testimony; thus our faith and hope will be in God, and we shall not come into condemnation. And may His voice reach the hearts of those dead in sin; that they may do works meet for repentance, and prepare for the solemn day.

Verses 30-38

Our Lord returns to his declaration of the entire agreement between the Father and the Son, and declared himself the Son of God. He had higher testimony than that of John; his works bore witness to all he had said. But the Divine word had no abiding-place in their hearts, as they refused to believe in Him whom the Father had sent, according to his ancient promises. The voice of God, accompanied by the power of the Holy Ghost, thus made effectual to the conversion of sinners, still proclaims that this is the beloved Son, in whom the Father is well pleased. But when the hearts of men are full of pride, ambition, and the love of the world, there is no room for the word of God to abide in them.

Verses 39-44

The Jews considered that eternal life was revealed to them in their Scriptures, and that they had it, because they had the word of God in their hands. Jesus urged them to search those Scriptures with more diligence and attention. "Ye do search the Scriptures," and ye do well to do so. They did indeed search the Scriptures, but it was with a view to their own glory. It is possible for men to be very studious in the letter of the Scriptures, yet to be strangers to its power. Or, "Search the Scriptures," and so it was spoken to them in the nature of an appeal. Ye profess to receive and believe the Scripture, let that be the judge. It is spoken to us as advising or commanding all Christians to search the Scriptures. Not only read them, and hear them, but search them; which denotes diligence in examining and studying them. We must search the Scriptures for heaven as our great end; For in them ye think ye have eternal life. We must search the Scriptures for Christ, as the new and living Way, that leads to this end. To this testimony Christ adds reproofs of their unbelief and wickedness; their neglect of him and his doctrine. Also he reproves their want of the love of God. But there is life with Jesus Christ for poor souls. Many who make a great profession of religion, yet show they want the love of God, by their neglect of Christ and contempt of his commandments. It is the love of God in us, the love that is a living, active principle in the heart, which God will accept. They slighted and undervalued Christ, because they admired and overvalued themselves. How can those believe, who make the praise and applause of men their idol! When Christ and his followers are men wondered at, how can those believe, the utmost of whose ambition is to make a fair show in the flesh!

Verses 45-47

Many trust in some form of doctrines or some parties, who no more enter into the real meaning of those doctrines, or the views of the persons whose names they bear, than the Jews did into those of Moses. Let us search and pray over the Scriptures, as intent on finding eternal life; let us observe how Christ is the great subject of them, and daily apply to him for the life he bestows.

Chapter 6

Chapter Outline

Many of disciples go back.

(66–71)

Verses 1-14

John relates the miracle of feeding the multitude, for its reference to the following discourse. Observe the effect this miracle had upon the people. Even the common Jews expected the Messiah to come into the world, and to be a great Prophet. The Pharisees despised them as not knowing the law; but they knew most of Him who is the end of the law. Yet men may acknowledge Christ as that Prophet, and still turn a deaf ear to him.

Verses 15-21

Here were Christ's disciples in the way of duty, and Christ was praying for them; yet they were in distress. There may be perils and afflictions of this present time, where there is an interest in Christ. Clouds and darkness often surround the children of the light and of the day. They see Jesus walking on the sea. Even the approaches of comfort and deliverance often are so mistaken, as to become the occasions of fear. Nothing is more powerful to convince sinners than that word, "I am Jesus whom thou persecutest;" nothing more powerful to comfort saints than this, "I am Jesus whom thou lovest." If we have received Christ Jesus the Lord, though the night be dark, and the wind high, yet we may comfort ourselves, we shall be at the shore before long.

Verses 22-27

Instead of answering the inquiry how he came there, Jesus blamed their asking. The utmost earnestness should be employed in seeking salvation, in the use of appointed means; yet it is to be sought only as the gift of the Son of man. Him the Father has sealed, proved to be God. He declared the Son of man to be the Son of God with power.

Verses 28-35

Constant exercise of faith in Christ, is the most important and difficult part of the obedience required from us, as sinners seeking salvation. When by his grace we are enabled to live a life of faith in the Son of God, holy tempers follow, and acceptable services may be done. God, even his Father, who gave their fathers that food from heaven to support their natural lives, now gave them the true Bread for the salvation of their souls. Coming to Jesus, and believing on him, signify the same. Christ shows that he is the true Bread; he is to the soul what bread is to the body, nourishes and supports the spiritual life. He is the Bread of God. Bread which the Father gives, which he has made to be the food of our souls. Bread nourishes only by the powers of a living body; but Christ is himself living Bread, and nourishes by his own power. The doctrine of Christ crucified is now as strengthening and comforting to a believer as ever it was. He is the Bread which came down from heaven. It denotes the Divinity of Christ's person and his authority; also, the Divine origin of all the good which flows to us through him. May we with understanding and earnestness say, Lord, evermore give us this Bread.

Verses 36-46

The discovery of their guilt, danger, and remedy, by the teaching of the Holy Spirit, makes men willing and glad to come, and to give up every thing which hinders applying to him for salvation. The Father's will is, that not one of those who were given to the Son, should be rejected or lost by him. No one will come, till Divine grace has subdued, and in part changed his heart; therefore no one who comes will ever be cast out. The gospel finds none willing to be saved in the humbling, holy manner, made known therein; but God draws with his word and the Holy Ghost; and man's duty is to hear and learn; that is to say, to receive the grace offered, and consent to the promise. None had seen the Father but his beloved Son; and the Jews must expect to be taught by his inward power upon their minds, and by his word, and the ministers whom he sent among them.

Verses 47-51

The advantage of the manna was small, it only referred to this life; but the living Bread is so excellent, that the man who feedeth on it shall never die. This bread is Christ's human nature, which he took to present to the Father, as a sacrifice for the sins of the world; to purchase all things pertaining to life and godliness, for sinners of every nation, who repent and believe in him.

Verses 52-59

The flesh and blood of the Son of man, denote the Redeemer in the nature of man; Christ and him crucified, and the redemption wrought out by him, with all the precious benefits of redemption; pardon of sin, acceptance with God, the way to the throne of grace, the promises of the covenant, and eternal life. These are called the flesh and blood of Christ, because they are purchased by the breaking his body, and the shedding of his blood. Also, because they are meat and drink to our souls. Eating this flesh and drinking this blood mean believing in Christ. We partake of Christ and his benefits by faith. The soul that rightly knows its state and wants, finds whatever can calm the conscience, and promote true holiness, in the redeemer, God manifest in the flesh. Meditating upon the cross of Christ gives life to our repentance, love, and gratitude. We live by him, as our bodies live by our food. We live by him, as the members by the head, the branches by the root: because he lives we shall live also.

Verses 60-65

The human nature of Christ had not before been in heaven, but being God and man, that wondrous Person was truly said to have come down from heaven. The Messiah's kingdom was not of this world; and they were to understand by faith, what he had said of a spiritual living upon him, and his fulness. As without the soul of man the flesh is of no value, so without the quickening Spirit of God all forms of religion are dead and worthless. He who made this provision for our souls, alone can teach us these things, and draw us unto Christ, that we may live by faith in him. Let us apply to Christ, thankful that it is declared that every one who is willing to come unto him shall be made welcome.

Verses 66-71

When we admit into our minds hard thoughts of the words and works of Jesus, we enter into temptation, which, if the Lord in mercy prevent not, will end in drawing back. The corrupt and wicked heart of man often makes that an occasion for offence, which is matter of the greatest comfort. Our Lord had, in the foregoing discourse, promised eternal life to his followers; the disciples fastened on that plain saying, and resolved to cleave to him, when others fastened on hard sayings, and forsook him. Christ's doctrine is the word of eternal life, therefore we must live and die by it. If we forsake Christ, we forsake our own mercies. They believed that this Jesus was the Messiah promised to their fathers, the Son of the living God. When we are tempted to backslide or turn away, it is good to remember first principles, and to keep to them. And let us ever remember our Lord's searching question; Shall we go away and forsake our Redeemer? To whom can we go? He alone can give salvation by the forgiveness of sins. And this alone brings confidence, comfort, and joy, and bids fear and despondency flee away. It gains the only solid happiness in this world, and opens a way to the happiness of the next.

Chapter 7

Chapter Outline

Christ goes to the feast of tabernacles.	(1–13)
His discourse at the feast.	(14–39)
The people dispute concerning Christ.	(40–53)

Verses 1-13

The brethren or kinsmen of Jesus were disgusted, when they found there was no prospect of worldly advantages from him. Ungodly men sometimes undertake to counsel those employed in the work of God; but they only advise what appears likely to promote present advantages. The people differed about his doctrine and miracles, while those who favoured him, dared not openly to avow their sentiments. Those who count the preachers of the gospel to be deceivers, speak out, while many who favour them, fear to get reproach by avowing regard for them.

Verses 14-24

Every faithful minister may humbly adopt Christ's words. His doctrine is not his own finding out, but is from God's word, through the teaching of his Spirit. And amidst the disputes which disturb the world, if any man, of any nation, seeks to do the will of God, he shall know whether the doctrine is of God, or whether men speak of themselves. Only those who hate the truth shall be given up to errors which will be fatal. Surely it was as agreeable to the design of the sabbath to restore health to the afflicted, as to administer an outward rite. Jesus told them to decide on his conduct according to the spiritual import of the Divine law. We must not judge concerning any by their outward appearance, but by their worth, and by the gifts and graces of God's Spirit in them.

Verses 25-30

Christ proclaimed aloud, that they were in error in their thoughts about his origin. He was sent of God, who showed himself true to his promises. This declaration, that they knew not God, with his claim to peculiar knowledge, provoked the hearers; and they sought to take him, but God can tie men's hands, though he does not turn their hearts.

Verses 31-36

The discourses of Jesus convinced many that he was the Messiah; but they had not courage to own it. It is comfort to those who are in the world, but not of it, and therefore are hated by it and weary of it, that they shall not be in it always, that they shall not be in it long. Our days being evil, it is well they are few. The days of life and of grace do not last long; and sinners, when in misery, will be glad of the help they now despise. Men dispute about such sayings, but the event will explain them.

Verses 37-39

On the last day of the feast of tabernacles, the Jews drew water and poured it out before the Lord. It is supposed that Christ alluded to this. If any man desires to be truly and for ever happy, let him apply to Christ, and be ruled by him. This thirst means strong desires after spiritual blessings, which nothing else can satisfy; so the sanctifying and comforting influences of the Holy Spirit, were intended by the waters which Jesus called on them to come to Him and drink. The comfort flows plentifully and constantly as a river; strong as a stream to bear down the opposition of doubts and fears. There is a fulness in Christ, of grace for grace. The Spirit dwelling and working in believers, is as a fountain of living, running water, out of which plentiful streams flow, cooling and cleansing as water. The miraculous gifts of the Holy Spirit we do not expect, but for his more common and more valuable influences we may apply. These streams have flowed from our glorified Redeemer, down to this age, and to the remote corners of the earth. May we be anxious to make them known to others.

Verses 40-53

The malice of Christ's enemies is always against reason, and sometimes the staying of it cannot be accounted for. Never any man spake with that wisdom, and power, and grace, that convincing clearness, and that sweetness, wherewith Christ spake. Alas, that many, who are for a time restrained, and who speak highly of the word of Jesus, speedily lose their convictions, and go on in their sins! People are foolishly swayed by outward motives in matters of eternal moment, are willing even to be damned for fashion's sake. As the wisdom of God often chooses things which men despise, so the folly of men commonly despises those whom God has chosen. The Lord brings forward his weak and timid disciples, and sometimes uses them to defeat the designs of his enemies.

Chapter 8

Chapter Outline

Verses 1-11

Christ neither found fault with the law, nor excused the prisoner's guilt; nor did he countenance the pretended zeal of the Pharisees. Those are self-condemned who judge others, and yet do the same thing. All who are any way called to blame the faults of others, are especially concerned to look to themselves, and keep themselves pure. In this matter Christ attended to the great work about which he came into the world, that was, to bring sinners to repentance; not to destroy, but to save. He aimed to bring, not only the accused to repentance, by showing her his mercy, but the prosecutors also, by showing them their sins; they thought to insnare him, he sought to convince and convert them. He declined to meddle with the magistrate's office. Many crimes merit far more severe punishment than they meet with; but we should not leave our own work, to take that upon ourselves to which we are not called. When Christ sent her away, it was with this caution, Go, and sin no more. Those who help to save the life of a criminal, should help to save the soul with the same caution. Those are truly happy, whom Christ does not condemn. Christ's favour to us in the forgiveness of past sins should prevail with us, Go then, and sin no more.

Verses 12-16

Christ is the Light of the world. God is light, and Christ is the image of the invisible God. One sun enlightens the whole world; so does one Christ, and there needs no more. What a dark dungeon would the world be without the sun! So would it be without Jesus, by whom light came into the world. Those who follow Christ shall not walk in darkness. They shall not be left without the truths which are necessary to keep them from destroying error, and the directions in the way of duty, necessary to keep them from condemning sin.

Verses 17-20

If we knew Christ better, we should know the Father better. Those become vain in their imaginations concerning God, who will not learn of Christ. Those who know not his glory and grace, know not the Father that sent him. The time of our departure out of the world, depends upon God. Our enemies cannot hasten it any sooner, nor can our friends delay it any longer, than the time appointed of the Father. Every true believer can look up and say with pleasure, My times are in thy hand, and better there than in my own. To all God's purposes there is a time.

Verses 21-29

Those that live in unbelief, are for ever undone, if they die in unbelief. The Jews belonged to this present evil world, but Jesus was of a heavenly and Divine nature, so that his doctrine, kingdom, and blessings, would not suit their taste. But the curse of the law is done away to all that submit to the grace of the gospel. Nothing but the doctrine of Christ's grace will be an argument powerful enough, and none but the Spirit of Christ's grace will be an agent powerful enough, to turn us from sin to God; and that Spirit is given, and that doctrine is given, to work upon those only who believe in Christ. Some say, Who is this Jesus? They allow him to have been a Prophet, an excellent Teacher, and even more than a creature; but cannot acknowledge him as over all, God blessed for evermore. Will not this suffice? Jesus here answers the question. Is this to honour him as the Father? Does this admit his being the Light of the world, and the Life of men, one with the Father? All shall know by their conversion, or in their condemnation, that he always spake and did what pleased the Father, even when he claimed the highest honours to himself.

Verses 30-36

Such power attended our Lord's words, that many were convinced, and professed to believe in him. He encouraged them to attend his teaching, rely on his promises, and obey his commands, notwithstanding all temptations to evil. Thus doing, they would be his disciples truly; and by the teaching of his word and Spirit, they would learn where their hope and strength lay. Christ spoke of spiritual liberty; but carnal hearts feel no other grievances than those that molest the body, and distress their worldly affairs. Talk to them of their liberty and property, tell them of waste committed upon their lands, or damage done to their houses, and they understand you very well; but speak of the bondage of sin, captivity to Satan, and liberty by Christ; tell of wrong done to their precious souls, and the hazard of their eternal welfare, then you bring strange things to their ears. Jesus plainly reminded them, that the man who practised any sin, was, in fact, a slave to that sin, which was the case with most of them. Christ in the gospel offers us freedom, he has power to do this, and those whom Christ makes free are really so. But often we see persons disputing about liberty of every kind, while they are slaves to some sinful lust.

Verses 37-40

Our Lord opposed the proud and vain confidence of these Jews, showing that their descent from Abraham could not profit those of a contrary spirit to him. Where the word of God has no place, no good is to be expected; room is left there for all wickedness. A sick person who turns from his physician, and will take neither remedies nor food, is past hope of recovery. The truth both heals and nourishes the hearts of those who receive it. The truth taught by philosophers has not this power and effect, but only the truth of God. Those who claim the privileges of Abraham, must do Abraham's works; must be strangers and sojourners in this world; keep up the worship of God in their families, and always walk before God.

Verses 41-47

Satan prompts men to excesses by which they murder themselves and others, while what he puts into the mind tends to ruin men's souls. He is the great promoter of falsehood of every kind.

He is a liar, all his temptations are carried on by his calling evil good, and good evil, and promising freedom in sin. He is the author of all lies; whom liars resemble and obey, with whom all liars shall have their portion for ever. The special lusts of the devil are spiritual wickedness, the lusts of the mind, and corrupt reasonings, pride and envy, wrath and malice, enmity to good, and enticing others to evil. By the truth, here understand the revealed will of God as to the salvation of men by Jesus Christ, the truth Christ was now preaching, and which the Jews opposed.

Verses 48-53

Observe Christ's disregard of the applause of men. those who are dead to the praises of men can bear their contempt. God will seek the honour of all who do not seek their own. In these verses we have the doctrine of the everlasting happiness of believers. We have the character of a believer; he is one that keeps the sayings of the Lord Jesus. And the privilege of a believer; he shall by no means see death for ever. Though now they cannot avoid seeing death, and tasting it also, yet they shall shortly be where it will be no more forever, Ex 14:13.

Verses 54-59

Christ and all that are his, depend upon God for honour. Men may be able to dispute about God, yet may not know him. Such as know not God, and obey not the gospel of Christ, are put together, 2Th 1:8. All who rightly know anything of Christ, earnestly desire to know more of him. Those who discern the dawn of the light of the Sun of Righteousness, wish to see his rising. "Before Abraham was, I AM." This speaks Abraham a creature, and our Lord the Creator; well, therefore, might he make himself greater than Abraham. I AM, is the name of God, Ex 3:14; it speaks his self-existence; he is the First and the Last, ever the same, Re 1:8. Thus he was not only before Abraham, but before all worlds, Pr 8:23; Joh 1:1. As Mediator, he was the appointed Messiah, long before Abraham; the Lamb slain from the foundation of the world, Re 13:8. The Lord Jesus was made of God Wisdom, Righteousness, Sanctification, and Redemption, to Adam, and Abel, and all that lived and died by faith in him, before Abraham. The Jews were about to stone Jesus for blasphemy, but he withdrew; by his miraculous power he passed through them unhurt. Let us stedfastly profess what we know and believe concerning God; and if heirs of Abraham's faith, we shall rejoice in looking forward to that day when the Saviour shall appear in glory, to the confusion of his enemies, and to complete the salvation of all who believe in him.

Chapter 9

Chapter Outline

Verses 1-7

Christ cured many who were blind by disease or accident; here he cured one born blind. Thus he showed his power to help in the most desperate cases, and the work of his grace upon the souls of sinners, which gives sight to those blind by nature. This poor man could not see Christ, but Christ saw him. And if we know or apprehend anything of Christ, it is because we were first known of him. Christ says of uncommon calamities, that they are not always to be looked on as special punishments of sin; sometimes they are for the glory of God, and to manifest his works. Our life is our day, in which it concerns us to do the work of the day. We must be busy, and not waste day-time; it will be time to rest when our day is done, for it is but a day. The approach of death should quicken us to improve all our opportunities of doing and getting good. What good we have an opportunity to do, we should do quickly. And he that will never do a good work till there is nothing to be objected against, will leave many a good work for ever undone, Ec 11:4. Christ magnified his power, in making a blind man to see, doing that which one would think more likely to make a seeing man blind. Human reason cannot judge of the Lord's methods; he uses means and instruments that men despise. Those that would be healed by Christ must be ruled by him. He came back from the pool wondering and wondered at; he came seeing. This represents the benefits in attending on ordinances of Christ's appointment; souls go weak, and come away strengthened; go doubting, and come away satisfied; go mourning, and come away rejoicing; go blind, and come away seeing.

Verses 8-12

Those whose eyes are opened, and whose hearts are cleansed by grace, being known to be the same person, but widely different in character, live as monuments to the Redeemer's glory, and recommend his grace to all who desire the same precious salvation. It is good to observe the way and method of God's works, and they will appear the more wonderful. Apply this spiritually. In the work of grace wrought upon the soul we see the change, but we see not the hand that makes it: the way of the Spirit is like that of the wind, which thou hearest the sound of, but canst not tell whence it comes, nor whither it goes.

Verses 13-17

Christ not only worked miracles on the sabbath, but in such a manner as would give offence to the Jews, for he would not seem to yield to the scribes and Pharisees. Their zeal for mere rites consumed the substantial matters of religion; therefore Christ would not give place to them. Also, works of necessity and mercy are allowed, and the sabbath rest is to be kept, in order to the sabbath work. How many blind eyes have been opened by the preaching of the gospel on the Lord's day! how many impotent souls cured on that day! Much unrighteous and uncharitable judging comes from men's adding their own fancies to God's appointments. How perfect in wisdom and holiness was our Redeemer, when his enemies could find nothing against him, but the oft-refuted charge of breaking the sabbath! May we be enabled, by well-doing, to silence the ignorance of foolish men.

Verses 18-23

The Pharisees vainly hoped to disprove this notable miracle. They expected a Messiah, but could not bear to think that this Jesus should be he, because his precepts were all contrary to their traditions, and because they expected a Messiah in outward pomp and splendour. The fear of man brings a snare, Pr 29:25, and often makes people deny and disown Christ and his truths and ways, and act against their consciences. The unlearned and poor, who are simple-hearted, readily draw proper inferences from the evidences of the light of the gospel; but those whose desires are another way, though ever learning, never come to the knowledge of the truth.

Verses 24-34

As Christ's mercies are most valued by those who have felt the want of them, that have been blind, and now see; so the most powerful and lasting affections to Christ, arise from actual knowledge of him. In the work of grace in the soul, though we cannot tell when, and how, and by what steps the blessed change was wrought, yet we may take the comfort, if we can say, through grace, Whereas I was blind, now I see. I did live a worldly, sensual life, but, thanks be to God, it is now otherwise with me, Eph 5:8. The unbelief of those who enjoy the means of knowledge and conviction, is indeed marvellous. All who have felt the power and grace of the Lord Jesus, wonder at the wilfulness of others who reject him. He argues strongly against them, not only that Jesus was not a sinner, but that he was of God. We may each of us know by this, whether we are of God or not. What do we? What do we for God? What do we for our souls? What do we more than others?

Verses 35-38

Christ owns those who own him and his truth and ways. There is particular notice taken of such a suffer in the cause of Christ, and for the testimony of a good conscience. Our Lord Jesus graciously reveals himself to the man. Now he was made sensible what an unspeakable mercy it was, to be cured of his blindness, that he might see the Son of God. None but God is to be worshipped; so that in worshipping Jesus, he owned him to be God. All who believe in him, will worship him.

Verses 39-41

Christ came into the world to give sight to those who were spiritually blind. Also, that those who see might be made blind; that those who have a high conceit of their own wisdom, might be sealed up in ignorance. The preaching of the cross was thought to be folly by such as by carnal wisdom knew not God. Nothing fortifies men's corrupt hearts against the convictions of the word, more than the high opinion which others have of them; as if all that gained applause with men, must obtain acceptance with God. Christ silenced them. But the sin of the self-conceited and self-confident remains; they reject the gospel of grace, therefore the guilt of their sin remains unpardoned, and the power of their sin remains unbroken.

Chapter 10

Chapter Outline

Verses 1-5

Here is a parable or similitude, taken from the customs of the East, in the management of sheep. Men, as creatures depending on their Creator, are called the sheep of his pasture. The church of God in the world is as a sheep-fold, exposed to deceivers and persecutors. The great Shepherd of the sheep knows all that are his, guards them by his providence, guides them by his Spirit and word, and goes before them, as the Eastern shepherds went before their sheep, to set them in the way of his steps. Ministers must serve the sheep in their spiritual concerns. The Spirit of Christ will set before them an open door. The sheep of Christ will observe their Shepherd, and be cautious and shy of strangers, who would draw them from faith in him to fancies about him.

Verses 6-9

Many who hear the word of Christ, do not understand it, because they will not. But we shall find one scripture expounding another, and the blessed Spirit making known the blessed Jesus. Christ is the Door. And what greater security has the church of God than that the Lord Jesus is between it and all its enemies? He is a door open for passage and communication. Here are plain directions how to come into the fold; we must come in by Jesus Christ as the Door. By faith in him as the great Mediator between God and man. Also, we have precious promises to those that observe this direction. Christ has all that care of his church, and every believer, which a good shepherd has of his flock; and he expects the church, and every believer, to wait on him, and to keep in his pasture.

Verses 10-18

Christ is a good Shepherd; many who were not thieves, yet were careless in their duty, and by their neglect the flock was much hurt. Bad principles are the root of bad practices. The Lord Jesus knows whom he has chosen, and is sure of them; they also know whom they have trusted, and are sure of Him. See here the grace of Christ; since none could demand his life of him, he laid it down of himself for our redemption. He offered himself to be the Saviour; Lo, I come. And the necessity of our case calling for it, he offered himself for the Sacrifice. He was both the offerer and the offering, so that his laying down his life was his offering up himself. From hence it is plain, that he died in the place and stead of men; to obtain their being set free from the punishment of sin, to obtain the pardon of their sin; and that his death should obtain that pardon. Our Lord laid not his life down for his doctrine, but for his sheep.

Verses 19-21

Satan ruins many, by putting them out of conceit with the word and ordinances. Men would not be laughed out of their necessary food, yet suffer themselves thus to be laughed out of what is far more necessary. If our zeal and earnestness in the cause of Christ, especially in the blessed work of bringing his sheep into his fold, bring upon us evil names, let us not heed it, but remember our Master was thus reproached before us.

Verses 22-30

All who have any thing to say to Christ, may find him in the temple. Christ would make us to believe; we make ourselves doubt. The Jews understood his meaning, but could not form his words into a full charge against him. He described the gracious disposition and happy state of his sheep; they heard and believed his word, followed him as his faithful disciples, and none of them should perish; for the Son and the Father were one. Thus he was able to defend his sheep against all their enemies, which proves that he claimed Divine power and perfection equally with the Father.

Verses 31-38

Christ's works of power and mercy proclaim him to be over all, God blessed for evermore, that all may know and believe He is in the Father, and the Father in Him. Whom the Father sends, he sanctifies. The holy God will reward, and therefore will employ, none but such as he makes holy. The Father was in the Son, so that by Divine power he wrought his miracles; the Son was so in the Father, that he knew the whole of His mind. This we cannot by searching find out to perfection, but we may know and believe these declarations of Christ.

Verses 39-42

No weapon formed against our Lord Jesus shall prosper. He escaped, not because he was afraid to suffer, but because his hour was not come. And He who knew how to deliver himself, knows how to deliver the godly our of their temptations, and to make a way for them to escape. Persecutors may drive Christ and his gospel our of their own city or country, but they cannot drive him or it out of the world. When we know Christ by faith in our hearts, we find all that the Scripture saith of him is true.

Chapter 11

Chapter Outline

Verses 1-6

It is no new thing for those whom Christ loves, to be sick; bodily distempers correct the corruption, and try the graces of God's people. He came not to preserve his people from these afflictions, but to save them from their sins, and from the wrath to come; however, it behoves us to apply to Him in behalf of our friends and relatives when sick and afflicted. Let this reconcile us to the darkest dealings of Providence, that they are all for the glory of God: sickness, loss, disappointment, are so; and if God be glorified, we ought to be satisfied. Jesus loved Martha, and her sister, and Lazarus. The families are greatly favoured in which love and peace abound; but those are most happy whom Jesus loves, and by whom he is beloved. Alas, that this should seldom be the case with every person, even in small families. God has gracious intentions, even when he seems to delay. When the work of deliverance, temporal or spiritual, public or personal, is delayed, it does but stay for the right time.

Verses 7-10

Christ never brings his people into any danger but he goes with them in it. We are apt to think ourselves zealous for the Lord, when really we are only zealous for our wealth, credit, ease, and safety; we have therefore need to try our principles. But our day shall be lengthened out, till our work is done, and our testimony finished. A man has comfort and satisfaction while in the way of his duty, as set forth by the word of God, and determined by the providence of God. Christ, wherever he went, walked in the day; and so shall we, if we follow his steps. If a man walks in the way of his heart, and according to the course of this world, if he consults his own carnal reasonings more than the will and glory of God, he falls into temptations and snares. He stumbles, because there is no light in him; for light in us is to our moral actions, that which light about us to our natural actions.

Verses 11-16

Since we are sure to rise again at the last, why should not the believing hope of that resurrection to eternal life, make it as easy for us to put off the body and die, as it is to put off our clothes and go to sleep? A true Christian, when he dies, does but sleep; he rests from the labours of the past day. Nay, herein death is better than sleep, that sleep is only a short rest, but death is the end of earthly cares and toils. The disciples thought that it was now needless for Christ to go to Lazarus, and expose himself and them. Thus we often hope that the good work we are called to do, will be done by some other hand, if there be peril in the doing of it. But when Christ raised Lazarus from the dead, many were brought to believe on him; and there was much done to make perfect the faith of those that believed. Let us go to him; death cannot separate from the love of Christ, nor put us out of the reach of his call. Like Thomas, in difficult times Christians should encourage one another. The dying of the Lord Jesus should make us willing to die whenever God calls us.

Verses 17-32

Here was a house where the fear of God was, and on which his blessing rested; yet it was made a house of mourning. Grace will keep sorrow from the heart, but not from the house. When God, by his grace and providence, is coming towards us in ways of mercy and comfort, we should, like Martha, go forth by faith, hope, and prayer, to meet him. When Martha went to meet Jesus, Mary sat still in the house; this temper formerly had been an advantage to her, when it put her at Christ's feet to hear his word; but in the day of affliction, the same temper disposed her to melancholy. It is our wisdom to watch against the temptations, and to make use of the advantages of our natural tempers. When we know not what in particular to ask or expect, let us refer ourselves to God; let him do as seemeth him good. To enlarge Martha's expectations, our Lord declared himself to be the Resurrection and the Life. In every sense he is the Resurrection; the source, the substance, the first-fruits, the cause of it. The redeemed soul lives after death in happiness; and after the resurrection, both body and soul are kept from all evil for ever. When we have read or heard the word of Christ, about the great things of the other world, we should put it to ourselves, Do we believe this truth? The crosses and comforts of this present time would not make such a deep impression upon us as they do, if we believed the things of eternity as we ought. When Christ our Master comes, he calls for us. He comes in his word and ordinances, and calls us to them, calls us by them, calls us to himself. Those who, in a day of peace, set themselves at Christ's feet to be taught by him, may with comfort, in a day of trouble, cast themselves at his feet, to find favour with him.

Verses 33-46

Christ's tender sympathy with these afflicted friends, appeared by the troubles of his spirit. In all the afflictions of believers he is afflicted. His concern for them was shown by his kind inquiry after the remains of his deceased friend. Being found in fashion as a man, he acts in the way and manner of the sons of men. It was shown by his tears. He was a man of sorrows, and acquainted with grief. Tears of compassion resemble those of Christ. But Christ never approved that sensibility of which many are proud, while they weep at mere tales of distress, but are hardened to real woe.

He sets us an example to withdraw from scenes of giddy mirth, that we may comfort the afflicted. And we have not a High Priest who cannot be touched with a feeling of our infirmities. It is a good step toward raising a soul to spiritual life, when the stone is taken away, when prejudices are removed, and got over, and way is made for the word to enter the heart. If we take Christ's word, and rely on his power and faithfulness, we shall see the glory of God, and be happy in the sight. Our Lord Jesus has taught us, by his own example, to call God Father, in prayer, and to draw nigh to him as children to a father, with humble reverence, yet with holy boldness. He openly made this address to God, with uplifted eyes and loud voice, that they might be convinced the Father had sent him as his beloved Son into the world. He could have raised Lazarus by the silent exertion of his power and will, and the unseen working of the Spirit of life; but he did it by a loud call. This was a figure of the gospel call, by which dead souls are brought out of the grave of sin: and of the sound of the archangel's trumpet at the last day, with which all that sleep in the dust shall be awakened, and summoned before the great tribunal. The grave of sin and this world, is no place for those whom Christ has quickened; they must come forth. Lazarus was thoroughly revived, and returned not only to life, but to health. The sinner cannot quicken his own soul, but he is to use the means of grace; the believer cannot sanctify himself, but he is to lay aside every weight and hinderance. We cannot convert our relatives and friends, but we should instruct, warn, and invite them.

Verses 47-53

There can hardly be a more clear discovery of the madness that is in man's heart, and of its desperate enmity against God, than what is here recorded. Words of prophecy in the mouth, are not clear evidence of a principle of grace in the heart. The calamity we seek to escape by sin, we take the most effectual course to bring upon our own heads; as those do who think by opposing Christ's kingdom, to advance their own worldly interest. The fear of the wicked shall come upon them. The conversion of souls is the gathering of them to Christ as their ruler and refuge; and he died to effect this. By dying he purchased them to himself, and the gift of the Holy Ghost for them: his love in dying for believers should unite them closely together.

Verses 54-57

Before our gospel passover we must renew our repentance. Thus by a voluntary purification, and by religious exercises, many, more devout than their neighbours, spent some time before the passover at Jerusalem. When we expect to meet God, we must solemnly prepare. No devices of man can alter the purposes of God: and while hypocrites amuse themselves with forms and disputes, and worldly men pursue their own plans, Jesus still orders all things for his own glory and the salvation of his people.

Chapter 12

Chapter Outline

Verses 1-11

Christ had formerly blamed Martha for being troubled with much serving. But she did not leave off serving, as some, who when found fault with for going too far in one way, peevishly run too far another way; she still served, but within hearing of Christ's gracious words. Mary gave a token of love to Christ, who had given real tokens of his love to her and her family. God's Anointed should be our Anointed. Has God poured on him the oil of gladness above his fellows, let us pour on him the ointment of our best affections. In Judas a foul sin is gilded over with a plausible pretence. We must not think that those do no acceptable service, who do it not in our way. The reigning love of money is heart-theft. The grace of Christ puts kind comments on pious words and actions, makes the best of what is amiss, and the most of what is good. Opportunities are to be improved; and those first and most vigorously, which are likely to be the shortest. To consult to hinder the further effect of the miracle, by putting Lazarus to death, is such wickedness, malice, and folly, as cannot be explained, except by the desperate enmity of the human heart against God. They resolved that the man should die whom the Lord had raised to life. The success of the gospel often makes wicked men so angry, that they speak and act as if they hoped to obtain a victory over the Almighty himself.

Verses 12-19

Christ's riding in triumph to Jerusalem is recorded by all the evangelists. Many excellent things, both in the word and providence of God, disciples do not understand at their first acquaintance with the things of God. The right understanding of spiritual nature of Christ's kingdom, prevents our misapplying the Scriptures which speak of it.

Verses 20-26

In attendance upon holy ordinances, particularly the gospel passover, the great desire of our souls should be to see Jesus; to see him as ours, to keep up communion with him, and derive grace from him. The calling of the Gentiles magnified the Redeemer. A corn of wheat yields no increase unless it is cast into the ground. Thus Christ might have possessed his heavenly glory alone, without becoming man. Or, after he had taken man's nature, he might have entered heaven alone, by his own perfect righteousness, without suffering or death; but then no sinner of the human race could have been saved. The salvation of souls hitherto, and henceforward to the end of time, is owing to the dying of this Corn of wheat. Let us search whether Christ be in us the hope of glory; let us beg him to make us indifferent to the trifling concerns of this life, that we may serve the Lord Jesus with a willing mind, and follow his holy example.

Verses 27-33

The sin of our souls was the troubled of Christ's soul, when he undertook to redeem and save us, and to make his soul an offering for our sin. Christ was willing to suffer, yet prayed to be saved from suffering. Prayer against trouble may well agree with patience under it, and submission to the will of God in it. Our Lord Jesus undertook to satisfy God's injured honour, and he did it by humbling himself. The voice of the Father from heaven, which had declared him to be his beloved Son, at his baptism, and when he was transfigured, was heard proclaiming that He had both glorified his name, and would glorify it. Christ, reconciling the world to God by the merit of his death, broke the power of death, and cast out Satan as a destroyer. Christ, bringing the world to God by the doctrine of his cross, broke the power of sin, and cast out Satan as a deceiver. The soul that was at a distance from Christ, is brought to love him and trust him. Jesus was now going to heaven, and he would draw men's hearts to him thither. There is power in the death of Christ to draw souls to him. We have heard from the gospel that which exalts free grace, and we have heard also that which enjoins duty; we must from the heart embrace both, and not separate them.

Verses 34-36

The people drew false notions from the Scriptures, because they overlooked the prophecies that spoke of Christ's sufferings and death. Our Lord warned them that the light would not long continue with them, and exhorted them to walk in it, before the darkness overtook them. Those who would walk in the light must believe in it, and follow Christ's directions. But those who have not faith, cannot behold what is set forth in Jesus, lifted up on the cross, and must be strangers to its influence as made known by the Holy Spirit; they find a thousand objections to excuse their unbelief.

Verses 37-43

Observe the method of conversion implied here. Sinners are brought to see the reality of Divine things, and to have some knowledge of them. To be converted, and truly turned from sin to Christ, as their Happiness and Portion. God will heal them, will justify and sanctify them; will pardon their sins, which are as bleeding wounds, and mortify their corruptions, which are as lurking diseases. See the power of the world in smothering convictions, from regard to the applause or censure of men. Love of the praise of men, as a by-end in that which is good, will make a man a hypocrite when religion is in fashion, and credit is to be got by it; and love of the praise of men, as a base principle in that which is evil, will make a man an apostate, when religion is in disgrace, and credit is to be lost for it.

Verses 44-50

Our Lord publicly proclaimed, that every one who believed on him, as his true disciple, did not believe on him only, but on the Father who sent him. Beholding in Jesus the glory of the Father, we learn to obey, love, and trust in him. By daily looking to Him, who came a Light into the world, we are more and more freed from the darkness of ignorance, error, sin, and misery; we learn that the command of God our Saviour is everlasting life. But the same word will seal the condemnation of all who despise it, or neglect it.

Chapter 13

Chapter Outline

Verses 1-17

Our Lord Jesus has a people in the world that are his own; he has purchased them, and paid dear for them, and he has set them apart for himself; they devote themselves to him as a peculiar people. Those whom Christ loves, he loves to the end. Nothing can separate a true believer from the love of Christ. We know not when our hour will come, therefore what we have to do in constant preparation for it, ought never to be undone. What way of access the devil has to men's hearts we cannot tell. But some sins are so exceedingly sinful, and there is so little temptation to them from the world and the flesh, that it is plain they are directly from Satan. Jesus washed his disciples' feet, that he might teach us to think nothing below us, wherein we may promote God's glory, and the good of our brethren. We must address ourselves to duty, and must lay aside every thing that would hinder us in what we have to do. Christ washed his disciples' feet, that he might signify to them the value of spiritual washing, and the cleansing of the soul from the pollutions of sin. Our Lord Jesus does many things of which even his own disciples do not for the present know the meaning, but they shall know afterward. We see in the end what was the kindness from events which seemed most cross. And it is not humility, but unbelief, to put away the offers of the gospel, as if too rich to be made to us, or too good news to be true. All those, and those only, who are spiritually washed by Christ, have a part in Christ. All whom Christ owns and saves, he justifies and sanctifies. Peter more than submits; he begs to be washed by Christ. How earnest he is for the purifying grace of the Lord Jesus, and the full effect of it, even upon his hands and head! Those who truly desire to be sanctified, desire to be sanctified throughout, to have the whole man, with all its parts and powers, made pure. The true believer is thus washed when he receives Christ for his salvation. See then what ought to be the daily care of those who through grace are in a justified state, and that is, to wash their feet; to cleanse themselves from daily guilt, and to watch against everything defiling. This should make us the more cautious. From yesterday's pardon, we should be strengthened against this day's temptation. And when hypocrites are discovered, it should be no surprise or cause of stumbling to us. Observe the lesson Christ here taught. Duties are mutual; we must both accept help from our brethren, and afford help to our brethren. When we see our Master serving, we cannot but see how ill it becomes us to domineer. And the same love which led Christ to ransom and reconcile his disciples when enemies, still influences him.

Verses 18-30

Our Lord had often spoken of his own sufferings and death, without such trouble of spirit as he now discovered when he spake of Judas. The sins of Christians are the grief of Christ. We are not to confine our attention to Judas. The prophecy of his treachery may apply to all who partake of God's mercies, and meet them with ingratitude. See the infidel, who only looks at the Scriptures with a desire to do away their authority and destroy their influence; the hypocrite, who professes to believe the Scriptures, but will not govern himself by them; and the apostate, who turns aside from Christ for a thing of naught. Thus mankind, supported by God's providence, after eating bread with Him, lift up the heel against Him! Judas went out as one weary of Jesus and his apostles. Those whose deeds are evil, love darkness rather than light.

Verses 31-35

Christ had been glorified in many miracles he wrought, yet he speaks of his being glorified now in his sufferings, as if that were more than all his other glories in his humbled state. Satisfaction was thereby made for the wrong done to God by the sin of man. We cannot now follow our Lord to his heavenly happiness, but if we truly believe in him, we shall follow him hereafter; meanwhile we must wait his time, and do his work. Before Christ left the disciples, he would give them a new commandment. They were to love each other for Christ's sake, and according to his example, seeking what might benefit others, and promoting the cause of the gospel, as one body, animated by one soul. But this commandment still appears new to many professors. Men in general notice any of Christ's words rather than these. By this it appears, that if the followers of Christ do not show love one to another, they give cause to suspect their sincerity.

Verses 36-38

What Christ had said concerning brotherly love, Peter overlooked, but spoke of that about which Christ kept them ignorant. It is common to be more eager to know about secret things, which belong to God only, than about things revealed, which belong to us and our children; to be more desirous to have our curiosity gratified, than our consciences directed; to know what is done in heaven, than what we may do to get thither. How soon discourse as to what is plain and edifying is dropped, while a doubtful dispute runs on into endless strife of words! We are apt to take it amiss to be told we cannot do this and the other, whereas, without Christ we can do nothing. Christ knows us better than we know ourselves, and has many ways of discovering those to themselves, whom he loves, and he will hide pride from them. May we endeavour to keep the unity of the Spirit in the bond of peace, to love one another with a pure heart fervently, and to walk humbly with our God.

Chapter 14

Chapter Outline

Verses 1-11

Here are three words, upon any of which stress may be laid. Upon the word troubled. Be not cast down and disquieted. The word heart. Let your heart be kept with full trust in God. The word your. However others are overwhelmed with the sorrows of this present time, be not you so. Christ's disciples, more than others, should keep their minds quiet, when everything else is unquiet. Here is the remedy against this trouble of mind, "Believe." By believing in Christ as the Mediator between God and man, we gain comfort. The happiness of heaven is spoken of as in a father's house. There are many mansions, for there are many sons to be brought to glory. Mansions are lasting dwellings. Christ will be the Finisher of that of which he is the Author or Beginner; if he have prepared the place for us, he will prepare us for it. Christ is the sinner's Way to the Father and to heaven, in his person as God manifest in the flesh, in his atoning sacrifice, and as our Advocate. He is the Truth, as fulfilling all the prophecies of a Saviour; believing which, sinners come by him the Way. He is the Life, by whose life-giving Spirit the dead in sin are quickened. Nor can any man draw nigh God as a Father, who is not quickened by Him as the Life, and taught by Him as the Truth, to come by Him as the Way. By Christ, as the Way, our prayers go to God, and his blessings come to us; this is the Way that leads to rest, the good old Way. He is the Resurrection and the Life. All that saw Christ by faith, saw the Father in Him. In the light of Christ's doctrine, they saw God as the Father of lights; and in Christ's miracles, they saw God as the God of power. The holiness of God shone in the spotless purity of Christ's life. We are to believe the revelation of God to man in Christ; for the works of the Redeemer show forth his own glory, and God in him.

Verses 12-17

Whatever we ask in Christ's name, that shall be for our good, and suitable to our state, he shall give it to us. To ask in Christ's name, is to plead his merit and intercession, and to depend upon that plea. The gift of the Spirit is a fruit of Christ's mediation, bought by his merit, and received by his intercession. The word used here, signifies an advocate, counsellor, monitor, and comforter. He would abide with the disciples to the end of time; his gifts and graces would encourage their hearts. The expressions used here and elsewhere, plainly denote a person, and the office itself includes all the Divine perfections. The gift of the Holy Ghost is bestowed upon the disciples of Christ, and not on the world. This is the favour God bears to his chosen. As the source of holiness and happiness, the Holy Spirit will abide with every believer for ever.

Verses 18-24

Christ promises that he would continue his care of his disciples. I will not leave you orphans, or fatherless, for though I leave you, yet I leave you this comfort, I will come to you. I will come speedily to you at my resurrection. I will come daily to you in my Spirit; in the tokens of his love, and visits of his grace. I will come certainly at the end of time. Those only that see Christ with an eye of faith, shall see him for ever: the world sees him no more till his second coming; but his disciples have communion with him in his absence. These mysteries will be fully known in heaven. It is a further act of grace, that they should know it, and have the comfort of it. Having Christ's commands, we must keep them. And having them in our heads, we must keep them in our hearts and lives. The surest evidence of our love to Christ is, obedience to the laws of Christ. There are spiritual tokens of Christ and his love given to all believers. Where sincere love to Christ is in the heart, there will be obedience. Love will be a commanding, constraining principle; and where love is, duty follows from a principle of gratitude. God will not only love obedient believers, but he will take pleasure in loving them, will rest in love to them. He will be with them as his home. These privileges are confined to those whose faith worketh by love, and whose love to Jesus leads them to keep his commandments. Such are partakers of the Holy Spirit's new-creating grace.

Verses 25-27

Would we know these things for our good, we must pray for, and depend on the teaching of the Holy Ghost; thus the words of Jesus will be brought to our remembrance, and many difficulties be cleared up which are not plain to others. To all the saints, the Spirit of grace is given to be a remembrancer, and to him, by faith and prayer, we should commit the keeping of what we hear and know. Peace is put for all good, and Christ has left us all that is really and truly good, all the promised good; peace of mind from our justification before God. This Christ calls his peace, for he is himself our Peace. The peace of God widely differs from that of Pharisees or hypocrites, as is shown by its humbling and holy effects.

Verses 28-31

Christ raises the expectations of his disciples to something beyond what they thought was their greatest happiness. His time was now short, he therefore spake largely to them. When we come to be sick, and to die, we may not be capable of talking much to those about us; such good counsel as we have to give, let us give while in health. Observe the prospect Christ had of an approaching conflict, not only with men, but with the powers of darkness. Satan has something in us to perplex us with, for we have all sinned; but when he would disturb Christ, he found nothing sinful to help him. The best evidence of our love to the Father is, our doing as he has commanded us. Let us rejoice in the Saviour's victories over Satan the prince of this world. Let us copy the example of his love and obedience.

Chapter 15

Chapter Outline

Verses 1-8

Jesus Christ is the Vine, the true Vine. The union of the human and Divine natures, and the fulness of the Spirit that is in him, resemble the root of the vine made fruitful by the moisture from a rich soil. Believers are branches of this Vine. The root is unseen, and our life is hid with Christ; the root bears the tree, diffuses sap to it, and in Christ are all supports and supplies. The branches of the vine are many, yet, meeting in the root, are all but one vine; thus all true Christians, though in place and opinion distant from each other, meet in Christ. Believers, like the branches of the vine, are weak, and unable to stand but as they are borne up. The Father is the Husbandman. Never was any husbandman so wise, so watchful, about his vineyard, as God is about his church, which therefore must prosper. We must be fruitful. From a vine we look for grapes, and from a Christian we look for a Christian temper, disposition, and life. We must honour God, and do good; this is bearing fruit. The unfruitful are taken away. And even fruitful branches need pruning; for the best have notions, passions, and humours, that require to be taken away, which Christ has promised to forward the sanctification of believers, they will be thankful, for them. The word of Christ is spoken to all believers; and there is a cleansing virtue in that word, as it works grace, and works out corruption. And the more fruit we bring forth, the more we abound in what is good, the more our Lord is glorified. In order to fruitfulness, we must abide in Christ, must have union with him by faith. It is the great concern of all Christ's disciples, constantly to keep up dependence upon Christ, and communion with him. True Christians find by experience, that any interruption in the exercise of their faith, causes holy affections to decline, their corruptions to revive, and their comforts to droop. Those who abide not in Christ, though they may flourish for awhile in outward profession, yet come to nothing. The fire is the fittest place for withered branches; they are good for nothing else. Let us seek to live more simply on the fulness of Christ, and to grow more fruitful in every good word and work, so may our joy in Him and in his salvation be full.

Verses 9-17

Those whom God loves as a Father, may despise the hatred of all the world. As the Father loved Christ, who was most worthy, so he loved his disciples, who were unworthy. All that love the Saviour should continue in their love to him, and take all occasions to show it. The joy of the hypocrite is but for a moment, but the joy of those who abide in Christ's love is a continual feast. They are to show their love to him by keeping his commandments. If the same power that first shed abroad the love of Christ's in our hearts, did not keep us in that love, we should not long abide in it. Christ's love to us should direct us to love each other. He speaks as about to give many things in charge, yet names this only; it includes many duties.

Verses 18-25

How little do many persons think, that in opposing the doctrine of Christ as our Prophet, Priest, and King, they prove themselves ignorant of the one living and true God, whom they profess to worship! The name into which Christ's disciples were baptized, is that which they will live and die by. It is a comfort to the greatest sufferers, if they suffer for Christ's name's sake. The world's ignorance is the true cause of its hatred to the disciples of Jesus. The clearer and fuller the discoveries of the grace and truth of Christ, the greater is our sin if we do not love him and believe in him.

Verses 26, 27

The blessed Spirit will maintain the cause of Christ in the world, notwithstanding the opposition it meets with. Believers taught and encouraged by his influences, would bear testimony to Christ and his salvation.

Chapter 16

Chapter Outline

Persecution foretold.	(1–6)
The promise of the Holy Spirit, and his office.	(7–15)
Christ's departure and return.	(16–22)
Encouragement to prayer.	(23–27)
Christ's discoveries of himself.	(28–33)

Verses 1-6

Our Lord Jesus, by giving his disciples notice of trouble, designed that the terror might not be a surprise to them. It is possible for those who are real enemies to God's service, to pretend zeal for it. This does not lessen the sin of the persecutors; villanies will never be changed by putting the name of God to them. As Jesus in his sufferings, so his followers in theirs, should look to the fulfilling of Scripture. He did not tell them sooner, because he was with them to teach, guide, and comfort them; they needed not then this promise of the Holy Spirit's presence. It will silence us to ask, Whence troubles come? It will satisfy us to ask, Whither go they? for we know they work for good. It is the common fault and folly of melancholy Christians to look only on the dark side of the cloud, and to turn a deaf ear to the voice of joy and gladness. That which filled the disciples' hearts with sorrow, was too great affection for this present life. Nothing more hinders our joy in God, than the love of the world, and the sorrow of the world which comes from it.

Verses 7-15

Christ's departure was necessary to the Comforter's coming. Sending the Spirit was to be the fruit of Christ's death, which was his going away. His bodily presence could be only in one place at one time, but his Spirit is every where, in all places, at all times, wherever two or three are gathered together in his name. See here the office of the Spirit, first to reprove, or to convince. Convincing work is the Spirit's work; he can do it effectually, and none but he. It is the method the Holy Spirit takes, first to convince, and then to comfort. The Spirit shall convince the world, of sin; not merely tell them of it. The Spirit convinces of the fact of sin; of the fault of sin; of the folly of sin; of the filth of sin, that by it we are become hateful to God; of the fountain of sin, the corrupt nature; and lastly, of the fruit of sin, that the end thereof is death. The Holy Spirit proves that all the world is guilty before God. He convinces the world of righteousness; that Jesus of Nazareth was Christ the righteous. Also, of Christ's righteousness, imparted to us for justification and salvation. He will show them where it is to be had, and how they may be accepted as righteous in God's sight. Christ's ascension proves the ransom was accepted, and the righteousness finished, through which believers were to be justified. Of judgment, because the prince of this world is judged. All will be well, when his power is broken, who made all the mischief. As Satan is subdued by Christ, this gives us confidence, for no other power can stand before him. And of the day of judgment. The coming of the Spirit would be of unspeakable advantage to the disciples. The Holy Spirit is our Guide, not only to show us the way, but to go with us by continued aids and influences. To be led into a truth is more than barely to know it; it is not only to have the notion of it in our heads, but the relish, and savour, and power of it in our hearts. He shall teach all truth, and keep back nothing profitable, for he will show things to come. All the gifts and graces of the Spirit, all the preaching, and all the writing of the apostles, under the influence of the Spirit, all the tongues, and miracles, were to glorify Christ. It behoves every one to ask, whether the Holy Spirit has begun a good work in his heart? Without clear discovery of our guilt and danger, we never shall understand the value of Christ's salvation; but when brought to know ourselves aright, we begin to see the value of the Redeemer. We should have fuller views of the Redeemer, and more lively affections to him, if we more prayed for, and depended on the Holy Spirit.

Verses 16-22

It is good to consider how near our seasons of grace are to an end, that we may be quickened to improve them. But the sorrows of the disciples would soon be turned into joy; as those of a mother, at the sight of her infant. The Holy Spirit would be their Comforter, and neither men nor devils, neither sufferings in life nor in death, would ever deprive them of their joy. Believers have joy or sorrow, according to their sight of Christ, and the tokens of his presence. Sorrow is coming on the ungodly, which nothing can lessen; the believer is an heir to joy which no one can take away. Where now is the joy of the murderers of our Lord, and the sorrow of his friends?

Verses 23-27

Asking of the Father shows a sense of spiritual wants, and a desire of spiritual blessings, with conviction that they are to be had from God only. Asking in Christ's name, is acknowledging our unworthiness to receive any favours from God, and shows full dependence upon Christ as the Lord our Righteousness. Our Lord had hitherto spoken in short and weighty sentences, or in parables, the import of which the disciples did not fully understand, but after his resurrection he intended plainly to teach them such things as related to the Father and the way to him, through his intercession. And the frequency with which our Lord enforces offering up petitions in his name, shows that the great end of the mediation of Christ is to impress us with a deep sense of our sinfulness, and of the merit and power of his death, whereby we have access to God. And let us ever remember, that to address the Father in the name of Christ, or to address the Son as God dwelling in human nature, and reconciling the world to himself, are the same, as the Father and Son are one.

Verses 28-33

Here is a plain declaration of Christ's coming from the Father, and his return to him. The Redeemer, in his entrance, was God manifest in the flesh, and in his departure was received up into glory. By this saying the disciples improved in knowledge. Also in faith; "Now are we sure." Alas! they knew not their own weakness. The Divine nature did not desert the human nature, but supported it, and put comfort and value into Christ's sufferings. And while we have God's favourable presence, we are happy, and ought to be easy, though all the world forsake us. Peace in Christ is the only true peace, in him alone believers have it. Through him we have peace with God, and so in him we have peace in our own minds. We ought to be encouraged, because Christ has overcome the world before us. But while we think we stand, let us take heed lest we fall. We know not how we should act if brought into temptation; let us watch and pray without ceasing, that we may not be left to ourselves.

Chapter 17

Chapter Outline

Verses 1-5

Our Lord prayed as a man, and as the Mediator of his people; yet he spoke with majesty and authority, as one with and equal to the Father. Eternal life could not be given to believers, unless Christ, their Surety, both glorified the Father, and was glorified of him. This is the sinner's way to eternal life, and when this knowledge shall be made perfect, holiness and happiness will be fully enjoyed. The holiness and happiness of the redeemed, are especially that glory of Christ, and of his Father, which was the joy set before him, for which he endured the cross and despised the shame; this glory was the end of the sorrow of his soul, and in obtaining it he was fully satisfied. Thus we are taught that our glorifying God is needed as an evidence of our interest in Christ, through whom eternal life is God's free gift.

Verses 6-10

Christ prays for those that are his. Thou gavest them me, as sheep to the shepherd, to be kept; as a patient to the physician, to be cured; as children to a tutor, to be taught: thus he will deliver up his charge. It is a great satisfaction to us, in our reliance upon Christ, that he, all he is and has, and all he said and did, all he is doing and will do, are of God. Christ offered this prayer for his people alone as believers; not for the world at large. Yet no one who desires to come to the Father, and is conscious that he is unworthy to come in his own name, need be discouraged by the Saviour's declaration, for he is both able and willing to save to the uttermost, all that come unto God by him. Earnest convictions and desires, are hopeful tokens of a work already wrought in a man; they begin to evidence that he has been chosen unto salvation, through sanctification of the Spirit and belief of the truth. They are thine; wilt thou not provide for thine own? Wilt thou not secure them? Observe the foundation on which this plea is grounded, All mine are thine, and thine are mine. This speaks the Father and Son to be one. All mine are thine. The Son owns none for his, that are not devoted to the service of the Father.

Verses 11-16

Christ does not pray that they might be rich and great in the world, but that they might be kept from sin, strengthened for their duty, and brought safe to heaven. The prosperity of the soul is the best prosperity. He pleaded with his holy Father, that he would keep them by his power and for his glory, that they might be united in affection and labours, even according to the union of the Father and the Son. He did not pray that his disciples should be removed out of the world, that they might escape the rage of men, for they had a great work to do for the glory of God, and the benefit of mankind. But he prayed that the Father would keep them from the evil, from being corrupted by the world, the remains of sin in their hearts, and from the power and craft of Satan. So that they might pass through the world as through an enemy's country, as he had done. They are not left here to pursue the same objects as the men around them, but to glorify God, and to serve their generation. The Spirit of God in true Christians is opposed to the spirit of the world.

Verses 17-19

Christ next prayed for the disciples, that they might not only be kept from evil, but made good. It is the prayer of Jesus for all that are his, that they may be made holy. Even disciples must pray for sanctifying grace. The means of giving this grace is, "through thy truth, thy word is truth." Sanctify them, set them apart for thyself and thy service. Own them in the office; let thy hand go with them. Jesus entirely devoted himself to his undertaking, and all the parts of it, especially the offering up himself without spot unto God, by the eternal Spirit. The real holiness of all true

Christians is the fruit of Christ's death, by which the gift of the Holy Ghost was purchased; he gave himself for his church, to sanctify it. If our views have not this effect on us, they are not Divine truth, or we do not receive them by a living and a working faith, but as mere notions.

Verses 20-23

Our Lord especially prayed, that all believers might be as one body under one head, animated by one soul, by their union with Christ and the Father in him, through the Holy Spirit dwelling in them. The more they dispute about lesser things, the more they throw doubts upon Christianity. Let us endeavour to keep the unity of the Spirit in the bond of peace, praying that all believers may be more and more united in one mind and one judgment. Thus shall we convince the world of the truth and excellence of our religion, and find more sweet communion with God and his saints.

Verses 24-26

Christ, as one with the Father, claimed on behalf of all that had been given to him, and should in due time believe on him, that they should be brought to heaven; and that there the whole company of the redeemed might behold his glory as their beloved Friend and Brother, and therein find happiness. He had declared and would further declare the name or character of God, by his doctrine and his Spirit, that, being one with him, the love of the Father to him might abide with them also. Thus, being joined to Him by one Spirit, they might be filled with all the fulness of God, and enjoy a blessedness of which we can form no right idea in our present state.

Chapter 18

Chapter Outline

Verses 1-12

Sin began in the garden of Eden, there the curse was pronounced, there the Redeemer was promised; and in a garden that promised Seed entered into conflict with the old serpent. Christ was buried also in a garden. Let us, when we walk in our gardens, take occasion from thence to mediate on Christ's sufferings in a garden. Our Lord Jesus, knowing all things that should come upon him, went forth and asked, Whom seek ye? When the people would have forced him to a crown, he withdrew, ch. 6:15, but when they came to force him to a cross, he offered himself; for he came into this world to suffer, and went to the other world to reign. He showed plainly what he could have done; when he struck them down he could have struck them dead, but he would not do so. It must have been the effect of Divine power, that the officers and soldiers let the disciples go away quietly, after the resistance which had been offered. Christ set us an example of meekness in sufferings, and a pattern of submission to God's will in every thing that concerns us. It is but a cup, a small matter. It is a cup that is given us; sufferings are gifts. It is given us by a Father, who has a father's authority, and does us no wrong; a father's affection, and means us no hurt. From the example of our Saviour we should learn how to receive our lighter afflictions, and to ask ourselves whether we ought to oppose our Father's will, or to distrust his love. We were bound with the cords of our iniquities, with the yoke of our transgressions. Christ, being made a sin-offering for us, to free us from those bonds, himself submitted to be bound for us. To his bonds we owe our liberty; thus the Son makes us free.

Verses 13-27

Simon Peter denied his Master. The particulars have been noticed in the remarks on the other Gospels. The beginning of sin is as the letting forth of water. The sin of lying is a fruitful sin; one lie needs another to support it, and that another. If a call to expose ourselves to danger be clear, we may hope God will enable us to honour him; if it be not, we may fear that God will leave us to shame ourselves. They said nothing concerning the miracles of Jesus, by which he had done so much good, and which proved his doctrine. Thus the enemies of Christ, whilst they quarrel with his truth, wilfully shut their eyes against it. He appeals to those who heard him. The doctrine of Christ may safely appeal to all that know it, and those who judge in truth bear witness to it. Our resentment of injuries must never be passionate. He reasoned with the man that did him the injury, and so may we.

Verses 28-32

It was unjust to put one to death who had done so much good, therefore the Jews were willing to save themselves from reproach. Many fear the scandal of an ill thing, more than the sin of it. Christ had said he should be delivered to the Gentiles, and they should put him to death; hereby that saying was fulfilled. He had said that he should be crucified, lifted up. If the Jews had judged him by their law, he had been stoned; crucifying never was used among the Jews. It is determined concerning us, though not discovered to us, what death we shall die: this should free us from disquiet about that matter. Lord, what, when, and how, thou hast appointed.

Verses 33-40

Art thou the King of the Jews? that King of the Jews who has been so long expected? Messiah the Prince; art thou he? Dost thou call thyself so, and wouldest thou be thought so? Christ answered this question with another; not for evasion, but that Pilate might consider what he did. He never took upon him any earthly power, never were any traitorous principles or practices laid to him. Christ gave an account of the nature of his kingdom. Its nature is not worldly; it is a kingdom within men, set up in their hearts and consciences; its riches spiritual, its power spiritual, and it glory within. Its supports are not worldly; its weapons are spiritual; it needed not, nor used, force to maintain and advance it, nor opposed any kingdom but that of sin and Satan. Its object and design are not worldly. When Christ said, I am the Truth, he said, in effect, I am a King. He conquers by the convincing evidence of truth; he rules by the commanding power of truth. The subjects of this kingdom are those that are of the truth. Pilate put a good question, he said, What is truth? When we search the Scriptures, and attend the ministry of the word, it must be with this inquiry, What is truth? and with this prayer, Lead me in thy truth; into all truth. But many put this question, who have not patience to preserve in their search after truth; or not humility enough to receive it. By this solemn declaration of Christ's innocence, it appears, that though the Lord Jesus was treated as the worst of evil-doers, he never deserved such treatment. But it unfolds the design of his death; that he died as a Sacrifice for our sins. Pilate was willing to please all sides; and was governed more by worldly wisdom than by the rules of justice. Sin is a robber, yet is foolishly chosen by many rather than Christ, who would truly enrich us. Let us endeavour to make our accusers ashamed as Christ did; and let us beware of crucifying Christ afresh.

Chapter 19

Chapter Outline

Christ condemned and crucified.	(1–18)
Christ on the cross.	(19–30)
His side pierced.	(31–37)
The burial of Jesus.	(38–42)

Verses 1-18

Little did Pilate think with what holy regard these sufferings of Christ would, in after-ages, be thought upon and spoken of by the best and greatest of men. Our Lord Jesus came forth, willing to be exposed to their scorn. It is good for every one with faith, to behold Christ Jesus in his sufferings. Behold him, and love him; be still looking unto Jesus. Did their hatred sharpen their endeavours against him? and shall not our love for him quicken our endeavours for him and his kingdom? Pilate seems to have thought that Jesus might be some person above the common order. Even natural conscience makes men afraid of being found fighting against God. As our Lord suffered for the sins both of Jews and Gentiles, it was a special part of the counsel of Divine Wisdom, that the Jews should first purpose his death, and the Gentiles carry that purpose into effect. Had not Christ been thus rejected of men, we had been for ever rejected of God. Now was the Son of man delivered into the hands of wicked and unreasonable men. He was led forth for us, that we might escape. He was nailed to the cross, as a Sacrifice bound to the altar. The Scripture was fulfilled; he did not die at the altar among the sacrifices, but among criminals sacrificed to public justice. And now let us pause, and with faith look upon Jesus. Was ever sorrow like unto his sorrow? See him bleeding, see him dying, see him and love him! love him, and live to him!

Verses 19-30

Here are some remarkable circumstances of Jesus' death, more fully related than before. Pilate would not gratify the chief priests by allowing the writing to be altered; which was doubtless owing to a secret power of God upon his heart, that this statement of our Lord's character and authority might continue. Many things done by the Roman soldiers were fulfilments of the prophecies of the Old Testament. All things therein written shall be fulfilled. Christ tenderly provided for his mother at his death. Sometimes, when God removes one comfort from us, he raises up another for us, where we looked not for it. Christ's example teaches all men to honour their parents in life and death; to provide for their wants, and to promote their comfort by every means in their power. Especially observe the dying word wherewith Jesus breathed out his soul. It is finished; that is, the counsels of the Father concerning his sufferings were now fulfilled. It is finished; all the types and prophecies of the Old Testament, which pointed at the sufferings of the Messiah, were accomplished. It is finished; the ceremonial law is abolished; the substance is now come, and all the shadows are done away. It is finished; an end is made of transgression by bringing in an everlasting righteousness. His sufferings were now finished, both those of his soul, and those of his body. It is finished; the work of man's redemption and salvation is now completed. His life was not taken from him by force, but freely given up.

Verses 31-37

A trial was made whether Jesus was dead. He died in less time than persons crucified commonly did. It showed that he had laid down his life of himself. The spear broke up the very fountains of life; no human body could survive such a wound. But its being so solemnly attested, shows there was something peculiar in it. The blood and water that flowed out, signified those two great benefits which all believers partake of through Christ, justification and sanctification; blood for atonement, water for purification. They both flow from the pierced side of our Redeemer. To Christ crucified we owe merit for our justification, and Spirit and grace for our sanctification. Let this silence the fears of weak Christians, and encourage their hopes; there came both water and blood out of Jesus' pierced side, both to justify and sanctify them. The Scripture was fulfilled, in Pilate's not allowing his legs to be broken, Ps 34:20. There was a type of this in the paschal lamb, Ex 12:46. May we ever look to Him, whom, by our sins, we have ignorantly and heedlessly pierced, nay, sometimes against convictions and mercies; and who shed from his wounded side both water and blood, that we might be justified and sanctified in his name.

Verses 38-42

Joseph of Arimathea was a disciple of Christ in secret. Disciples should openly own themselves; yet some, who in lesser trials have been fearful, in greater have been courageous. When God has work to do, he can find out such as are proper to do it. The embalming was done by Nicodemus, a secret friend to Christ, though not his constant follower. That grace which at first is like a bruised reed, may afterward resemble a strong cedar. Hereby these two rich men showed the value they had for Christ's person and doctrine, and that it was not lessened by the reproach of the cross. We must do our duty as the present day and opportunity are, and leave it to God to fulfil his promises in his own way and his own time. The grave of Jesus was appointed with the wicked, as was the case of those who suffered as criminals; but he was with the rich in his death, as prophesied, Isa

53:9; these two circumstances it was very unlikely should ever be united in the same person. He was buried in a new sepulchre; therefore it could not be said that it was not he, but some other that rose. We also are here taught not to be particular as to the place of our burial. He was buried in the sepulchre next at hand. Here is the Sun of Righteousness set for a while, to rise again in greater glory, and then to set no more.

Chapter 20

Chapter Outline

Verses 1-10

If Christ gave his life a ransom, and had not taken it again, it would not have appeared that his giving it was accepted as satisfaction. It was a great trial to Mary, that the body was gone. Weak believers often make that the matter of complaint, which is really just ground of hope, and matter of joy. It is well when those more honoured than others with the privileges of disciples, are more active than others in the duty of disciples; more willing to take pains, and run hazards, in a good work. We must do our best, and neither envy those who can do better, nor despise those who do as well as they can, though they come behind. The disciple whom Jesus loved in a special manner, and who therefore in a special manner loved Jesus, was foremost. The love of Christ will make us to abound in every duty more than any thing else. He that was behind was Peter, who had denied Christ. A sense of guilt hinders us in the service of God. As yet the disciples knew not the Scripture; they Christ must rise again from the dead.

Verses 11-18

We are likely to seek and find, when we seek with affection, and seek in tears. But many believers complain of the clouds and darkness they are under, which are methods of grace for humbling their souls, mortifying their sins, and endearing Christ to them. A sight of angels and their smiles, will not suffice, without a sight of Jesus, and God's smiles in him. None know, but those who have tasted it, the sorrows of a deserted soul, which has had comfortable evidences of the love of God in Christ, and hopes of heaven, but has now lost them, and walks in darkness; such a wounded spirit who can bear? Christ, in manifesting himself to those that seek him, often outdoes their expectations. See how Mary's heart was in earnest to find Jesus. Christ's way of making himself known to his people is by his word; his word applied to their souls, speaking to them in particular.

It might be read, Is it my Master? See with what pleasure those who love Jesus speak of his authority over them. He forbids her to expect that his bodily presence look further, than the present state of things. Observe the relation to God, from union with Christ. We, partaking of a Divine nature, Christ's Father is our Father; and he, partaking of the human nature, our God is his God. Christ's ascension into heaven, there to plead for us, is likewise an unspeakable comfort. Let them not think this earth is to be their home and rest; their eye and aim, and earnest desires, must be upon another world, and this ever upon their hearts, I ascend, therefore I must seek the things which are above. And let those who know the word of Christ, endeavour that others should get good from their knowledge.

Verses 19-25

This was the first day of the week, and this day is afterwards often mentioned by the sacred writers; for it was evidently set apart as the Christian sabbath, in remembrance of Christ's resurrection. The disciples had shut the doors for fear of the Jews; and when they had no such expectation, Jesus himself came and stood in the midst of them, having miraculously, though silently, opened the doors. It is a comfort to Christ's disciples, when their assemblies can only be held in private, that no doors can shut out Christ's presence. When He manifests his love to believers by the comforts of his Spirit, he assures them that because he lives, they shall live also. A sight of Christ will gladden the heart of a disciple at any time; and the more we see of Jesus, the more we shall rejoice. He said, Receive ye the Holy Ghost, thus showing that their spiritual life, as well as all their ability for their work, would be derived from him, and depended upon him. Every word of Christ which is received in the heart by faith, comes accompanied by this Divine breathing; and without this there is neither light nor life. Nothing is seen, known, discerned, or felt of God, but through this. After this, Christ directed the apostles to declare the only method by which sin would be forgiven. This power did not exist at all in the apostles as a power to give judgment, but only as a power to declare the character of those whom God would accept or reject in the day of judgment. They have clearly laid down the marks whereby a child of God may be discerned and be distinguished from a false professor; and according to what they have declared shall every case be decided in the day of judgment. When we assemble in Christ's name, especially on his holy day, he will meet with us, and speak peace to us. The disciples of Christ should endeavour to build up one another in their most holy faith, both by repeating what they have heard to those that were absent, and by making known what they have experienced. Thomas limited the Holy One of Israel, when he would be convinced by his own method or not at all. He might justly have been left in his unbelief, after rejecting such abundant proofs. The fears and sorrows of the disciples are often lengthened, to punish their negligence.

Verses 26-29

That one day in seven should be religiously observed, was an appointment from the beginning. And that, in the kingdom of the Messiah, the first day of the week should be that solemn day, was pointed out, in that Christ on that day once and again met his disciples in a religious assembly. The religious observance of that day has come down to us through every age of the church. There is not an unbelieving word in our tongues, nor thought in our minds, but it is known to the Lord Jesus;

and he was pleased to accommodate himself even to Thomas, rather than leave him in his unbelief. We ought thus to bear with the weak, Ro 15:1, 2. This warning is given to all. If we are faithless, we are Christless and graceless, hopeless and joyless. Thomas was ashamed of his unbelief, and cried out, My Lord and my God. He spoke with affection, as one that took hold of Christ with all his might; "My Lord and my God." Sound and sincere believers, though slow and weak, shall be graciously accepted of the Lord Jesus. It is the duty of those who read and hear the gospel, to believe, to embrace the doctrine of Christ, and that record concerning him, 1Jo 5:11.

Verses 30, 31

There were other signs and proofs of our Lord's resurrection, but these were committed to writing, that all might believe that Jesus was the promised Messiah, the Saviour of sinners, and the Son of God; that, by this faith, they might obtain eternal life, by his mercy, truth, and power. May we believe that Jesus is the Christ, and believing may we have life through his name.

Chapter 21

Chapter Outline

Christ appears to his disciples.	(1–14)
His discourse with Peter.	(15–19)
Christ's declaration concerning John.	(20–24)
The conclusion.	(25)

Verses 1-14

Christ makes himself known to his people, usually in his ordinances; but sometimes by his Spirit he visits them when employed in their business. It is good for the disciples of Christ to be together in common conversation, and common business. The hour for their entering upon action was not come. They would help to maintain themselves, and not be burdensome to any. Christ's time of making himself known to his people, is when they are most at a loss. He knows the temporal wants of his people, and has promised them not only grace sufficient, but food convenient. Divine Providence extends itself to things most minute, and those are happy who acknowledge God in all their ways. Those who are humble, diligent, and patient, though their labours may be crossed, shall be crowned; they sometimes live to see their affairs take a happy turn, after many struggles. And there is nothing lost by observing Christ's orders; it is casting the net on the right side of the ship. Jesus manifests himself to his people by doing that for them which none else can do, and things which they looked not for. He would take care that those who left all for him, should not want any good thing. And latter favours are to bring to mind former favours, that eaten bread may not be forgotten. He whom Jesus loved was the first that said, It is the Lord. John had cleaved most closely to his Master in his sufferings, and knew him soonest. Peter was the most zealous, and reached

Christ the first. How variously God dispenses his gifts, and what difference there may be between some believers and others in the way of their honouring Christ, yet they all may be accepted of him! Others continue in the ship, drag the net, and bring the fish to shore, and such persons ought not to be blamed as worldly; for they, in their places, are as truly serving Christ as the others. The Lord Jesus had provision ready for them. We need not be curious in inquiring whence this came; but we may be comforted at Christ's care for his disciples. Although there were so many, and such great fishes, yet they lost none, nor damaged their net. The net of the gospel has enclosed multitudes, yet it is as strong as ever to bring souls to God.

Verses 15-19

Our Lord addressed Peter by his original name, as if he had forfeited that of Peter through his denying him. He now answered, Thou knowest that I love thee; but without professing to love Jesus more than others. We must not be surprised to have our sincerity called into question, when we ourselves have done that which makes it doubtful. Every remembrance of past sins, even pardoned sins, renews the sorrow of a true penitent. Conscious of integrity, Peter solemnly appealed to Christ, as knowing all things, even the secrets of his heart. It is well when our falls and mistakes make us more humble and watchful. The sincerity of our love to God must be brought to the test; and it behoves us to inquire with earnest, preserving prayer to the heart-searching God, to examine and prove us, whether we are able to stand this test. No one can be qualified to feed the sheep and lambs of Christ, who does not love the good Shepherd more than any earthly advantage or object. It is the great concern of every good man, whatever death he dies, to glorify God in it; for what is our chief end but this, to die to the Lord, at the word of the Lord?

Verses 20-24

Sufferings, pains, and death, will appear formidable even to the experienced Christian; but in the hope to glorify God, to leave a sinful world, and to be present with his Lord, he becomes ready to obey the Redeemer's call, and to follow Him through death to glory. It is the will of Christ that his disciples should mind their own duty, and not be curious about future events, either as to themselves or others. Many things we are apt to be anxious about, which are nothing to us. Other people's affairs are nothing to us, to intermeddle in; we must quietly work, and mind our own business. Many curious questions are put about the counsels of God, and the state of the unseen world, as to which we may say, What is this to us? And if we attend to the duty of following Christ, we shall find neither heart nor time to meddle with that which does not belong to us. How little are any unwritten traditions to be relied upon! Let the Scripture be its own interpreter, and explain itself; as it is, in a great measure, its own evidence, and proves itself, for it is light. See the easy setting right such mistakes by the word of Christ. Scripture language is the safest channel for Scripture truth; the words which the Holy Ghost teaches, 1Co 2:13. Those who cannot agree in the same terms of art, and the application of them, may yet agree in the same Scripture terms, and to love one another.

Verse 25

Only a small part of the actions of Jesus had been written. But let us bless God for all that is in the Scriptures, and be thankful that there is so much in so small a space. Enough is recorded to direct our faith, and regulate our practice; more would have been unnecessary. Much of what is written is overlooked, much forgotten, and much made the matter of doubtful disputes. We may, however, look forward to the joy we shall receive in heaven, from a more complete knowledge of all Jesus did and said, as well as of the conduct of his providence and grace in his dealings with each of us. May this be our happiness. These are written that ye might believe that Jesus is the Christ, the Son of God; and that believing ye might have life through his name, ch. 20:31.

Acts

This book unites the Gospels to the Epistles. It contains many particulars concerning the apostles Peter and Paul, and of the Christian church from the ascension of our Saviour to the arrival of St. Paul at Rome, a space of about thirty years. St. Luke was the writer of this book; he was present at many of the events he relates, and attended Paul to Rome. But the narrative does not afford a complete history of the church during the time to which it refers, nor even of St. Paul's life. The object of the book has been considered to be, 1. To relate in what manner the gifts of the Holy Spirit were communicated on the day of Pentecost, and the miracles performed by the apostles, to confirm the truth of Christianity, as showing that Christ's declarations were really fulfilled. 2. To prove the claim of the Gentiles to be admitted into the church of Christ. This is shown by much of the contents of the book. A large portion of the Acts is occupied by the discourses or sermons of various persons, the language and manner of which differ, and all of which will be found according to the persons by whom they were delivered, and the occasions on which they were spoken. It seems that most of these discourses are only the substance of what was actually delivered. They relate nevertheless fully to Jesus as the Christ, the anointed Messiah.

Chapter 1

Chapter Outline

Verses 1-5

Our Lord told the disciples the work they were to do. The apostles met together at Jerusalem; Christ having ordered them not to depart thence, but to wait for the pouring out of the Holy Spirit. This would be a baptism by the Holy Ghost, giving them power to work miracles, and enlightening and sanctifying their souls. This confirms the Divine promise, and encourages us to depend upon it, that we have heard it from Christ; for in Him all the promises of God are yea and amen.

Verses 6-11

They were earnest in asking about that which their Master never had directed or encouraged them to seek. Our Lord knew that his ascension and the teaching of the Holy Spirit would soon end these expectations, and therefore only gave them a rebuke; but it is a caution to his church in all ages, to take heed of a desire of forbidden knowledge. He had given his disciples instructions for the discharge of their duty, both before his death and since his resurrection, and this knowledge is enough for a Christian. It is enough that He has engaged to give believers strength equal to their trials and services; that under the influence of the Holy Spirit they may, in one way or other, be witnesses for Christ on earth, while in heaven he manages their concerns with perfect wisdom, truth, and love. When we stand gazing and trifling, the thoughts of our Master's second coming should quicken and awaken us: when we stand gazing and trembling, they should comfort and encourage us. May our expectation of it be stedfast and joyful, giving diligence to be found of him blameless.

Verses 12-14

God can find hiding-places for his people. They made supplication. All God's people are praying people. It was now a time of trouble and danger with the disciples of Christ; but if any is afflicted, let him pray; that will silence cares and fears. They had now a great work to do, and before they entered upon it, they were earnest in prayer to God for his presence. They were waiting for the descent of the Spirit, and abounded in prayer. Those are in the best frame to receive spiritual blessings, who are in a praying frame. Christ had promised shortly to send the Holy Ghost; that promise was not to do away prayer, but to quicken and encourage it. A little company united in love, exemplary in their conduct, fervent in prayer, and wisely zealous to promote the cause of Christ, are likely to increase rapidly.

Verses 15-26

The great thing the apostles were to attest to the world, was, Christ's resurrection; for that was the great proof of his being the Messiah, and the foundation of our hope in him. The apostles were ordained, not to wordly dignity and dominion, but to preach Christ, and the power of his resurrection. An appeal was made to God; "Thou, Lord, who knowest the hearts of all men," which we do not; and better than they know their own. It is fit that God should choose his own servants; and so far as he, by the disposals of his providence, or the gifts of his Spirit, shows whom he was chosen, or what he has chosen for us, we ought to fall in with his will. Let us own his hand in the determining everything which befalls us, especially in those by which any trust may be committed to us.

Chapter 2

Chapter Outline

Verses 1-4

We cannot forget how often, while their Master was with them there were strifes among the disciples which should be the greatest; but now all these strifes were at an end. They had prayed more together of late. Would we have the Spirit poured out upon us from on high, let us be all of one accord. And notwithstanding differences of sentiments and interests, as there were among those disciples, let us agree to love one another; for where brethren dwell together in unity, there the Lord commands his blessing. A rushing mighty wind came with great force. This was to signify the powerful influences and working of the Spirit of God upon the minds of men, and thereby upon the world. Thus the convictions of the Spirit make way for his comforts; and the rough blasts of that blessed wind, prepare the soul for its soft and gentle gales. There was an appearance of something like flaming fire, lighting on every one of them, according to John Baptist's saying concerning Christ; He shall baptize you with the Holy Ghost, and with fire. The Spirit, like fire, melts the heart, burns up the dross, and kindles pious and devout affections in the soul; in which, as in the fire on the altar, the spiritual sacrifices are offered up. They were all filled with the Holy Ghost, more than before. They were filled with the graces of the Spirit, and more than ever under his sanctifying influences; more weaned from this world, and better acquainted with the other. They were more filled with the comforts of the Spirit, rejoiced more than ever in the love of Christ and the hope of heaven: in it all their griefs and fears were swallowed up. They were filled with the gifts of the Holy Ghost; they had miraculous powers for the furtherance of the gospel. They spake, not from previous though or meditation, but as the Spirit gave them utterance.

Verses 5-13

The difference in languages which arose at Babel, has much hindered the spread of knowledge and religion. The instruments whom the Lord first employed in spreading the Christian religion, could have made no progress without this gift, which proved that their authority was from God.

Verses 14-21

Peter's sermon shows that he was thoroughly recovered from his fall, and thoroughly restored to the Divine favour; for he who had denied Christ, now boldly confessed him. His account of the miraculous pouring forth of the Spirit, was designed to awaken the hearers to embrace the faith of Christ, and to join themselves to his church. It was the fulfilling the Scripture, and the fruit of Christ's resurrection and ascension, and proof of both. Though Peter was filled with the Holy Ghost, and spake with tongues as the Spirit gave him utterance, yet he did not think to set aside the Scriptures. Christ's scholars never learn above their Bible; and the Spirit is given, not to do away the Scriptures, but to enable us to understand, approve, and obey them. Assuredly none will escape the condemnation of the great day, except those who call upon the name of the Lord, in and through his Son Jesus Christ, as the Saviour of sinners, and the Judge of all mankind.

Verses 22-36

From this gift of the Holy Ghost, Peter preaches unto them Jesus: and here is the history of Christ. Here is an account of his death and sufferings, which they witnessed but a few weeks before. His death is considered as God's act; and of wonderful grace and wisdom. Thus Divine justice must be satisfied, God and man brought together again, and Christ himself glorified, according to an eternal counsel, which could not be altered. And as the people's act; in them it was an act of awful sin and folly. Christ's resurrection did away the reproach of his death; Peter speaks largely upon this. Christ was God's Holy One, sanctified and set apart to his service in the work of redemption. His death and sufferings should be, not to him only, but to all his, the entrance to a blessed life for evermore. This event had taken place as foretold, and the apostles were witnesses. Nor did the resurrection rest upon this alone; Christ had poured upon his disciples the miraculous gifts and Divine influences, of which they witnessed the effects. Through the Saviour, the ways of life are made known; and we are encouraged to expect God's presence, and his favour for evermore. All this springs from assured belief that Jesus is the Lord, and the anointed Saviour.

Verses 37-41

From the first delivery of that Divine message, it appeared that there was Divine power going with it; and thousands were brought to the obedience of faith. But neither Peter's words, nor the miracle they witnessed, could have produced such effects, had not the Holy Spirit been given. Sinners, when their eyes are opened, cannot but be pricked to the heart for sin, cannot but feel an inward uneasiness. The apostle exhorted them to repent of their sins, and openly to avow their belief in Jesus as the Messiah, by being baptized in his name. Thus professing their faith in Him, they would receive remission of their sins, and partake of the gifts and graces of the Holy Spirit. To separate from wicked people, is the only way to save ourselves from them. Those who repent of their sins, and give up themselves to Jesus Christ, must prove their sincerity by breaking off from the wicked. We must save ourselves from them; which denotes avoiding them with dread and holy fear. By God's grace three thousand persons accepted the gospel invitation. There can be no doubt that the gift of the Holy Ghost, which they all received, and from which no true believer has ever been shut out, was that Spirit of adoption, that converting, guiding, sanctifying grace, which is bestowed upon all the members of the family of our heavenly Father. Repentance and remission of sins are still preached to the chief of sinners, in the Redeemer's name; still the Holy Spirit seals the blessing on the believer's heart; still the encouraging promises are to us and our children; and still the blessings are offered to all that are afar off.

Verses 42-47

In these verses we have the history of the truly primitive church, of the first days of it; its state of infancy indeed, but, like that, the state of its greatest innocence. They kept close to holy ordinances, and abounded in piety and devotion; for Christianity, when admitted in the power of it, will dispose the soul to communion with God in all those ways wherein he has appointed us to meet him, and has promised to meet us. The greatness of the event raised them above the world, and the Holy Ghost filled them with such love, as made every one to be to another as to himself, and so made all things common, not by destroying property, but doing away selfishness, and causing charity. And God who moved them to it, knew that they were quickly to be driven from their possessions in Judea. The Lord, from day to day, inclined the hearts of more to embrace the gospel; not merely professors, but such as were actually brought into a state of acceptance with God, being made partakers of regenerating grace. Those whom God has designed for eternal salvation, shall be effectually brought to Christ, till the earth is filled with the knowledge of his glory.

Chapter 3

Chapter Outline

Verses 1-11

The apostles and the first believers attended the temple worship at the hours of prayer. Peter and John seem to have been led by a Divine direction, to work a miracle on a man above forty years old, who had been a cripple from his birth. Peter, in the name of Jesus of Nazareth, bade him rise up and walk. Thus, if we would attempt to good purpose the healing of men's souls, we must go forth in the name and power of Jesus Christ, calling on helpless sinners to arise and walk in the way of holiness, by faith in Him. How sweet the thought to our souls, that in respect to all the crippled faculties of our fallen nature, the name of Jesus Christ of Nazareth can make us whole! With what holy joy and rapture shall we tread the holy courts, when God the Spirit causes us to enter therein by his strength!

Verses 12-18

Observe the difference in the manner of working the miracles. Our Lord always spoke as having Almighty power, never hesitated to receive the greatest honour that was given to him on account of his Divine miracles. But the apostles referred all to their Lord, and refused to receive any honour, except as his undeserving instruments. This shows that Jesus was one with the Father, and co-equal with Him; while the apostles knew that they were weak, sinful men, and dependent for every thing on Jesus, whose power effected the cure. Useful men must be very humble. Not unto us, O Lord, not unto us, but to thy name, give glory. Every crown must be cast at the feet of Christ. The apostle showed the Jews the greatness of their crime, but would not anger or drive them to despair. Assuredly, those who reject, refuse, or deny Christ, do it through ignorance; but this can in no case be an excuse.

Verses 19-21

The absolute necessity of repentance is to be solemnly charged upon the consciences of all who desire that their sins may be blotted out, and that they may share in the refreshment which nothing but a sense of Christ's pardoning love can afford. Blessed are those who have felt this. It was not needful for the Holy Spirit to make known the times and seasons of these dispensations. These subjects are still left obscure. But when sinners are convinced of their sins, they will cry to the Lord for pardon; and to the penitent, converted, and believing, times of refreshment will come from the presence of the Lord. In a state of trial and probation, the glorified Redeemer will be out of sight, because we must live by faith in him.

Verses 22-26

Here is a powerful address to warn the Jews of the dreadful consequences of their unbelief, in the very words of Moses, their favourite prophet, out of pretended zeal for whom they were ready to reject Christianity, and to try to destroy it. Christ came into the world to bring a blessing with him. And he sent his Spirit to be the great blessing. Christ came to bless us, by turning us from our iniquities, and saving us from our sins. We, by nature cleave to sin; the design of Divine grace is to turn us from it, that we may not only forsake, but hate it. Let none think that they can be happy by continuing in sin, when God declares that the blessing is in being turned from all iniquity. Let none think that they understand or believe the gospel, who only seek deliverance from the punishment of sin, but do not expect happiness in being delivered from sin itself. And let none expect to be turned from their sin, except by believing in, and receiving Christ the Son of God, as their wisdom, righteousness, sanctification, and redemption.

Chapter 4

Chapter Outline

Verses 1-4

The apostles preached through Jesus the resurrection from the dead. It includes all the happiness of the future state; this they preached through Jesus Christ, to be had through him only. Miserable is their case, to whom the glory of Christ's kingdom is a grief; for since the glory of that kingdom is everlasting, their grief will be everlasting also. The harmless and useful servants of Christ, like the apostles, have often been troubled for their work of faith and labour of love, when wicked men have escaped. And to this day instances are not wanting, in which reading the Scriptures, social prayer, and religious conversation meet with frowns and checks. But if we obey the precepts of Christ, he will support us.

Verses 5-14

Peter being filled with the Holy Ghost, would have all to understand, that the miracle had been wrought by the name, or power, of Jesus of Nazareth, the Messiah, whom they had crucified; and this confirmed their testimony to his resurrection from the dead, which proved him to be the Messiah. These rulers must either be saved by that Jesus whom they had crucified, or they must perish for ever. The name of Jesus is given to men of every age and nation, as that whereby alone believers are saved from the wrath to come. But when covetousness, pride, or any corrupt passion, rules within, men shut their eyes, and close their hearts, in enmity against the light; considering all as ignorant and unlearned, who desire to know nothing in comparison with Christ crucified. And the followers of Christ should act so that all who converse with them, may take knowledge that they have been with Jesus. That makes them holy, heavenly, spiritual, and cheerful, and raises them above this world.

Verses 15-22

All the care of the rulers is, that the doctrine of Christ spread not among the people, yet they cannot say it is false or dangerous, or of any ill tendency; and they are ashamed to own the true reason; that it testifies against their hypocrisy, wickedness, and tyranny. Those who know how to put a just value upon Christ's promises, know how to put just contempt upon the world's threatenings. The apostles look with concern on perishing souls, and know they cannot escape eternal ruin but by Jesus Christ, therefore they are faithful in warning, and showing the right way. None will enjoy peace of mind, nor act uprightly, till they have learned to guide their conduct by the fixed standard of truth, and not by the shifting opinions and fancies of men. Especially beware of a vain attempt to serve two masters, God and the world; the end will be, you can serve neither fully.

Verses 23-31

Christ's followers do best in company, provided it is their own company. It encourages God's servants, both in doing work, and suffering work, that they serve the God who made all things, and therefore has the disposal of all events; and the Scriptures must be fulfilled. Jesus was anointed to be a Saviour, therefore it was determined he should be a sacrifice, to make atonement for sin. But sin is not the less evil for God's bringing good out of it. In threatening times, our care should not be so much that troubles may be prevented, as that we may go on with cheerfulness and courage in our work and duty. They do not pray, Lord let us go away from our work, now that it is become dangerous, but, Lord, give us thy grace to go on stedfastly in our work, and not to fear the face of man. Those who desire Divine aid and encouragement, may depend upon having them, and they ought to go forth, and go on, in the strength of the Lord God. God gave a sign of acceptance of their prayers. The place was shaken, that their faith might be established and unshaken. God gave them greater degrees of his Spirit; and they were all filled with the Holy Ghost, more than ever; by which they were not only encouraged, but enabled to speak the word of God with boldness. When they find the Lord God help them by his Spirit, they know they shall not be confounded, Isa 17.

Verses 32-37

The disciples loved one another. This was the blessed fruit of Christ's dying precept to his disciples, and his dying prayer for them. Thus it was then, and it will be so again, when the Spirit shall be poured upon us from on high. The doctrine preached was the resurrection of Christ; a matter of fact, which being duly explained, was a summary of all the duties, privileges, and comforts of Christians. There were evident fruits of Christ's grace in all they said and did. They were dead to this world. This was a great evidence of the grace of God in them. They did not take away others' property, but they were indifferent to it. They did not call it their own; because they had, in affection, forsaken all for Christ, and were expecting to be stripped of all for cleaving to him. No marvel that they were of one heart and soul, when they sat so loose to the wealth of this world. In effect, they had all things common; for there was not any among them who lacked, care was taken for their supply. The money was laid at the apostles' feet. Great care ought to be taken in the distribution of public charity, that it be given to such as have need, such as are not able to procure a maintenance for themselves; those who are reduced to want for well-doing, and for the testimony of a good conscience, ought to be provided for. Here is one in particular mentioned, remarkable for this generous charity; it was Barnabas. As one designed to be a preacher of the gospel, he disentangled himself from the affairs of this life. When such dispositions prevail, and are exercised according to the circumstances of the times, the testimony will have very great power upon others.

Chapter 5

Chapter Outline

Verses 1-11

The sin of Ananias and Sapphira was, that they were ambitious of being thought eminent disciples, when they were not true disciples. Hypocrites may deny themselves, may forego their worldly advantage in one instance, with a prospect of finding their account in something else. They were covetous of the wealth of the world, and distrustful of God and his providence. They thought they might serve both God and mammon. They thought to deceive the apostles. The Spirit of God in Peter discerned the principle of unbelief reigning in the heart of Ananias. But whatever Satan might suggest, he could not have filled the heart of Ananias with this wickedness had he not been consenting. The falsehood was an attempt to deceive the Spirit of truth, who so manifestly spoke and acted by the apostles. The crime of Ananias was not his retaining part of the price of the land; he might have kept it all, had he pleased; but his endeavouring to impose upon the apostles with an awful lie, from a desire to make a vain show, joined with covetousness. But if we think to put a cheat upon God, we shall put a fatal cheat upon our own souls. How sad to see those relations who should quicken one another to that which is good, hardening one another in that which is evil! And this punishment was in reality mercy to vast numbers. It would cause strict self-examination, prayer, and dread of hypocrisy, covetousness, and vain-glory, and it should still do so. It would prevent the increase of false professors. Let us learn hence how hateful falsehood is to the God of truth, and not only shun a direct lie, but all advantages from the use of doubtful expressions, and double meaning in our speech.

Verses 12-16

The separation of hypocrites by distinguishing judgments, should make the sincere cleave closer to each other and to the gospel ministry. Whatever tends to the purity and reputation of the church, promotes its enlargement; but that power alone which wrought such miracles by the apostles, can rescue sinners from the power of sin and Satan, and add believers to His worshippers. Christ will work by all his faithful servants; and every one who applies to him shall be healed.

Verses 17-25

There is no prison so dark, so strong, but God can visit his people in it, and, if he pleases, fetch them out. Recoveries from sickness, releases out of trouble, are granted, not that we may enjoy the comforts of life, but that God may be honoured with the services of our life. It is not for the preachers of Christ's gospel to retire into corners, as long as they can have any opportunity of preaching in the great congregation. They must preach to the lowest, whose souls are as precious to Christ as the souls of the greatest. Speak to all, for all are concerned. Speak as those who resolve to stand to it, to live and die by it. Speak all the words of this heavenly, divine life, in comparison with which the present earthly life does not deserve the name. These words of life, which the Holy Ghost puts into your mouth. The words of the gospel are the words of life; words whereby we may be saved. How wretched are those who are vexed at the success of the gospel! They cannot but see that the word and power of the Lord are against them; and they tremble for the consequences, yet they will go on.

Verses 26-33

Many will do an evil thing with daring, yet cannot bear to hear of it afterward, or to have it charged upon them. We cannot expect to be redeemed and healed by Christ, unless we give up ourselves to be ruled by him. Faith takes the Saviour in all his offices, who came, not to save us in our sins, but to save us from our sins. Had Christ been exalted to give dominion to Israel, the chief priests would have welcomed him. But repentance and remission of sins are blessings they neither valued nor saw their need of; therefore they, by no means, admitted his doctrine. Wherever repentance is wrought, remission is granted without fail. None are freed from the guilt and punishment of sin, but those who are freed from the power and dominion of sin; who are turned from it, and turned against it. Christ gives repentance, by his Spirit working with the word, to awaken the conscience, to work sorrow for sin, and an effectual change in the heart and life. The giving of the Holy Ghost, is plain evidence that it is the will of God that Christ should be obeyed. And He will surely destroy those who will not have Him to reign over them.

Verses 34-42

The Lord still has all hearts in his hands, and sometimes directs the prudence of the worldly wise, so as to restrain the persecutors. Common sense tells us to be cautious, while experience and observation show that the success of frauds in matters of religion has been very short. Reproach for Christ is true preferment, as it makes us conformable to his pattern, and serviceable to his interest. They rejoiced in it. If we suffer ill for doing well, provided we suffer it well, and as we should, we ought to rejoice in that grace which enabled us so to do. The apostles did not preach themselves, but Christ. This was the preaching that most offended the priests. But it ought to be the constant business of gospel ministers to preach Christ: Christ, and him crucified; Christ, and him glorified; nothing beside this, but what has reference to it. And whatever is our station or rank in life, we should seek to make Him known, and to glorify his name.

Chapter 6

Chapter Outline

The appointment of deacons.	(1–7)
Stephen falsely accused of blasphemy.	(8–15)

Verses 1-7

Hitherto the disciples had been of one accord; this often had been noticed to their honour; but now they were multiplied, they began to murmur. The word of God was enough to take up all the thoughts, cares, and time of the apostles. The persons chosen to serve tables must be duly qualified. They must be filled with gifts and graces of the Holy Ghost, necessary to rightly managing this trust; men of truth, and hating covetousness. All who are employed in the service of the church, ought to be commended to the Divine grace by the prayers of the church. They blessed them in the name of the Lord. The word and grace of God are greatly magnified, when those are wrought upon by it, who were least likely.

Verses 8-15

When they could not answer Stephen's arguments as a disputant, they prosecuted him as a criminal, and brought false witnesses against him. And it is next to a miracle of providence, that no greater number of religious persons have been murdered in the world, by the way of perjury and pretence of law, when so many thousands hate them, who make no conscience of false oaths. Wisdom and holiness make a man's face to shine, yet will not secure men from being treated badly. What shall we say of man, a rational being, yet attempting to uphold a religious system by false witness and murder! And this has been done in numberless instances. But the blame rests not so much upon the understanding, as upon the heart of a fallen creature, which is deceitful above all things and desperately wicked. Yet the servant of the Lord, possessing a clear conscience, cheerful hope, and Divine consolations, may smile in the midst of danger and death.

Chapter 7

Chapter Outline

Stephen's defence.	(1–50)
Stephen reproves the Jews for the death of Christ.	(51–53)
The martyrdom of Stephen.	(54–60)

Verses 1-16

Stephen was charged as a blasphemer of God, and an apostate from the church; therefore he shows that he is a son of Abraham, and values himself on it. The slow steps by which the promise made to Abraham advanced toward performance, plainly show that it had a spiritual meaning, and that the land intended was the heavenly. God owned Joseph in his troubles, and was with him by the power of his Spirit, both on his own mind by giving him comfort, and on those he was concerned with, by giving him favour in their eyes. Stephen reminds the Jews of their mean beginning as a check to priding themselves in the glories of that nation. Likewise of the wickedness of the patriarchs of their tribes, in envying their brother Joseph; and the same spirit was still working in them toward Christ and his ministers. The faith of the patriarchs, in desiring to be buried in the land of Canaan, plainly showed they had regard to the heavenly country. It is well to recur to the first rise of usages, or sentiments, which have been perverted. Would we know the nature and effects of justifying faith, we should study the character of the father of the faithful. His calling shows the power and freeness of Divine grace, and the nature of conversion. Here also we see that outward forms and distinctions are as nothing, compared with separation from the world, and devotedness to God.

Verses 17-29

Let us not be discouraged at the slowness of the fulfilling of God's promises. Suffering times often are growing times with the church. God is preparing for his people's deliverance, when their day is darkest, and their distress deepest. Moses was exceeding fair, "fair toward God;" it is the beauty of holiness which is in God's sight of great price. He was wonderfully preserved in his infancy; for God will take special care of those of whom he designs to make special use. And did he thus protect the child Moses? Much more will he secure the interests of his holy child Jesus, from the enemies who are gathered together against him. They persecuted Stephen for disputing in defence of Christ and his gospel: in opposition to these they set up Moses and his law. They may understand, if they do not wilfully shut their eyes against the light, that God will, by this Jesus, deliver them out of a worse slavery than that of Egypt. Although men prolong their own miseries, yet the Lord will take care of his servants, and effect his own designs of mercy.

Verses 30-41

Men deceive themselves, if they think God cannot do what he sees to be good any where; he can bring his people into a wilderness, and there speak comfortably to them. He appeared to Moses in a flame of fire, yet the bush was not consumed; which represented the state of Israel in Egypt, where, though they were in the fire of affliction, yet they were not consumed. It may also be looked upon as a type of Christ's taking upon him the nature of man, and the union between the Divine and human nature. The death of Abraham, Isaac, and Jacob, cannot break the covenant relation between God and them. Our Saviour by this proves the future state, Mt 22:31. Abraham is dead, yet God is still his God, therefore Abraham is still alive. Now, this is that life and immortality which are brought to light by the gospel. Stephen here shows that Moses was an eminent type of Christ, as he was Israel's deliverer. God has compassion for the troubles of his church, and the groans of his persecuted people; and their deliverance takes rise from his pity. And that deliverance was typical of what Christ did, when, for us men, and for our salvation, he came down from heaven. This Jesus, whom they now refused, as their fathers did Moses, even this same has God advanced to be a Prince and Saviour. It does not at all take from the just honour of Moses to say, that he was but an instrument, and that he is infinitely outshone by Jesus. In asserting that Jesus should change the customs of the ceremonial law. Stephen was so far from blaspheming Moses, that really he honoured him, by showing how the prophecy of Moses was come to pass, which was so clear. God who gave them those customs by his servant Moses, might, no doubt, change the custom by his Son Jesus. But Israel thrust Moses from them, and would have returned to their bondage; so men in general will not obey Jesus, because they love this present evil world, and rejoice in their own works and devices.

Verses 42-50

Stephen upbraids the Jews with the idolatry of their fathers, to which God gave them up as a punishment for their early forsaking him. It was no dishonour, but an honour to God, that the tabernacle gave way to the temple; so it is now, that the earthly temple gives way to the spiritual one; and so it will be when, at last, the spiritual shall give way to the eternal one. The whole world is God's temple, in which he is every where present, and fills it with his glory; what occasion has he then for a temple to manifest himself in? And these things show his eternal power and Godhead. But as heaven is his throne, and the earth his footstool, so none of our services can profit Him who made all things. Next to the human nature of Christ, the broken and spiritual heart is his most valued temple.

Verses 51-53

Stephen was going on, it seems, to show that the temple and the temple service must come to an end, and it would be the glory of both to give way to the worship of the Father in spirit and in truth; but he perceived they would not bear it. Therefore he broke off, and by the Spirit of wisdom, courage, and power, sharply rebuked his persecutors. When plain arguments and truths provoke the opposers of the gospel, they should be shown their guilt and danger. They, like their fathers, were stubborn and wilful. There is that in our sinful hearts, which always resists the Holy Ghost, a flesh that lusts against the Spirit, and wars against his motions; but in the hearts of God's elect, when the fulness of time comes, this resistance is overcome. The gospel was offered now, not by angels, but from the Holy Ghost; yet they did not embrace it, for they were resolved not to comply with God, either in his law or in his gospel. Their guilt stung them to the heart, and they sought relief in murdering their reprover, instead of sorrow and supplication for mercy.

Verses 54-60

Nothing is so comfortable to dying saints, or so encouraging to suffering saints, as to see Jesus at the right hand of God: blessed be God, by faith we may see him there. Stephen offered up two short prayers in his dying moments. Our Lord Jesus is God, to whom we are to seek, and in whom we are to trust and comfort ourselves, living and dying. And if this has been our care while we live, it will be our comfort when we die. Here is a prayer for his persecutors. Though the sin was very great, yet if they would lay it to their hearts, God would not lay it to their charge. Stephen died as much in a hurry as ever any man did, yet, when he died, the words used are, he fell asleep; he applied himself to his dying work with as much composure as if he had been going to sleep. He shall awake again in the morning of the resurrection, to be received into the presence of the Lord, where is fulness of joy, and to share the pleasures that are at his right hand, for evermore.

Chapter 8

Chapter Outline

Verses 1-4

Though persecution must not drive us from our work, yet it may send us to work elsewhere. Wherever the established believer is driven, he carries the knowledge of the gospel, and makes known the preciousness of Christ in every place. Where a simple desire of doing good influences the heart, it will be found impossible to shut a man out from all opportunities of usefulness.

Verses 5-13

As far as the gospel prevails, evil spirits are dislodged, particularly unclean spirits. All inclinations to the lusts of the flesh which war against the soul are such. Distempers are here named, the most difficult to be cured by the course of nature, and most expressive of the disease of sin. Pride, ambition, and desire after grandeur have always caused abundance of mischief, both to the world and to the church. The people said of Simon, This man is the great power of God. See how ignorant and thoughtless people mistake. But how strong is the power of Divine grace, by which they were brought to Christ, who is Truth itself! The people not only gave heed to what Philip said, but were fully convinced that it was of God, and not of men, and gave up themselves to be directed thereby. Even bad men, and those whose hearts still go after covetousness, may come before God as his people come, and for a time continue with them. And many wonder at the proofs of Divine truths, who never experience their power. The gospel preached may have a common operation upon a soul, where it never produced inward holiness. All are not savingly converted who profess to believe the gospel.

Verses 14-25

The Holy Ghost was as yet fallen upon none of these coverts, in the extraordinary powers conveyed by the descent of the Spirit upon the day of Pentecost. We may take encouragement from this example, in praying to God to give the renewing graces of the Holy Ghost to all for whose spiritual welfare we are concerned; for that includes all blessings. No man can give the Holy Spirit by the laying on of his hands; but we should use our best endeavours to instruct those for whom we pray. Simon Magus was ambitious to have the honour of an apostle, but cared not at all to have the spirit and disposition of a Christian. He was more desirous to gain honour to himself, than to do good to others. Peter shows him his crime. He esteemed the wealth of this world, as if it would answer for things relating to the other life, and would purchase the pardon of sin, the gift of the Holy Ghost, and eternal life. This was such a condemning error as could by no means consist with a state of grace. Our hearts are what they are in the sight of God, who cannot be deceived. And if they are not right in his sight, our religion is vain, and will stand us in no stead. A proud and covetous heart cannot be right with God. It is possible for a man to continue under the power of sin, yet to put on a form of godliness. When tempted with money to do evil, see what a perishing thing money is, and scorn it. Think not that Christianity is a trade to live by in this world. There is much wickedness in the thought of the heart, its false notions, and corrupt affections, and wicked projects, which must be repented of, or we are undone. But it shall be forgiven, upon our repentance. The doubt here is of the sincerity of Simon's repentance, not of his pardon, if his repentance was sincere. Grant us, Lord, another sort of faith than that which made Simon wonder only, and did not sanctify his heart. May we abhor all thoughts of making religion serve the purposes of pride or ambition.

And keep us from that subtle poison of spiritual pride, which seeks glory to itself even from humility. May we seek only the honour which cometh from God.

Verses 26-40

Philip was directed to go to a desert. Sometimes God opens a door of opportunity to his ministers in very unlikely places. We should study to do good to those we come into company with by travelling. We should not be so shy of all strangers as some affect to be. As to those of whom we know nothing else, we know this, that they have souls. It is wisdom for men of business to redeem time for holy duties; to fill up every minute with something which will turn to a good account. In reading the word of God, we should often pause, to inquire of whom and of what the sacred writers spake; but especially our thoughts should be employed about the Redeemer. The Ethiopian was convinced by the teaching of the Holy Spirit, of the exact fulfilment of the Scripture, was made to understand the nature of the Messiah's kingdom and salvation, and desired to be numbered among the disciples of Christ. Those who seek the truth, and employ their time in searching the Scriptures, will be sure to reap advantages. The avowal of the Ethiopian must be understood as expressing simple reliance on Christ for salvation, and unreserved devotion to Him. Let us not be satisfied till we get faith, as the Ethiopian did, by diligent study of the Holy Scriptures, and the teaching of the Spirit of God; let us not be satisfied till we get it fixed as a principle in our hearts. As soon as he was baptized, the Spirit of God took Philip from him, so that he saw him no more; but this tended to confirm his faith. When the inquirer after salvation becomes acquainted with Jesus and his gospel, he will go on his way rejoicing, and will fill up his station in society, and discharge his duties, from other motives, and in another manner than heretofore. Though baptized in the name of the Father, Son, and Holy Ghost, with water, it is not enough without the baptism of the Holy Ghost. Lord, grant this to every one of us; then shall we go on our way rejoicing.

Chapter 9

Chapter Outline

Verses 1-9

So ill informed was Saul, that he thought he ought to do all he could against the name of Christ, and that he did God service thereby; he seemed to breathe in this as in his element. Let us not despair of renewing grace for the conversion of the greatest sinners, nor let such despair of the pardoning mercy of God for the greatest sin. It is a signal token of Divine favour, if God, by the inward working of his grace, or the outward events of his providence, stops us from prosecuting or executing sinful purposes. Saul saw that Just One, ch. 22:14; 26:13. How near to us is the unseen world! It is but for God to draw aside the veil, and objects are presented to the view, compared with which, whatever is most admired on earth is mean and contemptible. Saul submitted without reserve, desirous to know what the Lord Jesus would have him to do. Christ's discoveries of himself to poor souls are humbling; they lay them very low, in mean thoughts of themselves. For three days Saul took no food, and it pleased God to leave him for that time without relief. His sins were now set in order before him; he was in the dark concerning his own spiritual state, and wounded in spirit for sin. When a sinner is brought to a proper sense of his own state and conduct, he will cast himself wholly on the mercy of the Saviour, asking what he would have him to do. God will direct the humbled sinner, and though he does not often bring transgressors to joy and peace in believing, without sorrows and distress of conscience, under which the soul is deeply engaged as to eternal things, yet happy are those who sow in tears, for they shall reap in joy.

Verses 10-22

A good work was begun in Saul, when he was brought to Christ's feet with those words, Lord, what wilt thou have me to do? And never did Christ leave any who were brought to that. Behold, the proud Pharisee, the unmerciful oppressor, the daring blasphemer, prayeth! And thus it is even now, and with the proud infidel, or the abandoned sinner. What happy tidings are these to all who understand the nature and power of prayer, of such prayer as the humbled sinner presents for the blessings of free salvation! Now he began to pray after another manner than he had done; before, he said his prayers, now, he prayed them. Regenerating grace sets people on praying; you may as well find a living man without breath, as a living Christian without prayer. Yet even eminent disciples, like Ananias, sometimes stagger at the commands of the Lord. But it is the Lord's glory to surpass our scanty expectations, and show that those are vessels of his mercy whom we are apt to consider as objects of his vengeance. The teaching of the Holy Spirit takes away the scales of ignorance and pride from the understanding; then the sinner becomes a new creature, and endeavours to recommend the anointed Saviour, the Son of God, to his former companions.

Verses 23-31

When we enter into the way of God, we must look for trials; but the Lord knows how to deliver the godly, and will, with the temptation, also make a way to escape. Though Saul's conversion was and is a proof of the truth of Christianity, yet it could not, of itself, convert one soul at enmity with the truth; for nothing can produce true faith, but that power which new-creates the heart. Believers are apt to be too suspicious of those against whom they have prejudices. The world is full of deceit, and it is necessary to be cautious, but we must exercise charity, 1Co 13:5. The Lord will clear up the characters of true believers; and he will bring them to his people, and often gives them opportunities of bearing testimony to his truth, before those who once witnessed their hatred to it. Christ now appeared to Saul, and ordered him to go quickly out of Jerusalem, for he must be sent to the Gentiles: see ch. 22:21. Christ's witnesses cannot be slain till they have finished their testimony.

The persecutions were stayed. The professors of the gospel walked uprightly, and enjoyed much comfort from the Holy Ghost, in the hope and peace of the gospel, and others were won over to them. They lived upon the comfort of the Holy Ghost, not only in the days of trouble and affliction, but in days of rest and prosperity. Those are most likely to walk cheerfully, who walk circumspectly.

Verses 32-35

Christians are saints, or holy people; not only the eminent ones, as Saint Peter and Saint Paul, but every sincere professor of the faith of Christ. Christ chose patients whose diseases were incurable in the course of nature, to show how desperate was the case of fallen mankind. When we were wholly without strength, as this poor man, he sent his word to heal us. Peter does not pretend to heal by any power of his own, but directs Eneas to look up to Christ for help. Let none say, that because it is Christ, who, by the power of his grace, works all our works in us, therefore we have no work, no duty to do; for though Jesus Christ makes thee whole, yet thou must arise, and use the power he gives thee.

Verses 36-43

Many are full of good words, who are empty and barren in good works; but Tabitha was a great doer, no great talker. Christians who have not property to give in charity, may yet be able to do acts of charity, working with their hands, or walking with their feet, for the good of others. Those are certainly best praised whose own works praise them, whether the words of others do so or not. But such are ungrateful indeed, who have kindness shown them, and will not acknowledge it, by showing the kindness that is done them. While we live upon the fulness of Christ for our whole salvation, we should desire to be full of good works, for the honour of his name, and for the benefit of his saints. Such characters as Dorcas are useful where they dwell, as showing the excellency of the word of truth by their lives. How mean then the cares of the numerous females who seek no distinction but outward decoration, and who waste their lives in the trifling pursuits of dress and vanity! Power went along with the word, and Dorcas came to life. Thus in the raising of dead souls to spiritual life, the first sign of life is the opening of the eyes of the mind. Here we see that the Lord can make up every loss; that he overrules every event for the good of those who trust in him, and for the glory of his name.

Chapter 10

Chapter Outline

The gifts of the Holy Spirit poured out.   (44–48)

Verses 1-8

Hitherto none had been baptized into the Christian church but Jews, Samaritans, and those converts who had been circumcised and observed the ceremonial law; but now the Gentiles were to be called to partake all the privileges of God's people, without first becoming Jews. Pure and undefiled religion is sometimes found where we least expect it. Wherever the fear of God rules in the heart, it will appear both in works of charity and of piety, neither will excuse from the other. Doubtless Cornelius had true faith in God's word, as far as he understood it, though not as yet clear faith in Christ. This was the work of the Spirit of God, through the mediation of Jesus, even before Cornelius knew him, as is the case with us all when we, who before were dead in sin, are made alive. Through Christ also his prayers and alms were accepted, which otherwise would have been rejected. Without dispute or delay Cornelius was obedient to the heavenly vision. In the affairs of our souls, let us not lose time.

Verses 9-18

The prejudices of Peter against the Gentiles, would have prevented his going to Cornelius, unless the Lord had prepared him for this service. To tell a Jew that God had directed those animals to be reckoned clean which were hitherto deemed unclean, was in effect saying, that the law of Moses was done away. Peter was soon made to know the meaning of it. God knows what services are before us, and how to prepare us; and we know the meaning of what he has taught us, when we find what occasion we have to make use of it.

Verses 19-33

When we see our call clear to any service, we should not be perplexed with doubts and scruples arising from prejudices or former ideas. Cornelius had called together his friends, to partake with him of the heavenly wisdom he expected from Peter. We should not covet to eat our spiritual morsels alone. It ought to be both given and taken as kindness and respect to our kindred and friends, to invite them to join us in religious exercises. Cornelius declared the direction God gave him to send for Peter. We are right in our aims in attending a gospel ministry, when we do it with regard to the Divine appointment requiring us to make use of that ordinance. How seldom ministers are called to speak to such companies, however small, in which it may be said that they are all present in the sight of God, to hear all things that are commanded of God! But these were ready to hear what Peter was commanded of God to say.

Verses 34-43

Acceptance cannot be obtained on any other ground than that of the covenant of mercy, through the atonement of Christ; but wherever true religion is found, God will accept it without regarding names or sects. The fear of God and works of righteousness are the substance of true religion, the effects of special grace. Though these are not the cause of a man's acceptance, yet they show it;

and whatever may be wanting in knowledge or faith, will in due time be given by Him who has begun it. They knew in general the word, that is, the gospel, which God sent to the children of Israel. The purport of this word was, that God by it published the good tidings of peace by Jesus Christ. They knew the several matters of fact relating to the gospel. They knew the baptism of repentance which John preached. Let them know that this Jesus Christ, by whom peace is made between God and man, is Lord of all; not only as over all, God blessed for evermore, but as Mediator. All power, both in heaven and in earth, is put into his hand, and all judgment committed to him. God will go with those whom he anoints; he will be with those to whom he has given his Spirit. Peter then declares Christ's resurrection from the dead, and the proofs of it. Faith has reference to a testimony, and the Christian faith is built upon the foundation of the apostles and prophets, on the testimony given by them. See what must be believed concerning him. That we are all accountable to Christ as our Judge; so every one must seek his favour, and to have him as our Friend. And if we believe in him, we shall all be justified by him as our Righteousness. The remission of sins lays a foundation for all other favours and blessings, by taking that out of the way which hinders the bestowing of them. If sin be pardoned, all is well, and shall end well for ever.

Verses 44-48

The Holy Ghost fell upon others after they were baptized, to confirm them in the faith; but upon these Gentiles before they were baptized, to show that God does not confine himself to outward signs. The Holy Ghost fell upon those who were neither circumcised nor baptized; it is the Spirit that quickeneth, the flesh profiteth nothing. They magnified God, and spake of Christ and the benefits of redemption. Whatever gift we are endued with, we ought to honour God with it. The believing Jews who were present, were astonished that the gift of the Holy Ghost was poured out upon the Gentiles also. By mistaken notions of things, we make difficult for ourselves as to the methods of Divine providence and grace. As they were undeniably baptized with the Holy Ghost, Peter concluded they were not to be refused the baptism of water, and the ordinance was administered. The argument is conclusive; can we deny the sign to those who have received the things signified? Those who have some acquaintance with Christ, cannot but desire more. Even those who have received the Holy Ghost, must see their need of daily learning more of the truth.

Chapter 11

Chapter Outline

Verses 1-18

The imperfect state of human nature strongly appears, when godly persons are displeased even to hear that the word of God has been received, because their own system has not been attended to. And we are too apt to despair of doing good to those who yet, when tried, prove very teachable. It is the bane and damage of the church, to shut out those from it, and from the benefit of the means of grace, who are not in every thing as we are. Peter stated the whole affair. We should at all times bear with the infirmities of our brethren; and instead of taking offence, or answering with warmth, we should explain our motives, and show the nature of our proceedings. That preaching is certainly right, with which the Holy Ghost is given. While men are very zealous for their own regulations, they should take care that they do not withstand God; and those who love the Lord will glorify him, when made sure that he has given repentance to life to any fellow-sinners. Repentance is God's gift; not only his free grace accepts it, but his mighty grace works it in us, grace takes away the heart of stone, and gives us a heart of flesh. The sacrifice of God is a broken spirit.

Verses 19-24

The first preachers of the gospel at Antioch, were dispersed from Jerusalem by persecution; thus what was meant to hurt the church, was made to work for its good. The wrath of man is made to praise God. What should the ministers of Christ preach, but Christ? Christ, and him crucified? Christ, and him glorified? And their preaching was accompanied with the Divine power. The hand of the Lord was with them, to bring that home to the hearts and consciences of men, which they could but speak to the outward ear. They believed; they were convinced of the truth of the gospel. They turned from a careless, carnal way of living, to live a holy, heavenly, spiritual life. They turned from worshipping God in show and ceremony, to worship him in the Spirit and in truth. They turned to the Lord Jesus, and he became all in all with them. This was the work of conversion wrought upon them, and it must be wrought upon every one of us. It was the fruit of their faith; all who sincerely believe, will turn to the Lord, When the Lord Jesus is preached in simplicity, and according to the Scriptures, he will give success; and when sinners are thus brought to the Lord, really good men, who are full of faith and of the Holy Ghost, will admire and rejoice in the grace of God bestowed on them. Barnabas was full of faith; full of the grace of faith, and full of the fruits of the faith that works by love.

Verses 25-30

Hitherto the followers of Christ were called disciples, that is, learners, scholars; but from that time they were called Christians. The proper meaning of this name is, a follower of Christ; it denotes one who, from serious thought, embraces the religion of Christ, believes his promises, and makes it his chief care to shape his life by Christ's precepts and example. Hence it is plain that multitudes take the name of Christian to whom it does not rightly belong. But the name without the reality will only add to our guilt. While the bare profession will bestow neither profit nor delight, the possession of it will give both the promise of the life that now is, and of that which is to come. Grant, Lord, that Christians may forget other names and distinctions, and love one another as the followers of Christ ought to do. True Christians will feel for their brethren under afflictions. Thus will fruit be brought forth to the praise and glory of God. If all mankind were true Christians, how cheerfully would they help one another! The whole earth would be like one large family, every member of which would strive to be dutiful and kind.

Chapter 12

Chapter Outline

Verses 1-5

James was one of the sons of Zebedee, whom Christ told that they should drink of the cup that he was to drink of, and be baptized with the baptism that he was to be baptized with, Mt 20:23. Now the words of Christ were made good in him; and if we suffer with Christ, we shall reign with him. Herod imprisoned Peter: the way of persecution, as of other sins, is downhill; when men are in it, they cannot easily stop. Those make themselves an easy prey to Satan, who make it their business to please men. Thus James finished his course. But Peter, being designed for further services, was safe; though he seemed now marked out for a speedy sacrifice. We that live in a cold, prayerless generation, can hardly form an idea of the earnestness of these holy men of old. But if the Lord should bring on the church an awful persecution like this of Herod, the faithful in Christ would learn what soul-felt prayer is.

Verses 6-11

A peaceful conscience, a lively hope, and the consolations of the Holy Spirit, can keep men calm in the full prospect of death; even those very persons who have been most distracted with terrors on that account. God's time to help, is when things are brought to the last extremity. Peter was assured that the Lord would cause this trial to end in the way that should be most for his glory. Those who are delivered out of spiritual imprisonment must follow their Deliverer, like the Israelites when they went out of the house of bondage. They knew not whither they went, but knew whom they followed. When God will work salvation for his people, all difficulties in their way will be overcome, even gates of iron are made to open of their own accord. This deliverance of Peter represents our redemption by Christ, which not only proclaims liberty to the captives, but brings them out of the prison-house. Peter, when he recollected himself, perceived what great things God had done for him. Thus souls delivered out of spiritual bondage, are not at first aware what God has wrought in them; many have the truth of grace, that want evidence of it. But when the Comforter comes, whom the Father will send, sooner or later, he will let them know what a blessed change is wrought.

Verses 12-19

God's providence leaves room for the use of our prudence, though he has undertaken to perform and perfect what he has begun. These Christians continued in prayer for Peter, for they were truly in earnest. Thus men ought always to pray, and not to faint. As long as we are kept waiting for a mercy, we must continue praying for it. But sometimes that which we most earnestly wish for, we are most backward to believe. The Christian law of self-denial and of suffering for Christ, has not done away the natural law of caring for our own safety by lawful means. In times of public danger, all believers have God for their hiding-place; which is so secret, that the world cannot find them. Also, the instruments of persecution are themselves exposed to danger; the wrath of God hangs over all that engage in this hateful work. And the range of persecutors often vents itself on all in its way.

Verses 20-25

Many heathen princes claimed and received Divine honours, but it was far more horrible impiety in Herod, who knew the word and worship of the living God, to accept such idolatrous honours without rebuking the blasphemy. And such men as Herod, when puffed with pride and vanity, are ripening fast for signal vengeance. God is very jealous for his own honour, and will be glorified upon those whom he is not glorified by. See what vile bodies we carry about with us; they have in them the seeds of their own dissolution, by which they will soon be destroyed, whenever God does but speak the word. We may learn wisdom from the people of Tyre and Sidon, for we have offended the Lord with our sins. We depend on him for life, and breath, and all things; it surely then behoves us to humble ourselves before him, that through the appointed Mediator, who is ever ready to befriend us, we may be reconciled to him, lest wrath come upon us to the utmost.

Chapter 13

Chapter Outline

Verses 1-3

What an assemblage was here! In these names we see that the Lord raises up instruments for his work, from various places and stations in life; and zeal for his glory induces men to give up flattering connexions and prospects to promote his cause. It is by the Spirit of Christ that his ministers are made both able and willing for his service, and taken from other cares that would hinder in it. Christ's ministers are to be employed in Christ's work, and, under the Spirit's guidance, to act for the glory of God the Father. They are separated to take pains, and not to take state. A blessing upon Barnabas and Saul in their present undertaking was sought for, and that they might be filled with the Holy Ghost in their work. Whatever means are used, or rules observed, the Holy Ghost alone can fit ministers for their important work, and call them to it.

Verses 4-13

Satan is in a special manner busy with great men and men in power, to keep them from being religious, for their example will influence many. Saul is here for the first time called Paul, and never after Saul. Saul was his name as he was a Hebrew; Paul was his name as he was a citizen of Rome. Under the direct influence of the Holy Ghost, he gave Elymas his true character, but not in passion. A fulness of deceit and mischief together, make a man indeed a child of the devil. And those who are enemies to the doctrine of Jesus, are enemies to all righteousness; for in it all righteousness is fulfilled. The ways of the Lord Jesus are the only right ways to heaven and happiness. There are many who not only wander from these ways themselves, but set others against these ways. They commonly are so hardened, that they will not cease to do evil. The proconsul was astonished at the force of the doctrine upon his own heart and conscience, and at the power of God by which it was confirmed. The doctrine of Christ astonishes; and the more we know of it, the more reason we shall see to wonder at it. Those who put their hand to the plough and look back, are not fit for the kingdom of God. Those who are not prepared to face opposition, and to endure hardship, are not fitted for the work of the ministry.

Verses 14-31

When we come together to worship God, we must do it, not only by prayer and praise, but by the reading and hearing of the word of God. The bare reading of the Scriptures in public assemblies is not enough; they should be expounded, and the people exhorted out of them. This is helping people in doing that which is necessary to make the word profitable, to apply it to themselves. Every thing is touched upon in this sermon, which might best prevail with Jews to receive and embrace Christ as the promised Messiah. And every view, however short or faint, of the Lord's dealings with his church, reminds us of his mercy and long-suffering, and of man's ingratitude and perverseness. Paul passes from David to the Son of David, and shows that this Jesus is his promised Seed; a Saviour to do that for them, which the judges of old could not do, to save them from their sins, their worst enemies. When the apostles preached Christ as the Saviour, they were so far from concealing his death, that they always preached Christ crucified. Our complete separation from sin, is represented by our being buried with Christ. But he rose again from the dead, and saw no corruption: this was the great truth to be preached.

Verses 32-37

The resurrection of Christ was the great proof of his being the Son of God. It was not possible he should be held by death, because he was the Son of God, and therefore had life in himself, which he could not lay down but with a design to take it again. The sure mercies of David are that everlasting life, of which the resurrection was a sure pledge; and the blessings of redemption in Christ are a certain earnest, even in this world. David was a great blessing to the age wherein he lived. We were not born for ourselves, but there are those living around us, to whom we must study to be serviceable. Yet here is the difference; Christ was to serve all generations. May we look to Him who is declared to be the Son of God by his resurrection from the dead, that by faith in him we may walk with God, and serve our generation according to his will; and when death comes, may we fall asleep in him, with a joyful hope of a blessed resurrection.

Verses 38-41

Let all that hear the gospel of Christ, know these two things: 1. That through this Man, who died and rose again, is preached unto you the forgiveness of sins. Your sins, though many and great, may be forgiven, and they may be so without any injury to God's honour. 2. It is by Christ only that those who believe in him, and none else, are justified from all things; from all the guilt and stain of sin, from which they could not be justified by the law of Moses. The great concern of convinced sinners is, to be justified, to be acquitted from all their guilt, and accepted as righteous in God's sight, for if any is left charged upon the sinner, he is undone. By Jesus Christ we obtain a complete justification; for by him a complete atonement was made for sin. We are justified, not only by him as our Judge but by him as the Lord our Righteousness. What the law could not do for us, in that it was weak, the gospel of Christ does. This is the most needful blessing, bringing in every other. The threatenings are warnings; what we are told will come upon impenitent sinners, is designed to awaken us to beware lest it come upon us. It ruins many, that they despise religion. Those that will not wonder and be saved, shall wonder and perish.

Verses 42-52

The Jews opposed the doctrine the apostles preached; and when they could find no objection, they blasphemed Christ and his gospel. Commonly those who begin with contradicting, end with blaspheming. But when adversaries of Christ's cause are daring, its advocates should be the bolder. And while many judge themselves unworthy of eternal life, others, who appear less likely, desire to hear more of the glad tidings of salvation. This is according to what was foretold in the Old Testament. What light, what power, what a treasure does this gospel bring with it! How excellent are its truths, its precepts, its promises! Those came to Christ whom the Father drew, and to whom the Spirit made the gospel call effectual, Ro 8:30. As many as were disposed to eternal life, as many as had concern about their eternal state, and aimed to make sure of eternal life, believed in Christ, in whom God has treasured up that life, and who is the only Way to it; and it was the grace of God that wrought it in them. It is good to see honourable women devout; the less they have to do in the world, the more they should do for their own souls, and the souls of others: but it is sad, when, under colour of devotion to God, they try to show hatred to Christ. And the more we relish the comforts and encouragements we meet with in the power of godliness, and the fuller our hearts are of them, the better prepared we are to face difficulties in the profession of godliness.

Chapter 14

Chapter Outline

Verses 1-7

The apostles spake so plainly, with such evidence and proof of the Spirit, and with such power; so warmly, and with such concern for the souls of men; that those who heard them could not but say, God was with them of a truth. Yet the success was not to be reckoned to the manner of their preaching, but to the Spirit of God who used that means. Perseverance in doing good, amidst dangers and hardships, is a blessed evidence of grace. Wherever God's servants are driven, they should seek to declare the truth. When they went on in Christ's name and strength, he failed not to give testimony to the word of his grace. He has assured us it is the word of God, and that we may venture our souls upon it. The Gentiles and Jews were at enmity with one another, yet united against Christians. If the church's enemies join to destroy it, shall not its friends unite for its preservation? God has a shelter for his people in a storm; he is, and will be their Hiding-place. In times of persecution, believers may see cause to quit a spot, though they do not quit their Master's work.

Verses 8-18

All things are possible to those that believe. When we have faith, that most precious gift of God, we shall be delivered from the spiritual helplessness in which we were born, and from the dominion of sinful habits since formed; we shall be made able to stand upright and walk cheerfully in the ways of the Lord. When Christ, the Son of God, appeared in the likeness of men, and did many miracles, men were so far from doing sacrifice to him, that they made him a sacrifice to their pride and malice; but Paul and Barnabas, upon their working one miracle, were treated as gods. The same power of the god of this world, which closes the carnal mind against truth, makes errors and mistakes find easy admission. We do not learn that they rent their clothes when the people spake of stoning them; but when they spake of worshipping them; they could not bear it, being more concerned for God's honour than their own. God's truth needs not the services of man's falsehood. The servants of God might easily obtain undue honours if they would wink at men's errors and vices; but they must dread and detest such respect more than any reproach. When the apostles preached to the Jews, who hated idolatry, they had only to preach the grace of God in Christ; but when they had to do with the Gentiles, they must set right their mistakes in natural religion. Compare their conduct and declaration with the false opinions of those who think the worship of a God, under any name, or in any manner, is equally acceptable to the Lord Almighty. The most powerful arguments, the most earnest and affectionate addresses, even with miracles, are scarcely enough to keep men from absurdities and abominations; much less can they, without special grace, turn the hearts of sinners to God and to holiness.

Verses 19-28

See how restless the rage of the Jews was against the gospel of Christ. The people stoned Paul, in a popular tumult. So strong is the bent of the corrupt and carnal heart, that as it is with great difficulty that men are kept back from evil on one side, so it is with great ease they are persuaded to evil on the other side. If Paul would have been Mercury, he might have been worshipped; but if he will be a faithful minister of Christ, he shall be stoned, and thrown out of the city. Thus men who easily submit to strong delusions, hate to receive the truth in the love of it. All who are converted need to be confirmed in the faith; all who are planted need to be rooted. Ministers' work is to establish saints as well as to awaken sinners. The grace of God, and nothing less, effectually establishes the souls of the disciples. It is true, we must count upon much tribulation, but it is encouragement that we shall not be lost and perish in it. The Person to whose power and grace the converts and the newly-established churches are commended, clearly was the Lord Jesus, "on whom they had believed." It was an act of worship. The praise of all the little good we do at any time, must be ascribed to God; for it is He who not only worketh in us both to will and to do, but also worketh with us to make what we do successful. All who love the Lord Jesus, will rejoice to hear that he has opened the door of faith wide, to those who were strangers to him and to his salvation. And let us, like the apostles, abide with those who know and love the Lord.

Chapter 15

Chapter Outline

Verses 1-6

Some from Judea taught the Gentile converts at Antioch, that they could not be saved, unless they observed the whole ceremonial law as given by Moses; and thus they sought to destroy Christian liberty. There is a strange proneness in us to think that all do wrong who do not just as we do. Their doctrine was very discouraging. Wise and good men desire to avoid contests and disputes as far as they can; yet when false teachers oppose the main truths of the gospel, or bring in hurtful doctrines, we must not decline to oppose them.

Verses 7-21

We see from the words "purifying their hearts by faith," and the address of St. Peter, that justification by faith, and sanctification by the Holy Ghost, cannot be separated; and that both are the gift of God. We have great cause to bless God that we have heard the gospel. May we have that faith which the great Searcher of hearts approves, and attests by the seal of the Holy Spirit. Then our hearts and consciences will be purified from the guilt of sin, and we shall be freed from the burdens some try to lay upon the disciples of Christ. Paul and Barnabas showed by plain matters of fact, that God owned the preaching of the pure gospel to the Gentiles without the law of Moses; therefore to press that law upon them, was to undo what God had done. The opinion of James was, that the Gentile converts ought not to be troubled about Jewish rites, but that they should abstain from meats offered to idols, so that they might show their hatred of idolatry. Also, that they should be cautioned against fornication, which was not abhorred by the Gentiles as it should be, and even formed a part of some of their rites. They were counselled to abstain from things strangled, and from eating blood; this was forbidden by the law of Moses, and also here, from reverence to the blood of the sacrifices, which being then still offered, it would needlessly grieve the Jewish converts, and further prejudice the unconverted Jews. But as the reason has long ceased, we are left free in this, as in the like matters. Let converts be warned to avoid all appearances of the evils which they formerly practised, or are likely to be tempted to; and caution them to use Christian liberty with moderation and prudence.

Verses 22-35

Being warranted to declare themselves directed by the immediate influence of the Holy Ghost, the apostles and disciples were assured that it seemed good unto God the Holy Spirit, as well as to them, to lay upon the converts no other burden than the things before mentioned, which were necessary, either on their own account, or from present circumstances. It was a comfort to hear that carnal ordinances were no longer imposed on them, which perplexed the conscience, but could not purify or pacify it; and that those who troubled their minds were silenced, so that the peace of the church was restored, and that which threatened division was removed. All this was consolation for which they blessed God. Many others were at Antioch. Where many labour in the word and doctrine, yet there may be opportunity for us: the zeal and usefulness of others should stir us up, not lay us asleep.

Verses 36-41

Here we have a private quarrel between two ministers, no less than Paul and Barnabas, yet made to end well. Barnabas wished his nephew John Mark to go with them. We should suspect ourselves of being partial, and guard against this in putting our relations forward. Paul did not think him worthy of the honour, nor fit for the service, who had departed from them without their knowledge, or without their consent: see ch. 13:13. Neither would yield, therefore there was no remedy but they must part. We see that the best of men are but men, subject to like passions as we are. Perhaps there were faults on both sides, as usual in such contentions. Christ's example alone, is a copy without a blot. Yet we are not to think it strange, if there are differences among wise and good men. It will be so while we are in this imperfect state; we shall never be all of one mind till we come to heaven. But what mischief the remainders of pride and passion which are found even in good men, do in the world, and do in the church! Many who dwelt at Antioch, who had heard but little of the devotedness and piety of Paul and Barnabas, heard of their dispute and separation; and thus it will be with ourselves, if we give way to contention. Believers must be constant in prayer, that they may never be led by the allowance of unholy tempers, to hurt the cause they really desire to serve. Paul speaks with esteem and affection both of Barnabas and Mark, in his epistles, written after this event. May all who profess thy name, O loving Saviour, be thoroughly reconciled by that love derived from thee which is not easily provoked, and which soon forgets and buries injuries.

Chapter 16

Chapter Outline

Paul takes Timothy to be his assistant.	(1–5)
Paul proceeds to Macedonia, The conversion of Lydia.	(6–15)
An evil spirit cast out, Paul and Silas scourged and imprisoned.	(16–24)
The conversion of the jailer at Philippi.	(25–34)
Paul and Silas released.	(35–40)

Verses 1-5

Well may the church look for much service from youthful ministers who set out in the same spirit as Timothy. But when men will submit in nothing, and oblige in nothing, the first elements of the Christian temper seem to be wanting; and there is great reason to believe that the doctrines and precepts of the gospel will not be successfully taught. The design of the decree being to set aside the ceremonial law, and its carnal ordinances, believers were confirmed in the Christian faith, because it set up a spiritual way of serving God, as suited to the nature both of God and man. Thus the church increased in numbers daily.

Verses 6-15

The removals of ministers, and the dispensing the means of grace by them, are in particular under Divine conduct and direction. We must follow Providence: and whatever we seek to do, if that suffer us not, we ought to submit and believe to be for the best. People greatly need help for their souls, it is their duty to look out for it, and to invite those among them who can help them. And God's calls must be complied with readily. A solemn assembly the worshippers of God must have, if possible, upon the sabbath day. If we have not synagogues, we must be thankful for more private places, and resort to them; not forsaking the assembling together, as our opportunities are. Among the hearers of Paul was a woman, named Lydia. She had an honest calling, which the historian notices to her praise. Yet though she had a calling to mind, she found time to improve advantages for her soul. It will not excuse us from religious duties, to say, We have a trade to mind; for have not we also a God to serve, and souls to look after? Religion does not call us from our business in the world, but directs us in it. Pride, prejudice, and sin shut out the truths of God, till his grace makes way for them into the understanding and affections; and the Lord alone can open the heart to receive and believe his word. We must believe in Jesus Christ; there is no coming to God as a Father, but by the Son as Mediator.

Verses 16-24

Satan, though the father of lies, will declare the most important truths, when he can thereby serve his purposes. But much mischief is done to the real servants of Christ, by unholy and false preachers of the gospel, who are confounded with them by careless observers. Those who do good by drawing men from sin, may expect to be reviled as troublers of the city. While they teach men to fear God, to believe in Christ, to forsake sin, and to live godly lives, they will be accused of teaching bad customs.

Verses 25-34

The consolations of God to his suffering servants are neither few nor small. How much more happy are true Christians than their prosperous enemies! As in the dark, so out of the depths, we may cry unto God. No place, no time is amiss for prayer, if the heart be lifted up to God. No trouble, however grievous, should hinder us from praise. Christianity proves itself to be of God, in that it obliges us to be just to our own lives. Paul cried aloud to make the jailer hear, and to make him heed, saying, Do thyself no harm. All the cautions of the word of God against sin, and all appearances of it, and approaches to it, have this tendency. Man, woman, do not ruin thyself; hurt not thyself, and then none else can hurt thee; do not sin, for nothing but that can hurt thee. Even as to the body, we are cautioned against the sins which do harm to that. Converting grace changes people's language of and to good people and good ministers. How serious the jailer's inquiry! His salvation becomes his great concern; that lies nearest his heart, which before was furthest from his thoughts. It is his own precious soul that he is concerned about. Those who are thoroughly convinced of sin, and truly concerned about their salvation, will give themselves up to Christ. Here is the sum of the whole gospel, the covenant of grace in a few words; Believe in the Lord Jesus Christ, and thou shalt be saved, and thy house. The Lord so blessed the word, that the jailer was at once softened and humbled. He treated them with kindness and compassion, and, professing faith in Christ, was baptized in that name, with his family. The Spirit of grace worked such a strong faith in them, as did away further doubt; and Paul and Silas knew by the Spirit, that a work of God was wrought in them. When sinners are thus converted, they will love and honour those whom they before despised and hated, and will seek to lessen the suffering they before desired to increase. When the fruits of faith begin to appear, terrors will be followed by confidence and joy in God.

Verses 35-40

Paul, though willing to suffer for the cause of Christ, and without any desire to avenge himself, did not choose to depart under the charge of having deserved wrongful punishment, and therefore required to be dismissed in an honourable manner. It was not a mere point of honour that the apostle stood upon, but justice, and not to himself so much as to his cause. And when proper apology is made, Christians should never express personal anger, nor insist too strictly upon personal amends. The Lord will make them more than conquerors in every conflict; instead of being cast down by their sufferings, they will become comforters of their brethren.

Chapter 17

Chapter Outline

Verses 1-9

The drift and scope of Paul's preaching and arguing, was to prove that Jesus is the Christ. He must needs suffer for us, because he could not otherwise purchase our redemption for us; and he must needs have risen again, because he could not otherwise apply the redemption to us. We are to preach concerning Jesus that he is Christ; therefore we may hope to be saved by him, and are bound to be ruled by him. The unbelieving Jews were angry, because the apostles preached to the Gentiles, that they might be saved. How strange it is, that men should grudge others the privileges they will not themselves accept! Neither rulers nor people need be troubled at the increase of real Christians, even though turbulent spirits should make religion the pretext for evil designs. Of such let us beware, from such let us withdraw, that we may show a desire to act aright in society, while we claim our right to worship God according to our consciences.

Verses 10-15

The Jews in Berea applied seriously to the study of the word preached unto them. They not only heard Paul preach on the sabbath, but daily searched the Scriptures, and compared what they read with the facts related to them. The doctrine of Christ does not fear inquiry; advocates for his cause desire no more than that people will fully and fairly examine whether things are so or not. Those are truly noble, and likely to be more and more so, who make the Scriptures their rule, and consult them accordingly. May all the hearers of the gospel become like those of Berea, receiving the word with readiness of mind, and searching the Scriptures daily, whether the things preached to them are so.

Verses 16-21

Athens was then famed for polite learning, philosophy, and the fine arts; but none are more childish and superstitious, more impious, or more credulous, than some persons, deemed eminent for learning and ability. It was wholly given to idolatry. The zealous advocate for the cause of Christ will be ready to plead for it in all companies, as occasion offers. Most of these learned men took no notice of Paul; but some, whose principles were the most directly contrary to Christianity, made remarks upon him. The apostle ever dwelt upon two points, which are indeed the principal doctrines of Christianity, Christ and a future state; Christ our way, and heaven our end. They looked on this as very different from the knowledge for many ages taught and professed at Athens; they desire to know more of it, but only because it was new and strange. They led him to the place where judges sat who inquired into such matters. They asked about Paul's doctrine, not because it was good, but because it was new. Great talkers are always busy-bodies. They spend their time in nothing else, and a very uncomfortable account they have to give of their time who thus spend it. Time is precious, and we are concerned to employ it well, because eternity depends upon it, but much is wasted in unprofitable conversation.

Verses 22-31

Here we have a sermon to heathens, who worshipped false gods, and were without the true God in the world; and to them the scope of the discourse was different from what the apostle preached to the Jews. In the latter case, his business was to lead his hearers by prophecies and miracles to the knowledge of the Redeemer, and faith in him; in the former, it was to lead them, by the common works of providence, to know the Creator, and worship Him. The apostle spoke of an altar he had seen, with the inscription, "TO THE UNKNOWN GOD." This fact is stated by many writers. After multiplying their idols to the utmost, some at Athens thought there was another god of whom they had no knowledge. And are there not many now called Christians, who are zealous in their devotions, yet the great object of their worship is to them an unknown God? Observe what glorious things Paul here says of that God whom he served, and would have them to serve. The Lord had long borne with idolatry, but the times of this ignorance were now ending, and by his servants he now commanded all men every where to repent of their idolatry. Each sect of the learned men would feel themselves powerfully affected by the apostle's discourse, which tended to show the emptiness or falsity of their doctrines.

Verses 32-34

The apostle was treated with more outward civility at Athens than in some other places; but none more despised his doctrine, or treated it with more indifference. Of all subjects, that which deserves the most attention gains the least. But those who scorn, will have to bear the consequences, and the word will never be useless. Some will be found, who cleave to the Lord, and listen to his faithful servants. Considering the judgement to come, and Christ as our Judge, should urge all to repent of sin, and turn to Him. Whatever matter is used, all discourses must lead to Him, and show his authority; our salvation, and resurrection, come from and by Him.

Chapter 18

Chapter Outline

Verses 1-6

Though Paul was entitled to support from the churches he planted, and from the people to whom he preached, yet he worked at his calling. An honest trade, by which a man may get his bread, is not to be looked upon with contempt by any. It was the custom of the Jews to bring up their children to some trade, though they gave them learning or estates. Paul was careful to prevent prejudices, even the most unreasonable. The love of Christ is the best bond of the saints; and the communings of the saints with each other, sweeten labour, contempt, and even persecution. Most of the Jews persisted in contradicting the gospel of Christ, and blasphemed. They would not believe themselves, and did all they could to keep others from believing. Paul hereupon left them. He did not give over his work; for though Israel be not gathered, Christ and his gospel shall be glorious. The Jews could not complain, for they had the first offer. When some oppose the gospel, we must turn to others. Grief that many persist in unbelief should not prevent gratitude for the conversion of some to Christ.

Verses 7-11

The Lord knows those that are his, yea, and those that shall be his; for it is by his work upon them that they become his. Let us not despair concerning any place, when even in wicked Corinth Christ had much people. He will gather in his chosen flock from the places where they are scattered Thus encouraged, the apostle continued at Corinth, and a numerous and flourishing church grew up.

Verses 12-17

Paul was about to show that he did not teach men to worship God contrary to law; but the judge would not allow the Jews to complain to him of what was not within his office. It was right in Gallio that he left the Jews to themselves in matters relating to their religion, but yet would not let them, under pretence of that, persecute another. But it was wrong to speak slightly of a law and religion which he might have known to be of God, and which he ought to have acquainted himself with. In what way God is to be worshipped, whether Jesus be the Messiah, and whether the gospel be a Divine revelation, are not questions of words and names, they are questions of vast importance. Gallio spoke as if he boasted of his ignorance of the Scriptures, as if the law of God was beneath his notice. Gallio cared for none of these things. If he cared not for the affronts of bad men, it was commendable; but if he concerned not himself for the abuses done to good men, his indifference was carried too far. And those who see and hear of the sufferings of God's people, and have no feeling with them, or care for them, who do not pity and pray for them, are of the same spirit as Gallio, who cared for none of these things.

Verses 18-23

While Paul found he laboured not in vain, he continued labouring. Our times are in God's hand; we purpose, but he disposes; therefore we must make all promises with submission to the will of God; not only if providence permits, but if God does not otherwise direct our motions. A very good refreshment it is to a faithful minister, to have for awhile the society of his brethren. Disciples are compassed about with infirmity; ministers must do what they can to strengthen them, by directing them to Christ, who is their Strength. Let us earnestly seek, in our several places, to promote the cause of Christ, forming plans that appear to us most proper, but relying on the Lord to bring them to pass if he sees good.

Verses 24-28

Apollos taught in the gospel of Christ, as far as John's ministry would carry him, and no further. We cannot but think he had heard of Christ's death and resurrection, but he was not informed as to the mystery of them. Though he had not the miraculous gifts of the Spirit, as the apostles, he made use of the gifts he had. The dispensation of the Spirit, whatever the measure of it may be, is given to every man to profit withal. He was a lively, affectionate preacher; fervent in spirit. He was full of zeal for the glory of God and the salvation of precious souls. Here was a complete man of God, thoroughly furnished for his work. Aquila and Priscilla encouraged his ministry, by attendance upon it. They did not despise Apollos themselves, or undervalue him to others; but considered the disadvantages he had laboured under. And having themselves got knowledge in the truths of the gospel by their long intercourse with Paul, they told what they knew to him. Young scholars may gain a great deal by converse with old Christians. Those who do believe through grace, yet still need help. As long as they are in this world, there are remainders of unbelief, and something lacking in their faith to be perfected, and the work of faith to be fulfilled. If the Jews were convinced that Jesus is Christ, even their own law would teach them to hear him. The business of ministers is to preach Christ. Not only to preach the truth, but to prove and defend it, with meekness, yet with power.

Chapter 19

Chapter Outline

Verses 1-7

Paul, at Ephesus, found some religious persons, who looked to Jesus as the Messiah. They had not been led to expect the miraculous powers of the Holy Ghost, nor were they informed that the gospel was especially the ministration of the Spirit. But they spake as ready to welcome the notice of it. Paul shows them that John never design that those he baptized should rest there, but told them that they should believe on Him who should come after him, that is, on Christ Jesus. They thankfully accepted the discovery, and were baptized in the name of the Lord Jesus. The Holy Ghost came upon them in a surprising, overpowering manner; they spake with tongues, and prophesied, as the apostles and the first Gentile coverts did. Though we do not now expect miraculous powers, yet all who profess to be disciples of Christ, should be called on to examine whether they have received the seal of the Holy Ghost, in his sanctifying influences, to the sincerity of their faith. Many seem not to have heard that there is a Holy Ghost, and many deem all that is spoken concerning his graces and comforts, to be delusion. Of such it may properly be inquired, "Unto what, then, were ye baptized?" for they evidently know not the meaning of that outward sign on which they place great dependence.

Verses 8-12

When arguments and persuasions only harden men in unbelief and blasphemy, we must separate ourselves and others from such unholy company. God was pleased to confirm the teaching of these holy men of old, that if their hearers believed them not, they might believe the works.

Verses 13-20

It was common, especially among the Jews, for persons to profess or to try to cast out evil spirits. If we resist the devil by faith in Christ, he will flee from us; but if we think to resist him by the using of Christ's name, or his works, as a spell or charm, Satan will prevail against us. Where there is true sorrow for sin, there will be free confession of sin to God in every prayer and to man whom we have offended, when the case requires it. Surely if the word of God prevailed among us, many lewd, infidel, and wicked books would be burned by their possessors. Will not these Ephesian converts rise up in judgement against professors, who traffic in such works for the sake of gain, or allow themselves to possess them? If we desire to be in earnest in the great work of salvation, every pursuit and enjoyment must be given up which hinders the effect of the gospel upon the mind, or loosens its hold upon the heart.

Verses 21-31

Persons who came from afar to pay their devotions at the temple of Ephesus, bought little silver shrines, or models of the temple, to carry home with them. See how craftsmen make advantage to themselves of people's superstition, and serve their worldly ends by it. Men are jealous for that by which they get their wealth; and many set themselves against the gospel of Christ, because it calls men from all unlawful crafts, however much wealth is to be gotten by them. There are persons who will stickle for what is most grossly absurd, unreasonable, and false; as this, that those are gods which are made with hands, if it has but worldly interest on its side. The whole city was full of confusion, the common and natural effect of zeal for false religion. Zeal for the honour of Christ, and love to the brethren, encourage zealous believers to venture into danger. Friends will often be raised up among those who are strangers to true religion, but have observed the honest and consistent behaviour of Christians.

Verses 32-41

The Jews came forward in this tumult. Those who are thus careful to distinguish themselves from the servants of Christ now, and are afraid of being taken for them, shall have their doom accordingly in the great day. One, having authority, at length stilled the noise. It is a very good rule at all times, both in private and public affairs, not to be hasty and rash in our motions, but to take time to consider; and always to keep our passions under check. We ought to be quiet, and to do nothing rashly; to do nothing in haste, of which we may repent at leisure. The regular methods of the law ought always to stop popular tumults, and in well-governed nations will do so. Most people stand in awe of men's judgments more than of the judgement of God. How well it were if we would thus quiet our disorderly appetites and passions, by considering the account we must shortly give to the Judge of heaven and earth! And see how the overruling providence of God keeps the public peace, by an unaccountable power over the spirits of men. Thus the world is kept in some order, and men are held back from devouring each other. We can scarcely look around but we see men act like Demetrius and the workmen. It is as safe to contend with wild beasts as with men enraged by party zeal and disappointed covetousness, who think that all arguments are answered, when they have shown that they grow rich by the practices which are opposed. Whatever side in religious disputes, or whatever name this spirit assumes, it is worldly, and should be discountenanced by all who regard truth and piety. And let us not be dismayed; the Lord on high is mightier than the noise of many waters; he can still the rage of the people.

Chapter 20

Verses 1-6

Tumults or opposition may constrain a Christian to remove from his station or alter his purpose, but his work and his pleasure will be the same, wherever he goes. Paul thought it worth while to bestow five days in going to Troas, though it was but for seven days' stay there; but he knew, and so should we, how to redeem even journeying time, and to make it turn to some good account.

Verses 7-12

Though the disciples read, and meditated, and prayed, and sung apart, and thereby kept up communion with God, yet they came together to worship God, and so kept up their communion with one another. They came together on the first day of the week, the Lord's day. It is to be religiously observed by all disciples of Christ. In the breaking of the bread, not only the breaking of Christ's body for us, to be a sacrifice for our sins, is remembered, but the breaking of Christ's body to us, to be food and a feast for our souls, is signified. In the early times it was the custom to receive the Lord's supper every Lord's day, thus celebrating the memorial of Christ's death. In this assembly Paul preached. The preaching of the gospel ought to go with the sacraments. They were willing to hear, he saw they were so, and continued his speech till midnight. Sleeping when hearing the word, is an evil thing, a sign of low esteem of the word of God. We must do what we can to prevent being sleepy; not put ourselves to sleep, but get our hearts affected with the word we hear, so as to drive sleep far away. Infirmity requires tenderness; but contempt requires severity. It interrupted the apostle's preaching; but was made to confirm his preaching. Eutychus was brought to life again. And as they knew not when they should have Paul's company again, they made the best use of it they could, and reckoned a night's sleep well lost for that purpose. How seldom are hours of repose broken for the purposes of devotion! but how often for mere amusement or sinful revelry! So hard is it for spiritual life to thrive in the heart of man! so naturally do carnal practices flourish there!

Verses 13-16

Paul hastened to Jerusalem, but tried to do good by the way, when going from place to place, as every good man should do. In doing God's work, our own wills and those of our friends must often be crossed; we must not spend time with them when duty calls us another way.

Verses 17-27

The elders knew that Paul was no designing, self-seeking man. Those who would in any office serve the Lord acceptably, and profitably to others, must do it with humility. He was a plain preacher, one that spoke his message so as to be understood. He was a powerful preacher; he preached the gospel as a testimony to them if they received it; but as a testimony against them if they rejected it. He was a profitable preacher; one that aimed to inform their judgments, and reform their hearts and lives. He was a painful preacher, very industrious in his work. He was a faithful preacher; he did not keep back reproofs when necessary, nor keep back the preaching of the cross. He was a truly Christian, evangelical preacher; he did not preach notions or doubtful matters; nor affairs of state or the civil government; but he preached faith and repentance. A better summary of these things, without which there is no salvation, cannot be given: even repentance towards God, and faith towards our Lord Jesus Christ, with their fruits and effects. Without these no sinner can escape, and with these none will come short of eternal life. Let them not think that Paul left Asia for fear of persecution; he was in full expectation of trouble, yet resolved to go on, well assured that it was by Divine direction. Thanks be to God that we know not the things which shall befall us during the year, the week, the day which has begun. It is enough for the child of God to know that his strength shall be equal to his day. He knows not, he would not know, what the day before him shall bring forth. The powerful influences of the Holy Spirit bind the true Christian to his duty. Even when he expects persecution and affliction, the love of Christ constrains him to proceed. None of these things moved Paul from his work; they did not deprive him of his comfort. It is the business of our life to provide for a joyful death. Believing that this was the last time they should see him, he appeals concerning his integrity. He had preached to them the whole counsel of God. As he had preached to them the gospel purely, so he had preached it to them entire; he faithfully did his work, whether men would bear or forbear.

Verses 28-38

If the Holy Ghost has made ministers overseers of the flock, that is, shepherds, they must be true to their trust. Let them consider their Master's concern for the flock committed to their charge. It is the church He has purchased with his own blood. The blood was his as Man; yet so close is the union between the Divine and human nature, that it is there called the blood of God, for it was the blood of Him who is God. This put such dignity and worth into it, as to ransom believers from all evil, and purchase all good. Paul spake about their souls with affection and concern. They were full of care what would become of them. Paul directs them to look up to God with faith, and commends them to the word of God's grace, not only as the foundation of their hope and the fountain of their joy, but as the rule of their walking. The most advanced Christians are capable of growing, and will find the word of grace help their growth. As those cannot be welcome guests to the holy God who are unsanctified; so heaven would be no heaven to them; but to all who are born again, and on whom the image of God is renewed, it is sure, as almighty power and eternal truth make it so. He recommends himself to them as an example of not caring as to things of the present world; this they would find help forward their comfortable passage through it. It might seem a hard saying, therefore Paul adds to it a saying of their Master's, which he would have them always remember; "It is more blessed to give than to receive:" it seems they were words often used to his disciples. The opinion of the children of this world, is contrary to this; they are afraid of giving, unless in hope of getting. Clear gain, is with them the most blessed thing that can be; but Christ tell us what is more blessed, more excellent. It makes us more like to God, who gives to all, and receives from none; and to the Lord Jesus, who went about doing good. This mind was in Christ Jesus, may it be in us also. It is good for friends, when they part, to part with prayer. Those who exhort and pray for one another, may have many weeping seasons and painful separations, but they will meet before the throne of God, to part no more. It was a comfort to all, that the presence of Christ both went with him and stayed with them.

Chapter 21

Chapter Outline

Verses 1-7

Providence must be acknowledged when our affairs go on well. Wherever Paul came, he inquired what disciples were there, and found them out. Foreseeing his troubles, from love to him, and concern for the church, they wrongly thought it would be most for the glory of God that he should continue at liberty; but their earnestness to dissuade him from it, renders his pious resolution the more illustrious. He has taught us by example, as well as by rule, to pray always, to pray without ceasing. Their last farewell was sweetened with prayer.

Verses 8-18

Paul had express warning of his troubles, that when they came, they might be no surprise or terror to him. The general notice given us, that through much tribulation we must enter into the kingdom of God, should be of the same use to us. Their weeping began to weaken and slacken his resolution Has not our Master told us to take up our cross? It was a trouble to him, that they should so earnestly press him to do that in which he could not gratify them without wronging his conscience. When we see trouble coming, it becomes us to say, not only, The will of the Lord must be done, and there is no remedy; but, Let the will of the Lord be done; for his will is his wisdom, and he doeth all according to the counsel of it. When a trouble is come, this must allay our griefs, that the will of the Lord is done; when we see it coming, this must silence our fears, that the will of the Lord shall be done; and we ought to say, Amen, let it be done. It is honourable to be an old disciple of Jesus Christ, to have been enabled by the grace of God to continue long in a course of duty, stedfast in the faith, growing more and more experienced, to a good old age. And with these old disciples one would choose to lodge; for the multitude of their years shall teach wisdom. Many brethren at Jerusalem received Paul gladly. We think, perhaps, that if we had him among us, we should gladly receive him; but we should not, if, having his doctrine, we do not gladly receive that.

Verses 19-26

Paul ascribed all his success to God, and to God they gave the praise. God had honoured him more than any of the apostles, yet they did not envy him; but on the contrary, glorified the Lord. They could not do more to encourage Paul to go on cheerfully in his work. James and the elders of the church at Jerusalem, asked Paul to gratify the believing Jews, by some compliance with the ceremonial law. They thought it was prudent in him to conform thus far. It was great weakness to be so fond of the shadows, when the substance was come. The religion Paul preached, tended not to destroy the law, but to fulfil it. He preached Christ, the end of the law for righteousness, and repentance and faith, in which we are to make great use of the law. The weakness and evil of the human heart strongly appear, when we consider how many, even of the disciples of Christ, had not due regard to the most eminent minister that even lived. Not the excellence of his character, nor the success with which God blessed his labours, could gain their esteem and affection, seeing that he did not render the same respect as themselves to mere ceremonial observances. How watchful should we be against prejudices! The apostles were not free from blame in all they did; and it would be hard to defend Paul from the charge of giving way too much in this matter. It is vain to attempt to court the favour of zealots, or bigots to a party. This compliance of Paul did not answer, for the very thing by which he hoped to pacify the Jews, provoked them, and brought him into trouble. But the all-wise God overruled both their advice and Paul's compliance with it, to serve a better purpose than was intended. It was in vain to think of pleasing men who would be pleased with nothing but the rooting out of Christianity. Integrity and uprightness will be more likely to preserve us than insincere compliances. And it should warn us not to press men to doing what is contrary to their own judgment to oblige us.

Verses 27-40

In the temple, where Paul should have been protected as in a place of safety, he was violently set upon. They falsely charged him with ill doctrine and ill practice against the Mosaic ceremonies. It is no new thing for those who mean honestly and act regularly, to have things laid to their charge which they know not and never thought of. It is common for the wise and good to have that charged against them by malicious people, with which they thought to have obliged them. God often makes those a protection to his people, who have no affection to them, but only have compassion for sufferers, and regard to the public peace. And here see what false, mistaken notions of good people and good ministers, many run away with. But God seasonably interposes for the safety of his servants, from wicked and unreasonable men; and gives them opportunities to speak for themselves, to plead for the Redeemer, and to spread abroad his glorious gospel.

Chapter 22

Chapter Outline

Verses 1-11

The apostle addressed the enraged multitude, in the customary style of respect and good-will. Paul relates the history of his early life very particularly; he notices that his conversion was wholly the act of God. Condemned sinners are struck blind by the power of darkness, and it is a lasting blindness, like that of the unbelieving Jews. Convinced sinners are struck blind as Paul was, not by darkness, but by light. They are for a time brought to be at a loss within themselves, but it is in order to their being enlightened. A simple relation of the Lord's dealings with us, in bringing us, from opposing, to profess and promote his gospel, when delivered in a right spirit and manner, will sometimes make more impression that laboured speeches, even though it amounts not to the full proof of the truth, such as was shown in the change wrought in the apostle.

Verses 12-21

The apostle goes on to relate how he was confirmed in the change he had made. The Lord having chosen the sinner, that he should know his will, he is humbled, enlightened, and brought to the knowledge of Christ and his blessed gospel. Christ is here called that Just One; for he is Jesus Christ the righteous. Those whom God has chosen to know his will, must look to Jesus, for by him God has made known his good-will to us. The great gospel privilege, sealed to us by baptism, is the pardon of sins. Be baptized, and wash away thy sins; that is, receive the comfort of the pardon of thy sins in and through Jesus Christ, and lay hold on his righteousness for that purpose; and receive power against sin, for the mortifying of thy corruptions. Be baptized, and rest not in the sign, but make sure of the thing signified, the putting away of the filth of sin. The great gospel duty, to which by our baptism we are bound, is, to seek for the pardon of our sins in Christ's name, and in dependence on him and his righteousness. God appoints his labourers their day and their place, and it is fit they should follow his appointment, though it may cross their own will. Providence contrives better for us than we do for ourselves; we must refer ourselves to God's guidance. If Christ send any one, his Spirit shall go along with him, and give him to see the fruit of his labours. But nothing can reconcile man's heart to the gospel, except the special grace of God.

Verses 22-30

The Jews listened to Paul's account of his conversion, but the mention of his being sent to the Gentiles, was so contrary to all their national prejudices, that they would hear no more. Their frantic conduct astonished the Roman officer, who supposed that Paul must have committed some great crime. Paul pleaded his privilege as a Roman citizen, by which he was exempted from all trials and punishments which might force him to confess himself guilty. The manner of his speaking plainly shows what holy security and serenity of mind he enjoyed. As Paul was a Jew, in low circumstances, the Roman officer questioned how he obtained so valuable a distinction; but the apostle told him he was free born. Let us value that freedom to which all the children of God are born; which no sum of money, however large, can purchase for those who remain unregenerate. This at once put a stop to his trouble. Thus many are kept from evil practices by the fear of man, who would not be held back from them by the fear of God. The apostle asks, simply, Is it lawful? He knew that the God whom he served would support him under all sufferings for his name's sake. But if it were not lawful, the apostle's religion directed him, if possible, to avoid it. He never shrunk from a cross which his Divine Master laid upon his onward road; and he never stept aside out of that road to take one up.

Chapter 23

Chapter Outline

Paul's defence before the council of the Jews. (1–5)

Paul's defence. He receives a Divine assurance that he shall go to Rome. (6–11)

The Jews conspire to kill Paul, Lysias sends him to Cesarea. (12–24)

Lysias's letter to Felix. (25–35)

Verses 1-5

See here the character of an honest man. He sets God before him, and lives as in his sight. He makes conscience of what he says and does, and, according to the best of his knowledge, he keeps from whatever is evil, and cleaves to what is good. He is conscientious in all his words and conduct. Those who thus live before God, may, like Paul, have confidence both toward God and man. Though the answer of Paul contained a just rebuke and prediction, he seems to have been too angry at the treatment he received in uttering them. Great men may be told of their faults, and public complaints may be made in a proper manner; but the law of God requires respect for those in authority.

Verses 6-11

The Pharisees were correct in the faith of the Jewish church. The Sadducees were no friends to the Scripture or Divine revelation; they denied a future state; they had neither hope of eternal happiness, nor dread of eternal misery. When called in question for his being a Christian, Paul might truly say he was called in question for the hope of the resurrection of the dead. It was justifiable in him, by this profession of his opinion on that disputed point, to draw off the Pharisees from persecuting him, and to lead them to protect him from this unlawful violence. How easily can God defend his own cause! Though the Jews seemed to be perfectly agreed in their conspiracy against religion, yet they were influenced by very different motives. There is no true friendship among the wicked, and in a moment, and with the utmost ease, God can turn their union into open enmity. Divine consolations stood Paul in the most stead; the chief captain rescued him out of the hands of cruel men, but the event he could not tell. Whoever is against us, we need not fear, if the Lord stand by us. It is the will of Christ, that his servants who are faithful, should be always cheerful. He might think he should never see Rome; but God tells him, even in that he should be gratified, since he desired to go there only for the honour of Christ, and to do good.

Verses 12-24

False religious principles, adopted by carnal men, urge on to such wickedness, as human nature would hardly be supposed capable of. Yet the Lord readily disappoints the best concerted schemes of iniquity. Paul knew that the Divine providence acts by reasonable and prudent means; and that, if he neglected to use the means in his power, he could not expect God's providence to work on his behalf. He who will not help himself according to his means and power, has neither reason nor revelation to assure him that he shall receive help from God. Believing in the Lord, we and ours shall be kept from every evil work, and kept to his kingdom. Heavenly Father, give us by thy Holy Spirit, for Christ's sake, this precious faith.

Verses 25-35

God has instruments for every work. The natural abilities and moral virtues of the heathens often have been employed to protect his persecuted servants. Even the men of the world can discern between the conscientious conduct of upright believers, and the zeal of false professors, though they disregard or understand not their doctrinal principles. All hearts are in God's hand, and those are blessed who put their trust in him, and commit their ways unto him.

Chapter 24

Chapter Outline

Verses 1-9

See here the unhappiness of great men, and a great unhappiness it is, to have their services praised beyond measure, and never to be faithfully told of their faults; hereby they are hardened and encouraged in evil, like Felix. God's prophets were charged with being troublers of the land, and our Lord Jesus Christ, that he perverted the nation; the very same charges were brought against Paul. The selfish and evil passions of men urge them forward, and the graces and power of speech, too often have been used to mislead and prejudice men against the truth. How different will the characters of Paul and Felix appear at the day of judgement, from what they are represented in the speech of Tertullus! Let not Christians value the applause, or be troubled at the revilings of ungodly men, who represent the vilest of the human race almost as gods, and the excellent of the earth as pestilences and movers of sedition.

Verses 10-21

Paul gives a just account of himself, which clears him from crime, and likewise shows the true reason of the violence against him. Let us never be driven from any good way by its having an ill name. It is very comfortable, in worshipping God, to look to him as the God of our fathers, and to set up no other rule of faith or practice but the Scriptures. This shows there will be a resurrection to a final judgment. Prophets and their doctrines were to be tried by their fruits. Paul's aim was to have a conscience void of offence. His care and endeavour was to abstain from many things, and to abound in the exercises of religion at all times; both towards God. and towards man. If blamed for being more earnest in the things of God than our neighbours, what is our reply? Do we shrink from the accusation? How many in the world would rather be accused of any weakness, nay, even of wickedness, than of an earnest, fervent feeling of love to the Lord Jesus Christ, and of devotedness to his service! Can such think that He will confess them when he comes in his glory, and before the angels of God? If there is any sight pleasing to the God of our salvation, and a sight at which the angels rejoice, it is, to behold a devoted follower of the Lord, here upon earth, acknowledging that he is guilty, if it be a crime, of loving the Lord who died for him, with all his heart, and soul, and mind, and strength. And that he will not in silence see God's word despised, or hear his name profaned; he will rather risk the ridicule and the hatred of the world, than one frown from that gracious Being whose love is better than life.

Verses 22-27

The apostle reasoned concerning the nature and obligations of righteousness, temperance, and of a judgment to come; thus showing the oppressive judge and his profligate mistress, their need of repentance, forgiveness, and of the grace of the gospel. Justice respects our conduct in life, particularly in reference to others; temperance, the state and government of our souls, in reference to God. He who does not exercise himself in these, has neither the form nor the power of godliness, and must be overwhelmed with the Divine wrath in the day of God's appearing. A prospect of the judgment to come, is enough to make the stoutest heart to tremble. Felix trembled, but that was all. Many are startled by the word of God, who are not changed by it. Many fear the consequences of sin, yet continue in the love and practice of sin. In the affairs of our souls, delays are dangerous. Felix put off this matter to a more convenient season, but we do not find that the more convenient season ever came. Behold now is the accepted time; hear the voice of the Lord to-day. He was in haste to turn from hearing the truth. Was any business more urgent than for him to reform his conduct, or more important than the salvation of his soul! Sinners often start up like a man roused from his sleep by a loud noise, but soon sink again into their usual drowsiness. Be not deceived by occasional appearances of religion in ourselves or in others. Above all, let us not trifle with the word of God. Do we expect that as we advance in life our hearts will grow softer, or that the influence of the world will decline? Are we not at this moment in danger of being lost for ever? Now is the day of salvation; tomorrow may be too late.

Chapter 25

Chapter Outline

Verses 1-12

See how restless malice is. Persecutors deem it a peculiar favour to have their malice gratified. Preaching Christ, the end of the law, was no offence against the law. In suffering times the prudence of the Lord's people is tried, as well as their patience; they need wisdom. It becomes those who are innocent, to insist upon their innocence. Paul was willing to abide by the rules of the law, and to let that take its course. If he deserved death, he would accept the punishment. But if none of the things whereof they accused him were true, no man could deliver him unto them, with justice. Paul is neither released nor condemned. It is an instance of the slow steps which Providence takes; by which we are often made ashamed, both of our hopes and of our fears, and are kept waiting on God.

Verses 13-27

Agrippa had the government of Galilee. How many unjust and hasty judgments the Roman maxim, ver. #(16), condemn! This heathen, guided only by the light of nature, followed law and custom exactly, yet how many Christians will not follow the rules of truth, justice, and charity, in judging their brethren! The questions about God's worship, the way of salvation, and the truths of the gospel, may appear doubtful and without interest, to worldly men and mere politicians. See how slightly this Roman speaks of Christ, and of the great controversy between the Jews and the Christians. But the day is at hand when Festus and the whole world will see, that all the concerns of the Roman empire were but trifles and of no consequence, compared with this question of Christ's resurrection. Those who have had means of instruction, and have despised them, will be awfully convinced of their sin and folly. Here was a noble assembly brought together to hear the truths of the gospel, though they only meant to gratify their curiosity by attending to the defence of a prisoner. Many, even now, attend at the places of hearing the word of God with "great pomp," and too often with no better motive than curiosity. And though ministers do not now stand as prisoners to make a defence for their lives, yet numbers affect to sit in judgment upon them, desirous to make them offenders for a word, rather than to learn from them the truth and will of God, for the salvation of their souls But the pomp of this appearance was outshone by the real glory of the poor prisoner at the bar. What was the honour of their fine appearance, compared with that of Paul's wisdom, and grace, and holiness; his courage and constancy in suffering for Christ! It is no small mercy to have God clear up our righteousness as the light, and our just dealing as the noon-day; to have nothing certain laid to our charge. And God makes even the enemies of his people to do them right.

Chapter 26

Chapter Outline

Verses 1-11

Christianity teaches us to give a reason of the hope that is in us, and also to give honour to whom honour is due, without flattery or fear of man. Agrippa was well versed in the Scriptures of the Old Testament, therefore could the better judge as to the controversy about Jesus being the Messiah. Surely ministers may expect, when they preach the faith of Christ, to be heard patiently. Paul professes that he still kept to all the good in which he was first educated and trained up. See here what his religion was. He was a moralist, a man of virtue, and had not learned the arts of the crafty, covetous Pharisees; he was not chargeable with any open vice and profaneness. He was sound in the faith. He always had a holy regard for the ancient promise made of God unto the fathers, and built his hope upon it. The apostle knew very well that all this would not justify him before God, yet he knew it was for his reputation among the Jews, and an argument that he was not such a man as they represented him to be. Though he counted this but loss, that he might win Christ, yet he mentioned it when it might serve to honour Christ. See here what Paul's religion is; he has not such zeal for the ceremonial law as he had in his youth; the sacrifices and offerings appointed by that, are done away by the great Sacrifice which they typified. Of the ceremonial cleansings he makes no conscience, and thinks the Levitical priesthood is done away in the priesthood of Christ; but, as to the main principles of his religion, he is as zealous as ever. Christ and heaven, are the two great doctrines of the gospel; that God has given to us eternal life, and this life is in his Son. These are the matter of the promise made unto the fathers. The temple service, or continual course of religious duties, day and night, was kept up as the profession of faith in the promise of eternal life, and in expectation of it. The prospect of eternal life should engage us to be diligent and stedfast in all religious exercises. Yet the Sadducees hated Paul for preaching the resurrection; and the other Jews joined them, because he testified that Jesus was risen, and was the promised Redeemer of Israel. Many things are thought to be beyond belief, only because the infinite nature and perfections of Him that has revealed, performed, or promised them, are overlooked. Paul acknowledged, that while he continued a Pharisee, he was a bitter enemy to Christianity. This was his character and manner of life in the beginning of his time; and there was every thing to hinder his being a Christian. Those who have been most strict in their conduct before conversion, will afterwards see abundant reason for humbling themselves, even on account of things which they then thought ought to have been done.

Verses 12-23

Paul was made a Christian by Divine power; by a revelation of Christ both to him and in him; when in the full career of his sin. He was made a minister by Divine authority: the same Jesus who appeared to him in that glorious light, ordered him to preach the gospel to the Gentiles. A world that sits in darkness must be enlightened; those must be brought to know the things that belong to their everlasting peace, who are yet ignorant of them. A world that lies in wickedness must be sanctified and reformed; it is not enough for them to have their eyes opened, they must have their hearts renewed; not enough to be turned from darkness to light, but they must be turned from the power of Satan unto God. All who are turned from sin to God, are not only pardoned, but have a grant of a rich inheritance. The forgiveness of sins makes way for this. None can be happy who are not holy; and to be saints in heaven we must be first saints on earth. We are made holy, and saved by faith in Christ; by which we rely upon Christ as the Lord our Righteousness, and give up ourselves to him as the Lord our Ruler; by this we receive the remission of sins, the gift of the Holy Ghost, and eternal life. The cross of Christ was a stumbling-block to the Jews, and they were in a rage at Paul's preaching the fulfilling of the Old Testament predictions. Christ should be the first that should rise from the dead; the Head or principal One. Also, it was foretold by the prophets, that the Gentiles should be brought to the knowledge of God by the Messiah; and what in this could the Jews justly be displeased at? Thus the true convert can give a reason of his hope, and a good account of the change manifest in him. Yet for going about and calling on men thus to repent and to be converted, vast numbers have been blamed and persecuted.

Verses 24-32

It becomes us, on all occasions, to speak the words of truth and soberness, and then we need not be troubled at the unjust censures of men. Active and laborious followers of the gospel often have been despised as dreamers or madmen, for believing such doctrines and such wonderful facts; and for attesting that the same faith and diligence, and an experience like their own, are necessary to all men, whatever their rank, in order to their salvation. But apostles and prophets, and the Son of God himself, were exposed to this charge; and none need be moved thereby, when Divine grace has made them wise unto salvation. Agrippa saw a great deal of reason for Christianity. His understanding and judgment were for the time convinced, but his heart was not changed. And his conduct and temper were widely different from the humility and spirituality of the gospel. Many are almost persuaded to be religious, who are not quite persuaded; they are under strong convictions of their duty, and of the excellence of the ways of God, yet do not pursue their convictions. Paul urged that it was the concern of every one to become a true Christian; that there is grace enough in Christ for all. He expressed his full conviction of the truth of the gospel, the absolute necessity of faith in Christ in order to salvation. Such salvation from such bondage, the gospel of Christ offers to the Gentiles; to a lost world. Yet it is with much difficulty that any person can be persuaded he needs a work of grace on his heart, like that which was needful for the conversion of the Gentiles. Let us beware of fatal hesitation in our own conduct; and recollect how far the being almost persuaded to be a Christian, is from being altogether such a one as every true believer is.

Chapter 27

Chapter Outline

Paul's voyage towards Rome.	(1–11)
Paul and his companions endangered by a tempest.	(12–20)
He receives a Divine assurance of safety.	(21–29)
Paul encourages those with him.	(30–38)
They are shipwrecked.	(39–44)

Verses 1-11

It was determined by the counsel of God, before it was determined by the counsel of Festus, that Paul should go to Rome; for God had work for him to do there. The course they steered, and the places they touched at, are here set down. And God here encourages those who suffer for him, to trust in him; for he can put it into the hearts of those to befriend them, from whom they least expect it. Sailors must make the best of the wind: and so must we all in our passage over the ocean of this world. When the winds are contrary, yet we must be getting forward as well as we can. Many who are not driven backward by cross providences, do not get forward by favourable providences. And many real Christians complain as to the concerns of their souls, that they have much ado to keep their ground. Every fair haven is not a safe haven. Many show respect to good ministers, who will not take their advice. But the event will convince sinners of the vanity of their hopes, and the folly of their conduct.

Verses 12-20

Those who launch forth on the ocean of this world, with a fair gale, know not what storms they may meet with; and therefore must not easily take it for granted that they have obtained their purpose. Let us never expect to be quite safe till we enter heaven. They saw neither sun nor stars for many days. Thus melancholy sometimes is the condition of the people of God as to their spiritual matters; they walk in darkness, and have no light. See what the wealth of this world is: though coveted as a blessing, the time may come when it will be a burden; not only too heavy to be carried safely, but heavy enough to sink him that has it. The children of this world can be prodigal of their goods for the saving their lives, yet are sparing of them in works of piety and charity, and in suffering for Christ. Any man will rather make shipwreck of his goods than of his life; but many rather make shipwreck of faith and a good conscience, than of their goods. The means the sailors used did not succeed; but when sinners give up all hope of saving themselves, they are prepared to understand God's word, and to trust in his mercy through Jesus Christ.

Verses 21-29

They did not hearken to the apostle when he warned them of their danger; yet if they acknowledge their folly, and repent of it, he will speak comfort and relief to them when in danger. Most people bring themselves into trouble, because they do not know when they are well off; they come to harm and loss by aiming to mend their condition, often against advice. Observe the solemn profession Paul made of relation to God. No storms or tempests can hinder God's favour to his people, for he is a Help always at hand. It is a comfort to the faithful servants of God when in difficulties, that as long as the Lord has any work for them to do, their lives shall be prolonged. If Paul had thrust himself needlessly into bad company, he might justly have been cast away with them; but God calling him into it, they are preserved with him. They are given thee; there is no greater satisfaction to a good man than to know he is a public blessing. He comforts them with the same comforts wherewith he himself was comforted. God is ever faithful, therefore let all who have an interest in his promises be ever cheerful. As, with God, saying and doing are not two things, believing and enjoying should not be so with us. Hope is an anchor of the soul, sure and stedfast, entering into that within the veil. Let those who are in spiritual darkness hold fast by that, and think not of putting to sea again, but abide by Christ, and wait till the day break, and the shadows flee away.

Verses 30-38

God, who appointed the end, that they should be saved, appointed the means, that they should be saved by the help of these shipmen. Duty is ours, events are God's; we do not trust God, but tempt him, when we say we put ourselves under his protection, if we do not use proper means, such as are within our power, for our safety. But how selfish are men in general, often even ready to seek their own safety by the destruction of others! Happy those who have such a one as Paul in their company, who not only had intercourse with Heaven, but was of an enlivening spirit to those about him. The sorrow of the world works death, while joy in God is life and peace in the greatest distresses and dangers. The comfort of God's promises can only be ours by believing dependence on him, to fulfil his word to us; and the salvation he reveals must be waited for in use of the means he appoints. If God has chosen us to salvation, he has also appointed that we shall obtain it by repentance, faith, prayer, and persevering obedience; it is fatal presumption to expect it in any other way. It is an encouragement to people to commit themselves to Christ as their Saviour, when those who invite them, clearly show that they do so themselves.

Verses 39-44

The ship that had weathered the storm in the open sea, where it had room, is dashed to pieces when it sticks fast. Thus, if the heart fixes in the world in affection, and cleaving to it, it is lost. Satan's temptations beat against it, and it is gone; but as long as it keeps above the world, though tossed with cares and tumults, there is hope for it. They had the shore in view, yet suffered shipwreck in the harbour; thus we are taught never to be secure. Though there is great difficulty in the way of the promised salvation, it shall, without fail, be brought to pass. It will come to pass that whatever the trials and dangers may be, in due time all believers will get safely to heaven. Lord Jesus, thou hast assured us that none of thine shall perish. Thou wilt bring them all safe to the heavenly shore. And what a pleasing landing will that be! Thou wilt present them to thy Father, and give thy Holy Spirit full possession of them forever.

Chapter 28

Chapter Outline

Paul kindly received at Melita.	(1–10)
He arrives at Rome.	(11–16)
His conference with the Jews.	(17–22)
Paul preaches to the Jews, and abides at Rome a prisoner.	(23–31)

Verses 1-10

God can make strangers to be friends; friends in distress. Those who are despised for homely manners, are often more friendly than the more polished; and the conduct of heathens, or persons called barbarians, condemns many in civilized nations, professing to be Christians. The people thought that Paul was a murderer, and that the viper was sent by Divine justice, to be the avenger of blood. They knew that there is a God who governs the world, so that things do not come to pass by chance, no, not the smallest event, but all by Divine direction; and that evil pursues sinners; that there are good works which God will reward, and wicked works which he will punish. Also, that murder is a dreadful crime, one which shall not long go unpunished. But they thought all wicked people were punished in this life. Though some are made examples in this world, to prove that there is a God and a Providence, yet many are left unpunished, to prove that there is a judgment to come. They also thought all who were remarkably afflicted in this life were wicked people. Divine revelation sets this matter in a true light. Good men often are greatly afflicted in this life, for the trial and increase of their faith and patience. Observe Paul's deliverance from the danger. And thus in the strength of the grace of Christ, believers shake off the temptations of Satan, with holy resolution. When we despise the censures and reproaches of men, and look upon them with holy contempt, having the testimony of our consciences for us, then, like Paul, we shake off the viper into the fire. It does us no harm, except we are kept by it from our duty. God hereby made Paul remarkable among these people, and so made way for the receiving of the gospel. The Lord raises up friends for his people in every place whither he leads them, and makes them blessings to those in affliction.

Verses 11-16

The common events of travelling are seldom worthy of being told; but the comfort of communion with the saints, and kindness shown by friends, deserve particular mention. The Christians at Rome were so far from being ashamed of Paul, or afraid of owning him, because he was a prisoner, that they were the more careful to show him respect. He had great comfort in this. And if our friends are kind to us, God puts it into their hearts, and we must give him the glory. When we see those even in strange places, who bear Christ's name, fear God, and serve him, we should lift up our hearts to heaven in thanksgiving. How many great men have made their entry into Rome, crowned and in triumph, who really were plagues to the world! But here a good man makes his entry into Rome, chained as a poor captive, who was a greater blessing to the world than any other merely a man. Is not this enough to put us for ever out of conceit with worldly favour? This may encourage God's prisoners, that he can give them favour in the eyes of those that carry them captives. When God does not soon deliver his people out of bondage, yet makes it easy to them, or them easy under it, they have reason to be thankful.

Verses 17-22

It was for the honour of Paul that those who examined his case, acquitted him. In his appeal he sought not to accuse his nation, but only to clear himself. True Christianity settles what is of common concern to all mankind, and is not built upon narrow opinions and private interests. It aims at no worldly benefit or advantage, but all its gains are spiritual and eternal. It is, and always has been, the lot of Christ's holy religion, to be every where spoken against. Look through every town and village where Christ is exalted as the only Saviour of mankind, and where the people are called to follow him in newness of life, and we see those who give themselves up to Christ, still called a sect, a party, and reproached. And this is the treatment they are sure to receive, so long as there shall continue an ungodly man upon earth.

Verses 23-31

Paul persuaded the Jews concerning Jesus. Some were wrought upon by the word, and others hardened; some received the light, and others shut their eyes against it. And the same has always been the effect of the gospel. Paul parted with them, observing that the Holy Ghost had well described their state. Let all that hear the gospel, and do not heed it, tremble at their doom; for who shall heal them, if God does not? The Jews had afterwards much reasoning among themselves. Many have great reasoning, who do not reason aright. They find fault with one another's opinions, yet will not yield to truth. Nor will men's reasoning among themselves convince them, without the grace of God to open their understandings. While we mourn on account of such despisers, we should rejoice that the salvation of God is sent to others, who will receive it; and if we are of that number, we should be thankful to Him who hath made us to differ. The apostle kept to his principle, to know and preach nothing but Christ and him crucified. Christians, when tempted from their main business, should bring themselves back with this question, What does this concern the Lord Jesus? What tendency has it to bring us to him, and to keep us walking in him? The apostle preached not himself, but Christ, and he was not ashamed of the gospel of Christ. Though Paul was placed in a very narrow opportunity for being useful, he was not disturbed in it. Though it was not a wide door that was opened to him, yet no man was suffered to shut it; and to many it was an effectual door, so that there were saints even in Nero's household, Php 4:22. We learn also from Php 1:13, how God overruled Paul's imprisonment for the furtherance of the gospel. And not the residents at Rome only, but all the church of Christ, to the present day, and in the most remote corner of the globe, have abundant reason to bless God, that during the most mature period of his Christian life and experience, he was detained a prisoner. It was from his prison, probably chained hand to hand to the soldier who kept him, that the apostle wrote the epistles to the Ephesians, Philippians, Colossians, and Hebrews; epistles showing, perhaps more than any others, the Christian love with which his heart overflowed, and the Christian experience with which his soul was filled. The believer of the present time may have less of triumph, and less of heavenly joy, than the apostle, but every follower of the same Saviour, is equally sure of safety and peace at the last. Let us seek to live more and more in the love of the Saviour; to labour to glorify Him by every action of our lives; and we shall assuredly, by his strength, be among the number of those who now overcome our enemies; and by his free grace and mercy, be hereafter among the blessed company who shall sit with Him upon his throne, even as He also has overcome, and is sitting on his Father's throne, at God's right hand for evermore.

96733431R00248

Made in the USA
San Bernardino, CA
20 November 2018